Remains of Old Latin

(Volume I)

Ennius And Caecilius

E. H. Warmington

Alpha Editions

This edition published in 2020

ISBN : 9789354033407

Design and Setting By
Alpha Editions
email - alphaedis@gmail.com

CONTENTS

PAGE

INTRODUCTION vii

ENNIUS 1

CAECILIUS 467

WORDS FROM ENNIUS AND CAECILIUS NOT INCLUDED
IN THE TEXT OR THE NOTES OF THIS VOLUME. 562

CONCORDANCES—

    I.—ENNIUS (*for ref. from Vahlen's ed. to this*) . . 565

    II.—ENNIUS (*for ref. from this ed. to Vahlen's*) . . 575

    I.—CAECILIUS (*for ref. from Ribbeck's ed. to this*) . 585

    II.—CAECILIUS (*for ref. from this ed. to Ribbeck's*) . 587

INDEX. 591

INTRODUCTION

Scope of this work. Limits of the archaic period.
Archaic spelling. Contents

In three volumes entitled *Remains of Old Latin*,
of which this is the first volume, my object is to
present a Latin text and an English translation of
Latin remnants, literary and epigraphic, which
belong to the archaic period of Roman literary history.
I have fixed the limit of this archaic period at 81—80
B.C., which are the years of Sulla's dictatorship.
It is indeed true that the limit cannot really be
defined with precision, partly because archaisms
in spelling and in form survive, especially in epigraphic records, during many years after the date
here given. However, for practical purposes, the
time of Sulla's supremacy has been found to be the
best, even though some of the inscriptions, which
will be included in the third volume, may belong to
a somewhat later period; for the year 80, in which
Sulla resigned his powers, may be taken to mark
the beginning of the golden age in Latin literature,
and the archaisms which persist during this age
and the early imperial era are natural survivals,
some conscious, some unconscious; while some are
definitely mistakes or false archaisms. I therefore
claim to present, so far as the remains allow, a picture
of Latin in the making; but there is one important

thing which must be stated here. I have not tried to reconstruct the spelling used by the old writers,[a] but have retained the 'modernised' spelling which our sources for the literary fragments normally show. Sometimes indeed these sources present or seem to present the true archaic spelling. In such cases I have reproduced it. With the exception of remnants like those of the Twelve Tables of Roman Law, the most valuable of the literary remains belonging to the archaic period, as defined above, are fragments from the works of poets; it is the poetic fragments which give the best idea of Latin in the process of development. Hence the literary remains in these three volumes consist of the fragments of seven poets, namely, Livius Andronicus, Naevius, Ennius, Caecilius, Pacuvius, Accius, and Lucilius. These poets are not taken in chronological order, owing to the necessity of producing volumes of manageable size; but each poet is complete in his volume, this first volume containing Ennius and Caecilius. The inscriptions present both poetry and prose; further introductory matter about them will be found in the third volume.

Sources

Our sources for old literary fragments are nearly all later writers of prose. These writers vary very much in nature, belong to widely different eras, and

[a] The inscriptions are an obvious exception from this general ruling, for in them the archaisms in spelling and form are nearly all in their original state. Many actual archaisms of Latin will thus be best apprehended by readers if they will study the inscriptions; these include some documents which are much older than most of the literary remains.

INTRODUCTION

differ greatly in the reasons for which they quote the old Latin. Some of them, especially those nearest to the archaic period, quote archaic predecessors largely because the renown of these was still great, and their plays were still widely performed or read, and their whole work had some meaning in the public life of Rome and Italy; while others, especially writers from the beginning of the imperial epoch onwards, were interested chiefly in linguistic peculiarities of various kinds, and, in a few important cases, in the imitation of the archaic poets by later ones. There is no need to review all these sources, but I have thought it advisable to give here some information about certain late sources which are not often read but which are the most fruitful in giving us fragments of archaic Latin. The point of view of these writers is that of grammarians, or of persons who want at the moment to deal with a point of grammar or philology.[a]

(i) Nonius. This is the grammarian and lexicographer Nonius Marcellus, who in his *De Compendiosa Doctrina* in twenty books, written about the beginning of the fourth century after Christ, provides us with more ancient literary fragments than any other source does. He consulted a limited number of 'classical' writers, and also other grammarians and lexicographers, and first made large catalogues of words occurring in them, and then compiled his *Doctrina* from these catalogues, in such

---

[a] I wish to point out here that ancient philology was largely ignorant and fanciful, so that many of the derivations given by the sources are absurd and even fantastic; and in quoting them I have not thought it worth while to point this out unless the fact is relevant to the right interpretation of an archaic fragment.

a way that the order of the fragments as he finally
quotes them is sometimes the same as their order
in the original writer; this is a matter of greatest
importance in considering the fragments of Lucilius
which will be given in our third volume; further
details on this point will be found there. The text
of Nonius tends to be very corrupt in the quotations
from old writers, and I have thus felt it advisable
to give fuller critical notes on his passages than
on most of those which come from other sources.
The extant manuscripts all come (possibly by way of
an intervening MS. now lost) from a lost archetype,
and are indicated in these volumes by *sigla* as
follows :

Lu. Lugdunensis (Voss., lat. fol. 73); 9th cent.;
   best of all. Well corrected by two hands
   (*L2, L3*).
F., Flor. Florentinus (Laur., xlviii, 1); 9th cent.;
   copied from *Lu*; corrected by two hands.
   Books I–III only.
Harl. Harleianus (Mus. Brit. 2719); 9th–10th
   cent.; copied partly from *F* and from *Gen.*
   (see below) in book IV; corrections by *H2, H3.*
Escorial. Escorialensis (M III, 14); 10th cent.;
   copied partly from the same source as *Par.* 7667
   (see below), partly from *F* (corrected).
G. Gudianus (Wolfenb. 96); 10th cent. (source for
   correctors *H2, L3*).
Lugd. Lugdunensis (Voss., 4to. 116); 10th–11th
   cent.
Bamb. Bambergensis (M.V. 18); 9th–10th cent.
Turic. Turicense fragmentum (C796) 10th cent.
   (bad).

Par. 7666. Parisinus 7666; 10th cent.
Par. 7665   } Parisinus 7665. Bernensis 347, 357,
Bern. 347, 357 } 10th cent. All portions of one *cd.*
Montepess. Montepessulanus (212); 9th–10th cent.
Ox. Oxoniensis (Bibl. Bodl. Can. Cl. Lat. 279);
  10th cent.
Gen. Genevensis (84); 9th cent. (good).
Bern. 83. Bernensis 83; 10th cent. (bad).
Par 7667. Parisinus 7667; 10th cent.

There is also Cantabrigiensis (Mm. V. 22); 9th
cent.; copied from *Gen.*
The edition which I have used is that of W. M.
Lindsay, Leipzig, Teubner, 1903, and the numeration
that of Mercier.
(ii) Festus. This is Sextus Pompeius Festus
(probably of the second century after Christ), whose
work is an abridgment of an earlier work entitled
De Verborum Significatu and written by M. Verrius
Flaccus, a famous grammarian of Augustus' time.
Only the latter part of Festus' abridgment has
survived, and there is only one manuscript of it—
the Codex Farnesianus IV. A. 3 (11th cent.) at Naples.
Even in this there are large gaps, which can be restored in part from copies of the codex made before
it was damaged so much as it is now, and in part
from an abridgment of Festus' own work made by
Paulus Diaconus (c. 720—c. 800). Paulus' work is
extant in a number of codices. The edition used in
these volumes is the combined Paulus and Festus
edited by W. M. Lindsay, Leipzig, Teubner, 1913.
(iii) Servius. The elaborate commentary on
Virgil by Maurus (Marius ?) Servius Honoratus—
these names occur in varying order—who gives us

xi

many fragments, was composed about the end of the fourth century after Christ, and is extant in very different groups of manuscripts. One group gives apparently the original commentary of Servius, who is in these volumes referred to simply as Servius. But another group shows the same commentary embedded in other matter, so to speak, or rather supplemented or augmented from an anonymous writer of about the same date. Where the source of an old fragment comes from one of these supplemented contexts, the author is referred to as 'Servius auctus,' 'Servius (supplemented).' Readers will further understand from this the meaning of the phrase *augmenter of Servius*.[a]

The edition used for these volumes is that of G. Thilo and H. Hagen, Leipzig, Teubner, 1878–1902, re-issued in 1923.

(iv) Several late grammarians, in particular Charisius, Diomedes, and Priscianus, who give us many fragments at second hand.[b] These are all to be found in *Grammatici Latini*, ed. H. Keil (and others), Leipzig, 1857–1880, referred to in these volumes as G. L. K.

(v) Some fragments given by one or two scholars of the medieval and early modern eras have been included, but they differ in trustworthiness. For example, Ekkehart or Ekkehard (there are four with this name), a monk of St. Gall, who died *c.* 1061; and Osbern of Gloucester (*c.* 1123–1200) are worthy

---

[a] Note that J. J. H. Savage, in *Harvard Studies in Classical Philology*, 1932, 77, maintains that the ' Servius auctus ' commentary is a mixture or conflation of two commentaries—that of Servius and another of Aelius Donatus who wrote about 25 years before Servius.

[b] Priscianus appears to quote directly from Ennius.

of belief. But it is not easy to decide about the German philologist Kaspar von Barth (1587–1658). In his *Adversaria* and his commentary on Statius he professes to quote fragments of Ennius from old sources. In 1636 his library and manuscripts were destroyed by fire, so that, even when he wrote in good faith, he often depended upon his memory. It is thus difficult to trust his authority.

This point leads me naturally to mention the groups of fragments which I have classed doubtfully as spurious; I have included only such as readers who are already familiar with the old poets may expect to find in these volumes. There are others which I have omitted altogether. Amongst these are a number given as genuine by Merula, who acted apparently in good faith. They will be found in Vahlen's third edition of Ennius, on pp. 240–242.

Method of quotation from sources

In presenting each literary fragment, the method used in these three volumes is to give, as a separate ' item,' either the whole passage of the source by which the fragment of old Latin is quoted or referred to, or so much of the passage as may reveal the old author of the quotation (with or without the title or other details of the old author's work), the reason for the quotation, and maybe something of its meaning and context, or of the nature of the work from which it is quoted. These items fall into two classes :

(i) Passages which quote actual words of the old author. These passages give true fragments and form the bulk of the text and translation in the first two volumes of this series. They are numbered by figures placed over the middle of each item, the numeration representing the lines, or parts of lines, which, printed in distinctive type, are thus deemed to survive from among the lost works of the author.[a] Single words not placed in the text or given in a note are collected at the end of each volume.

(ii) Passages which do not give words as actually written by the old author. Some of these reveal a ' hidden fragment ' by a paraphrase; others tell us something about the old poet's work, or about its context at some particular point. Such items as these are not numbered, but they are placed in what is apparently the best position for them; where they are separated by spaces from numbered items of class (i), they are to be taken as separate items. In view of the meagre nature of our knowledge about the lost poets, it was felt advisable to include these passages.[b]

A word must be said here about C. Iulius Hyginus, from whom I have incorporated a number of important extracts belonging to this second class. Under Hyginus' name has come down to us a mythological treatise written in Latin[c] and entitled *Fabulae* or *Fabularum Liber*. This contains about three hundred old Greek legends and gene-

---

[a] With the exception of Ennius' *Euhemerus*, the lines are lines of poetry; in Euhemerus the numeration is of lines of text as printed in this volume.

[b] Many ' testimonia ' about the old author's life, or criticising his work as a whole or a particular work, have not been included. But references to the sources for the lives of the old authors have been given in the introductions to the volumes.

[c] There are also fragments of a version or original in Greek.

xiv

alogies, and consists of an abridgment, or possibly
a union of two abridgments, of the original work.
The extant text shows a poor knowledge of good
Latin and Greek ; if this reflects the mind of the
original author, then Professor H. J. Rose, the
latest editor, is probably right in rejecting the belief
that the author was that Hyginus who was a learned
freedman of Augustus. Although it is not easy to
decide in every case, Iulius Hyginus' sources appear
to have been very often epic poems and Alexandrian
works written in prose, less often old Greek
tragedies, or hypotheses of these. Sometimes a
Fabula has been produced from the plots of two or
more Greek tragedies 'contaminated.' In a few
cases Hyginus' source for a legend appears to be
a separate old Latin play or its hypothesis. Where
this happens I have incorporated Hyginus' plot into
the extant fragments of the Latin play ; but the
correctness of this use of Hyginus should not be
regarded as wholly certain.

The references added at the end of any item in
the Latin (not the English) text, and prefixed by
the abbreviation Cf. or Cp., generally indicate
other sources which give all or part of the old fragment, but are not quoted in this text.

Where several fragments have survived from one
book (for example, of Ennius' *Annals*) or one play
or other named work of an old poet—especially
where the fragments of this particular work are all
or mostly quoted by one or two sources (for example,
by Nonius)—there the ascription, by the source,
to 'Ennius in such and such a book' has, as a rule,
only been included in the text of that passage which
gives the *first* fragment of a group as arranged by

XV

me. After that, the ascription has been omitted unless there was a special reason; this method has excluded some needless repetition. Where no work of, for example, Ennius is named by the source in quoting a fragment, and yet the fragment is ascribed in this edition to a definite work, the lack of any ascription by the source has been indicated in some way; so also where neither the old work nor the old author of a fragment is mentioned by the source, yet the author or his work, or both are known or can be deduced with probability.

In a good many places the Greek model or source of an old Latin fragment is known or deduced; in such cases the Greek original has been quoted or referred to at the beginning of the relevant item on the Latin page, but not translated. Again, in some cases the source which quotes a substantial fragment shows how the old Latin poet not only drew upon some older Greek source, but also inspired some later Latin poet; thus we have fragments of Ennius which imitated Homer and were imitated by Virgil. In such cases the passages from the original Greek author, from the old Latin poet, and from the later Latin poet, have been given in full, both in text and in translation.

Throughout the literary fragments the reconstruction is mine, save where it is established, well known, and indisputable. There was no room to give the full evidence for various allocations of fragments to probable contexts; but the English translation of many of the items is provided with a heading in italic letters giving the known context, or indicating a probable context, of the old fragment. In those cases where the context cannot be regarded as known,

INTRODUCTION

I do not vouch for the correctness of these headings ; but most of them have a better foundation than mere conjecture. Their function is to indicate the reason why I have put various items in the places where they now stand, and to be if possible a help and a guide. In order to make the series more useful, I have compiled two concordances, which will be found near the end of the volumes. One is intended for the use of persons who possess a standard complete Latin text of any old author and wish to compare, at any point, that text with this; while the other is intended to assist those who wish to turn from the present text and translation and to consult the latest standard predecessor.

Life of Ennius

Quintus Ennius was born in 239 [a] B.C. at Rudiae, now Rugge, in Calabria,[b] or Messapia, and claimed, as a Messapian, to be descended from King Messapus.[c] It was probably because this Italian district had been deeply influenced by Greek culture that Ennius was in later ages called ' Greek ' or ' Half-Greek.' [d] He was probably quite young when he learnt to speak not only Greek but Latin, for the colony of

---

[a] Gellius, XVII, 21, 43; Cicero, *Brut.*, 18, 72; *Tusc. Disp.*, I, 1, 3. Jerome, Euseb. *Chron.*, anno ab Abraham 1777, 240 B.C. and Abr. 1849, 168 B.C. is wrong.
[b] Cic., *pro Archia*, 9, 22; Schol. Bob., *ad loc.*; Cic., *de Orat.*, III, 42, 168; Ausonius, *Technopaegn.*, XIV, 17; Silius, XII, 393 ff.; Strabo, 281-2c. Mela, II, 66 gives the wrong Rudiae near Canusium.
[c] Silius, *l.c.*; Ovid, *Ars Amat.*, III, 409; Serv., ad *Aen.*, VII, 691; Suidas, s.v. Έννιος; Horace, *C.*, IV, 8, 20 and Acro, *ad* loc.
[d] Festus, 412, 33; Suetonius, *de grammaticis*, 1.

INTRODUCTION

Brundisium was only twenty miles or so from Rudiae; he spoke Oscan also, and used to say that he had three 'hearts' because he could speak Greek, Oscan, and Latin.[a] From Jerome's mistake in saying that Ennius was born at Tarentum[b] it is perhaps right to conclude that he was educated there.

He joined the Roman army and, according to Silius, rose to the rank of centurion. While he was serving in Sardinia in 204 B.C., he was there brought to the notice of M. Porcius Cato, who was at that time quaestor. He is alleged to have instructed Cato in 'Greek letters,'[c] which means that he introduced Cato to Greek literature if not to the Greek language. In any case he made a great impression on Cato, and was brought by him to Rome.[d] There he lived on the Aventine, according to Jerome, and apparently tended grounds (*loca coluit*) sacred to Tutilina or 'Guardian Goddess,' according to Porcius (Licinus?) in a passage of Varro.[e] He was doubtless attracted to the Aventine because in that region had been built, in honour of Livius Andronicus, a temple of Minerva for the use of poets and actors. During the first years of his residence in Rome (which lasted during all the rest of his life) he appears to have earned his living chiefly by teaching Greek to Romans[f]; but at the same time he took to writing original poetry which increased his income, the death of Livius Andronicus and the banishment of Naevius giving him a good opportunity within the range of

[a] Gellius, XVII, 17, 1.
[b] Jerome, ann. 1777, 240.
[c] Sil., *l.c.*; 'Aurel Vict.,' *de vir. illustr.*, 47.
[d] 'Cornel. Nepos,' *Cato*, 1, 4; Jerome, ann. 1777, 240.
[e] Jerome, *l.c.*; Varro, *L.L.*, V, 163.
[f] Suet., *l.c.*

xviii

drama. In the course of his writing he did much to
establish a reasonable system of long and short
syllables in poetry, and introduced into Latin the
Greek hexameter. In due course he made friends
with some of the most enlightened and influential
Romans of the day, as is shown below. We can
obtain a few glimpses of his character, and in this
connexion it is worth while noting the good story
which Cicero tells of him [a] : Scipio Nasica, who was
consul in 191, when he once went to call on Ennius,
was put off by the statement of Ennius' maidservant
that the master was not at home. But Nasica had
his suspicions that, at Ennius' orders, she had not
told the truth. So a few days later when Ennius
called on Nasica, and asked for him at the front door,
Nasica, unseen within, shouted that he was not at
home. When Ennius claimed to recognise Nasica's
voice, Nasica replied ' Shame on you. When *I*
asked for *you*, I believed your maidservant that
you weren't at home; don't you believe *me* in
person ? ' It is probably this story which gave rise
to the tradition that on the Aventine Ennius lived a
thrifty life and kept only one maidservant for his
needs.[b] However, it is probably a true tradition
with regard to his early years in Rome, and it may
be that Ennius never became a rich man; for he
appears to have been poor even at seventy years of
age.[c] He was of a convivial nature, and perhaps
drank more wine than was good for him. He said
of himself ' I never poetise unless I have the gout,'
and Horace says of him that he never ' leaped

[a] Cic., *de Oratore*, II, 68, 276.
[b] Jerome, ann. 1777, 240.
[c] Cic., *de Senect.*, 5, 14.

forward to sing of arms ' (that is, he never went ahead with the composition of his *Annals*) unless he was drunk.[a] Gellius quotes a fragment of Ennius in which the poet is alleged to describe his own character as that of a loyal, trustworthy, and intimate friend of those statesmen who chose to know him.[b]

Ennius became indeed a close friend with some of the best Romans of this period, above all perhaps with Scipio Africanus, whom he celebrated in his poetry[c]; and with Marcus Fulvius Nobilior and his son Quintus. When Marcus, consul in 189 B.C., went to Aetolia, he took Ennius with him.[d] Ennius went not to fight but doubtless because Marcus was a man of culture and Ennius intended to celebrate the coming campaign, as he afterwards did.[e] Marcus doubtless rewarded Ennius well; a very late record[f] states that, to his discredit, Marcus did no more than give to Ennius one military cloak out of the spoils taken at Ambracia. In 184 B.C. Marcus' son Quintus caused Ennius to be made a full Roman citizen with a grant of land either at Potentia in Picenum or at Pisaurum in Umbria; for it was apparently this Quintus Fulvius who was concerned in the foundation

[a] Ennius, *Satires*, 21, pp. 390–1 of this book; Horace, *Epist.*, I, 19, 7–8, Q. Serenus Sammonicus, XXXVI, 706–7.

[b] Gell., XII, 4, 4; Ennius, *Annals*, 210—27, as given in full on pp. 78–81.

[c] Horace, *C.*, IV, 8, 15 ff.; Cic., *pro Arch.*, 9, 22, and Schol. Bob., *ad loc.*; Ennius' own work *Scipio*; see pp. 394 ff. In later ages the tradition, apparently a true one, of this friendship was much exaggerated—Claudian, XXIII.

[d] Cic., *pro Arch.*, 11, 27; *Tusc. Disp.*, I, 2, 3; *Brut.*, 20, 79, where Cic. inaccurately says of E. ' militaverat.'

[e] In *Ambracia* and Book XV of the *Annals*; see pp. 142 ff., 358-61. Cp. ' Aurel. Vict.,' *de vir. illustr.*, 52, 3.

[f] Symmachus, *Epist.*, I, 20, 2.

INTRODUCTION

of a colony at both places in that year.[a] Ennius'
friendship with Scipio Nasica has already been indicated above. In the case of Cato, I think we can
trace a loss of that old friendship which had been the
making of Ennius. Cicero, in maintaining that the
Romans were slow to appreciate poetry and did not
honour poets as they should have done, shows [b]
that Cato in a speech laid it to Marcus Fulvius'
charge that he had taken poets (Ennius of course is
meant) into his province. Now it might be said that
Cato may simply have used this argument insincerely
and merely as a political expedient against an un-
friendly statesman; or that Cato implied that Rome
and not a province was the right place for a good poet,
especially one whom Cato himself had brought to
Rome in the first place. But Cicero did not thus
interpret Cato's speech, which was apparently
extant in Cicero's time; and we must remember that
Cato had developed an abiding hatred of new manners
and especially of Greek culture amongst Romans,
and conclude that Ennius had ceased to be a friend
of Cato. There were two reasons, I think, for this
estrangement: Cato found that Ennius was, after
all, for his taste much too deeply engaged in
Greek culture and in expounding of it to Romans
and in transferring it into Latin; Ennius had shown
himself to be something of an Epicurean, and in
works like *Epicharmus* and *Euhemerus*, and elsewhere,
was expressing opinions which Cato believed to be
subversive of Roman religion and manners. And
further, Cato had already quarrelled with Ennius'

[a] Cic., *Brut.*, 20, 79; Livy, XXXIX, 44, 10; Cic., *pro Arch.*,
10, 22; *de Orat.*, III, 42, 168.
[b] *Tusc. Disp.*, I, 2, 3.

friends such as the Scipios, partly again because of their love of Greek culture.

There is one other man of affairs between whom and Ennius we can certainly trace some connexion. One of Ennius' neighbours was Servius Galba.[a] This was probably Servius Sulpicius Galba who was praetor urbanus in 187 B.C. and was a friend of M. Fulvius. There is, however, much doubt concerning A. Postumius Albinus, who was praetor in 155, consul in 151. He, according to an isolated manuscript, dedicated[b] to Ennius, who must have been growing old then, a history written by Albinus (obviously as a young man) in Greek.

Of friendship between Ennius and other primarily literary men we can discover little. We do not know that he was ever acquainted personally with his older contemporaries, the poets Livius Andronicus and Naevius, for the former's death and the latter's exile came about the time in which Ennius reached Rome. Still, years after Naevius' death, Ennius did, in his *Annals*, rightly disparage the ruder style of Naevius' *Punic War* while recognising its value as an historical record, and imitating a phrase or two.[c] Nor, again, is there evidence that he was acquainted with Plautus, who lived for twenty years after Ennius first came to Rome, though we know that Plautus was acquainted with Ennius' plays.[d] Plautus was a writer of comedies, whereas Ennius' dramatic talent was expended almost entirely on

[a] Cic., *Ac. Pr.*, II, 16, 51.
[b] Buecheler, *Rhein. Mus.*, XXXIX, 623; cp. *Riv. di fil. class.*, XII, 396. But the document is justly suspected of being a forgery.
[c] Cic., *Brut.*, 19, 75–6. On this, see pp. 82–3.
[d] Plaut., *Poen.*, prol., 1 ff. See pp. 218–21.

tragedies. But Ennius does indeed appear to have
made friends with the comic writer Caecilius Statius,
an Insubrian Gaul; his life is described, so far as we
know it, below, and the remains of his work are
included in this book. Jerome says that Caecilius
was ' at first ' (that is, at one time) a ' contubernalis '
or close comrade of Ennius. In fact Caecilius
appears to have remained a friend until Ennius'
death which came first, and to have been cremated
near the place where Ennius' body also was burnt.[a]
And lastly, Ennius must presumably have known
the tragic poet M. Pacuvius, a Calabrian of Brundisium (220 B.C.–c. 132), because he was a son of Ennius'
sister.[b] But it is doubtful whether Pacuvius, who
was for many years a painter, not a playwright, by
profession, had done much by way of composition of
tragedies before his uncle's death in 169 (see below).
According to one Pompilius,[c] Pacuvius was a
' discipulus ' of Ennius. This may mean that
Pacuvius was merely inspired to emulate Ennius in
the composition of tragedy and possibly too of satire,
in which Pacuvius is known to have indulged.

In the year 169, at the age of seventy, just after
he had produced the tragedy *Thyestes*, and still,
according to Cicero, calmly bearing and almost
enjoying poverty and old age, Ennius died of gout.[d]
His body was apparently cremated on the Ianiculum;
and some authorities stated that his bones were taken

[a] Jerome, ann. Abr. 1838, 179 B.C.
[b] Pliny, *N.H.*, XXXV, 19; Jerome, ann. Abr. 1863, 154
B.C. (who wrongly makes P. son of E.'s daughter).
[c] In Nonius, 88, 5–7.
[d] Cic., *Brut.*, 20, 78; *de senect.*, 5, 14; Jerome, ann. Abr.
1849, 168 B.C., a year out.

to his birthplace Rudiae.[a] This at any rate was a
common custom. But the connexion of Ennius
with the sepulchre of the Scipios is doubtful. Thus,
according to Cicero, a statue of Ennius in marble
was, in Cicero's time, *believed* to have been set up in
the Scipios' sepulchre because of Africanus' affection
for him;[b] in Livy's time, of three statues then to be
seen in the sepulchre, one was *said* at that time to be
a statue of Ennius;[c] later on again, the elder Pliny
says that Africanus *ordered* that a statue of Ennius
be put in his tomb, and that Ennius' name could still
be read on it;[d] yet again, as a fourth stage in the
development of what is, from beginning to end,
apparently a falsehood, Jerome, following Suetonius,
says that Ennius himself was cremated (*sepultus*)
in Scipio's sepulchre.[e] Lastly, we may mention
the ascription to Ennius by Woelfflin, in modern
times, of at least some of the old *elogia* still extant
on the monuments of the Scipios. The existence of
such a statue as the Romans described was probably
an assumption without foundation. A sculptured
portrait inscribed 'Q. Ennius' has been found[f]
at Rome, but unfortunately it is headless. No
portrait of Ennius has been found in the Scipios'
sepulchre.

With regard to Ennius' poetic remains, I propose,

[a] Jerome, *l.c.*, and ann. Abr. 1838, 179.
[b] Cic., *pro Arch.*, 9, 22.
[c] Livy, XXXVIII, 56; Ovid, *Ars Amat.*, III, 409, assumes
the statement to be one of fact.
[d] Pliny, *N.H.*, VII, 114; Solinus, I, 122 (from Pliny);
cp. Val. Max., VIII, 14, 1.
[e] Jerome, ann. Abr. 1849, 168; cp. Schol. Bob., ad Cic.,
pro Arch., 9, 22.
[f] *Not. d. scav.*, 1903, 600 ff.

with the help of notes and headings given in the text and translation, to let the fragments in the main speak for themselves, but I give here a few probabilities and known facts about his various works, though we can trace the date of hardly one of them. He produced tragedies at various times up to the year of his death, while the epic poem the *Annals*, by far his greatest single work, was apparently composed over a long period, being once or twice resumed, as time went on, after a tentative ending. His minor works were composed for special occasions or as the spirit moved him. Thus, his poem *Scipio* in praise of Africanus, victor of Hannibal in the battle of Zama, and possibly the *Satires* (of which the third book apparently alludes to Scipio), were written soon after the triumph celebrated by Scipio in 201 in honour of that last contest of the Second Punic War; and *Ambracia*, in honour of M. Fulvius, very soon after 188. A number of tragedies were probably composed before the *Annals* were begun or had gone very far, because dramatic composition would more than any poetry except comedies enable or help Ennius to live independently of literary ' patrons ' so far as he could. The tragedy *Achilles after Aristarchus*, was written before the composition of Plautus' *Poenulus* in 189. The *Annals* had reached no farther than the twelfth book (which was perhaps intended to be the last) in 172, for in that book Ennius mentioned his age as being sixty-seven years; thus books thirteen to eighteen were composed between 172 and 168; Ennius intended again to finish with book fifteen, and indeed made an end there; but added three more books for a particular reason. The eighteenth was probably unfinished. Lastly, in the year of his death, 169, Ennius produced the tragedy *Thyestes*, which was his last work.[a]

The list of Ennius' complete works comprises eighteen [b] books of *Annals*, at least twenty tragedies, two historical Roman plays (*fabulae praetextae*), two comedies (*fabulae palliatae* ?), at least four books of *Satires*, the poems *Scipio*, *Sota*, *Protrepticum* (?), *Hedyphagetica* (?), *Epicharmus*, *Euhemerus or Holy History*, and *epigrams*. There was a later grammarian, named Ennius (fl. c. 100 B.C.), whom it is difficult to distinguish from the poet. Two books on 'letters and syllables' and one (?) on 'metres' were generally attributed by later Romans to this grammarian.[c] I have assumed that the first development of shorthand writing [d] is also to be ascribed to the grammarian. But that the doubling of consonants was begun or established by the poet Ennius (and not the grammarian) as Festus indicates,[e] I take to be a true tradition; for in Latin inscriptions the double consonants do not appear (except in one name where the Greek is transliterated) until 189 B.C., as will be seen in the third volume of this series.

[a] For further particulars about the points dealt with in this paragraph, reference should be made to the text and translation.

[b] Diomedes, ap. *G. L.*, I, 484, 3 K. From this passage it appears that at one time (in the Augustan age ?) the *Annals* of E. were called ' *Romais* ' (cp. Virgil's *Aeneis*).

[c] Suet., *de grammat.*, 1.

[d] Suet., fragm. p. 135 Reiff., 289 Roth; Isid., *Orig.*, I, 22, 1; cd. *Cass.* W. Schmitz, *Symb. Philol. Bonn*, 532.

[e] Fest., 412, 30.

INTRODUCTION

Life of Caecilius

About Caecilius Statius we cannot say much. We do not know the date of his birth at all, while the date of his death is doubtful; but he was probably born about the year 220 b.c. He was one Statius, a Gaul or Celt of the Insubrian tribe in northern Italy; according to some, his birthplace was Mediolanum [a] (Milan). He was brought to Rome a slave, probably as a prisoner of war, between 200 and 194. We may presume that he then came into the hands of a Roman Caecilius, by whom he was freed from slavery. He henceforth bore Caecilius' gentile name, according to the custom of men who were manumitted; the name Statius, as Gellius tells us, becoming thus a kind of surname.[b] After he was made a freedman, he became a friend of Ennius,[c] as we described above, and took to writing comedies from Greek models (*fabulae palliatae*) belonging to the ' New Attic ' type and apparently wrote nothing else besides plays of this kind. It is not unreasonable to suggest that Caecilius chose this department of drama because Ennius was already composing tragedies; and thus the two poets were able to be friends without being rivals in the same sphere. At first Caecilius was not successful, for, says Lucius Ambivius Turpio,[d] the stage-manager and actor, ' at first, in new plays of Caecilius which I produced,

---

[a] Jerome, ann. Abr. 1838, 179.
[b] Gell., IV, 20, 13. By Cicero's time he was generally referred to simply as Caecilius; he is hardly ever called Statius alone in extant authorities.
[c] Jerome, *l.c.*
[d] According to the words put into his mouth by Terence in the second prologue to *Hecyra*, 14–15.

I was in some cases hissed off the stage, in others maintained my ground with difficulty.' This was perhaps because Caecilius as an Insubrian had not yet mastered Latin fully.[a] But in course of time, as we know, he became famous, reaching, according to Jerome, the height of his renown in 179, and was regarded as a person fit to judge plays offered for exhibition. In his own stage-work some thought him especially skilful in handling of plots, others remarked on his power to stir up the emotions, others again admired his surpassing dignity or weight (*gravitas*[b]). Some indeed, like Vulcacius Sedigitus (c. 130 B.C.), put Caecilius at the head of Roman writers of comedies; Cicero too was inclined to do the same.[c] Much later, Gellius (c. A.D. 130–180), in a severe criticism which will be found in this book in connexion with the fragments of Caecilius' *Plocium*, seems to have found him effective enough when read without reference to his Greek model Menander, but, in comparison with the Greek original, much inferior to it. It has been argued that, since the titles of his comedies show three classes—plays with Latin titles, like the plays of Plautus; plays with both a Latin and a Greek title; and plays with simply a Greek title,—and since the last kind form a majority, Caecilius was at first very free with his models but tended later to keep closer to them; but we can see from extant fragments of Menander's Πλόκιον that Caecilius was very free even in plays which are quoted under a Greek title only.

---

[a] Cic., *ad Att.*, VII, 3, 10; cp. *Brut.*, 74, 258.
[b] His plots: Varro, in Nonius, 374, 6; emotions: Charisius, in *G. L.*, I, 41K; ' gravitas ': Horace, *Epist.*, II, 1, 59.
[c] Sedigitus in Gell., XV, 24, 1.

Caecilius died soon after Ennius, perhaps in the year after, that is, in 168, for Jerome [a] seems to say that he died 'anno post mortem Ennii.' But Suetonius [b] says (with how much truth we cannot tell) that Terence was officially ordered to read his first play *Andria* to Caecilius, who, uninterested at the beginning, approved of it as Terence read on. But this play was not exhibited until 166 B.C., so that some add III or IIII after 'Ennii' in the text of Jerome. Caecilius' remains were apparently cremated near the Ianiculum or near if not at the same place in which those of Ennius had been burnt before him.

EDITIONS AND TRANSLATIONS

Ennius

R. and H. Stephanus. *Fragmenta Poetarum Veterum Latinorum quorum opera non extant. Ennii . . . a Rob. Stephano . . . congesta, ab Henrico . . . digesta.* 1564. pp. 78 ff.

H. Colonna. *Q. Ennii poetae . . . quae supersunt Fragmenta ab Hieronymo Columna conquisita, disposita, et explicata.* Naples. 1590.

M. A. Del Rio (Delrius). *Syntagma Tragoediae Latinae, I. Fragmenta veterum tragicorum*, pp. 96 ff. Paris. 1593.

P. Merula.[c] *Q. Ennii . . . Annalium libb. XIIX quae apud varios auctores superant fragmenta conlecta . . . ab P. . . . Merula.* Leyden. 1595.

---

[a] ann. Abr. 1838, 179.   [b] *vita Terentii*, 28, 8.
[c] To be distinguished from G. Merula or Mirlani.

INTRODUCTION

P. Schrijver. P. Scriverius. *Collectanea Veterum Tragicorum. . . . Q. Ennii . . . aliorumque fragmenta. Castigationes et notae. . . . G. J. Vossii.* Leyden. 1620 (bound up with Schrijver's *Seneca Tragicus*).

F. Hesselius. *Q. Ennii . . . Fragmenta . . . ab H. Columna conquisita . . . recusa accurante F. H. i.c. Accedunt. . . . M. A. Delrii opinationes. . . . G. J. Vossii castigationes et notae . . .* Amsterdam. 1707.

E. P. J. Spangenberg. *Q. Enii Annalium libb. XVIII fragmenta. Post P. Merulae curas iterum recensita. . . . Opera et studio E. S.* Leipzig. 1825.

F. H. Bothe. *Poetae Latii Sceneci,* V–VI. 1834.

L. Mueller. *Q. Ennii Carminum Reliquiae. . . . Emendavit et adnotavit L. M.* (St. Petersburg). 1885.

Corpus Poetarum Latinorum. ed. J. P. Postgate. 1894. I. contains L. Mueller's revision (in 1888) of his text of 1885.

A. Bachrens. *Fragmenta Poetarum Romanorum.* Leipzig. 1886. (Does not include Ennius' plays.)

O. Ribbeck. *Scaenicae Romanorum Poesis Fragmenta.* I. *Tragicorum Rom. Fr.*; II. *Comicorum Rom. Fr. praeter Plautum et Terentium.* Leipzig; 1st edition, 1852; 2nd edition, trag. 1871, com. 1873; 3rd edition ('Teubner Texts'), trag., 1897, com., 1898.

J. Vahlen. *Ennianae Poesis Reliquiae.* Leipzig; 1st edition, 1854; 2nd edition, 1903; 3rd edition, 1928.

L. Valmaggi. *Q. Ennio; i frammenti degli Annali*

INTRODUCTION

editi e illustrati da Luigi Valmaggi. Turin.
1900.
E. Diehl. *Poetarum Romanorum Veterum Reliquiae.*
Selegit E. D. Bonn: Weber. 1911. *Kleine*
Texte, 69, pp. 17–49.
G. Pascoli. *Epos*, I. Livorno: Giusti; 2nd edition.
1911. pp. 13 ff. (*Annals.*)
Ethel M. Steuart. *The Annals of Quintus Ennius;*
edited by E. M. S. Cambridge. 1925.

There are also R. Estienne, *Fragmenta Poetarum*
Veterum Latinorum. 1564; *Corpus Omnium veterum*
poetarum Latinorum, I. 1611. Geneva; *Opera et*
Fragmenta Veterum Poetarum Latinorum. II. pp.
1457 ff. Q. *Ennii Fragmenta*, ed. M. Maittaire.
London, 1713, 1721; *Collectio Pisaurensis omnium*
poematum. . . . Latinorum. IV. 1766, ed. P. Amati,
pp. 264 ff; J. B. Levée et G. A. Le Monnier, *Théâtre*
complet des Latins (Latin and French), XV. Paris,
1823. But these are not important.
There are selections from the fragments in J.
Wordsworth, *Fragments and Specimens of Early Latin.*
Oxford. 1874; and in W. W. Merry, *Selected Frag-*
ments of Roman Poetry. Oxford. 2nd ed., 1898.

Caecilius

Fragments will be found in the following, all of
which are mentioned above under *Ennius*: R. and
H. Stephanus, *Fragmenta Poetarum Veterum Latinorum*,
1564; F. H. Bothe, *Poetae Latii Scenici*, 1834;
O. Ribbeck, *Comicorum Rom. Fr.* (1st ed., 1852;
2nd ed., 1873; 3rd ed., 1898); E. Diehl, *Poet. Rom.*
Vet. Rel. 1911, pp. 59-65; also in the unimportant
works cited above at the end of the Ennian list,

INTRODUCTION

especially in Merry's *Selected Fragments.* Lastly, the fragments were edited separately by L. Spengel, *Caecilii Statii deperditarum fabularum fragmenta.* Monachii. 1829.

Abbreviations

A large amount of important work in restoring and annotating fragments of the old poets has been done by scholars such as editors and emendators in their studies on the later writers who quote the fragments; and by scholars who have recorded their labours on the poets themselves in separate books or in periodical publications. It is not possible to give a full list of these here. With regard to Ennius and Caecilius, the following are two works which have been often referred to in abbreviated form in notes : O. Ribbeck, *Die römische Tragödie im Zeitalter der Republik,* 1875 (*Röm. Trag.*); and E. Norden, *Ennius und Vergilius* (Norden). Readers who refer to Ribbeck's editions of the dramatic fragments (*Scaenica Romanorum Poesis*) will find that it is his second edition (not his third, prepared for a special purpose) which contains the completest *apparatus critici* and the best introductions (*corollaria*) to the tragic and the comic fragments respectively. For this reason, where this work of Ribbeck is cited or referred to, without indication of the edition, the second edition is meant. In the case of Vahlen's Ennius, it is the third edition, published in 1928, which is meant; the Roman figures refer to his *praefatio,* other figures to the pages of his text, except in the concordances, where the figures refer to his lines of Ennius' poetry.

With regard to the critical notes on the Latin

text, in designating the names of scholars, the following abbreviations have been used: B = Baehrens; D(I.) = Dousa (Ianus); D(F.) = Dousa (Franciscus); H = Housman; Iun. = Iunius (*i.e.* Adriaan de Jonghe); L = Lachmann; Linds. = Lindsay; M = Marx; Mr. = L. Mueller (the others of that name are given with their initials); Palmer. (*Spic.*) = J. M. Palmerius, *Spicilegia*; Quich. = Quicherat; R *or* Ribb. = Ribbeck; S = Scaliger; St. = Ethel Steuart; T = Turnebus; V = Vahlen; Voss. = Vossius (G. J. Voss). In some cases I have given the original name (for example, Colonna, Mercier, Saumaise) instead of a Latinised form of it; but I shrank from giving, for example, Jonghe for Iunius, Schrijver for Scriverius; while the original name of Turnebus is, I believe, not known. Emendations suggested by me are marked W. Variant readings, and the names or initials of scholars, have been shown in Roman type; codices and their sigla, and all other words, in italic type.

I give sincere thanks to Mr. G. Noël-Armfield of Cambridge who put these three volumes into typescript; and to the printers and publishers for their care and skill in producing a very difficult piece of printing.

E. H. WARMINGTON.

King's College, University of London,
Strand,
   London, W.C. 2.
      29*th of May,* 1935.

ENNIUS

B

ENNIUS

LIBER I

1

Varro, *L.L.*, VII, 19 : Ennii . . . —

Musae quae pedibus magnum pulsatis Olympum ;

caelum dicunt Graeci Olympum.

Cp. Varr., *R.R.*, I, 1, 4; Serv., ad *Aen.*, XI., 660; Hom. *Il.*, II, 484 Ἔσπετε νῦν μοι Μοῦσαι Ὀλύμπια δώματ᾽ ἔχουσαι.

2-3

[Probus], ap. *G.L.*, IV, 23, 11 K : Neutro genere . . . brevis est (syllaba). . . . Ennius in I—

Nam populos . . .
. . . Italos res atque poemata nostra cluebunt.

Fronto, *de Eloq.*, 146 N : Magistra Homeri Calliopa, magister Enni Homerus et Somnus.

²⁻³ Italos . . . cluebunt W *coll. Lucret.*, I, 119, ' per gentes Italas hominum quae clara clueret ' cluebunt D (I.) *fort.* Namque Italos . . . clarabunt (cp. *Hor.*, *C.*, IV, 3, 4 —clarabit). *alii alia* nam latos p. res *cd*.

---

a This is clear from Varro, *R.R.* I, 1, 4. Vahlen's second line must go—see p. 463.

2

ANNALS

BOOK I

1

The first ᵃ line ; invocation of the Muses :
Varro : In Ennius there is . . . —

Muses, who with your feet beat mighty Olympus ;

by Olympus the Greeks mean the sky.

2–3

Exhortation to readers :
Probus : As for the neuter gender the syllable ᵇ is short. . . . .
Ennius in the first book—

ᶜ for my subject and my poem shall have renown
among the peoples of Italy.

*Homer, seen by Ennius on Mount Helicon in a dream, was the
source of inspiration :*
Fronto : Homer's instructress was Calliope ; Ennius'
instructors were Homer and Sleep.

ᵇ *sc.* the final syllable, nom. voc. acc. pl.
ᶜ The readings and all proposals are doubtful (V., CXLVII).
Miss Steuart puts this fr. later, joining it with line 14. St.,
pp. 95–7.

ENNIUS

Fronto, *Epp.*, Vol. I, p. 94 (cp. 98) Haines : Transeo nunc ad Q. Ennium nostrum, quem tu ais ex somno et somnio initium sibi scribendi fecisse. Sed profecto nisi ex somno suscitatus esset, numquam somnium suum narrasset.

4

Fronto, *Epp.*, Vol. I, pp. 204 H : Si quando te—

somno leni

ut poeta ait—

placidoque revinctus

video in somnis, numquam est quin amplectar et exosculer . . . hoc unum ex Annalibus sumptum amoris mei argumentum poeticum et sane somniculosum.

5

Cicero, *Ac. Pr.*, II, 16, 51 : Cum somniavit (*Ennius*) narravit—

visus Homerus adesse poeta.

Cp. *Ac. Pr.*, 27, 88 : de Re Pub., VI, 10, 10.

6

Cicero, *Ac. Pr.*, II, 27, 88 : Nisi vero Ennium non putamus ita totum illud audivisse—

'O pietas animi !

si modo id somniavit ut si vigilans audiret.

Cp. Donat. in Ter., *Eun.*, III, 5, 12.

7–10

Epicharmus, ap. *Com. Cr. Fr.* I, 123 Kaibel : καὶ γὰρ τὸ θῆλυ τῶν ἀλεκτορίδων γένος, | αἰ λῇς καταμαθεῖν, ἀτενὲς οὐ τίκτει τέκνα | ζῶντ' ἀλλ' ἐπῴζει καὶ ποιεῖ ψυχὰν ἔχειν.

Varro, *L.L.*, V, 59 : Haec duo caelum et terra quod anima et corpus. Humidum et frigidum terra, eaque corpus, caldor caeli et inde anima, sive—

---

⁵ < In somnis mihi > visus Colonna, Merula *coll. Aen. II*, 270, *fortasse recte*.

ANNALS

Marcus Aurelius to Fronto: And now I pass to our poet Ennius, who you say began to write after sleeping and dreaming. But surely if he had not been roused out of his sleep he would never have told the tale of his dream.

4

Fronto writes to Marcus Aurelius: If ever,—

Fettered in soft calm sleep

as the poet says, I see you in dreams,[a] there is no time when I do not embrace you and fondly kiss you . . . this is one proof of my love, which I take from the *Annals*, a poetic and dreamy one indeed.

5

Homer appears :

Cicero: When Ennius had dreamed, this is what he told of it—

Homer the poet appeared at my side.

6

Opening of Homer's speech :

Cicero: Unless indeed we choose to believe that Ennius, merely because he dreamed it, did not hear the whole of that famous speech—

' O loving kindness of thy heart. . . .'[b]

as well as he would have heard it if he had been awake.

7–10

Homer tells how his soul migrated into Ennius' body :

Varro: These two, sky and earth, correspond with life and body. The wet and cold masses form the earth, and she is body; heat is the essence of the sky, whence comes life, whether we assume that—

---

[a] This suggests that the fr. is rightly placed here.
[b] Thus Miss Steuart.

ENNIUS

' Ova parire solet genus pennis condecoratum
non animam,

ut ait Ennius—

' et post inde venit divinitus pullis
ipsa anima ;

sive, ut Zenon Citieus, animalium semen ignis isque anima et
mens.

Cp. Diomed., ap. *G.L.*, I, 383, 5 K; Priscian., ap. *G.L.*, II,
401, 3 K.

11–12

Varro, *L.L.*, V, 60 : Recte igitur . . . quod ait . . . Ennius—

' terraque corpus
quae dedit ipsa capit neque dispendi facit hilum.

Cp. V, 111 ; IX, 53.

13

Donatus, in Ter., *Andr.*, II, 5, 18 : ' Memini videre ' pro
' vidisse ' Ennius—

' Memini me fiere pavum.

Cp. Ter., in *Adelph.*, I, 2, 26; in *Phorm.*, I, 2, 24; Charis.,
ap. *G.L.*, I, 98, 4 K ; Tertull., *de An.*, 33 pavum se meminit
Homerus Ennio somniante. Lucret., I, 112–126.

Schol. *ad Pers.*, *Prol.*, 2–3 : Tangit Ennium qui dixit se
vidisse per somnium in Parnaso Homerum sibi dicentem quod
eius anima in suo esset corpore.

ᵃ It is difficult to believe that these fragments belong to anything but *Epicharmus* (see pp. 410 ff.). In this part of his work
Varro quotes several passages from Ennius' *Epicharmus*, and

6

ANNALS

' The feather-furbished tribe is wont to be delivered of eggs, not of life,

according to the words of Ennius *—

' and after that time life itself comes to the chicks by a god's will;

or, according to Zenon of Cition, that the seed of living things is fire and this is their life and soul.

11–12

Varro : Right therefore is the statement of . . . Ennius *—

' And earth who herself bestowed the body takes it back and wastes not a whit.

13

Donatus : ' I remember seeing ' instead of ' having seen ' : Ennius—

' I remember becoming *c* a peacock.

A scholiast : Persius alludes to Ennius, who states that in a dream he saw a vision of Homer on Parnassus (*mistake for Helicon*); Homer said that his soul was in Ennius' body.

---

not from the *Annals*. Yet we must agree with those who assign them to the first book of the *Annals* (V., CXLVIII; and 3–4). The metre is not the same as that of known frs. of *Epicharmus*, and an allusion in Lucretius points to the *Annals*.

b See preceding note.

c Macrob., *G.L.*, V., 645, notes *fiere* for *fieri* in the tenth book also.

7

ENNIUS

14

Persius, S., VI, 9–11 : —

' Lunai portum, est operae, cognoscite, cives.'

Cor iubet hoc Enni posquam destertuit esse | Maeonides,
Quintus pavone ex Pythagoreo.

Schol., *ad loc.* : Hunc versum ad suum carmen de Ennii
carminibus transtulit. Merito ergo ait ' cor iubet hoc Enni
postquam destertuit.' Sic Ennius ait in Annalium suorum
principio, ubi dicit se vidisse in somnis Homerum dicentem
fuisse quondam pavonem et ex eo translatam in se animam
esse secundum Pythagorae philosophi definitionem.

Cp. Porphyr., ad Hor., *Ep.* II, 1, 50–3; Comment. in Stat.,
Theb., III, 484; Ov., *Met.*, XV, 160 *s.*; Hor., *C.*, I, 28–9 *s.*

15

Priscianus, ap. *G.L.*, II, 97–8 K. : ' Veterrimus quasi a
' veter.' . . . Ennius—

Quom veter occubuit Priamus sub Marte Pelasgo,

16–17

Servius (auctus) ad *Georg.*, III, 35 : Assaracus avus Anchisae.
Ennius—

Assaraco natus Capys optimus isque pium ex se
Anchisen generat.

Il., XX, 239 : Ἀσσάρακος δὲ Κάπυν, ὅδ' ἄρ' Ἀγχίσην τέκε παῖδα.

¹⁴ *trib. Saturis* H
¹⁷ Anchisen *Serv. auct.*   Anchisam Valmaggi *prob.* St.

ᵃ I agree with Vahlen (CXLIX : cp. V., ' Über die A. des E.'
in *Abh. Kön. Ak.*, 1886, 37, 38), who concludes from Persius'
language that the mention of Luna (Spezia) came after the
tale of the dream.   But Housman (*C.R.*, 1934, 50–1) may well
be right in assigning this fr. to the Satires. Cf. also St., pp.
95 ff. ' cor ' might be translated here ' a heart '; I suggest that
Ennius' statement (Gellius, XVII, 17, 1) that he had three
hearts because he spoke Greek, Oscan, and Latin, was made
here in the *Annals.*

8

ANNALS

14

Romans must remember the place where Ennius dreamed :

Persius :—

'Take note, ye citizens, of Luna's harbour—it is worth while.

Thus commanded Ennius in his senses after he had [a] snored out his dream that he was the Man of Maeonia—Quintus at last out of a Pythagorean peacock.

A scholiast on this passage: This line he took from the poems of Ennius to put into his own poem. It is well then that he says, ' thus commanded Ennius in his senses after he had snored out.' That is what Ennius says in the beginning of his *Annals* where he states that in the course of a dream he saw a vision of Homer who said that he was once a peacock and from it, according to a rule [b] laid down by the philosopher Pythagoras, his soul had been conveyed into Ennius.

15

Beginning of the narrative. The Fall of Troy :

Priscianus : ' Veterrimus ' is as it were derived from a positive ' veter.' . . . Ennius has—

When aged Priam was laid low beneath the warring Pelasgian,

16–17

The Lineage of Aeneas : Assaracus, Capys, and Anchises :

Servius (supplemented) : Assaracus was grandfather of Anchises. . . . Ennius—

From Assaracus sprang Capys best of men : and he was from his loins begetter of Anchises the loyal.[c]

[b] See pp. 5–7.
[c] In the story followed by Ennius, Achilles was the rescuer. V., CLII makes Aeneas (as in Homer) speak this line to the King of Alba.

9

ENNIUS

18–19

Probus in Verg., *Ecl.*, VI, 31 : Ennius Anchisen augurii ac
per hoc divini quoddam habuisse praesumit sic—

Doctusque Anchisa, Venus quem pulcherruma
dium
fari donavit, divinum pectus habere.

Cp. Schol. Ver. ad *Aen.*, II, 687.

20

Servius (auctus) ad *Georg.*, IV, 59 : ' Nare ' pro volare ut apud
Ennium in primo—

transnavit cita per teneras caliginis auras.

21

Festus, 428, 11 : ' Sos ' pro ' cos ' . . . ut Ennius lib. I—

Constitit inde loci propter sos dia dearum.

Cp. Paul., ex F., 429, 11. Cp. *Il.*, XVIII, 388, etc., δῖα
θεάων.

22–3

Festus, 234, 23 : ' Orare ' antiquos dixisse pro agere testimonio. . . . Ennius quoque cum dixit in lib. I Annalium—

                                                    ' face vero
quod tecum precibus pater orat.'

[18] doctusque Anchisa Fleckeisen   atque Anchises doctus
S   doctus parens Anchisa Mr.   doctusque Anchises *Prob.*
doctus Anchisa *Schol. Ver.*   pulcherruma dium Fleckeisen
pulchra dearum *Prob.*   pulcherrima diu *Schol. Ver.*
[19] fari donavit *Prob.*   fata docet *Schol. Ver.*   fari
Bernays   fari fata docet *coni.* V
[22] face vero Colonna   facere vero *cdd.*   tu face vero
August.   tum face vero (*olim* tu vero face) V *qui un. vers.
constit.*

10

ANNALS

18-19

Anchises :

Probus : Ennius pictures to himself Anchises as having
some power of soothsaying by bird-lore, and, through this,
something of the prophet in him : thus—

and shrewd Anchises to whom Venus, loveliest of
goddesses, granted power to foretell, yea to have
a godly heart of prophecy.[a]

20

An approach [b] of Venus :

Servius (supplemented) : ' To float ' instead of ' to fly,' as
in a passage of E. in the first book—

Along she floated swiftly through rare wafts of
mistiness.

21

Venus appears to Aeneas and his companions :

Festus : ' Sos ' for ' eos '; for example Ennius in Book I—

Thereupon she, hallowed among the holy goddesses, took her stand close to them.

22-3

*She [e] tries to persuade Aeneas to obey Anchises and retire to
Mount Ida :*

Festus : That the ancients used the term ' to plead ' [d] for ' to
deal.' Ennius also was a witness when he wrote in the first
book of the *Annals*—

' But be sure to do what your father pleads for
in prayers with you.'

[a] St., pp. 101-3.
[b] Cf. the excellent note of Miss St., pp. 103-4; cp. V., CL.
[e] For this variation of the legend cf. Dionys. Halic., I, 48, 2;
V., CLXIX; St., pp. 104, 105.
[d] Festus means the use of *orare cum aliquo* (like *agere c. a.*)
instead of *orare aliquem.*

ENNIUS

24

Macrobius, VI, I, 11 : ' Est locus, Hesperiam Grai cogno-
mine dicunt ' (*Aen.*, I, 530; III, 163). Ennius in I—

Est locus, Hesperiam quam mortales perhibebant,[a]

25

Varro, *L.L.*, VII, 28 : ' Cascum ' vetus esse significat E.
quod ait—

quam prisci casci populi tenuere Latini.

Cp. Cic., *Tusc. Disp.*, I, 12, 27.

26

Varro, *L.L.*, V, 42 (*de Capitolio*) : Hunc antea montem
Saturnium appellatum prodiderunt et ab eo late Saturniam
terram ut etiam Ennius appellat—

Saturnia terra[b]

27–8

Nonius, 197, 2 : ' Caelum ' neutro. Masculino ... Ennius—

Saturno

quem Caelus genuit.

Cp. Charis., ap. *G.L.*, I, 72, 13 K.

29

Nonius, 216, 31 : ' Obsidio ' . . . neutro Ennius—

Quom saevo obsidio magnus Titanus premebat,[c]

---

[24] quam *Macrob.*   quem St. *lapsu typograph. ; sed recte?*
[29] saevo Iun.   sos Havet   suo *cdd.*

---

[a] Sc. Greeks, V., CL.   [b] V., CL–CLI.
[c] V., CLI.

ANNALS

24

Italy and the Latins :

Macrobius : ' There is a region which the Greeks call by name " Western Land." ' Ennius in the first book—

There is a region which mortals^a used to call
' Western Land,'

25

Varro : That ' cascus ' means ' old ' is shown by Ennius because he says—

which the ancient Latin folk of eld did hold.^b

26

The early connexion of Latium with Saturn : ^c

Varro says of the Capitoline Hill : Men have recorded that once upon a time this hill was called ' Saturn's ' and hence in a broad sense they record—

Saturn's Land

as Ennius among others calls it.

27-8

The fortunes of Saturn :

Nonius : ' Caelum ' neuter. In a masculine form . . . Ennius—

To Saturn whom Sky begat.

29

Why he fled to Italy :

Nonius : ' Obsidio ' . . . neuter in Ennius—

When great Titan was afflicting him with cruel duress.^d

^d Ennius himself in *Euhemerus* (see pp. 420-3) told how Titan kept Saturn imprisoned, and how Saturn fled to Italy. This line, however, is a hexameter and surely belongs to the *Annals*, not to *Euhemerus*, which was written in *septenarii*.

ENNIUS

30

Priscianus, ap. *G.L.*, II, 337, 26 K : ' Laurentis ' etiam pro
' Laurens.' Ennius in A.—

quos homines quondam Laurentis terra recepit.

31

Atilius Fortunat., ap. *G.L.*, VI, 284, 20 K : Maximus qui est
versus syllabas habet XVII . . . minimus habet XII ut est
Ennianus—

Olli respondit rex Albai Longai.

Cp. Donat., ap. *G.L.*, IV, 396, 19 K : Pompeius, ap. *G.L.*,
V, 297, 30 K : *Explanat. in Donat.*, ap. *G.L.*, IV, 548, 2 K.

Servius, ad *Aen.*, VI, 777 : . . . Secundum Ennium, referetur
(Romulus) inter deos cum Aenea.

Servius, ad *Aen.*, VI, 777 : Dicit . . . Iliam fuisse filiam
Aeneae.

32-48

Cicero, *de Div.*, I, 20, 40 : Narrat . . . apud Ennium Vestalis
illa—

Excita quom tremulis anus attulit artubus lumen,
talia tum memorat lacrumans exterrita somno :
' Euridica prognata, pater quam noster amavit,
vires vitaque corpus meum nunc deserit omne.   35
Nam me visus homo pulcher per amoena salicta
et ripas raptare locosque novos ; ita sola
postilla, germana soror, errare videbar,
tardaque vestigare et quaerere te, neque posse

[32] excita, et cita *cdd. Cic. de Div.*   *fortasse* Vestalis
Ilia ' excita

---

[a] This is Vahlen's decision (V., CLIII); but St., p. 111,
includes the fr. in the story of Ilia's fate.
[b] Cp. p. 39.
   Cf. St., pp. 106 ff.; V., CLIII ff.

ANNALS

30

Aeneas and his followers arrive at Laurentum in Latium :

Priscianus : 'Laurentis' for 'Laurens.' Ennius in the *Annals*—

These men one day Laurentum's land received.

31

Concourse of Aeneas and the King of Alba : [a]

Atilius : The shortest hexameter has 12 syllables like this of Ennius—

To him answer made the King of Alba Longa.

Aeneas is deified :

Servius : According to Ennius, he (Romulus) will be reckoned with Aeneas among the gods.[b]

The story of Ilia :

Servius goes on : He says that Ilia was a daughter of Aeneas.

32–48

The dream of Ilia,[c] daughter of Aeneas, after his death :

Cicero : in Ennius the famous vestal tells her story—

When the old woman[d] roused up, had with limbs a-tremble brought a light, then the maid,[e] frightened out of sleep, spoke thus in tears :—' O daughter of Eurydica,[f] you whom our father loved, now strength and life too leave all my body. For a man of beautiful looks seemed to hurry me away among pleasant sallow-thickets and banks and places strange ; so, my own sister, after that did I seem to wander alone, and slow-footed to track and search for you, but to be unable to catch you to

[d] Probably some attendant or nurse.   [e] Ilia.
[f] According to Ennius, wife of Aeneas and mother not of Ilia but only of Ilia's step-sister, though both sisters were daughters of Aeneas.

15

corde capessere ; semita nulla pedem stabilibat. 40
Exin conpellare pater me voce videtur
his verbis : " O gnata, tibi sunt ante ferendae
aerumnae, post ex fluvio fortuna resistet."
Haec ecfatus pater, germana, repente recessit,
nec sese dedit in conspectum corde cupitus, 45
quamquam multa manus ad caeli caerula templa
tendebam lacrumans et blanda voce vocabam.
Vix aegro tum corde meo me somnus reliquit.

Ovidius, *Tr.* II, 259–260 :

Sumpserit annales (nihil est hirsutius illis)
facta sit undа parens Ilia nempe leget.

Servius (auctus) ad *Aen.*, I, 273 Naevius et Ennius Aeneae
ex filia nepotem Romulum conditorem urbis tradunt.
Cp. Serv., ad *Aen.*, VI, 777.

49–50

Nonius, 378, 15 : 'Parumper,' cito ac velociter. . . . Ennius
Annali lib. I—

' Te nunc sancta precor Venus, te genetrix patris
        nostri
ut me de caelo visas cognata parumper,'

[42] ferendae Davis   gerendae *cdd. prob.* V
[46] tum *Voss. A.*   cum *Voss. B. Vind. fortasse recte*
[49] nunc sancta Colonna   sale nata V   sane alta
Pascoli   dea sancta Ilberg   venerata B   te te
sancta *coni.* St.   sane neta *cdd.*
[50] rogitata Haupt

16

my heart: no path made sure my stepping. Then it was father who seemed to lift up his voice and speak to me in these words:—" O daughter, first there are hardships to be borne by you; but after that, your fortunes will rise[a] again from a river." With these words, my own sister, did father suddenly withdraw, and no longer gave himself to my gaze though my heart longed for him; no, even though many a time and with tears did I keep holding out my hands towards the blue precincts of the sky, and called and called him with caressing voice. Even then did sleep scarcely leave me all sick at heart.

Ilia, loved by Mars, gives birth to Romulus and Remus :

Ovid :

If a woman should take the *Annals* (there's no poem shaggier than they) she will perforce read how Ilia became a mother.[b]

Servius (supplemented) : Naevius and Ennius record that the founder of the city was Romulus, grandson of Aeneas through his daughter.

49-50

Ilia, arraigned for her fault, appeals to Venus :

Nonius : ' Parumper,' speedily[c] and quickly. . . . Ennius in the first book of the *Annals*—

' Thee, hallowed Venus, thee now the mother of my father, I pray look down on me from heaven a little while, my kinswoman.'

[a] A very rare use of the verb. The vision mysteriously prophesies the salvation of Romulus by a flooding of the Tiber. This might imply that the council of the gods had taken place already; but see note on line 57, p. 20.
[b] Cf. S. G. Owen, *Ov. Nas. Trist.*, II, pp. 164-5.
[c] Nonius here mistakes the meaning of *parumper*.

17

ENNIUS

51

Macrobius VI, 1, 12: 'Tuque o Thybri, tuo genitor cum flumine sancto' (*Aen.*, VIII, 72). Ennius in I—

'Teque pater Tiberine tuo cum flumine sancto,

52

Charisius, ap. *G.L.*, I, 90, 26 K.: 'Neptis' grammatici nolunt dici . . . et advocant Ennium quod dixerit ita—

'Ilia dia nepos, quas aerumnas tetulisti

Cp. Non., 215, 8: Fest., 402, 15; Serg., *Explanat. in Donat.*, ap. *G.L.*, IV, 563, 14 K.

53–4

Servius (auctus) ad *Aen.*, IX, 653: 'Cetera' id est in ceterum; est autem Ennianum—

'cetera quos peperisti

ne cures.

55

Nonius, 306, 26: 'Facessere' est facere. . . .—

Haec ecfatus, ibique latrones dicta facessunt.

Porphyrio, ad Hor., C., I, 2, 17: Ilia auctore Ennio in amnem Tiberim iussu Amulii regis Albanorum praecipitata; antea enim Anieni matrimonio iuncta est.

---

a Aeneas, according to Norden, 162, because he is the speaker in Virgil's line. But cf. St., pp. 109–10, V., CLIX. The speaker might be even Horatius Cocles (Livy, II, 10, 11—tum Cocles 'Tiberine pater' inquit 'te sancte precor. . . .').

b If these are words of comfort to Ilia, we might conclude that the council of the gods had already taken place (cp.

51

Ilia ^a appeals also to Tiber :

Macrobius : ' And thou, sire Thybris with thy hallowed
stream '; Ennius in the first book—

' And thee, Father of the Tiber, with thy hallowed
stream,

52

Venus answers Ilia's prayer :

Charisius : The grammarians would have it that the form
' neptis ' should not be used . . . and Ennius is appealed to
because he wrote ' nepos ' as a feminine, thus—

' Ilia, godly granddaughter, the hardships you
have borne . . .

53-4

Servius (supplemented), on ' cetera ' in Virgil : ' Cetera
that is, ' in ceterum '; and it is an Ennian usage—

' For the rest, take ^b you no care for the boys to
whom you gave birth.

55

Amulius orders Ilia to be thrown into the Tiber :

Nonius : ' Facessere ' means ' to do.' . . .—

Thus he spake out; and then the hireling warriors
sprang to carry ^c out his word.

Porphyrio : According to Ennius' account Ilia was thrown
headlong into the river Tiber by order of Amulius, King of
the Albans; but before this she was joined in marriage to
the Anio.

---

p. 17, n. *a*). But I have put this debate later. See below,
p. 20.

^c *facessere* means more than merely *facere.*

ENNIUS

56

Servius (auctus) ad *Aen.*, III, 333 : 'Reddita' more veteri
pro 'data' accipiendum est . . . Ennius Annalibus—

At Ilia reddita nuptum,

57

Tertullianus, *adv. Val.*, 7 : Ennius poeta—

cenacula maxima caeli

simpliciter pronuntiavit de elati situs nomine vel quia Iovem
illic epulantem legerat apud Homerum.

Cp. Schol. Ver. ad *Aen.*, X, 1.

58

Servius, ad *Aen.*, X, 5 :—

bipatentibus

Est tem sermo Ennianus, tractus ab ostiis quae ex utraque
parte aperiuntur.

59

Macrobius, *S.*, VI, 1, 9 : 'Axem humero torquet stellis
ardentibus aptum.' (*Aen.*, IV, 482, VI, 797.) Ennius in I—

qui caelum versat stellis fulgentibus aptum.

[56] At Ilia Commelinus   ut illa Daniel   ut Ilia V
ad illa *cd.*   nuptum *vulg.*   nupta B   nuptam *cd.*
[57-8] *trib. Ann. I ed. Lips.*

---

a It is not known where the debate of the gods should be
placed. I put it here because the strange preservation of
the twins might well be the result of divine intervention.
Cp. V., CLIX ff. I suggest that the passage in Ovid, *Met.*,
XIV, 812 ff. leads us to put the council a long while before
Romulus' death; Mars speaks at a time when Rome was well

ANNALS

56

Ilia is married to Tiber :

Servius (supplemented) on ' reddita ' in Virgil: ' reddita ' must, as an archaic usage, be taken to mean ' data '; Ennius in the *Annals*—

But Ilia, rendered into wedlock,

57

The gods assemble to decide [a] *the fate of Romulus :*

Tertullian : Ennius the poet spoke simply of—

most mighty dining-halls of heaven

either on account of their lofty position or because in a passage of Homer [b] he had read of Jupiter feasting there.

58

Servius, on ' bipatentibus ' in Virgil :—

with twin openings [c]

This mode of expression is Ennian, and is drawn from the use of doors which we unclose both to right and left.

59

The assembled gods ; Jupiter : [d]

Macrobius : (Atlas) ' whirls on his shoulders the sky dotted ' with blazing stars. Ennius in the first book—

who spins round the sky dotted with shining stars.

established, and he refers to a *concilium* held *quondam* and can only recall Jupiter's promise by an effort of memory.
[b] Not in the extant poems.
[c] The attribution to this context is suggested by the passage in which Virgil (*Aen.*, X, 1 ff.) uses the word.
[d] Or Atlas; if so, we should place this fr. among those which describe the ancestors of Aeneas, p. 9 (V., CLII).
[e] ' tangled in a skein of '—Miss Steuart. But Ennius was a man, and he meant simply dotted.

ENNIUS

60–1

Martianus Capella, I, 42 : Ipsius collegae Iovis . . . bis seni cum eodem Tonante numerantur quos . . . distichum complectitur Ennianum—

Iuno Vesta Minerva Ceres Diana Venus Mars
Mercurius Iovis Neptunus Vulcanus Apollo

Cp. Apulei., *de deo Socr.*, 2, 6, 23.

62

Servius ad *Aen.*, IV, 576 : Aut distinguendum ' sancte ' aut ' sancte deorum ' secundum Ennium dixit—

Respondit Iuno Saturnia sancta dearum.

Cp. Donat., ap. *G.L.*, IV, 394, 1 K. : Serg., *explanat. in Donat.*, ap. *G.L.*, IV, 563, 20 K. : Pompei., ap. *G.L.*, V, 291, 17 K. : Mar. Plot. Sac., ap. *G.L.*, VI, 450, 20 K. (*pulchra dearum*).

63–4

Varro, *L.L.*, VII, 5 : Dicam in hoc libro de verbis quae a poetis sunt posita . . . incipiam hinc—

' Unus erit quem tu tolles in caerula caeli templa.'

Cp. Ovid., *Met.*, XIV, 812 ff.; Fasti., II, 485 ff.

[60–2] *trib. Ann. lib. I* Merula

ANNALS

60–1

Martianus Capella: The colleagues of Jupiter himself amount to twice six in number, including the Thunderer just mentioned; whose names are contained in a pair of lines in Ennius [a]—

Juno Vesta Minerva Ceres Diana Venus Mars
Mercury Jupiter Neptune Vulcan Apollo

62

Speech of Juno ; she agrees [b] *to the deification of Romulus :*

Servius, on ' sancte deorum ' in Virgil : We must either put a comma after ' sancte ' or else he used the phrase ' sancte deorum ' after Ennius—

Juno, hallowed among goddesses, daughter of Saturn, made answer.

63–4

Jupiter foretells to Mars that only one of his sons shall be deified :

Varro : In this book I shall speak of words which find a place in the poets. . . . I will begin with this—

' One there will be whom thou shalt raise up to the blue precincts of the sky.[c]

[a] If, as is probable, there was only one council, this list of gods is rightly placed here.
[b] This fr. may belong to Book VIII; see p. 109. But cf. Hor. O., III, 3, 16 :
Quirinus | Martis equis Acheronta fugit | gratum elocuta consiliantibus | Iunone divis. . . .
[c] The attribution to Ennius is not certain, but provided that this is right, the fr. certainly belongs to the description of the council, if we may judge from the passage in Ovid, *Met.*, XIV, 812 ff. Ovid seems to recall the unplaced fr. ' divumque hominumque pater rex ' (see p. 168), which might be placed somewhere in this context.

ENNIUS

65

Festus, 392, 35 : ' Remanant,' repetunt. Ennius lib. I—

. . . destituunt rivos camposque remanant

Cp. Paul., ex F., 393, 11.

66–9

Fronto, *de Orat.*, 160 N : ' Factum est ' : eodem hoc verbo Enni†. urmiak . . . —

⟨lo⟩ ca claudi :

ait—

factum est . . . ⟨Tiberis⟩

. . . et facinus commemorabile. Tiberis est Tusce Tiber quem iubes cludi. Tiber amnis et dominus et fluentium circa regnator undarum. Ennius—

Postquam

constituit sese fluvius qui est omnibus princeps

. . . . cui succidit Ilia

Cp. Cic., *Orat.*, 48, 161.

---

[65] destituunt S clivis decedunt *olim* V desubito linquent Bergk desunt Fest. *prob.* V *qui* (*Rh. Mus.* XIV, 552) < iam stabulis d.> *add.* rivos camposque *Fest., Paul.* campos ripisque Mr. (*qui* undae *add.*) campos rivoque B (*an recte* ?) *alii alia.*

[66] *Fronto, de Orat.*, 160 *fortasse* verbo Ennius utitur in I A. < lo > ca *supplevi.* *vocabula* loca claudi . . . factum est. . . . Tiberis *puto esse Ennii* postquam constituit sese W postquam consistit Bekker Postquamconsisiiiiseiluuiu *cd.*

[69] cui succidit (*vel* subiacet, succubat, succinit) Ilia W *lac.* *indicavi sec. Kuebler* qui sub civilia *cd.* *trib. Ann. lib. I ed. Lips.*

24

ANNALS

65

The Tiber overflows a second time :

Festus: 'Remanant,' they seek again.   E. in the first book—

The waters left their channels and flowed back into the plains.[a]

66–9

Jupiter orders [b] Tiber to subside :

Fronto: 'It was done.' This same verb is used by Ennius . . . —

the broken places to be dammed up ;

he says—

it was done . . . the Tiber

. . . and a noteworthy act. 'Tiberis' is in Tuscan dialect 'Tiber,' which you order to be dammed up. The river Tiber is lord and ruler of all flowing waters round those parts. Ennius—

After the river which is chief over all settled down . . . for whose sake Ilia did sink beneath

---

[a] I keep the order of Festus—*rivos camposque*—which points to a second flooding of the river; otherwise the fr. expresses the return of flooding waters to their right channel. V., CLXI seems to me to be wrong.

[b] I suggest that we have here fragments of Ennius describing how Jupiter commanded Tiber to draw back his waters, and how Tiber obeyed. However, even such meagre scraps as I have added to Fronto's text are quite uncertain. But compare Horace, *Odes*, I, 2, 17–20 :

Iliae dum se nimium querenti
iactat ultorem vagus et sinistra
labitur ripa Iove non probante u-
xorius amnis.

Cp. also Virgil, *E.*, III, 14; Claudite iam rivos pueri; sat prata biberunt.

ENNIUS

70

Charisius, ap. *G.L.*, I, 128, 31 K : ' Fici.' Ennius—
fici dulciferae lactantes ubere toto

71

Servius (auctus) ad *Aen.*, II, 355 : 'Sane apud veteres
' lupus ' promiscuum erat, ut Ennius—
lupus femina feta repente

Cp. Fest., 402, 4; Quintil., I, 6, 12.
Servius, ad *Aen.*, VIII, 631 Sane totus hic locus Ennianus
est.

72–4

Nonius, 378, 15 : ' Parumper ' cito ac velociter . . .—
Indotuetur ibi lupus femina, conspicit omnis :
hinc campum celeri passu permensa parumper
coniicit in silvam sese.

75–6

Nonius, 134, 11 : ' Licitari,' congredi, pugnare. Ennius—
pars ludicre saxa
iactant, inter se licitantur

70–71 *trib. lib. I* Colonna
73 hinc campum Colonna   in campo *cdd.*
75–6 *trib. lib. I ed. Lips.*

---

a *ubere*, perhaps an udder-shaped mass; cp. Pall., *Jun.*,
7, 6, 9 ; so that Ennius maybe simply completes a metaphor
of milk and udder. But the tree was indeed ' *ruminalis* '
and I take *ubere* as the tree's udders of figs.

70

The trough holding Ilia's twins Romulus and Remus is cast up by a fig-tree which was later called the ' Fig-Tree of the Paps.'

Charisius : ' Fici.' Ennius—

sweet-bearing figs, dripping milk from the whole udder.[a]

71

The she-wolf :

Serviusn (supplemented): The noun 'lupus' was in old writers certainly common to both genders, as in Ennius—

Suddenly a she-wolf big with young

She suckles Romulus and Remus :

Servius : The whole [b] of this passage (*Aen.*, VIII, 630-4) is certainly modelled on Ennius.

72-4

The wolf sees the shepherds and flees :

Nonius : ' Parumper,' speedily and quickly . . . —

Thereupon the she-wolf gazed and saw them all; then she, passing over the plain with quick lope, hurriedly betook herself into a wood.

75-6

Romulus and Remus sport with the shepherds :

Nonius : ' Licitari,' to engage in battle, to fight. E.—

Some hurled stones in play and justled one with another.

[b] I suggest that in that passage the words *tereti cervice reflexam* (cp. Lucret., I, 35) are directly copied from Ennius, for Cicero, in a passage of translation from the *Phaenomena* (*de Nat. Deor.*, II, 41), has *obstipum caput a tereti cervice reflexum* where *obstipum* is a word favoured by Ennius (see lines 278, 398).

ENNIUS

77

Festus, 376, 22 : ' Ratus sum ' significat ' putavi ': sed alioqui pro ' firmo,' ' certo,' ponitur ' ratus est,' et ' ratum.' Ennius—

Occiduntur ubi potitur ratus Romulus praedam.

78

Macrobius, S., VI, 1, 13 : ' Accipe daque fidem, sunt nobis fortia bello | pectora ' (Aen., VIII, 150). Ennius in I—

' Accipe daque fidem foedusque feri bene firmum.

79

Macrobius, VI, 1, 14 : ' Et lunam in nimbo nox intempesta tenebat ' (Aen., III, 597). Ennius in I—

Quom superum lumen nox intempesta teneret,

80-100

Cicero, de Div., I, 48, 107 ff. : Itaque Romulus augur ut apud Ennium est, cum fratre item augure—

---

[a] Or perhaps as a defender of the shepherds against the attacks of robbers, whose spoils Romulus captured. V., CLXII. Miss St. takes the incident as one in a conflict with royal shepherds (St., 113). Some take *occiduntur* as the last word of a sentence. *Ratus* was probably a permanent nickname of Romulus.

[b] V., CLIX sees in this fr. an agreement between Aeneas and the King of Alba ; Miss Steuart makes it a part of Hersilia's speech (see below) ; there can be little doubt, however, that Macrobius, in his quotations from Ennius in VI, 1, 11-15, has given them in the order of Ennius' text (cf. G. Regel, *De Vergilio poetarum imitatore testimonia*, 37, n. 36), which Miss Steuart (Pref., X) admits as a possibility. This forces

77

Romulus as a hunter [a] :

Festus : ' Ratus sum ' means ' I thought ' : but apart from this ' ratus ' and ' ratum ' are put for ' firm,' ' sure.' Ennius—

They were cut down when Romulus the Resolved won his quarry.

78

Romulus is reconciled [b] with Numitor :

Macrobius quoting Virgil : ' Give and take you plighted troth : there are within us hearts brave in war.' Ennius in the first book—

' Give and take you plighted troth and make a treaty truly firm.

79

Romulus and Remus are about to take the auspices for founding a city ; [c] they wait for daybreak :

Macrobius : ' And the dead of night held hid the moon in a black mist.' Ennius in the first book—

When the dead of night held hid the light above,

80–100

Romulus and Remus take the auspices at dawn ; Romulus stands on the Aventine, Remus on the Remuria.[d]

Cicero : And thus Romulus, as augur with his brother, likewise as augur, as takes place in a passage of Ennius—

---

us to put this fr. earlier than that which is rightly believed to refer to Remus (p. 32). The context which I suggest here seems to me to be the most natural one.

[c] St., 113 is I think right (V., CXIV differs). On the position of this fr., cf. preceding note.

[d] On this point, cf. St., 113 ff. The Remuria may have been part of the Aventine. Cf. also V., CLXII ff., and in *Sitzungsber. d. k. Ak* 1894, 1143 ff. ; and Mommsen, *Herm.*, XVI, 13 ff.

ENNIUS

Curantes magna cum cura tum cupientes
regni dant operam simul auspicio augurioque;
. . . . in monte . . . .
. . . Remus auspicio se devovet atque secundam
solus avem servat. At Romulus pulcher in alto
quaerit Aventino, servat genus altivolantum.   85
Certabant urbem Romam Remoramve vocarent.
Omnibus cura viris uter esset induperator :
expectant, veluti consul quom mittere signum
volt, omnes avidi spectant ad carceris oras
quam mox emittat pictis e faucibus currus :   90
sic exspectabat populus atque ora tenebat,
rebus utri magni victoria sit data regni.
Interea sol albus recessit in infera noctis.
Exin candida se radiis dedit icta foras lux ;
et simul ex alto longe pulcherruma praepes   95
laeva volavit avis, simul aureus exoritur sol.
Cedunt de caelo ter quattuor corpora sancta
avium, praepetibus sese pulchrisque locis dant.
Conspicit inde sibi data Romulus esse propritim
auspicio regni stabilita scamna solumque.   100

    Cp. Gell., VI, 6, 9.

Excerpta ex cod. Cassin. 90 C, ap. *C.G.L.*, V, 578, 3 : Romae
conditor certus nescitur. Ennius et alii a Romulo.
    Cp. Servius (auct.) ad *Aen.*, I, 273.

---

[91] ore timebat *cdd. opt.*
[99] propritim Mr.   propriam *Voss A Vind.*   priora
Voss B

---

    [a] Here *sol* has been taken to mean the moon. But if
Ennius meant moon, why did he not write '*luna alba*' ?
It may be that Romulus and Remus went out at night and

ANNALS

Then, careful with a great care, each in eagerness
for royal rule, they are intent on the watching and
soothsaying of birds . . . on a hill. . . . Remus
devotes himself to watching and apart looks out for
a favourable bird. But handsome Romulus makes
his search on high Aventine and so looks out for
the soaring breed. Whether they should call the
city Roma or Remora—this was their contest.
Anxiety filled all the men as to which of the two
should be ruler. As, when the consul means to
give the signal, all men look eagerly at the barrier's
bounds to see how soon he will send the chariots
forth from the painted mouths—so they waited.
Thus were the people waiting, and held their tongues,
wondering to which of the two the victory of right
royal rule should be given by the event. Meanwhile
the white sun *a* withdrew into depths of night. Then
clear shot forth, struck out in rays, a light: just
when, winging to the left, there flew from the height
a bird, the luckiest far of flying prophets, just then
all golden there rose up the sun. Thrice four
hallowed forms of birds moved down from the sky,
and betook themselves to places lucky and of happy
omen. From this saw Romulus that to him, to be
his own, were duly given the chair and throne *b* of
royalty, established firm by the watching of birds.

Romulus founds the city of Rome :

An excerpt from a glossary : Of Rome there is no known
founder common to tradition. . . . Ennius and others say
it was founded by Romulus.

---

waited; at dawn came the crowd of followers. The sun has
risen; is hidden by a cloud (*infera noctis*); it shines again
brightly. Then come the birds.
  b Or perhaps 'land,' 'territory.' Cp. Bk. III, line 155.

ENNIUS

101

Festus, 348, 4 : ' Quamde ' pro quam . . . —

' Iuppiter, ut muro fretus magis quamde manus vi ! '

102–3

Macrobius, *S.*, VI, 1, 15 : Tu tamen interea calido mihi sanguine poenas | persolves (*Aen.*, IX, 420). Ennius in I—

' Nec pol homo quisquam faciet inpune animatus hoc nec tu ; nam mi calido dabis sanguine poenas.'

Cp. Serv. auct. ad *Aen.*, IX, 420.

104

Nonius, 516, 11 : ' Torviter ' . . . —

' Ast hic quem nunc tu tam torviter increpuisti

105

Festus, 426, 2 : ' Sum ' pro ' eum '—

' At tu non, ut sum summam servare decet rem,

101 manus vi S   manu stat *Lambinus*   manu sa imperat *olim* O. Mueller   manus vi idē in secundo V manus impe . . . secto *cd.*   *fortasse* manum vi
103 nec B *prob.* St.   neque Merula   nisi *cdd. prob.* V dabis *Serv. auct.*   das *Macrob. prob.* V
105 at tu *cd.*   astu non vi *coni.* V   at te non ut Colonna

ANNALS

101

Remus scoffs at Romulus and his wall on the Palatine :

Festus : ' Quamde,' for quam . . . —

' Jupiter ! Yes, truly relies he more on a wall
than the might of his arm ! '

102–3

Romulus threatens Remus with death :

Macrobius, quoting Virgil : Meanwhile you shall none the
less pay full recompense to me with your life-blood.   Ennius
in the first book—

' Neither you nor any man alive shall do this
unpunished : no, you shall give recompense to me
with your life-blood.'

104

A mediator (or Romulus ?) seeks to heal the quarrel : [a]

Nonius : ' Torviter ' . . . —

' But he whom you just now so fiercely noised at

105

Festus : ' Sum ' for ' eum ' . . . —

' But it is not your part to guard the state, as it
behoves him to do.[b]

[a] V., CLXII doubtfully assigns this to Romulus upbraiding
Amulius for treating Remus roughly before he was recognised.
[b] V., CLXIII and p. 15.

106

Grammat., *Brevis Expos. Verg. Georg.*, ad II, 384 : Romulus cum aedificasset templum Iovi Feretrio pelles unctas stravit et sic ludos edidit ut caestibus dimicarent et cursu contenderent, quam rem Ennius in Annalibus testatur.

Servius (auctus) ad *Aen.*, III, 384 : Et quidam ' lentandus ' nove verbum fictum putant, sed in Annalibus legitur—

conque fricati oleo lentati adque arma parati.

Paulus, F., 25, 17 : ' Bellicrepam ' saltationem dicebant quando cum armis saltabant, quod a Romulo institutum est, ne simile pateretur quod fecerat ipse cum a ludis Sabinorum virgines rapuit.

107

Festus, 476, 17 : ' Sas ' Verrius putat significare ' eas ' testo Ennio qui dicat in lib. I—

[' virgines ;] nam sibi quisque domi Romanus habet sas.'

Paul., 25, 17 bellicrepa *vocab. trib. Enn.* O. Mueller, *Ann. lib.* I Ilberg.

[106] confricati o. l. paratique a. a. *Serv. auct. corr.* B confricti . . . et ad a. p. Ilberg   confricati . . . paratique ad arma *Servius auct.*   *fortasse* cumque ficati *trib. Enn. Ann.* Barth, *lib.* I, Ilberg

[107] virgini *sive* virgine L   *fortasse secludend. ut gloss.*

---

* V. in his first ed. (p. 16) kept this fr. in Bk. I of Ennius' *Annals* but rejected it in the 3rd ed. (p. 16). Valmaggi may

34

ANNALS

106

The war with the Sabines. Having built temples after the defeat of the Sabines, Romulus celebrates public games and dances :

A grammarian: When Romulus had built a temple to Jupiter Feretrius, he caused greased hides to be spread out and held games in such a manner that men fought with gauntlets and competed in running races; Ennius bears witness to this fact in the *Annals.*

Servius (supplemented) on 'lentandus' in Virgil: And some think that 'lentandus' is a coined word of Virgil's; but in the *Annals* [a] we read—

Rubbed down with oil, suppled and ready for taking arms.

Paulus [b]: 'Noise o' War' was a term the Romans were wont to use of dancing when they danced with weapons; this was an institution of Romulus so that he should not suffer the like of what he himself did when he dragged off the maidens of the Sabines at their public games.

107

Rape of the Sabine women. A Sabine speaks :

Festus: 'Sas.' Verrius believes it means 'eas,' his witness being Ennius on the ground that he says in the first book—

' maidens ; for the Romans have each their own at home.

where it seems rather to mean 'suas.' [c]

---

be right in his belief (cp. Müller) that what Servius' augmenter quotes is prose.
   [b] Paulus probably alludes to a passage of Ennius.
   [c] It is impossible to decide this matter.

ENNIUS

108

Priscianus, ap. *G.L.*, II, 591, 5 K : . . . nominativo . . .
brevem te syllabam pro met . . . addere solent auctores.
. . . Ennius—

O Tite tute Tati tibi tanta tyranne tulisti!

Cp. Pompei., ap. *G.L.*, V, 303, 33 K : Priscian. ap. III,
492, 25 K : al.

109

Festus, 460, 12 : 'Stolidus' stultus . . .—

nam vi depugnare sues stolidi soliti sunt.

110

Charisius, ap. *G.L.*, I, 196, 15 K : 'Concorditer' . . .—

'Aeternum seritote diem concorditer ambo.'

111

Gellius, XIII, 23, 19 : Ennius . . . in primo Annali . . .—

'Nerienem Mavortis et Herem

si quod minime solet numerum servavit, primam syllabam
intendit, tertiam corripuit.

---

[108] *trib. Lucil.* St., *C.Q.*, *XVIII*, 24.
[109] soliti S   solidi *cd.*

---

^a Steuart (*Ann.*, 235; and *C.Q.*, XCIII, 24) attributes
this fr. to Lucilius as one of the hundred solecisms which
he enumerated. I suggest that we have here a scornful
speech (of Romulus?) uttered against Tatius during one
of the indecisive struggles of which tradition tells. I would
point out that Sophocles (*Oed. Tyr.*, 371) makes Oedipus in a
rage say to Teiresias, with a similar alliteration, τυφλὸς τά τ'

36

ANNALS

108

Rage of the Romans against Titus Tatius :

Priscian : In the nominative . . . authors are wont to add the short syllable *te* instead of *met*. . . . Ennius— [a]

' Thyself to thyself, Titus Tatius the tyrant, thou tookest those terrible troubles.'

109

Hersilia mediates between the Romans and the Sabines :

Festus : ' Stolidus,' silly . . . —

' for to fight out a quarrel by force—it is a thing of boorish boars beloved.

110

Charisius : ' Concorditer ' . . . —

' Both of you, while away your days in friendliness for ever.'

111

Hersilia's prayer : [b]

Gellius : Ennius also in the first book of *Annals*—

' Nerio, consort of Mars, and Here likewise '

if he has preserved the metre (which is certainly not always the case with him), has lengthened the first syllable and shortened [c] the third.

---

[a] ὦτα τόν τε νοῦν τά τ' ὅμματ' εἰ. Cp. Homer's πολλὰ δ' ἄναντα κ.τ.λ., quoted on p. 70. Others refer the fr. to the death of Tatius.

[b] Cp. Gell., XIII, 23, 13 : V., CLXIV : St., p. 121, suggests settlement of Sabines on the Aventine or a general gift of land to citizens.

[c] Gellius scans Nērĭĕnem ; but the true scansion is Nērĭēnem.

ENNIUS

112–13

Nonius, III, 39 : ' Fortunatim,' prospere . . . —

' Quod mihi reique fidei regno vobisque, Quirites,
se fortunatim feliciter ac bene vortat.

Varro, *L.L.*, V, 55: Ut ait Ennius, Titienses a Tatio,
Ramnenses a Romulo, Lucerus, ut Iunius, ab Lucumone.

Servius, ad *Aen.*, VI, 777 : secundum Ennium, referetur
(*Romulus*) inter deos cum Aenea.

114–15

Servius, ad *Aen.*, VI, 763 : ' Aevum, proprie aeternitas est
quae non nisi in deos venit. Ennius—

' Romulus in caelo cum dis genitalibus aevum
degit.

Cp. Cic., *Tusc., Disp.*, I, 12, 29. *C.I.L.*, IV, 3135.

116

Nonius, 120, 1 : ' Hora,' iuventutis dea . . . —

' Teque Quirine pater veneror Horamque Quirini.

[112] quod *olim* V   ea *cdd*.   reique fide M   (reique
Roth) reliquae fidei *cdd*.   quod mihi meaeque fide et *olim* V
(mique meaeque *vel* quae mihi meaeque fide et Grauert)
et postea ea uti res (*vel* ea res ut)   mique meaeque fidei *vel*
resque ea mi, fidei B
[114-15] *trib. Ann. lib. II* Colonna
[116] <teque> *add.* Colonna   <bene> Hŏramque Mr.

ANNALS

112-13

Romulus to Titus Tatius after the establishment of double kingship? :

Nonius : ' Fortunatim,' prosperously . . . —

' And may this, I pray, turn out in fortune prosperous and fair for me, our task, our plighted troth, our kingdom, and for you, my citizens.[a]

The Sabines form a new tribe at Rome :

Varro : According to Ennius, the Titienses were so called from Tatius, the Ramnes from Romulus; the Luceres, according to Junius, from Lucumon.

Romulus is deified :

Servius : According to Ennius, Romulus will be reckoned with Aeneas among the gods.

114-15

Proculus tells the people of his vision of Romulus :

Servius : ' Aevum ' properly means eternity, which comes to none but gods. Ennius—

' Romulus lives from age to age in heaven with the gods that gave him birth.'

116

Romulus and Hersilia are worshipped by the Romans :

Nonius says : ' Hora,' goddess of youth. . . .

' Thee I worship, sire Quirinus, and thee, Hora,[b] consort of Quirinus.'

[a] Cp. V., CLXV.
[b] Hersilia deified. Quirinus was the name given to deified Romulus.

LIBER II

117-21

Cicero, *de Rep.*, I, 41, 61 : Iusto quidem rege cum est populus orbatus pectora diu tenet desiderium, sicut ait Ennius, post optimi regis obitum—

           simul inter
sese sic memorant: ' O Romule Romule die
qualem te patriae custodem di genuerunt!
O pater o genitor o sanguen dis oriundum!

Non eros nec dominos appellabant eos quibus iuste paruerunt denique ne reges quidem, sed patriae custodes sed patres et deos. Nec sine causa; quid enim addunt ?—

' Tu produxisti nos intra luminis oras.

Cp. Lactant., *Div. Inst.*, I, 15, 30 : Priscian., ap. *G.L.*, II, 250, 15 K.

122

Festus, 492, 6 : ' Speres ' antiqui pluraliter dicebant, ut E. lib. II—

' Et simul effugit speres ita funditus nostras . . .

---

117 *tt. trib. lib. II Prisc., lib. I* Colonna *sec. vetus exemplar Prisc.*   *vocabula* pectora tenet desiderium *fortasse Ennio tribuenda.* diu *cd. m.* 1 dia *m.* 2 dura Steinacker   fida Krarup

---

ᵃ There is no need to question Priscian's authority for putting this fr. in Bk. II. I make the direct quotation begin from *simul.* At any rate it is clear that Cicero began by

ANNALS

BOOK II

117–20

The people mourn Romulus :

Cicero : Indeed when a people is bereaved of a just king, then even as Ennius says,[a] after the passing of the best of kings, for many days longing filled their breasts—

And at the same time they talked thus among themselves—' O Romulus, godly Romulus, what a guardian of your country did the gods beget you ! O father and begetter, O blood sprung from the gods !

They used to call those whom they had lawfully obeyed not lords and masters, nor yet again kings, but guardians of their country, yes and fathers and gods. Nor was this without reason. For what do they say next ?—

' You it was who brought us forth into the world of light.

122

Festus : ' Speres.' The archaic writers used this plural form, for example Ennius in the second book [b]—

' And so soon as he fled away, our hopes he thus utterly . . .

---

[a] paraphrase which slips into the real quotation, and all changes are doubtful. St., p. 123.
[b] V., CLXVI suggests the combat of the triplets as the context—see lines 131 ff.

ENNIUS

123

Festus, 346, 5 : 'Quadrata Roma' in Palatio ante templum
Apollinis dicitur . . . eius loci Ennius meminit cum ait—

Et qui se sperat Romae regnare Quadratae?

124

Varro, *L.L.*, VII, 42 : Apud Ennium—

Olli respondit suavis sonus Egeriai,

'olli' valet dictum 'illi' ab 'olla' et 'ollo.'

Cp. Serv., ad *Aen.*, XI, 236.

125-6

Varro, *L.L.*, VII, 4 : 3 Apud Ennium—

Mensas constituit idemque ancilia;

dicta ab ambecisu quod ea arma ab utraque parte ut
Thracum incisa;—

libaque fictores Argeos et tutulatos.

Liba quod libandi causa fiunt : fictores dicti a fingendis
libis, Argei ab Argis . . . tutulati dicti hi qui in sacris in
capitibus habere solent ut metam.

---

[123] qui se sperat Saumaise qui sextus erat Hertz quis
est erat *cd*.

[125] ancilia <primus> S <bis sex> Corssen

ANNALS

123

Question of a successor to Romulus : [a]

Festus : 'Square Rome,' a name given to a site on the Palatine in front of the temple of Apollo. . . . Ennius has this place in mind when he says—

And what man hopes that he will be king of Square Rome ?

124

The reign of Numa Pompilius. Intercourse of Numa and Egeria :

Varro : In a passage of Ennius—

To him replied Egeria with sweet sound,

The word 'olli' has the force of 'illi,' from 'ollus,' 'olla.'

125-6

The religious institutions of Numa :

Varro : In a passage of Ennius—

He established the Tables, he also the Shields . . .

'ancilia' is a word derived from 'ambicisus,' because those arms were indented on either edge like those of Thracians ;—

. . . and the Pancakes, the Bakers, the Rush-Dummies, and the cone-haired Priests.

'Liba' are so called because they are made to be used at libations. The 'fictores' are so called 'a fingendis libis'; the term Argei is derived from Argos. . . . 'tutulati' is a term used for those who at sacrifices are accustomed to wear a kind of cone on their heads.

---

[a] My chief reason for not reading *sextus erat* and putting the fr. in Bk. III (V., CLXIX–CLX) is that when Servius Tullius came to rule, the city was no longer *Square* Rome.

ENNIUS

127-9

Varro, *L.L.*, VII, 45 : Eundem Pompilium ait fecisse flamines qui cum omnes sunt a singulis deis cognominati . . . sunt in quibus flaminum cognominibus latent origines ut in his qui sunt versibus plerique—

Volturnalem Palatualem Furinalem
Floralemque Falacrem et Pomonalem fecit
hic idem.

130

Festus, 156, 5 : ' Me ' pro ' mihi ' dicebant antiqui ut Ennius cum ait lib. II—

' Si quid me fuerit humanitus ut teneatis.

Propertius, III, 3 (IV, 2), 5-7 :

Parvaque tam magnis admoram fontibus ora
  unde pater sitiens Ennius ante bibit :
et cecinit Curios fratres et Horatia pila. . . .

131

Priscianus, ap. *G.L.*, III, 3, 6 K : Sic ergo ἐμοῦ σοῦ οὗ mei tui sui ἐμοῦς σοῦς οὗς mis tis si . . . Ennius—

' Ingens cura mis cum concordibus aequiperare ;

[127-9] *hexam. constit.* O. Mueller   *iamb. scaz.* T *saturn.*
alii   Volturnales | Palatuales Furinales Floralesque |
Falacres et Pomonales f. h. i. L   *alii alia*

---

[a] It is not certain whether Varro has here quoted Ennius; if he has, then this is clearly the right place for the fr. The proper names excuse the ugliness of the lines. Cf. Skutsch, in *Pauly*, s.v. *Ennius*, 2623; Norden, 78.

[b] Elsewhere called Curiatii. Whether we read *cecinit* or *cecini* we can assume that the examples given by Propertius were incidents which Ennius described in noteworthy passages of poetry.

ANNALS

127-9

He institutes the flamines :

Varro : Ennius states that Pompilius also established the ' special priests '; although all are surnamed from individual gods . . . there are special priests whose surnames remain obscure in origin . . . as is the case with most of the following which are enumerated in these verses—

He likewise established the priests of Volturnus, of Palatua, of Furina, of Flora, of Falacer, and of Pomona.[a]

130

Numa desires that his institutions be maintained :

Festus : The ancients used to say ' me ' instead of ' mihi,' as does Ennius when he says in the second book—

' If something of man's fate should happen to me, do you keep my ordinances.

The reign of Tullus Hostilius. War between Rome and Alba, which agree to settle their quarrels by a combat between two sets of triplet brothers.

Propertius :

And I had already put puny lips to mighty fountains, whence once father Ennius did slake his thirst and sang of the brothers Curii[b] and of the Horatii and their spears. . . .

131

The triplets are ready to fight[c] :

Priscianus : In this way, therefore, ἐμοῦ σοῦ and οὐ correspond to mei tui and sui, ἐμοῦς, σοῦς, οὐς to mis tis sis. . . . Ennius—

' A great and strong anxiety is mine to do equal deeds with my heartfellows.

[c] I take it one of them speaks. Others (St., p. 127 and V., CLXVI-CLXVII) put this later as spoken by the surviving Horatius. Certainly the meaning is doubtful; Ennius seems to use *concordes* in a special sense—' men nearest to my heart.' Note that the *s* in *mis* is elided in recitation.

ENNIUS

132

Festus, 194, 12 : 'Occasus' interitus vel solis cum decidit a superis infra terras; quo vocabulo Ennius pro occasione est usus in lib. II—

Hic occasus datust: at Horatius inclutus saltù . . .

133

Priscianus, ap. *G.L.*, II, 504, 22 K : Vetustissimi inveniuntur etiam produxisse . . . paenultimam. . . .—

' Adnuit sese mecum decernere ferro.

134

Festus, 540, 10 : ' Tolerare,' patienter ferre . . .—

ferro se caedi quam dictis his toleraret.

135

Festus, 348, 4 : ' Quamde ' pro quam . . .—

' quamde tuas omnes legiones ac populares.

136

Festus, 426, 2 : ' Sum ' pro ' eum '. . .—

At sese, sum quae dederat in luminis oras,

[132] datus est *cd.*   *trib. lib. IV* Ilberg (*de Horatio Coclite cogitans*)

---

[a] St., p. 126, refers this fr. to the conference between Mettius and Tullus in Livy, I, 23. Cf. also V., CLXVI, CLXVII, who refers the words to Tullus.

ANNALS

132

The fight : the surviving Horatius escapes a thrust :

Festus : ' Occasus,' a passing away of the sun, for example, when it drops down from the heights to regions beneath the earth; Ennius used this noun for ' occasio ' in the second book—

This chance was given him, but renowned Horatius with a leap . . .

133

Horatius justifies himself to his sister, who loved one of the Curiatii :

Priscianus : We find very ancient writers who even lengthened the penultimate (*sc. of perfects in -ui*) . . .—

' He agreed that he would join issue with me by the sword.

134

Horatius' sister heaps reproaches on him ?

Festus : ' Tolerare,' to bear patiently . . .—

She would fain suffer slaughter by the sword rather than by words such as these.

135

She cares more for her dead Curiatius than for all the Romans : ª

Festus : ' Quamde ' . . . for ' quam ' . . .—

' than for all your legions and commoners.

136

Horatius' father pleads for his son at his trial for killing his sister ; he pictures the mother's grief ? :

Festus : ' Sum ' for ' eum ' . . .—

' But that him whom she gave forth into the world of light, she . . .

47

ENNIUS

137

Festus, 188, 30 : ' Ningulus ' nullus . . .—

' qui ferro minitere atque in te ningulus . . .'

138

Festus, 530, 25 : ' ⟨Tu⟩ditantes,' tundentes, ⟨negotium id est ag⟩entes . . .—

Haec inter se totum egere diem tuditantes.

139

Quintilianus, I, 5, 12 : Nam duos in uno nomine faciebat barbarismos Tinga Placentinus . . . preculam pro pergula dicens. . . . At in eadem vitii geminatione—

Mettoeoque Fufetioeo

dicens Ennius poetico iure defenditur.

140

Macrobius, ap. *G.L.*, V, 651, 32 K : ' Tractare ' saepe trahere. . . . Ennius—

tractatus per aequora campi

[138] egere diem (*olim* tum certabant) V   se tota vi tuditantes S   tota tum vi Mr.   sese t.v. illi tuditantes O. Mueller   sese tuditant vi contendentes Ilberg   se totum . . . tes *cd*.
[139] Mettoeoque Fufetioeo Skutsch   *alii alia, cf. St. ad loc.*
[140] *trib. Ann. lib. II* Colonna

48

ANNALS

137

The prosecutor (or one of the two judges ? [a]) accuses Horatius :

Festus : ' Ningulus,' no one . . . —

' Who are one to threaten with the sword, while against you no one . . .'

138

Progress of the trial :

Festus : ' Tuditantes' means ' tundentes,' that is, conducting an affair . . . —

They spent the whole day threshing out this trial among themselves.

139

The punishment of Mettius Fufettius by Tullus for refusing to help Rome :

Quintilian : Tinga of Placentia . . . by writing ' precula ' for ' pergula ' was guilty of two barbarisms in one noun. . . . But Ennius arraigned on a like charge of a double mistake [b] by saying—

Mettoeoque Fufetioeo

is defended on the plea of poet's licence.

140

He is torn apart by horses :

Macrobius : ' Tractare ' means to pull again and again. . . . Ennius—

Dragged over the smooth flat plain

---

[a] Or it may be Horatius' sister.

[b] I translate Gellius ambiguously here because it is not certain in what form Ennius really wrote the names Mettius Fufettius. If Ennius committed two faults in the names, then *vitii geminatione* means ' with the commission of two faults.' Perhaps *eiusdem* should be read. Ennius apparently imitates the Homeric genitive—μεγάλοιο Κρόνοιο and the like.

ENNIUS

141-2

Priscianus, ap. *G.L.*, II, 206, 22 K : Vetustissimi . . .
' homo homonis ' declinaverunt. Ennius—

Vulturus in silvis miserum mandebat homonem.
Heu! Quam crudeli condebat membra sepulchro!

Cp. Charis., ap. *G.L.*, I, 147, 15 K : Serv., ad *Aen.*, VI, 595.
Schol. Bamb., ad Stat., *Theb.*, III, 508.

143

Servius, ad *Aen.*, II, 313 : ' Clangor ' : Plerumque . . .'. ad
tubam evertuntur civitates sicut Albam Tullus Hostilius
iussit everti.
Priscianus, ap. *G.L.*, II, 450, 2 K : . . . in nominationibus
id est ὀνοματοποιίαις, sive nominum seu verborum novis
conformationibus non omnes declinationes motus sunt
quaerendi . . . taratantara Ennius—

At tuba terribili sonitu taratantara dixit.

Cp. Serv., ad *Aen.*, IX, 501 : ' At tuba terribilem sonitum.'

Servius ad 486 : ' At domus interior ' : de Albano excidio
translatus est locus.

144

Servius (auctus) ad *Aen.*, III, 333 : ' Reddita ' more veteri
pro ' data ' accipiendum est . . .—

isque dies postquam Ancus Marcius regna recepit,

pro ' accepit.'

[141-2] *trib. Ann. lib. II* Merula
[141] silvis *Prisc.*, *Serv. cdd. CSM* campo *cdd. HFC* in campos
cd. R spineto *Charis.*   spinis Koch *coll. Aen. VIII*, 645
[143] *trib. Ann. lib. II* V
[144] *trib. lib. II* Ilberg   postquam A. M., Ilberg   post
aut Marcus quam *Serv. auct.*

ANNALS

141-2

and birds devour his corpse :

Priscianus: The oldest writers declined 'homo,' gen. 'homonis.' Ennius—

A vulture did craunch the poor wight in the forest. Ah! In what a cruel tomb buried he his limbs!

143

The destruction of Alba Longa by Tullus :

Servius, on 'clangor' in Virgil: States are generally overthrown to the sound of a trumpet, in the way in which Tullus Hostilius ordered Alba to be overthrown.[a]
Priscianus: In 'nominationes,' that is in onomatopoeias whether nouns or verbs, of unusual structure, we must not look for all the turns of inflexion . . . 'taratantara.' Ennius—

And the trumpet in terrible tones taratantara blared.

Servius on Virg., *Aen.*, II, 486 : 'And the dwelling within.' This passage (II, 486 ff.) is taken from the *Sack of Alba.*

144

The reign of Ancus Marcius. His accession :

Servius (supplemented), on ' reddita ' in Virgil : ' Reddita' must, as an archaic usage, be taken to mean ' data ' . . .—

and that day when Ancus Marcius [b] received the kingship,

Here ' recepit ' stands for accepit.

---

[a] Servius is probably thinking here of Ennius' narrative in the *Annals.*
[b] The text is not clear, but the reference is certain.

ENNIUS

145

Macrobius, *S.*, VI, 4, 3 (ad *Georg.*, II, 462): Pulchre ' vomit undam ' et antique : nam Ennius ait—

et Tiberis flumen vomit in mare salsum,

146–7

Festus, 346, 14 : ' Quaesere' ponitur ab antiquis pro quaerere . . . —

Ostia munita est : idem loca navibus celsis
munda facit nautisque mari quaesentibus vitam.

Cp. Paul., ex F., 397, 3; 121, 3; Fest., 20, 7.

148

Servius (auctus) ad *Aen.*, XI, 326 : Quidam ' texamus' proprie dictum tradunt quia loca in quibus naves fiunt Graeco ναυπήγια Latine textrina dici : Ennius—

Isdem campus habet textrinum navibus longis.

Cp. Cic., *Orat.*, 47, 157.

149

Festus, 400, 29 : Ennius iocatus videtur . . . et lib. II—

i caerula prata.

[146] celsis *Fest.*, 120   pulchris *Fest.*, 346
[148] *Cf. St.*, *pp.* 129–30 : *V.* 85–6
[149] pont>i S   Neptuni T   caeli Lindsay   campi Reichardt

---

[a] V., p. 25, attributes this fr. to Bk. II of the *Annals*, and cites Ov., *Fast.*, IV, 291–2; Fest., 228, 14.

ANNALS

145

The foundation of Ostia : fortifications and other works :

Macrobius : A most happy expression of Virgil's is ' belches
forth a flood,' and archaic too, for Ennius [a] says—

and the river Tiber belches into the salt sea,

146-7

Festus : ' Quaesere ' is put by archaic writers instead of
' quaerere ' . . .—

Ostia was fortified.   He likewise made the channel
clear for tall ships and for sailors seeking a livelihood
on the sea.

148

Servius (supplemented) : Some say that ' texamus ' is the
right term to use because the places in which ships are made
are called in Greek ναυπήγια, in Latin ' textrina.'   Ennius [b]—

for them too the plain holds a workshop for their
long ships.

149

Festus : Ennius [c] seems to have made a jest . . . and in
the second book—

the blue-dark plains.

[b] St., pp. 129–30 rightly, I think, says that the harbour
works are contrasted with others further inland.
[c] The jest or joke is lost and may have belonged to the
Satires.   As for this passage from the *Annals,* it is not clear
what Ennius was describing, but it is tempting to supply
⟨pont⟩i (Scaliger) and to refer the fr. to the sailors of line 147.
It is just possible that i is a complete word—' go tramp the
blue meadows.'

53

ENNIUS

LIBER III

150

Nonius, 51, 7 : 'Laevum' significari veteres putant quasi a levando. . . . Ennius annali lib. III—

Olim de caelo laevum dedit inclutus signum.

151-2

Probus, ad Verg., *Ecl.*, VI, 31 : Pro aere venti hic extrinsecus accipiuntur : ad quod argumentum collegimus Ennii exemplum de Annalium tertio—

et densis aquila pinnis obnixa volabat
vento quem perhibent Graium genus aera lingua.

153

Schol. Bern. ad *Georg.*, IV, 7 : 'Laeva,' prospera . . . ut Ennius ait—

ab laeva rite probatum.

154

Festus, 428, 11 : 'Sos' . . . interdum pro suos . . . Ennius—

Postquam lumina sis oculis bonus Ancus reliquit,

Cp. Paul, ex F., 429, 10. Lucret., III, 1025 : Lumina sis oculis etiam bonus Ancus reliquit.

---

[153] *trib. lib. III* St.

ANNALS

BOOK III

150

Jupiter's omen to Priscus on his way to Rome :

Nonius : 'Laevum.' The old critics believe this word to take its meaning as it were from 'levare.' . . . Ennius in the third book of *Annals*—

The All-glorious sent down one day from the sky a favourable sign.

151-2

The omen :

Probus, on 'anima' in Virgil : 'Air' is here taken, by inductive reasoning, to mean 'winds'; in proof of this we have taken an example of Ennius from the third book of the *Annals*—

and there came flying on thick-set wings an eagle, battling with the breeze which the Greek nation calls in its tongue 'aer.' [a]

153

Tanaquil (?) accepts the omen as favourable :

A scholiast : 'Laeva,' prosperous . . . as Ennius says—

on the left hand and duly taken as good.

154

The death of Ancus Marcius :

Festus : 'Sos' . . . now and then writers put it for suos . . . Ennius—

After good Ancus quitted the light with his eyes,

---

[a] Ennius' philology was here more accurate than he knew— Greek root a*F*, Sanscrit vä 'blow,' vatas 'wind.'

ENNIUS

155

Festus, 426, 33 : ' Solum,' terram.   Ennius lib. III—

Tarquinio dedit imperium simul et sola regni.

156

Festus, 428, 11 : ' Sos ' pro ' eos.' . . . Ennius lib. III—

Circum sos quae sunt magnae gentes opulentae.

157

Servius, ad *Aen.*, VI, 219 : ' lavant frigentis et ungunt ' :
versus Ennii, qui ait—

Tarquinii corpus bona femina lavit et unxit.

Cp. Donat., in Ter., *Hec.*, I, 2, 60.

158

Festus, 284, 22 : ' Prodinunt,' prodeunt . . . —

Prodinunt famuli : tum candida lumina lucent.

Cp. Paul., ex F., 285, 8.

159

Macrobius, *S.*, I, 4, 17 : Animadvertendum est . . .
quod etiam ' qua noctu ' dixerit (*Ennius*). Et hoc posuit in
annalium septimo, in quorum tertio clarius idem dixit—

' Hac noctu filo pendebit Etruria tota.

[157] Tarquinii corpus *Serv.*   Exin Tarquinium bona
Donat.

---

[a] It is more likely, however, that *sŏla* (from *sŏlum*) means
throne.

ANNALS

155

Tarquinius Priscus is made King :

Festus: 'Solum,' earth. Ennius in the third book—

gave to Tarquin both sway and soil [a] of the kingdom.

156

War of Priscus with the Latins [b] (or Etruscans ?) :

Festus: 'Sos' for 'eos.' . . . E. in the third book—

The clans of might and wealth which are around them.

157

Tanaquil decks dead Priscus :

Servius, on ' And they wash and anoint his body in the chill of death' in Virgil: a line from Ennius, who says—

The good woman washed and anointed Tarquin's body.

158

The funeral of Priscus :

Festus: ' Prodinunt,' the same as 'prodeunt' . . . —

The thralls moved on: then beamed bright lights.

159

The reign of Servius Tullius ; wars with Etruria. Speech of an Etruscan (?) general before battle ? : [c]

Macrobius: We must notice that he used even ' qua noctu.' And this he put in the seventh book of the *Annals*, in the third book of which he wrote the same sort of thing more clearly—

' On this night all Etruria's fate will hang by a thread.

[b] V., CLXIX (Dion. Halic., III, 51 : 57): St., pp. 133–4, suggests the Etruscan wars of Servius Tullius (Livy, I, 42).
[c] St. suggests the battle noticed by Livy in I, 42.

ENNIUS

160-61

Macrobius, *S.*, VI, 1, 16 : Concurrunt undique telis | indomiti agricolae ' (*Aen.*, VII, 520–1).   Ennius in III—

Postquam defessi sunt stare et spargere sese
hastis ansatis, concurrunt undique telis.

162

Macrobius, *S.*, VI, 1, 9 : ' Axem humero torquet stellis ardentibus aptum ' (*Aen.* IV, 482 ; VI, 797) . . . —

Caelum prospexit stellis fulgentibus aptum.

163

Gellius, I, 22, 14 : An ' superesse ' dixerint veteres pro ' restare et perficiendae rei deesse ' quaerebamus . . . invenimus in tertio Enni Annalium in hoc versu—

Inde sibi memorat unum superesse laborem :

id est reliquum esse et restare, quod quia id est, divise pronuntiandum est.

---

[160] stare et V   stando Pontanus   stantes Scriver.
stant et *cdd.*
[162] prospexit *Macrob.*   suspexit V

ANNALS

160–61

A battle [a] *in Servius' Etruscan wars :*

Macrobius : ' The unruly husbandmen engage with javelins on all sides.' Ennius in the third book—

After they were tired out from standing and spattering each other with loop-handled lances, they engaged with javelins on all sides.

162

Tarquinius Superbus. Lucretia outraged lies on a roof :

Macrobius : (Atlas) ' whirls on his shoulder the sky dotted with blazing stars ' . . . —

She looked up at the sky dotted with shining stars.

163

Lucretia [b] *prepares for death :*

Gellius : We used to investigate the question whether ' superesse ' in the archaic writers was a term used for ' remain and be lacking for the completion of a thing ' . . . we find in the third book of Ennius' *Annals* this line—

Then she says that for herself one labour still waits over :

' superesse,' ' is left ' and ' remains ' undone; this being the meaning, it must be spoken as two words.

---

[a] See previous note; V., CLXIX compares Dion. Halic., III, 52, 2–3.

[b] Thus St., p. 133. Others refer the fr. to the foundation of a temple of Diana by Servius Tullius, or to the building of the *area* of the temple of Jupiter by Tarquinius Priscus; cf. V., CLXX.

ENNIUS

LIBER IV

164

Macrobius, S., VI, I, 17: 'Summa nituntur opum vi' (*Aen.*, XII, 552). Ennius in quarto—

Romani scalis summa nituntur opum vi.

Cp. Serv., ad *Aen.*, XII, 552.

165

Paulus, ex F., 16, 22: Anxur vocabatur quae nunc Tarracina dicitur Vulscae gentis, sicut ait Ennius—

Vulsculus perdidit Anxur.

166

Cicero, *de Re Pub.*, I, 16, 25: Id . . . postea ne nostrum quidem Ennium fugit, qui ut scribit, anno trecentesimo quinquagesimo fere post Romam conditam—

— nonis Iunis soli luna obstitit et nox.

165 *trib. Ann. lib. IV* Merula
166 <quom> nonis Bergk   *trib. Ann. lib. IV ed. Lips.*

---

[a] This number, according to the year (753 B.C.) accepted in Cicero's time for the foundation of Rome, leads us to the year 400 B.C. when there was an eclipse of the sun on the 21st of June; 5th must be a mistake of Ennius. Note that since Ennius put the foundation of Rome in the ninth century

ANNALS

BOOK IV

THE EARLY REPUBLIC, PROBABLY TO THE
GALLIC INVASION OF 390 OR 387 B.C.

164

The siege of Anxur by the Romans :

Macrobius : ' They strain with all their might and main '
(Virgil). Ennius in the fourth book—

The Romans on their ladders strain with all their
might and main.

165

Anxur is stormed, 406 B.C.

Paulus : The town which is now spoken of as Tarracina,
belonging to the Volscian tribe, used to be called Anxur, as
Ennius' words show—

The wretched Volscians lost Anxur.

166

Eclipse of the sun, 21st of June, 400 B.C. :

Cicero, *on the true cause of solar eclipses :*

In later times this did not escape the notice even of our
Ennius, who writes that, about three hundred and fifty [a] years
after the foundation of Rome—

On June's fifth day the moon blocked out the sun
in darkness.

B.C., he must have given a much larger number than 353 or
350 for the year of this eclipse. On this problem cf. St.,
135; Beloch, in *H.,* LVII, 119 ff.; another view: Soltau,
Woch. f. Kl. Phil., III, 979 ff.

61

ENNIUS

LIBER V

167

Festus, 194, 12 : 'Occasus' . . . E. pro occasione est usus
. . . in lib. V—

Inicit inritatus, tenet occasus, iuvat res.

168

Nonius, 556, 19 : 'Ansatae' iaculamenta cum ansis . . . —

ansatas mittunt de turribus

169

Priscianus, ap. *G.L.*, II, 428, 14 K : 'Misereo' . . .
vetustissimi sunt usi . . . —

Cogebant hostes lacrumantes ut misererent.

170

Acro, ad Hor., *Ep.*, II, 2, 98 : . . . Romani quondam
pugnaverunt cum hostibus Samnitibus usque ad noctem ;
unde et Ennius inquit—

Bellum aequis manibus nox intempesta diremit.

[168] hastas *add.* Colonna   altis Quich.
[170] aequum St. *fortasse recte*

---

[a] The context of all the frs. is uncertain.
[b] Livy, VII, 10; or Titus Manlius and a Tusculan ? Livy,
VIII, 7 : Vahlen, CLXXIV.

ANNALS

BOOK V

SAMNITE WARS AND THE RISE OF PYRRHUS, TO B.C. 295 [a]

167

A single combat ; Manlius and a Gaul ? : [b]

Festus : ' Occasus.' . . . E. used it for ' occasio ' . . . in the fifth book—

Vexation drives him on, the chance holds him to it, the fact helps him.

168

Defence of Fregellae against the Romans ? :

Nonius : ' Ansatae,' missiles with loop-handles . . .—

They send down loop-handled lances from the towers.

169

Appeal of women at Fregellae at its capture, 313 B.C. [c]

Priscianus : ' Misereo ' . . . was used by the oldest writers . . .—

They caused even the enemy to have pity on them shedding tears.

170

A battle between the Romans and the Samnites ? : [d]

Acro : At one time the Romans fought with Samnite enemies until nightfall; whence Ennius also says—

The dead of night wrested from them a drawn battle.

[c] St., p. 137.
[d] Livy, X, 12; or Livy, VII, 33; Vahlen, CLXXII.

ENNIUS

171

Macrobius, *S.*, VI, 4, 4 : ' Agmen ' pro actu et ductu quodam ponere non inelegans est, ut ' leni fluit agmine Thybris ' (*Aen.*, II, 782). Immo et antiquum est. Ennius enim in quinto ait—

quod per amoenam urbem leni fluit agmine flumen.

172

Nonius, 226, 29 : ' Stirpem ' . . . masculino E. Annalium lib. V—

nomine Burrus uti memorant a stirpe supremo.

Cp. Fest., 454, 28 : 402, 16.

NOTE ON BOOKS

There can be no doubt that Ennius did not include the First Punic War in the detailed narrative of his *Annals*; the statement of Cicero (see pp. 82–83) is explicit, and it is unreasonable to believe that we know better than he did. He tells us that Ennius did not desire to rival Naevius, who had already written a poem about this war (see *Remains of Old Latin*, Vol. II); it is further probable (see St., pp. 163–4) that Ennius had before him other poems covering the same ground. It is quite possible that in Book VII Ennius gave a mere sketch, or enumerated only the chief events of this war; but I have no hesitation in following Miss Steuart in her refusal to attribute to it a number of fragments on which she offers attractive suggestions (St., pp. 149 ff.). Cf. also Norden, *Enn. u. Verg.*, 63 ff., 143 ff., 170. For the old view, which goes back to Merula, see V., CLXXIX ff.; Müller, *Q. Enn.*, 166 and *C. Q.* XIII, 113 ff.; Skutch, *Pauly*, s.v. Ennius, 2607, etc.

Non. 226 lib. V *cdd.* VI Merula   [172] numine *Fest.* Pyrrhus *cdd.*   Burrus *Ennius*—cf. *Cic.*, *Orat.*, 48, 160

64

ANNALS

171

The River Liris at Interamna [a] *Lirenas, where the fields were laid waste in* 294 B.C. :

Macrobius: It is not inelegant to put ' agmen ' in the sense of a certain ' actus ' and ' ductus '; for example, ' Thybris flows with gentle train.' Indeed it is also an antique usage; for Ennius in the fifth book says—

because the river flows with gentle train through the pleasant town.

172

Rise of Pyrrhus : [b]

Nonius: ' Stirps ' . . . Ennius has it in the masculine in the fifth book of the *Annals*—

by name **Burrus**, a man they say of highest stock.

VI AND VII

On the other hand, I cannot believe that Ennius allowed his history of Pyrrhus to extend into the seventh book so that at the beginning of that book it was interrupted by three things : (i) the elaborate prologue to the book; (ii) an account of the origin of Carthage; (iii) an apology for not describing the First Punic War. I suggest that the war with Pyrrhus was contained wholly in Book VI, which was thus devoted to a man whom Ennius, it is clear, admired; and that Book VII, after a prologue and an apology, sketched the origins of Carthage, brushed aside, as it were, the First Punic War with a short outline, and narrated the winning of Sardinia [c] and Corsica by Rome, her reduction of the piratic

---

[a] Thus St., pp. 137–8, who explains *quod* as introducing an etymological remark. But *quod* could go with *flumen* and the town could be Minturnae, where a colony was founded in 295 B.C.

[b] We may keep this fr. in the book to which Nonius apparently assigns it (St., p. 138).

[c] Where Ennius himself served as a soldier.

ENNIUS

Illyrians to submission (here we may put some of the disputed fragments), and the conquest of Cisalpine Gaul. It is possible that the achievements of Hamilcar, Hasdrubal, and Hannibal in Spain were also sketched. Thus Book VIII began with

LIBER VI

173

Servius, ad *Aen.*, IX, 526 (528): ('ingentis) oras evolvite belli.' Hoc est . . . 'narrate non tantum initia sed etiam extrema bellorum'; nam orae sunt extremitates. *Servius auctus*: Est autem Ennianum—

Quis potis ingentis oras evolvere belli?

Cp. Quintil., VI, 3, 36 (. . . annali sexto 'quis e.q.s.); Macrob., *S.*, VI, 1, 18; Diomed., ap. *G.L.*, I, 386, 1 K.

174–6

Cicero, *de Div.*, II, 56, 116: Herodotum cur veraciorem ducam Ennio? Num minus ille potuit de Croeso quam de Pyrrho fingere Ennius? Quis enim est qui credat Apollinis ex oraculo Pyrrho esse responsum?—

' Aio te Aiacida Romanos vincere posse.'

Primum Latine Apollo numquam locutus est; deinde ista sors inaudita Graecis est; praeterea Pyrrhi temporibus iam Apollo versus facere desierat; postremo, quamquam semper fuit, ut apud Ennium est,—

' stolidum genus Aeacidarum
bellipotentes sunt magis quam sapientipotentes;

[173] oras *Serv. auct.*　causas *Quintil.*
[174-6] *trib. lib. VI* Merula

---

[a] Here again I disagree with Steuart. Other views— Norden, 75, 128, 131 ff.

ANNALS

the outbreak of the Second Punic War and carried events down to the departure of Scipio Africanus for Africa in 204 B.C.[a] This left Ennius free to devote all Book IX to the crowning achievement of his friend Scipio.

BOOK VI

THE WAR WITH PYRRHUS, 281–271 B.C.

173

Prologue :

Servius, on ' Unroll ye this great war from end to end,' in Virgil : that is . . . Tell ye not only the beginnings, but also the conclusions of these wars; for by ' orae ' is meant ' extremities.' *An augmenter of Servius adds :* It is further an expression of Ennius—

Who can unroll this great war from end to end ?

174–6

Pyrrhus receives an oracle of Apollo :

Cicero : Why should I take Herodotus to be more truthful than Ennius ? Surely he was quite as capable of inventing stories about Croesus as Ennius was about Pyrrhus. For who is there who could believe that Apollo's oracle gave this answer to Pyrrhus ?—

' I say that you, O man sprung from Aeacus,
The Romans can defeat.'[b]

In the first place, Latin is a tongue in which Apollo never spoke; again, that particular reply is not known among the Greeks; and, moreover, in the time of Pyrrhus Apollo had already ceased to make verses; and lastly, although it has always held good, as we find in Ennius, that—

' That tribe of blockheads, stock of Aeacus
Are war-strong more than wisdom-strong ';

[b] A famous example of advice which can be taken in two opposite ways.

tamen hanc amphiboliam versus intellegere potuisset ' vincere te Romanos ' nihilo magis in se quam in Romanos valere.

Cp. (*vers.* 174): Quintil., VII, 9, 6 : ' Aurel. Vict.,' *de vir. illustr.*, 35, 1; Ammian. Marcell., XXIII, 5, 9; Porphyr. ad Hor., *A.P.*, 403; Charisius, ap. *G.L.*, I, 271, 28 K : *et alibi.*

177

Valla, ad Iuv., VII, 134 : ' Stlataria.' Probus exponit illecebrosa. Ennius—

et melior navis quam quae stlataria portat.

178

Festus, 170, fin. : ' Navus ' celer ac strenuus. . . . Ennius, lib. VI—

Navus repertus homo, Graio patre Graius homo, rex.

179

Festus, 424, 27: <Summ>ussi dicebantur <murmura-tores>. . . . Ennius in sexto . . .—

Intus in occulto mussabant.

Cp. Paul., ex F., 425, 5 : 127, 6.

180

Macrobius, *S.*, VI, 1, 54 : ' Pulverulentus eques furit; omnes arma requirunt ' (*Aen.*, VII, 625) . . .—

Balantum pecudes quatit; omnes arma requirunt.

---

[177] *trib. lib. VI* St.   *VII* Merula
[180] balatum *vel* balantum *cdd.*   palatur *vel* palatus B

---

[a] The line is commonly taken to refer to the model ship used for training the Romans in the First Punic War (V., CLXXX).

still, Pyrrhus would have had the sense to see that the double
meaning of the line ' you the Romans . . . defeat ' applied
equally to himself and to the Romans.

177

Pyrrhus' stormy crossing to Italy ; his ship : [a]
Valla : ' Stlataria.'   Probus   expounds :   ' alluring.'
Ennius—

and a better ship than such as carries foreign
fripperies.

178

Pyrrhus was at first welcomed in Tarentum, 281 B.C. :
Festus : ' Navus,' swift and active. . . . E. in the sixth
book—

A man of deeds they found him, a Greek son of a
Greek father, and a very king.[b]

179

but he shewed himself a stern master :
Festus : ' Summussi ' is a term which was applied to
murmurers. . . . Ennius in the sixth book . . .—

Within they grumbled in secret.

180

A sudden raid near Tarentum by Lucius Aemilius Barbula ? :
Macrobius, quoting Virgil[c] : ' Through the dust the horsemen
raged ; all cried for weapons.' . . .—

He harried the bleating sheep ; all cried for
weapons.

---

[b] This fr. might refer to Pyrrhus' promised help to
Tarentum.
[c] V., CLXXVI. But cf. Havet, *Rev. de Phil.,* IX, 166.

ENNIUS

181-5

Macrobius, S., VI, 2, 27 :

Itur in antiquam silvam stabula alta ferarum.
Procumbunt piceae, sonant icta securibus ilex
fraxincaeque trabes cuneis, et fissile robur
scinditur; advolvunt ingentes montibus ornos.

(*Aen.*, VI, 179 ff.; cp. *Aen.*, XI, 134 ff.)

Ennius in VI—

Incedunt arbusta per alta, securibus caedunt.
Percellunt magnas quercus, exciditur ilex,
fraxinus frangitur atque abies consternitur alta,
pinus proceras pervortunt; omne sonabat
arbustum fremitu silvai frondosai.

Homerus, *Il.*, XXIII, 114 :

οἱ δ' ἴσαν ὑλοτόμους πελέκεας ἐν χερσὶν ἔχοντες
σειράς τ' εὐπλέκτους· πρὸ δ' ἄρ' οὐρῆες κίον αὐτῶν·
πολλὰ δ' ἄναντα κάταντα πάραντά τε δόχμιά τ' ἦλθον.
ἀλλ' ὅτε δὴ κνημοὺς προσέβαν πολυπίδακος Ἴδης,
αὐτίκ' ἄρα δρῦς ὑψικόμους ταναήκεϊ χαλκῷ
τάμνον ἐπειγόμενοι· ταὶ δὲ μεγάλα κτυπέουσαι
πῖπτον. τὰς μὲν ἔπειτα διαπλήσσοντες Ἀχαιοὶ
ἔκδεον ἡμιόνων· ταὶ δὲ χθόνα ποσσὶ δατεῦντο
ἐλδόμεναι πεδίοιο διὰ ῥωπήϊα πυκνά.

186-93

Cicero, *de Off.*, I, 12, 38 : Pyrrhi quidem de captivis reddendis illa praeclara—

' Nec mi aurum posco nec mi pretium dederitis
nec cauponantes bellum sed belligerantes

[187] non *Pal. Harl.* nec *rell.*

ANNALS

181-5

Preparations for burning the dead after the battle of Heraclea, 280 B.C. :

Macrobius, quoting Virgil :

They went into an old forest, deep dens of the wild ; forward fell pitch-pines, clattered holms under hatchet-blows, clattered beams of ash-trees against wedges ; splitting oakwood too they cleft, and rolled along lofty rowans of the mountains.

Ennius in the sixth book—

Then strode they through deep thicket-woods and hewed
With hatchets ; mighty oaks they overset ;
Down crashed the holm and shivered ash outhacked ;
Felled was the stately fir ; they wrenched right down
The lofty pines ; and all the thicketwood
Of frondent forest rang and roared and rustled.

Homer has :

And they went holding in their hands hatchets for cutting wood, and ropes well twisted, while mules walked on in front of them. And oft strode they uphill and downhill, and sideways and crossing. But when they came nigh unto the shoulders of Ida which is full of fountains, then straightway they hewed leafy-topped oaks, pressing on with the long edge of bronze ; and the trees crashing mightily fell ; whereon these the Achaeans split up and hung from the mules, and these tore up the ground with their feet through thick underwood, eager for the plain.

186-93

Pyrrhus replies to Fabricius, who came to ransom prisoners taken at Heraclea :

Cicero : And of Pyrrhus too there is that illustrious speech on the restoration of prisoners—

' Gold for myself I ask not ; no, to me ye shall not pay a price. Not chaffering war but waging war,

ferro non auro vitam cernamus utrique;
vosne velit an me regnare era, quidve ferat Fors,
virtute experiamur. Et hoc simul accipe dictum: 190
quorum virtuti belli fortuna pepercit,
eorundem libertati me parcere certum est.
Dono, ducite, doque volentibus cum magnis dis.'

Cp. Serv. ad *Aen.*, X, 532; XII, 709; Verg., *Aen.*, V, 385:
Ducere dona iube. III, 12 cum sociis natoque Penatibus et
magnis dis. VIII, 679 cum . . . magnis dis.

194-5

Cicero, *de Senect.*, 6, 16: Ad Appii Claudii senectutem
accedebat etiam ut caecus esset; tamen is cum sententia
senatus inclinaret ad pacem cum Pyrrho foedusque faciendum,
non dubitavit dicere illa quae versibus persecutus est Ennius—

' Quo vobis mentes rectae quae stare solebant
ante hac, dementes sese flexere viai?

Hom., *Il.*, XXIV, 201: ὦ μοι, πῇ δή τοι φρένες οἴχονθ' ἧς
τὸ πάρος περ | ἔκλε' ἐπ' ἀνθρώπους;

196

Donatus, ad Ter., *Phorm.*, V, 4, 2: 'Parare animo'; et
venuste additum animo. Ennius sexto—

' Sed, quid ego hic animo lamentor?

Od., XI, 418: ὀλοφύραο θυμῷ.

197

Varro, *L.L.*, VII, 41: Apud Ennium—

Orator sine pace redit regique refert rem,

orator dictus ab oratione.

---

not with gold but with iron—thus let us of both
sides make trial for our lives. To see what Mistress
Chance may bring, whether it be you or I she wishes
to be king—let it be by bravery that we make the
test. And withal hear this word of mine : of those
warriors to whose bravery war's fortune has been
kind, to the freedom of those same have I too
planned to be kind. I give them to you, take them
home—and with them I give you the blessing of the
great gods.'

194–5

*Fruitless embassy of Cineas to Rome. Appius Claudius
Caecus protests against any acceptance of Cineas' offers :*

Cicero : When Appius Claudius was in old age it happened
that he was also blind; nevertheless, when the opinion of the
Senate was inclined towards peace and alliance with Pyrrhus
he did not hesitate to utter those famous thoughts which
Ennius set forth in poetry—

' Whither on your road have senseless turned your
senses which hitherto were wont to stand upright?

196

Donatus on ' in animo parare ' in Terence : the addition of
' animo ' is graceful. Ennius in the sixth book—

' But wherefore do I grieve now in my heart?

197

Cineas reports to Pyrrhus his failure at Rome :

Varro : In a passage of Ennius—

The spokesman came back without a peace, and
brought the news to the king,

' spokesman ' is a term derived from speech.

ENNIUS

198–9

Schol. Veron., ad *Aen.*, V, 473 : ' Hic victor superans (animis tauroque superbus '). . . . . Ennius in VI—

' aut animos superant atque aspera prima ◡ _ _
. . . fera belli spernunt . . .

200–2

Nonius, 150, 5 : ' Prognariter,' strenue fortiter et constanter.
. . . ‒

' Divi hoc audite parumper
ut pro Romano populo prognariter armis
certando prudens animam de corpore mitto.

203

Festus, 488, 28 : <Scitae alias quae sunt> bona facie,
a<li>as bonis <artibus mulieres a p>oetis usurpantur.
. . . Ennius in lib. VI—

Iumen ⟨ta . . . .⟩ scitus agaso

---

[198] aut *cd*. ast *olim* V   animos *cd*.   animo Keil *fort*.
animis   aspera prima Keil (*Rh. Mus. VI*, 375) asperrima
Mai   asp . . . rima *cd*.
[203] iumenta Ilberg   lumen *Fest*.   iumentisque parum
iam prodest scitus agaso *coni*. Havet, *Rev. de Phil., IX*, 167

ANNALS

198–9

The courage of the Romans ? : [a]

A scholiast, on ' Here the conqueror towering in pride of soul ' in Virgil : Ennius in the sixth book—

' Or they mount high in pride, and the rough beginnings . . . of war they spurn.

200–2

The battle of Ausculum, 279 B.C. Decius Mus devotes himself to the ' di manes ' :

Nonius : ' Prognariter,' actively, valiantly and steadfastly. . . . —

' Ye gods, hear this my prayer a little while as from my body I breathe my last for the Roman people's sake, knowingly and steadfastly, in arms and in battle.

203

Pyrrhus' mahouts cut the traces of the Roman chariot-horses in the battle of Ausculum : [b]

Festus : ' Scitae ' is a term applied by poets sometimes to women of good looks, sometimes to women who are of good accomplishments. . . . Ennius in the sixth book—

The skilled driver . . . . . . the beasts.

[a] Spoken by Cineas to Pyrrhus ? or it may be part of Appius' speech at Rome.
[b] Thus Steuart, pp. 148–9. *iumenta* is surely right. Havet (*Rev. de Phil.*, IX, 167) refers the fr. to plague-ridden flocks and connects it with fr. 180.

75

ENNIUS

204

Macrobius, *S.*, VI, 22 : ' Quadrupedante putrem sonitu quatit ungula campum ' (*Aen.*, VIII, 596). Ennius in VI—

Explorant Numidae, totam quatit ungula terram

205

Macrobius, *S.*, VI, 1, 8 : ' Vertitur interea caelum et ruit Oceano nox ' (*Aen.*, II, 250). Ennius in libro VI—

Vertitur interea caelum cum ingentibus signis.

206

Achilles Tatius, ad Catull., LXIII, 40 : ' Lustravit aethera album ' : . . . Ennius de sole . . . in VI—

Ut primum tenebris abiectis indalbabat,

Cp. Apulei., *Met.*, VII, 1.

207-8

Macrobius, *S.*, VI, 1, 10 : ' Conciliumque vocat divum pater atque hominum rex ' (*Aen.*, X, 2). Ennius in VI—

Tum cum corde suo divum pater atque hominum rex effatur.

Hom., *Il*, I, 544 : πατὴρ ἀνδρῶν τε θεῶν τε.

---

²⁰⁴ totum $\overset{m}{cdd}$. (tota *Par.*)   tostam Stowasser   *trib. lib.*
VII Kuypers
²⁰⁶ inalbabat dies *Ach.*   dies inalbebat *Apulei.*   indal-
babat | orta dies Wakefield   cuncta dies *coni.* V.   *reicit*
hoc fr. Bergk *prob.* Norden

ᵃ So I take it. The fr. is generally put in Book VII (Norden, 128).

76

204

*Operations of Pyrrhus against the Carthaginians in Sicily,
277–276 B.C. : * [a]

Macrobius, quoting Virgil: 'The four-footed beat of the
hoofs shook the crumbling plain.' Ennius in the sixth book—

The Numidians went scouting; their hoofs shook
the whole ground.

205

*The battle of Beneventum, 275 B.C.; Pyrrhus moves to attack
the Roman camp by night? : * [b]

Macrobius, quoting Virgil: 'Meanwhile round rolls the
sky and night sets in from the Ocean.' Ennius in the sixth
book—

Meanwhile the sky rolls round with its vast
constellations.

206

and dawn reveals his approach :

Achilles Tatius: 'He scanned the white ether'...
Ennius on the sun ... in the sixth book ...—

When darkness was cast away and the day was
first whitening, [c]

207–8

*A soliloquy of Jupiter (during the battle of Beneventum ?) * [d] *:*

Macrobius, quoting Virgil: 'and the father of the gods and
king of men called a council.' Ennius in the sixth book—

Then with all his heart the father of the gods and
king of men spoke forth.

[b] V., CLXXVIII–CLXXIX (Plut., *Pyrrh.*, 25). Miss St.
(p. 148) points to the battle of Ausculum.
[c] *indalbabat* is archaic for *inalbabat*; cp. *indaudio* for
inaudio; *indu* for *in.*
[d] Compare Homer, *Il.*, XVII, 441–2: Κρονίων . . . προτὶ ὃν
μυθήσατο θυμόν, but 'cum corde suo effatur' can hardly mean
'converses with his own heart.' Cf. also *Il.*, XVII, 200.

ENNIUS

209

Cicero, *de Re Publ.*, III, 3, 6 : ex qua vita (*sc.* civili) sic
summi viri ornantur, ut vel M' Curius—

quem nemo ferro potuit superare nec auro.

Note on

The clash between Rome and Carthage.

On this book see pp. 64–5. Steuart includes in it the end
of the war with Pyrrhus. Norden, pp. 143–52 has devoted
special attention to a reconstruction of the book; he would

LIBER VII

210-27

Gellius, XII, 4, 4 : Descriptum definitumque est a Quinto
Ennio in Annali septimo graphice admodum sciteque sub
historia Gemini Servilii, viri nobilis, quo ingenio, qua comitate
qua modestia . . . amicum esse conveniat hominis genere
et fortuna superioris—

Haece locutus vocat quocum bene saepe libenter
mensam sermonesque suos rerumque suarum
comiter inpertit, magnam cum lassus diei
partem trivisset de summis rebus regendis,

²⁰⁹ *trib. lib. XII* V (*trib. olim lib. VI*)
²¹³ trivisset B   fuvisset Lips   fuisset *cdd.* (fuisse
cd. B) magna cum lapsa dies iam | parte fuisset T

ᵃ Or 3rd consulship (274) or censorship (272). Or the fr.
may be a later reminiscence. At any rate Ennius was
probably the author.
ᵇ Servilius is rightly supposed to be Cn. Servilius Geminus
who was consul in 217 and was killed at the battle of Cannae

ANNALS

209

Triumph (275 ?) or death (270) ᵃ of Manius Curius Dentatus :

Cicero: From such a life (*i.e.* of a statesman) men of the highest rank are honoured, as for example Manius Curius—

whom none could overcome with iron or gold.

Book VII

Events leading to the Second Punic War

carry the narrative at least as far as the battle at the Trebia. Vahlen, CLXXIX ff., believes that Ennius did include a fairly detailed narrative of the First Punic War.

BOOK VII

210–27

Prologue :

Gellius: There is a very clever and graphic description and definition by Ennius in the seventh book of the *Annals* (in a sketch of Geminus Servilius, a man of noble birth), of what temper and cheerfulness and modesty . . . it is seemly a man should show who is a friend of another his superior in birth and fortunes ᵇ—

So saying he called to one with whom he shared willingly and cheerfully and right often his table, his talks, and his affairs, when, tired out, he had spent long hours of the day in managing the

(in 216); but the fr. is supposed to be connected in some way with that battle. This, however, forces us either to upset the probable construction of Books VII and VIII or to alter the book-number given by Gellius. Perhaps E. honoured Servilius by representing him as a special source of inspiration to a poet dealing with the Punic Wars. See Norden, 131 ff.; Vahlen, CLXXXIII–CLXXXIV; Steuart, 152 f.; Havet, *Rev. de Phil.*, II, 93–96.

consilio indu foro lato sanctoque senatu ;
quoi res audacter magnas parvasque iocumque   215
eloqueretur sed cura, malaque et bona dictu
evomeret si qui vellet tutoque locaret ;
quorum multa volup ac gaudia clamque palamque,
ingenium quoi nulla malum sententia suadet
ut faceret facinus levis aut malus ; doctus fidelis 220
suavis homo facundus, suo contentus, beatus,
scitus, secunda loquens in tempore, commodus,
     verbum
paucum, multa tenens antiqua, sepulta vetustas
quae facit, et mores veteresque novosque, tenens res
multorum veterum, leges divumque hominumque, 225
prudenter qui dicta loquive tacereve posset.
Hunc inter pugnas Servilius sic conpellat.

L. Aelium Stilonem dicere solitum ferunt, Q. Ennium de
semet ipso haec scripsisse picturamque istam morum et
ingenii ipsius Q. Ennii factam esse.

228

Festus, 340, 24 : ' Quianam ' pro quare . . . —

— quianam dictis nostris sententia flexa est ?

Cp. Paul., ex F., 341, 9.

---

[216] sed cura malaque Hosius   et haud cunctans Bergk   nec
cunctans M   et incunctans Huschke   tincta malis et
quae bona Lips   et cuncta simul malaque Hug   eloqu. et
unose *olim* V   et cuncta malaque et bona *vel* et cuncta
malusq. (cunctam aliisq *N*) et bona *cdd*.
[218] volup ac gaudia Colonna   volup sibi fecit *coni. olim*
V (*qui* gaudia *seclud.*)   voluptate gaudia *T*, *Y*   volup
gaudia *cett*.
[224] tenens res *olim* V.   tenentem *cdd. prob.* Havet
[226] prudenter *olim* V.   prudentem *cdd. prob.* Havet
[227] S. s. c. Dousa (F.)   c. S. s. *cdd*.
[228] < heu > quianam *Augustinus*, S

greatest affairs, by counsel given in the wide mart
and sacred senate-house; one to whom care-free [a]
he would often speak out boldly matters great
and small, and joke the while, and blurt out words
good and bad to say, if so he wished at all, and store
them in loyal keeping; one with whom he could
share many a pleasure and many a joy both openly
and secretly; whose nature no thought of mind led
to do a bad deed lightly or with wrong intent;
a learned, trusty, winsome man and a fine talker,
content with his own, happy and shrewd; one who
spoke the right thing at the right time, and
obliging; of few words; keeping many old-time
ways of which a bygone age long buried is the
maker, and manners old and new; keeping also
to the modes of many a one of our elders, and the
laws too of gods and men; one who could prudently
speak out hearsay or keep it to himself. Him did
Servilius, in the midst of battles,[b] thus address.

They say that Lucius Aelius Stilo used to state that
Quintus Ennius wrote this about none other than himself,[c]
and that the passage given here is a picture of the manners
and temper of Quintus Ennius himself.

228

Prologue continued ? [d]

Festus: ' Quianam ' for ' quare ' and ' cur ' . . . —

For why has your intent been turned by my words ? [e]

[a] *sed* is an archaic word for *sine*.
[b] Apparently metaphorical ' battles.'
[c] *i.e.* that Servilius' friend was Ennius himself. But
cf. V., p. 43; Norden, 131 ff.
[d] Steuart (159) refers the fr. to the war with Pyrrhus—his
Italian allies resent his plan to withdraw to Sicily.
[e] Or, ' why has the meaning of our words been distorted ? '
(Norden 46).

81

ENNIUS

229–30

Festus, 476, 17 : ' Sas.' . . . Eiusdem lib. VII fatendum
est eam significari cum ait—

nec quisquam sophiam sapientia quae perhibetur
in somnis vidit prius quam sam discere coepit.

Cp. Paul., ex F., 477, 4.

231–2

Cicero, *Brut.*, 19, 76 : Tamen illius quem in vatibus et
Faunis adnumerat Ennius, Bellum Punicum quasi Myronis
opus delectat. Sit Ennius sane ut est certe perfectior : qui
si illum ut simulat contemneret, non omnia bella persequens
primum illud Punicum acerrimum bellum reliquisset. Sed
ipse dicit cur id faciat—

Scripsere alii rem

versibus

et luculente quidem scripserunt etiam si minus quam tu
polite : nec vero tibi aliter videri debet, qui a Naevio vel
sumpsisti multa, si fateris, vel si negas, surripuisti.

232–4

Cicero, *Brut.*, 18, 71 : Quid ? Nostri veteres versus ubi sunt ?

quos olim Fauni vatesque canebant,

quom neque Musarum scopulos. . . .

. . . nec dicti studiosus quisquam erat ante hunc

ait ipse de se nec mentitur in gloriando.

[229–30] philosophiam quae doctrina Latina lingua non (*vel*
nomen) habet *Fest.*   sophiam S *qui vocabula* q. d. L. l. n. h.
seclud.

[231–5] *sic constit.* V. ('*Über die Annal. des E.*') *Abh. B. Akad.
d. W.*, 1886, 12 *s.*   [231] scripsere inquit *Cic.*

[233] scopulos < quisquam superarat > *ed. Victor.* auxilio s.
superarat Pascoli   *fortasse* superaverat ullus | umquam
nec d. s. erat *ed. Victor.*

---

[a] St., 156 : V., CLXXXI, and in *Abh. Berl. Akad.*, 1886, 13.
[b] Naevius; cf. Norden, 145 ff.; Steuart, 157–9; V.,
CLXXXI, and in *Abh. Berl. Akad.*, 1886, 12–14.

ANNALS

229-30

Prologue continued : Ennius alludes [a] *to his tale of his dream in the first book :*

Festus: 'Sas.' . . . In the seventh book of the same poet it must be confessed that 'eam' is meant when he says—

nor has any man seen in his dreams Wisdom (a name we give to knowledge) before he has begun to learn her secrets.

231-2

The first Punic War ; Ennius chooses to omit a detailed narrative of the war because Naevius and others have already sung about it :

Cicero : Nevertheless, the *Punic War* of this poet,[b] whom Ennius counts among the seers and Fauns, gives delight as though it were a work of Myron.[c] I grant you, to be sure, that Ennius is the more perfect poet as he certainly is; but if he really scorned Naevius, as he pretends, he would not, in working through all our wars, have left undone the famous First Punic War, a most bitter one. But in his own words he tells us why he does it. He says—

Others have written of the matter [d] in verses

And nobly indeed they wrote, even though they did it in less finished fashion than you did ; nor indeed ought it to appear otherwise to you who took many points from Naevius, if you confess it ; or if you deny it, filched them.

232-4

Cicero : Well ? Our old verses, where are they ? In his own words he speaks of himself (nor lies in his boasting)—

which once upon a time the Fauns and Seers used to sing, when no one had surmounted [e] the rough rocks of the Muses . . . nor was anyone mindful of style before this man . . .

[c] The sculptor, of Eleutherae in Attica.
[d] The First Punic War, in Saturnians. (See Naevius, in *Remains of Old Latin*, Vol. II.)
[e] We might supply 'superaverat ullus umquam.'

ENNIUS

235

Cicero, *Orat.*, 51, 171 : Ergo Ennio licuit vetera contemnenti dicere 'versibus quos olim Fauni vatesque canebant,' mihi de antiquis eodem modo non licebit ? Praesertim cum dicturus non sim 'ante hunc,' ut ille, nec quae sequuntur—

Nos ausi reserare

Cp. Cic., *Orat.*, 47, 157; *de Div.*, I, 50, 114; Varro, *L.L.*, VII, 36; Quintil., IX, 4, 115; Serv. auct., ad *Georg.*, I, 11; Fest., 476, 10.

236

Probus, ad *Georg.*, II, 506 : 'Sarrano dormiat ostro.' Tyriam purpuram vult intelligi Sarranum ostrum. Tyron enim Sarram appellatam Homerus docet, quem etiam Ennius sequitur auctorem cum dicit—

Poenos Sarra oriundos

237

Festus, 324, 15 : 'Puelli' per deminutionem a pueris dicti sunt. Itaque et Ennius ait—

Poeni suos soliti dis sacrificare puellos

Cp. Paul., ex F., 325, 5; Nonius, 158, 20.

[234-5] . . . quisquam, nec dicti studiosus erat. . . . | ante hunc. . . . | nos ausi reserare St. (*pp.* 157-8)
[237] Poeni suos soliti dis V   dis soliti sos Hug   dis Poeni s. s. Mr.   penisolitis vos *Fest.*   Poeni soliti suos *Paul.*   Ennius suos divis *Non.*

ANNALS

235

Cicero : Therefore since it was allowed to Ennius, when he scorned the old poetry, to say ' in verses which once upon a time the Fauns and seers used to sing,' must I be forbidden to speak of archaic writers in the same fashion? Especially since I am not going to say ' before me ' as *he* does, nor what follows—

'Twas I durst unbar . . .

236

The origins of Carthage. The Carthaginian stock ; [a] *the worship of Moloch :*

Probus, on ' that he may sleep on shell-dye of Sarra ' in Virgil: By shell-dye of ' Sarra' he wishes us to understand Tyrian purple. For that Tyre was called Sarra we are informed by Homer; [b] Ennius also follows him as an authority when he says—

Phoenicians [c] sprung from Sarra

237

Festus : ' Puelli' is a word derived in a diminutive form from ' pueri.' Thus Ennius [d] says—

Phoenicians accustomed to offer up to the gods their own little sons

[a] Norden, 77 ff., 89, 92, 150.
[b] Not in the extant poems.
[c] Generally meaning Carthaginians, but here probably the original race.
[d] Norden, 77 ff., 89 ff. He refers the fr. to a definite occasion in 310 B.C. The fr. might belong to Book VIII— embassy to Hannibal demanding his sons for sacrifice— St., 157.

238

Cicero, *de Inv.*, I, 19, 27 : Historia est gesta res ab aetatis nostrae memoria remota, quod genus—

Appius indixit Karthaginiensibus bellum.

239–40

Servius (auctus) ad *Georg.*, II, 449 : ' Buxum ' lignum non arborem dixit, quamvis Ennii exemplo et arborem potuerit dicere neutro genere.   Ille enim sic in septimo—

longique cupressi
stant sectis foliis et amaro corpore buxum.

241

Charisius, ap. *G.L.*, I, 130, 29 K : ' Frus.' ' Haec frus' quia sic ab Ennio est declinatum Annalium libro VII—

russescunt frundes

238 *trib. Enn. ed. Lips.*
240 sectis *cdd.* rectis Ursinus

---

[a] Provided that Ennius wrote this line and that it was in the *Annals* and not in *Scipio*, the fr. is perhaps best placed here.   It does not follow that Ennius went on to tell the story of the war in detail. Cf. Norden, 71 ff. for another view (also St., 150–1); it may well be a ' reference back ' (preceded by ' postquam ') made near the end of Book IX in which the end of the Second Punic War was described.
[b] Sc. by his actions, not as an envoy.

ANNALS

238

How the Romans and the Carthaginians first came into conflict ? ; [a] Appius Claudius Caudex enters Sicily, 264 B.C. :

Cicero : ' History ' means public events remote from the recollection of our own age; such as—

Appius proclaimed [b] war against the Carthaginians.

239–40

Events between the First and Second Punic Wars. Rome obtains Corsica (239 B.C.) and Sardinia [c] (238) :

Servius (supplemented): By ' box ' Virgil meant the wood and not the tree, although in using the neuter gender he could have meant even the tree after the example of Ennius; for that poet has it thus in the seventh book—

and tapering cypresses with crenelled leaves,[d] and the box too, with bitter body,[e] stand straight.

241

Charisius : ' Frus.' Fem. gender because it is thus inflected by E. in the seventh book of the *Annals*—

the leaves turn ruddy

[c] Ennius himself served in Sardinia (see *introd.*) and so may have introduced personal impressions into his narrative.

[d] *sectis* means divided up into small parts. Cypress-leaves appear so, being scale-like and imbricated. In line 565 *rectosque cupressos*, ' upright cypresses,' is quite right. We may note these expressions as good examples of Ennius' verbal accuracy.

[e] Because honey from the flowers is bitter; it was especially true of Corsican honey (Pliny, XVI, 70).

ENNIUS

242-3

Nonius, 385, 5 : ' Rumor,' favor, auxiliatio . . . —

Legio aggreditur Romana ruinas,
mox auferre domos, populi rumore secundo.

244

Festus, 428, 1 : ' Sos ' pro eos . . . —

Dum censent terrere minis, hortantur ibi sos.

245-6

Festus, 538, 34 : ' Tonsam ' Ennius significat remum, quod
quasi tondeatur ferro, cum ait lib. VII—

' Poste recumbite vestraque pectora pellite tonsis.'

Item—

Pone petunt, exim referunt ad pectora tonsas.

Cp. Paul., ex. F., 539, 13.

---

[242] aggreditur Romana W   reducta ruinis Hug   red-
ditu rumore ruinas mox a. d. p. r. s. *Non.*   reddit murumque
ruinas V   reddit urbemque Ribb.   redit ut B   rediit
olim V
[243] rumore secundo (*deinde ut init. alterius citationis*)
ruina | mox *e.q.s.* Mr. *prob.* St.   Cf. V., *Sitz.-Ber. K. Ak.,*
1888, 48.   ' legio rediit rumore ' et ' ruina mox a. d. *e.q.s.*
Linds. (de legionis reditu ' ruina *e.q.s. coni.*)
[244] ibei O. Mr.   ibe *cd.*
[246] premunt Mr.   ferunt B *prob.* Valmaggi

---

a In the following fr. I keep one quotation; and suggest that
it describes a scene in the narrative where the Romans helped
the Carthaginian mutineers (*populus*) in Sardinia.

88

ANNALS

242-3

Rome obtains Sardinia (238 B.C.): [a]

Nonius : ' Rumor,' favour, aid. . . . —

The Roman army, cheered on by the crowd, attacked the ruins, and soon made away with the dwellings.

244

War with the Illyrian pirates, 230–228 B.C. Complaints of the Greeks about half-hearted measures ? :

Festus : ' Sos ' for ' eos ' . . . —

While they were minded to startle them with threats, therewith they encouraged them.

245-6

Advance of the Roman fleet under Cn. Fulvius and L. Postumius : [b]

Festus : ' Tonsa.' By this word Ennius, when he says in the seventh book—

' Lean ye right backward and beat ye your breasts with the trimmers ';

means an oar, because as it were ' tonditur,' it is trimmed, with a knife; again—

Backward they reach, then again pull the trimmers to their breasts.

[b] This seems to me to be the only possible context. These frs. are usually assigned to a narrative of the First Punic War (cf. Vahlen, CLXXX ; Norden, 66–71, 76, 94 ff., 151 is suggestive). But this can hardly be right (see pp. 64–5 and St., 150–2), though at first sight it does look as if Ennius is describing the building of the first Roman fleet, and the training of the crews, in 260 B.C.

ENNIUS

247

Festus, 170, 28 : 'Nare' a nave ductum Cornificius ait . . . —

Alter nare cupit, alter pugnare paratust.

248

Priscianus, ap. *G.L.*, II, 486, 13 K : 'Mulgeo' quoque mulsi facit . . . —

· Mulserat huc navem compulsam fluctibus pontus.

249

Paulus, ex F., 500, 10 : 'Sibynam' appellant Illyrii telum venabuli simile. Ennius—

Illyrii restant sicis sibynisque fodentes.

250

Nonius, 116, 2 : 'Gracilentum' pro gracili . . . —

Deducunt habiles gladios filo gracilento.

[249] *trib. lib. VII* Merula

---

[a] Pun on *nare, pugnare*. St., p. 152, would attribute this fr. also to the history of Pyrrhus; I take *alter* as referring to an Illyrian *lembos*. But cf. Norden, 67–70, 151; Kvičala, *Eos*, VIII, 8 ff. refers the fr. to Hannibal at the Tagus in 220 B.C.

[b] So I interpret this fr., which is usually attributed to the First Punic War (Norden, 65 ff., 69, 151—a stranded Carthaginian ship which served the Romans as a model in 260 B.C. Cp. Vahlen, CLXXX; on p. 41 he says 'Mulserat Ennii ad mulcendum h. e. leniter movendum referri oportet ').

247

A sea-fight ; Illyrians hard-pressed :

Festus : ' Nare.' Cornificius states that this word is derived from ' navis ' . . . —

The one [a] wishes to float in flight; the other is ready to fight.

248

An Illyrian ship is driven ashore : [b]

Priscianus : ' Mulgeo ' likewise takes ' mulsi ' for its perfect tense . . . —

Hither the sea had gently washed a ship buffeted by the billows.

249

The Illyrians resist stoutly :

Paulus : ' Sibyna,' a name given by the Illyrians to a javelin resembling a hunting-spear. Ennius [c]—

The Illyrians stood fast and stabbed with curving knives and hunting-spears.

250

War of the Boii and other Cisalpine and Transalpine Celts against Rome, 226–222 B.C. Preparations of the Gauls ? : [d]

Nonius : ' Gracilentum ' for ' gracilis.' . . . —

They beat out handy swords like slender thread.

St., 151 suggests that the reference is to the storm which Pyrrhus experienced on his voyage to Italy, and puts the fr. in Book VI.

[c] This fragment should perhaps be assigned to a later book—cf. V., CLXXXV (Livy, XXXI, 34; 200 B.C.).

[d] Or possibly Spanish swords are meant; they were used by the Romans. Cf. Norden, 119 ff., 152.

ENNIUS

251-2

Macrobius, *S.*, I, 4, 17 : . . . —

qua Galli furtim noctu summa arcis adorti
moenia concubia vigilesque repente cruentant.

Quo in loco animadvertendum est non solum quod ' noctu,'
' concubia ' sed quod etiam ' qua noctu ' dixerit (*Ennius*);
et hoc ponit in Annalium septimo. . . .

253

Macrobius, *S.*, VI, 1, 19 : ' Ne qua meis dictis esto mora :
Iuppiter hac stat ' (*Aen.*, XII, 565). Ennius in VII—

' Non semper vestra evertit; nunc Iuppiter hac stat.'

254

Macrobius, *S.*, VI, 1, 52 : 'Audentes fortuna iuvat.' (*Aen.*,
X, 284). E. in VII—

' Fortibus est fortuna viris data.

255

Priscianus, ap. *G.L.*, II, 223, 4 K : Sed Nar servavit *a*
productam etiam in obliquis . . . —

Sulphureas posuit spiramina Naris ad undas.

---

[a] The Gauls were ultimately not successful.
[b] *qua* is generally taken as *qua via*.
[c] 'To men of pluck is given luck.' See last fragm. for the
context, and cf. Norden, 43 ff.

ANNALS

251–2

The Gauls near Clusium, 225 B.C.; *terror at Rome;*
reminiscence of the invasion of 390 (? 387) B.C. :

Macrobius :—

on that night the Gauls with stealth attacked the
wall-tops of the citadel in the sleep-time, and on a
sudden brought bloodshed [a] on the sentinels.

In this passage we must notice that Ennius not only used
'noctu' and 'concubia' but also 'qua noctu';[b] he puts
this expression in the seventh book of the *Annals.* . . .

253

Defeat of the Gauls at Telamon ? 225 B.C.   *Speech of Gaius*
Atilius or of Lucius Aemilius :

Macrobius, quoting Virgil: 'Let there be no delay to my
commands. Jupiter stands on our side.' Ennius in the
seventh book—

Not always does Jupiter upset your plans; now
he stands on our side.

254

Macrobius, quoting Virgil: 'Fortune favours the daring.'
E. in the seventh book—

To men of fortitude is fortune granted.[c]

255

The Via Flaminia is completed by Flaminius as far as
Ariminum (220 B.C.); *works built at the crossing of the river*
Nar between Narnia and Carsulae ? :

Priscianus : But 'Nar' has kept the *a* long even in oblique
cases. . . . —

He built blow-holes by Nar's sulphury waters.

ENNIUS

Propertius, III, 3, 9 :

Et cecinit . . .

Regiaque Aemilia vecta tropaea rate

256-7

Servius (auctus) ad *Georg.*, III, 116 : Hic equitem . . .
equum dicit. . . . Ennius Annalium septimo—

Denique vi magna quadrupes eques atque elephanti
proiciunt sese.

Cp. Gell., XVIII, 5, 2; Non., 106, 30; Macrob., *S.*, VI,
9, 10.

Praeconia ex libris VIII–XV

Cicero, *pro Archia*, 9, 22 : Carus fuit Africano superiori
noster Ennius, itaque etiam in sepulchro Scipionum putatur
is esse constitutus ex marmore; cuius laudibus certe non
solum ipse qui laudatur sed etiam populi Romani nomen
ornatur. In caelum huius proavus Cato tollitur; magnus
honos populi Romani rebus adiungitur. Omnes denique
illi Maximi, Marcelli, Fulvii non sine communi omnium nostrum
laude decorantur. Ergo illum qui haec fecerat, Rudinum
hominem, maiores nostri in civitatem receperunt.

---

[a] See p. 44. It is, of course, tempting to see an allusion
by Propertius to the victory of Aemilius Paullus over Perseus
in 168 B.C. (which Ennius did not live to see); but such an
intrusion between the event of Tullius' reign and a reference
to Fabius of the Second Punic War would be inartistic.

[b] It is possible that the reference is to the battle at the
Trebia in 218; cf. Norden, 126 ff., 152. The attribution to
a narrative of the First Punic War (V., CLXXIX ff.;
CLXXXIV) is not acceptable. St., pp. 151–2, suggests that
we have here the stampede of Pyrrhus' elephants at the
battle of Beneventum. But apart from what I have said
above, the words of Gellius show that this was nearly at the
end of the book.

ANNALS

Second Illyrian War, 219 B.C.; *suppression of Demetrius of Pharos by L. Aemilius Paullus :*

Propertius [a] says :

And he sang . . . of the royal trophies carried by Aemilius' ship.

256-7

Second Punic War begins ; [b] *Hannibal advances from ' New Carthage,' spring* 218 B.C. :

Servius (supplemented) : Here by ' equitem ' Virgil means ' equum.' . . . Ennius in the seventh book of the *Annals*—

At last with mighty rush the horseman at a four-footed gallop [c] and the elephants too hurl themselves onwards.

Some great men of whom Ennius wrote in Books VIII–XV

Cicero : Our poet Ennius was a dear friend of the elder Africanus, and that is why a marble statue of him, it is thought, was set up in the tomb of the Scipios. But his verses of praise are surely an adornment not only for him who is praised but also for the name of the Roman people. Cato, ancestor of Cato here, is extolled to the skies; this carries with it great honour for the history of the Roman people. In short, all those great names—the Maximi, Marcelli, Fulvii—are honoured by praise which is shared by all of us. Hence it was that he who had done [d] all this, a native of Rudiae, was received by our ancestors into their citizenship.

---

[c] On this use of ' eques ' cf. St., p. 160. Later Roman writers were themselves at variance whether *eques* could be used of the horse only. Gellius, XVIII, 5, insists that Ennius really did write *quadrupes eques*.

[d] Ennius told of the achievements and sang the praises of Scipio Africanus chiefly in Book IX and *Scipio* (pp. 394 ff.); of Cato in Book XI; of Q. Fabius Max. Rullianus in Book V and of Fabius Cunctator in Book VIII (and, by reminiscence, in Book XII); of M. Claudius Marcellus in Book VIII; and of M. Fulvius Nobilior in Book XV and *Ambracia* (pp. 358 ff.).

ENNIUS

LIBER VIII

258–9

Horatius, *S.*, I, 4, 60 : Non, ut si solvas—

Postquam Discordia taetra
belli ferratos postes portasque refregit,

invenias etiam disiecti membra poetae.

Porphyrio *ad loc.* Est sensus : Si dissolvas versus vel meos
vel Lucilii, non invenies eadem membra quae sunt in Ennianis
versibus, qui magno scilicet spiritu et verbis altioribus com-
positi sunt, velut hi sunt ' Postquam e.q.s.

Cp. Verg., *Aen.*, VII, 622 : Belli ferratos rupit Saturnia
postes. Serv., ad 622; Acro, ad Hor., *l.c.*

260–1

Probus, ad Verg., *Ecl.*, VI, 31 . . . Hic (*aer*) est . . . qui
nobis vivendi spirituum commeatum largitur. Hoc illud et
Ennius appellavit in Annalibus—

corpore tartarino prognata paluda virago,
cui par imber et ignis spiritus et gravis terra.

Cp. Varr., *L.L.*, VII, 37; Fest., 546, 2.

---

²⁵⁸⁻⁹ *trib. Ann. lib. VII* Norden
²⁶⁰⁻¹ *trib. lib. VIII* St., *VII* Norden

ª St. takes the narrative to the departure of Hannibal
from Italy—see notes on pp. 65–7. But fr. 300–5 of Book IX
rules this out (see p. 112).

ANNALS

BOOK VIII

The Second Punic War to the Departure [a] of Scipio for Africa

258-9

Outbreak of Discord :

Horace: You would not still find the limbs of a dismembered poet as you would if you were to break up the following—

After foul Discord broke open the ironclad doors and doorposts of war,

Porphyrio on this passage : The sense is : If you analyse my verses or Lucilius', you will not find the same sort of ' limbs ' as you would in Ennius [b] verses, which are to be sure composed with mighty inspiration, with the use of a loftier diction as these are : ' After . . .

260-1

Probus : Air surely is the thing which gives us supplies of the breath of life. 'Spiritus' is the name given to it by Ennius [c] also in the *Annals*—

⟨Discord,⟩ of hellish body daughter bred, woman of war in warrior's cloak, for whom water and fire and breath and heavy earth are equal.

[b] This fr. is doubtless rightly put in the eighth book— St., 171; V., CLXXXV, CLXXXVI (but Norden, 146, puts it in the seventh).
[c] On this fr. cf. St., 170–171. *Discordia* is here ' an incarnation of chaos '; only when Empedocles' four elements (here mentioned by Ennius) were *unequally* mixed did separate things come into being—cf. Norden 10 ff. (esp. 12–14). Festus, 456, 2, explains *tartarino* as horrible and fearful.

97

ENNIUS

262-8

Gellius, XX, 10, 1 : ' Ex iure manum consertum ' verba
sunt ex antiquis actionibus. . . . Ennius . . . verbis hisce
usus est . . . tum ego hos versus ex octavo Annali absentes
dixi . . . —

⟨proeliis promulgatis⟩
pellitur e medio sapientia, vi geritur res,
spernitur orator bonus, horridus miles amatur ;
haud doctis dictis certantes, sed maledictis   265
miscent inter sese inimicitiam agitantes ;
non ex iure manum consertum, sed magis ferro
rem repetunt regnumque petunt, vadunt solida vi.

Cp. Cic., *Pro Mur.*, 14, 30 (proeliis promulgatis ' pellitur . . .) ;
Cic., *ad Fam.*, VII, 13, 2 ; Lactant., *Div. Inst.*, V, 1, 5.

269

Priscianus, ap. *G.L.*, II, 209, 6 K : Dido, Didonis. . . .
(210, 10 K) Ennius in VIII—

Poenos Didone oriundos

270

Gellius, VI, 12, 7 : Q . . . Ennius Carthaginiensium—

tunicatam iuventutem

non videtur sine probro dixisse.

Cp. Non., 536, 31.

---

[262] promulgatis *add. ex Cic., pro Mur.*, 14, ⟨si sunt
proelia promulgata⟩ B [263] tollitur *Cic., pro Mur.*
[265] sed Colonna nec *cdd.* (ñ Z)

---

[a] This clause is supplied from Cic., *pro Mur.*, 14, 30, and
may belong to Ennius.

ANNALS

262–8

The people in time of war :

Gellius says: ' Ex iure manum consertum' are words drawn from ancient cases at law. . . . Ennius used these words . . . Then I myself recited from memory these lines from the eighth book of the *Annals* . . . —

When news of battles is proclaimed,[a] away from view is Wisdom thrust, with violence is action done, scorned is the speaker of good counsel, dear is the rude warrior. Not with learned speeches do men strive, but [b] with evil speaking fall foul one of another, brewing unfriendliness. They rush to make joint seizure [c]—not by law; rather by the sword do they seek a due return and aim at the first place, and move on with pack and press.

269

Rome thinks lightly of the Carthaginians ? :

Priscianus: Dido, Didonis. . . . E. in the eighth book—

Phoenicians sprung from Dido

270

Gellius: Quintus Ennius does not appear to have spoken of the Carthaginians as—

petticoated lads

without scorn.

---

[b] *nec* may be right—men strive, not with speech of any kind, but with force.

[c] *consertum,* supine (after *vadunt*) as the ' end of motion '; or supply ' *vocant* '—the legal phrase was ' *vocare consertum.*' There may likewise be a legal sense in *agitantes* ' pressing accusations of . . .

ENNIUS

271

Ekkehart, ad Oros., VI, 6, 21 (*de Hamilcare Rhodano*):
Ennius—

qualis consiliis quantumque potesset in armis.

272-3

Ekkehart (?), ad Oros., IV, 14, 3 (*de Hannibale*): De quo
Ennius—

at non sic duplex fuit hostis
Aeacida Burrus.

Propertius, III, 3, 9-10:

Et cecinit . . .
victricesque moras Fabii pugnamque sinistram
Cannensem et versos ad pia vota deos.

274

Nonius, 150, 18: ' Praecox ' et ' praecoca ' . . . —

' praecox pugna est.

[271] *trib. Ann. lib. VIII* St., *VII* V
[272] duplex B   dirus Mr   dubius Ekk.? *prob.* V.,
Norden   *fortasse* durus
[273] phyrrus Ekk. (?)   at n.s. dubius Pyrrhus (Burrus)
fuit A.h. *coni.* V   *trib. Ann. VIII* Mr.
[274] *Non.*, 150 *seclud.* et Linds. (*coni.* praecox est p. *vel*
praecox et praecoquis)   praecox *Non.*   praecoca Mr.

---

[a] It is possible that this fr. should be put in Book VII as
part of the *primordia Carthaginis*; it is generally referred to
the mission of Hamilcar Rhodanus (given by Orosius in the
passage against which Ekkehart wrote the fr. of Ennius) in

ANNALS

271

The Romans were unaware of Hannibal's character :

Over a passage of Orosius, in a *codex Sangallensis*, referring to Hamilcar Rhodanus, Ekkehart wrote the following: Ennius *a* has—

what kind of man he was in counsels, and how great his prowess in arms.

272-3

Over another passage of Orosius, in the same codex, referring to Hannibal, Ekkehart (?) wrote the following: On Hannibal Ennius *b* has—

But not such a double-faced foe was Burrus sprung from Aeacus.

Election in 217 B.C. of Quintus Fabius Maximus (Cunctator) as dictator : Battle of Cannae, 216 B.C. ; crisis of the war :

Propertius: And he sang . . . of Fabius' delays that were fraught with victory: and of the ill-starred fight of Cannae; and how the gods were turned to hear our heartfelt prayers.

274

*The Battle of Cannae.*c* Aemilius Paullus, on the eve of Cannae, tries to persuade Terentius Varro not to accept battle :* *d*

Nonius : ' Praecox ' and ' praecoca ' . . .—

' Time is unripe for fighting.

331 to inquire into Alexander's achievements. Cf. Norden, 80 ff., 86-7, 150. But cf. St., p. 173.
b Norden, 80 ff., 87-8, 151, retains the reading *dubius* and puts the fr. in Book VII, referring it to Hannibal's oath.
c A probable order for some of the fragments can be deduced from Livy's account, references to which are given below where they seem to apply.
d Livy, XXII, 44; Polyb., III, 110, 4, 8 ; Silius, IX, 44 ff.
' *Praecox* ' generally means ripening early.

ENNIUS

275

Diomedes, ap. *G.L.*, I, 382, 11 K : Apud veteres et abnueo dictum annotamus . . . —

' Certare abnueo ; metuo legionibus labem.

276–7

Cicero, *pro Balbo*, 22, 51 : Neque enim ille summus poeta noster Hannibalis illam magis cohortationem quam communem imperatoriam voluit esse—

' Hostem qui feriet mihi erit Karthaginiensis,
quisquis erit ; quoiatis siet . . .

278

Festus, 220, 25 : ' Obstipum,' obliquum . . . —

amplius exaugere obstipo lumine solis

279

Nonius, 217, 7 : ' Pulvis ' generis . . . feminini . . . —

iamque fere pulvis ad caelum vasta videtur

[276] feriet erit inquit mihi *Par.*   feriet inquit mihi erit *rell.*
[277] quoiatis siet < non anxius quaero > *coni.* V   siet, quoiatis siet Merula
[279] vegetur Bergk

---

[a] Silius, IX, 209–211.   Or possibly the battle at the Ticinus —Livy, XXII, 45.   On both occasions Hannibal made promises of Carthaginian citizenship.

ANNALS

275

Fears of Paullus :

Diomedes : In the old writers we notice that ' abnueo '
is used . . . —

' I refuse to join issue ; I fear ruin for my legions.

276–7

Hannibal to his troops on the occasion of the battle of Cannae,
B.C. 216 : [a]

Cicero : And further our renowned and greatest poet did
not wish that famous encouragement to be Hannibal's any
more than one common to all commanders—

' He who will strike a blow at the enemy—hear
me ! he will be a Carthaginian, whatever his name
will be ; whatever his country,

278

The battle. The position of the sun favours [b] both sides :

Festus : ' Obstipum,' slanting. . . . —

to grow much greater because of the slanting sunlight

279

But the wind raised dust-clouds which hindered the Romans : [c]

Nonius : ' Pulvis ' in the feminine gender . . . —

and just then a huge dust-cloud was seen to reach
the sky.

[b] Livy, XXII, 46 sol . . . peropportune utrique parti
obliquus erat.   In Ennius' fr. we might supply *vires* or *umbrae.*
(Cp. Val. Max., VII, 4, ext. 2.   Hannibal takes account of the
sunlight and the dust.)
[c] Livy, *l.c.* ventus . . . adversus Romanis coortus multo
pulvere . . . prospectum ademit.

ENNIUS

280

Priscianus, ap. *G.L.*, III, 479, 4 K : 'Denseo' . . . (480, 5)
'denso' . . . —

Densantur campis horrentia tela virorum.

281

Macrobius, *S.*, VI, 1, 52 : 'Ac ferreus ingruit imber'
(*Aen.*, XII, 284). Ennius in VIII—

Hastati spargunt hastas; fit ferreus imber.

282

Paulus, ex F., 439, 7 : 'Suppernati' dicuntur quibus
femina sunt succisa in modum suillarum pernarum. Ennius—

His pernas succidit iniqua superbia Poeni.

Cp. Fest., 438, 14.

283

Macrobius, *S.*, XI, 1, 22 : 'Quadrupedante putrem sonitu
quatit ungula campum' (*Aen.*, VIII, 596). Ennius . . .
in VIII—

Consequitur; summo sonitu quatit ungula terram.

Livius, XXII, 50 : Haec ubi dicta dedit stringit gladium,
cuneoque facto per medios vadit hostes.

---

[282] his *Paul.* is *Fest.*

---

^a Probably as described by Livy, XXII, 47; cp. especially :
Romani . . . aequa fronte acieque densa impulere hostium
cuneum.

^b I compare Livy, XXII, 48, adversum adoriuntur
Romanam aciem, tergaque ferientes ac poplites caedentes
stragem ingentem . . . fecerunt. Cp. Val. Max., CII, 4,
ext. 2. But it may be that he describes how the Roman
wounded were found mutilated after the battle—Livy, *id.*,
51 quosdam et iacentes vivos succisis feminibus poplitibusque
invenerunt. *Perna* (= *poples*) is not used elsewhere of a man.

104

ANNALS

280

The infantry engagement : [a]

Priscian : ' Denseo ' inflected as from ' denso ' . . . —

The bristling spears of the warriors crowded thick
upon the plain.

281

Macrobius, quoting Virgil : ' And a shower of iron comes
thick.' Ennius in the eighth book—

The line of lancers scattered its lances; came a
shower of iron.

282

Attack of the Numidians ; Romans are mutilated :

Paulus : Men are called ' suppernati ' (ham-strung) whose
upper thighs are cut through in the manner of pigs' haunches.
Ennius—

These the Poeni houghed, wicked haughty foes.[b]

283

Hasdrubal sends the Numidians in pursuit of the Romans : [c]

Macrobius, quoting Virgil : ' The four-footed beat of the
hoofs shook the crumbling plain.' Ennius in the eighth
book—

They gave chase : with mightiest clatter their
hoofs shook the ground.

*The military tribune, P. Sempronius Tuditanus, leads a
remnant through to Canusium :*

Livy : When he had made this speech, he drew his sword,
formed the men into a wedge, and charged through the
midst of the enemy.[d]

---

[c] I would compare Livy, XXII, 48, Hasdrubal . . . sub-
actos ex media acie Numidas . . . ad persequendos passim
fugientes mittit.

[d] It seems probable that Livy has really preserved fragments of two lines.—V., CXC; Norden, 141.

ENNIUS

284-6

Macrobius, *S.*, VI, 2, 16 : ' Multa dies variusque labor mutabilis aevi | rettulit in melius, multos alterna revisens | lusit et in solido rursus fortuna locavit (*Aen.*, XI, 425-7). Ennius in VIII—

' Multa dies in bello conficit unus . . .
et rursus multae fortunae forte recumbunt;
haudquaquam quemquam semper fortuna secuta est.

287

Nonius, 435, 13 : ' Quartum' et ' quarto' . . . Ennius recte—

Quintus pater quartum fit consul.

Cp. Gell., X, 1, 6.

288

Paulus, ex F., 193, 7 : ' Ob ' . . . pro ' ad,' ut E.—

Ob Romam noctu legiones ducere coepit

Cp. Fest., 192, 15; *id.*, 218, 9; Exc. ex cd. Cassin. 90, ap. *C.G.L.*, V, 573, 45.

Propertius, III, 3, 11 :

Et cecinit . . .
Hannibalemque Lares Romana sede fugantes.

289

Festus, 234, 29 : ' Oscos ' quos dicimus ait Verrius Opscos ante dictos teste Ennio cum dicat—

De muris rem gerit Opscus.

[284] < infit > multa *coni.* V   *post* 284 *spatium stat.* V
[287-90] *trib. Ann. lib. VIII* Merula

ANNALS

284-6

The Senators prevent panic at Rome ? :

Macrobius, quoting Virgil: 'Many a day and change of
work in ever-varying life have brought back countless men
to better state; and fortune, her eye now here now there,
has had the laugh and set men anew on foundation form.'
Ennius in the eighth book—

' Many things does one day bring about in war . . .
and many fortunes through chance sink low again.
In no wise has fortune followed any man all his days.

287

The fourth consulship of Fabius, 214 B.C. :

Nonius: 'Quartum' and 'quarto.' E. rightly has
'quartum' in—

Quintus the father[a] was made consul for the
fourth time.

288

During the siege of Capua. Hannibal marches on Rome,
211 B.C.

Paulus: 'Ob,' . . . for 'ad'; for example Ennius—

He began by night to lead his hosts against Rome.

His retreat :

Propertius: And he sang . . . how our Guardian Gods[b]
put Hannibal to flight from their Roman home.

289

Capua is stormed, 211 B.C. :

Festus says: 'Oscans.' Verrius states that the people we
call by this name were formerly called the 'Opscians,' his
witness being Ennius, since he says—

The Opscan gives battle from the wall.

---

[a] As distinguished from his son, who was made praetor
at the same time.
[b] Especially the god Tutanus (Non., 47, 26).

ENNIUS

290

Paulus, ex F., 88, 34 : 'Meddix' apud Oscos nomen magistratus est. E.—

Summus ibi capitur meddix, occiditur alter.

291

Schol. Bern. ad *Georg.*, IV, 67 : Ennius in VIII ait—

Tibia Musarum pangit melos,

292

Priscianus, ap. *G.L.*, III, 192, 9 K : Solent auctores variare figuras . . . ut Ennius—

Optima caelicolum, Saturnia, magna dearum

293

Servius, ad *Aen.*, I, 281 : 'Consilia in melius referet' quia bello Punico secundo, ut ait Ennius—

Romanis Iuno coepit placata favere.

Servius, ad *Aen.*, I, 20; In Ennio . . . inducitur Iuppiter promittens Romanis excidium Carthaginis.

---

[293] *hexametr. constit.* Hug *non prob.* Norden   placata Iuno coepit favere Romanis *Serv.*

---

[a] *ad Iunonem Reginam* (Livy, XXVII, 37) attributed to Livius Andronicus (see *Remains, etc.*, Vol. II, Loeb)—St., pp. 177–8. Vahlen, CXC and p. 52 sees a reference to Mar-

ANNALS

290

Fate of Seppius Loesius and others of Capua :

Paulus : ' Meddix ' is among the Oscans the name of a magistrate. Ennius—

There the chief magistrate was made prisoner, the other was put to death.

291

Hymn of Livius Andronicus (?) to Juno, 207 B.C. ? : [a]

A scholiast : Ennius says in the eighth book—

The flute composed a song of music,

292

Juno begins to favour the Romans :

Priscianus : Authors are wont to vary their figures . . . for example, Ennius—

Saturn's daughter, mighty among goddesses, dearest of those that dwell in heaven,

293

Servius : ' She will change her counsels for the better,' because in the Second Punic War, according to Ennius—

Juno was appeased and began to shew the Romans [b] her good-will.

And Jupiter promises that destruction awaits Carthage :

Servius : In Ennius Jupiter is introduced as promising the Romans that Carthage shall be overthrown.

---

cellus, who, after the recovery of Syracuse in 212, was granted an ovation only.

[b] Servius, however, perhaps gave a paraphrase, not a jumbled line of Ennius—Norden, 169.

ENNIUS

294

Macrobius, *S.*, VI, 1, 20 : 'Invadunt urbem somno vinoque sepultam ' (*Aen.*, II, 265). Ennius in VIII—

Nunc hostes vino domiti somnoque sepulti,

Cp. Lucret., V, 974, somnoque sepulti.

295

Festus, 194, 12 : ' Occasus ' . . . pro occasione . . .—

Ast occasus ubi tempusve audere repressit,

296

Servius (auctus), ad *Aen.*, IX, 641 : ' Mactus.' Etiam mactatus dicebatur, ut Ennius—

Livius inde redit magno mactatus triumpho.

297-9

Nonius, 151, 18 : ' Portisculus ' proprie est hortator remigum, id est qui eam perticam tenet quae portisculus dicitur qua et cursum et exhortamenta moderatur . . .—

                tonsam ante tenentes
parerent, observarent, portisculus signum
quom dare coepisset.

[294] sepulti | <consiluere> *add.* V *ex Paul.*, 41, 5 (' consiluere ' Ennius pro conticuere posuit) *coll. Aen.*, IX, 234 somno vinoque soluti | conticuere
[295] ast Colonna aut *cd.*
[297] tonsam ante S   tonsas Colonna   tonsam arte Merula   tonsamque Carrio   tusam Linds.   tusante *cdd.*   *fortasse* tunsam ante   *trib. lib. VIII Non. VII* Merula

---

[a] I would compare Livy, XXVII, 48. But Steuart, p. 179, suggests the attack by Scipio in 203 on the camps of the Carthaginians and the Numidians.

ANNALS

294

The drunken Gauls at the Battle of the Metaurus, 207 B.C. : [a]

Macrobius, quoting Virgil : 'They rushed on the city, which was buried in sleep and wine.' Ennius in the eighth book—

And now the enemy, mastered by wine and buried in sleep,

295

Festus : ' Occasus ' . . . for ' occasio ' . . .—

But when the occasion or the time smothered their daring,

296

Triumphant return of the two consuls :

Servius (supplemented) : ' Mactus.' Even the form ' mactatus ' was used for this; for example, Ennius—

Thence returned Livius [b] magnified with a great triumph.

297–9

New fleet of Scipio Africanus (consul, 205) in training ? : [c]

Nonius : ' Portisculus ' is, in its proper sense, the term for the time-beater of a ship's oarsmen; that is to say, the man who holds the staff for which the term ' portisculus ' is used; by means of this he times the rhythm and ' lay to ' . . .—

that, holding the oar forward, they should obey and watch when the boatswain began to give them the signal.

[b] Almost certainly Livius Salinator is meant; after the battle of Metaurus he enjoyed a triumph superior to Claudius Nero's (Livy, XXVIII, 9). It is, however, possible that the reference is to Livius' earlier triumph over the Illyrians (Polyb., III, 19, 12), in which case the fr. belongs to Book VII—V., CXCI.

[c] So I suggest; St., 151, points to the sham fights whereby the Romans kept up their training. This is one of the frs. usually put in Book VII—V., CLXXIX; Norden, 66-7, 151.

ENNIUS

LIBER IX

300-5

Cicero, *Brut.*, 15, 58 : Est . . . sic apud illum (Ennium) in nono ut opinor Annali—

Additur orator Cornelius suaviloquenti
ore, Cethegus Marcus, Tuditano collega,
Marci filius.

Et oratorem appellat et suaviloquentiam tribuit . . . sed est ea laus eloquentiae certe maxima—

. . . Is dictust ollis popularibus olim
qui tum vivebant homines atque aevum agitabant,
' Flos delibatus populi

Probe vero. Ut enim hominis decus ingenium sic ingeni ipsius lumen est eloquentia, qua virum excellentem praeclare tum illi homines florem populi esse dixerunt—

Suadaeque medulla.'

. . . hic Cethegus consul cum P. Tuditano fuit bello Punico secundo quaestorque is consulibus M. Cato modo plane annis CXL ante me consulem, et ipsum nisi unius esset Ennii testimonio cognitum, hunc vetustas, ut alios fortasse multos, oblivione obruisset.

Cp. Cic., *de Senect.*, 14; Gell., XII, 2, 3 ff.; Quintil., II, 15, 4; XI, 3, 31; Serv. auct., ad *Aen.*, VIII, 500; et fortasse Hor., *Ep.*, II, 2, 115 ff.

---

[303] dictus popularibus *Cic. cdd.* dictus tollis p. *cdd. Gell.* dictust ollis p. Gronov.
[304] agitabant *Gell.*   agebant *Cic.*

---

[a] It seems natural to take the fr. as describing either the election of the two consuls for 204 in the summer of 205, or to their entry into office on 15th of March, 204. Thus we could not, as Steuart does, extend Book VIII down to Hannibal's recall from Italy, which took place in 203. She suggests that

ANNALS

BOOK IX

300–5

M. Cornelius and P. Sempronius consuls, 204 B.C. : [a]

Cicero : The following is a passage in Ennius' work, in the ninth book, I think, of the *Annals*—

Then Marcus Cornelius Cethegus, son of Marcus, an orator whose mouth spoke winsome speech, is put in as a colleague to Tuditanus.

He calls him an orator and also grants him winsomeness of speech . . . but the greatest stroke in praise of his eloquence is surely this—

. . . By those fellow-countrymen who were then alive and had their being he was once upon a time called the ' choice flower ' of the people,

Well said indeed. For, as the glory of a man is his natural talents, so the lustre of those very talents is eloquence; and a man surpassing in eloquence was admirably called by the men of that time ' flower of the people—

and the marrow of Persuasion.' [b]

. . . This Cethegus was consul with Publius Tuditanus in the Second Punic War, and Marcus Cato was a quaestor in their consulship, in round numbers only one hundred and fifty years before my own consulship; and were this fact not known through the testimony of Ennius alone, antiquity would have buried this very Cethegus, as maybe it has buried many others, in oblivion.

Cethegus and Tuditanus were connected with some mission, possibly the negotiations for peace begun in 203. Cicero's uncertainty about Book IX is feigned; on this cf. St., pp. 180–81. They were both censors in 209, so that the fr. may belong to Book VIII.

[b] Suada, Πειθώ, goddess of Persuasion.

ENNIUS

306

Festus, 140, 21 : ' Metonymia ' . . . quae continet quod continetur, ut Ennius ait—

Africa terribili tremit horrida terra tumultu.

307

Nonius, 472, 5 : ' Luctant ' pro luctantur . . . —

Viri validis cum viribus luctant.

308

Nonius, 217, 8 : ' Pulvis ' . . . Feminini . . . —

Pulvis fulva volat

309

Nonius, 95, 30 : ' Debil,' debilis . . . —

debil homo

310-11

Priscianus, ap. *G.L.*, II, 485, 17 K : In *geo* desinentia . . . (486)—

Cyclopis venter velut olim turserat alte
carnibus humanis distentus

312

Servius (?) ad *Georg.*, II, 437 : ' Undantem,' abundantem . . . E. lib. IX—

praeda exercitus undat.

[306] *trib. lib. IX* Hug
[307] viri *ed. princ.* <fortuna> varia V Illyria Havet (*Rev. de Phil.*, *XV*, 72) varia vel viri a *cdd.* cum *add.* D (I.)
[308] iamque fere pulvis f.v. *cdd.* iamque fere *nata ex priore citat. seclud.* Hug
[310] alte D (I.) alti Prisc.

ANNALS

306

Scipio's campaigns in Africa? [a]

Festus: 'Metonymia' . . . when the meaning of a word contains exactly the contents of its equivalent; for example, Ennius when he says—

Trembled Africa, land rough and rude, with a terrible tumult.

307

Battle of Zama? 202 B.C. :

Nonius: ' Luctant ' for ' luctantur ' . . .—

The soldiers struggled with sturdy strength.

308

Nonius: ' Pulvis ' . . . of the feminine gender . . .

Brown dust flies aloft

309

Nonius: ' Debil,' the same as ' debilis ' . . .—

a feeble fellow

310-11

Priscianus: Verbs ending in *geo* . . .—

Just as the Cyclops' belly once swelled high, stretched tight with human flesh

312

The spoils won after the battle of Zama :

Servius (?): ' Undantem,' the same as ' abundantem.' . . . Ennius in the ninth book of the *Annals*—

the army billowed in booty.

[a] Cf. Hug, *Q. Enn. Annal.*, VII–IX, p. 10. The fr. may belong to Book VIII (Carthage's war with her mercenaries) or to ' *Scipio* ' (pp. 394 ff.).

ENNIUS

313-14

Nonius, 110, 8 : ' Famul,' famulus . . . —

   . . . Mortalem summum Fortuna repente
reddidit e summo regno ut famul oltimus esset.

Lucret., III, 1034-5 :

Scipiadas belli fulmen Carthaginis horror,
Ossa dedit terrae proinde ac famul infimus esset.

315

Priscianus, ap. *G.L.*, II, 278, 12 K : Ennius . . . in IX
pro frugi homo frux ponit quod est adiectivum—

' Sed quid ego haec memoro ? Dictum factumque
facit frux.

316

Varro, *L.L.*, V, 182 : ' Militis stipendia ' ideo quod eam
stipem pendebant ; ab eo etiam Ennius scribit—

    Poeni stipendia pendunt.

317

Macrobius, S., VI, 4, 17 : (Vergilius) inseruit operi suo et
Graeca verba, . . . auctorum . . . veterum audaciam secutus
. . . Ennius in IX—

    lychnorum lumina bis sex

[314] reddidit e s. r. ut famul V   oltimus Linds.   ultimus
Faber   infimus Lips. *prob.* V   reddiderit s. ut r. f.   *vel*
reddidit ut s. (e) r. f. *edd.*   reddidit summo regno famul
ut optimus *edd.* (cf. V. *Sitz.-Ber. B. Ak.*, 1888, 45)
[316] *trib. lib. VII* Merula
[317] < florebant flammis > *suppl.* V, *Sitz.-Ber. B. Ak.*, 1896,
720, *coll. Serv., ad Aen., VII*, 804 Ennius et Lucretius florere
dicunt omne quod nitidum est ; *et Lucret., IV*, 450 bina lucernarum florentia lumina flammis

ANNALS

313-14

Nonius : ' Famul,' the same as ' famulus ' . . . —

Fortune on a sudden casts down the highest mortal from the height of his sway, to become the lowliest thrall.

315

Scipio to Hannibal ? :

Priscianus : Ennius . . . in the ninth book puts ' frux,' which is an adjective, for ' frugi homo '—

' But to what end do I speak so ? " No sooner said than done "—so acts your man of worth.[b]

316

Terms of peace imposed on Carthage, 201 B.C. :

Varro says : ' Militis stipendia ' (soldier's pay) is a term used because[c] they paid it as a ' stips ' (small coins in piles). This is the derivation of ' stipendia ' as used by Ennius among others—

The Poeni paid payments of money.

317

Funeral of the slain ? :

Macrobius : Virgil inserted into his work even Greek words . . . following the daring of ancient authors. . . . Ennius in the ninth book—

twice six lighted lamps

[a] Lucretius (see opposite) had this passage in mind. It is possible that Ennius was thinking of the downfall of Hannibal in 195 B.C., an event which would come in Book XI.

[b] ' Proverbium celeritatis ' says Donatus, ad Ter. *Andr.*, 381. Cp. ' suits the action to the word.'

[c] Varro means that since ' stipendia ' is used here of a payment in coin, it shows its derivation from *stips*.

ENNIUS

318–19

Nonius, 66, 18 : Politiones agrorum cultus diligentes . . . —

' Rastros dentiferos capsit causa poliendi
agri.

320–21

Nonius, 150, 37 : ' Perpetuassit ' sit perpetua, aeterna . . . —

' libertatemque, ut perpetuassit
quaeque axim

LIBER X

322–3

Gellius, XVIII, 9 : ' Inseque ' quasi ' perge dicere ' . . .
itaque ab Ennio scriptum in his versibus—

Insece, Musa, manu Romanorum induperator
quod quisque in bello gessit cum rege Philippo.

Alter autem . . . perseverabat Velio Longo . . . fidem
esse habendam, qui . . . scripserit non ' inseque ' apud
Ennium legendum sed ' inseçe ' . . . Cp. Paul., ex F., 79, 29.
Hom., *Od.*, I, 1 . . . ἔννεπε Μοῦσα

324

Priscianus, ap. *G.L.*, II, 541, 13 K : ' Campso, campsas '
solebant vetustissimi dicere. Ennius in X—

Leucatan campsant.

[318] dentiferos Hug dentifabres Roeper dentifabros
Onions dentefabres *cdd. fortasse recte*
[320] *vide Linds. ad loc.*
[322] inseçe *prob. Gell.* inseque *Gell.* XVIII, 9, 5 *Paul.*

---

 [a] *capsit*, fut. perf. ; *perpetuassit*, *axim*, perf. subj.

ANNALS

318–19

Italy after the war ? the soldiers must return to the soil :

Nonius : ' Politiones,' diligent cultivations of fields . . .

' He will take toothed rakes for to dress the fields.

320–21

Let Rome's liberty be maintained :

Nonius : ' Perpetuassit,' may it be perpetual, eternal . . . —

. . . ' and liberty, that it may last for ever and all that I may have done [a]

BOOK X

Wars with Macedon to the settlement with Philip, 196 b.c., after the Battle of Cynoscephalae

322–3

Prologue :

Gellius : ' Inseque ' has the sense of ' go on to tell,' and this therefore is the form used by Ennius in these verses—

Go on to tell what each commander of the Romans wrought with his troops in war with King Philip.

But the other . . . insisted that we must trust Velius Longus, . . . who wrote that in Ennius we should read not ' inseque ' but ' insece.' . . .

324

First Macedonian War (214–205 b.c.); expedition of Valerius Laevinus (214) :

Priscianus : The oldest writers used to say also ' campso,[b] campsas,' bend. Ennius in the tenth book—

They doubled Leucate.

[b] Clearly derived from κάμπτω.

ENNIUS

325

Isidorus, *Orig.*, I, 35, 3 : ' Zeugma ' est clausula dum plures sensus uno verbo clauduntur . . . ut—

Graecia Sulpicio sorti data, Gallia Cottae.

326

Cicero, *de Re Publ.*, I, 18, 30:—

Egregie cordatus homo catus Aelius Sextus

qui egregie cordatus et catus fuit et ab Ennio dictus est non quod ea quaerebat quae numquam inveniret, sed quod ea respondebat quae eos qui quaesissent et cura et negotio solverent.

Cp. Cic., *Tusc. Disp.*, I, 9, 18; *de Orat.*, I, 45, 198; Varro, *L.L.*, VII, 46; Pomponius, *in Dig.*, I, 2, 2, 38.

327-9

Cicero, *de Senect.*, 1, 1 :—

' O Tite si quid ego adiuvero, curamve levasso
  quae nunc te coquit et versat in pectore fixa,
  ecquid erit praemi?

[325] *trib. Enn. Ann.* X Mr.
[326] *trib. Ann. lib.* X Merula
[327] ego te adiuto *Donat.*

---

[a] That the author is Ennius we can hardly doubt. P. Sulpicius Galba, C. Aurelius Cotta. Cf. Livy, XXXI, 5, 1; 6, 1. There is no real *zeugma* here.

ANNALS

325

Second Macedonian War, 200-196 B.C.   Consuls of 200 :

Isidore : ' Zeugma ' is a period when more than one idea
is completed by one verb . . . for example *a* . . . —

Greece was given by lot to Sulpicius, Gaul to
Cotta.

326

Sextus Aelius Paetus, consul with Flamininus, 198 : b

Cicero :—

A man uncommonly well-witted, shrewd Sextus
Aelius

who was a man of more than common wit and shrewd, and
called such by Ennius not because he used to search for
things which he could never discover, but because he used to
give such answers as freed from anxiety and trouble those who
had asked him questions.

327-9

*Activities c of T. Quinctius Flamininus in 198.   A shepherd
sent by the Epirote King Charopus to guide the Romans, asks :*

Cicero :—

O Titus, if it is I can help you in anything and
lighten you of the worry which, stubborn in your
breast, now sears and haunts you, will there be any
reward ?

b Livy, XXXII, 8; Flamininus only was sent to Macedonia.
c I have given the quotations in the order in which they
appear in Cicero, in case this should be right. For the
occasion cf. Livy, XXXII, 11-2. We need not doubt that it
was from Ennius that Cicero quoted.

ENNIUS

330-1

Cicero, *loc. cit.*: Licet enim mihi versibus eisdem affari te, Attice, quibus affatur Flamininum—

' Ille vir haud magna cum re sed plenus fidei,

quamquam certo scio non ut Flamininum—

' sollicitari te Tite sic noctesque diesque.

Cp. Donat., ad Ter., *Phorm.*, prol, 34 ' Adiutans ' . . . Ennius.

332

Macrobius, *S.*, VI, 1, 9 : ' Axem humero torquet stellis ardentibus aptum ' (*Aen.*, IV, 482). Ennius . . . in X—

Hinc nox processit stellis ardentibus apta

333-5

Servius (auctus), ad *Georg.*, IV, 188 : ' Mussant ' autem murmurant . . . —

Aspectabat virtutem legionis suai
exspectans si mussaret, ' quae denique pausa
pugnandi fieret aut duri finis laboris ? '

336

Diomedes, ap. *G.L.*, I, 382, 24 K : Veteres nonnulli ' horitatur ' dixerunt . . . —

. . . horitatur . . . induperator

quasi specie iterativa.

[333-4] suai exspectans Bergk   legionis suspectans D (I.) sive spectans *cdd.*
[334] mussaret quae D (I.)   mussaret dubitaretque *cd.* pausa Bergk *prob.* St.   causa D (I.) *prob.* V causam *cd.*
[335] finis *add.* Bergk   pausa D (I.)
[336] horitatur Hug   horitur *cdd.*

ANNALS

330–1

Flamininus sent to Charopus to ask if the shepherd were trustworthy ; the reply :

Cicero continues : for I may be allowed to address to you, Atticus, the same verses as those in which Flamininus is addressed by—

'That man not blessed with wealth but full of loyalty,

although I know for certain it is not, like Flamininus—

'that you are care-worn, Titus, thus day and night.

332

The night-march of Flamininus, guided by the shepherd : [a]

Macrobius, quoting Virgil : 'Atlas on his shoulder turns the heaven dotted with blazing stars' . . . Ennius in the tenth book—

And then the night came on, dotted with blazing stars

333–5

The Battle of Cynoscephalae, 197 B.C.; [b] *anxiety of Flamininus :*

Servius (supplemented) : 'Mussant' also means 'they murmur' . . . —

He was watching the mettle of his army, waiting to see if they would grumble, saying 'what rest will there be at last from our fighting, or end to our hard toil?'

336

Speech of Flamininus before the battle : [c]

Diomedes says : Some old writers used the form 'horitatur' . . . —

The commander . . . cheers and cheers them on

'horitatur' being as it were in iterative form.

[a] Livy, XXXII, 11, 9.   [b] St., p. 187.
[c] St., p. 187; Livy, XXXIII, 8.

ENNIUS

337–8

Priscianus, ap. *G.L.*, II, 30, 4 K : Vetustissimi non semper eam (*sc. m*) subtrahebant . . . —

Insignita fere tum milia militum octo
duxit delectos, bellum tolerare potentes.

339–41

Festus, 188, 16 : ' Nictit ' canis in odorandis ferarum vestigiis leviter ganniens . . . —

Veluti si quando vinclis venatica velox
apta solet si forte feras ex nare sagaci
sensit, voce sua nictit ululatque ibi acute.

Cp. Paul., ex F., 189, 2.

342

Diomedes, ap. *G.L.*, I, 373, 5 K : ' Pinsit ' secundum tertium ordinem . . . —

pinsunt terram genibus.

[339] vĕlūtī si *cd.* (cp. '*Hedyph.*' mĕlănūrŭm, p. 408) vinculis *cd.* veluti quando vinclis T   sicuti si S (cp. fr. 553) *fortasse* is veluti W   venatica velox apta T   venatica veneno xapta *cd.*   vinclo venatica aeno S   solet *Fest.*   dolet B   feras *add.* O. Mueller (si forte feras ea) a. s. cani ' forte feram si ex S, T

ANNALS

337-8

The battle: special troop of Philip? :

Priscianus: The oldest writers did not always elide *m*; . . . —

Then he led some eight thousand warriors, wearing badges, chosen men, strong to bear war well.

339-41

Impatience of Flamininus' army? :

Festus: 'Nictit' is a term used of a dog gently whimpering as he scents the tracks of wild animals . . . —

And just[a] as sometimes a fleet hunting-dog, tied up by a chain, is wont to do if by chance her keen-scented nostril has caught scent of wild quarry— she lifts her voice in a whimper and straightway loudly gives tongue.

342

Fighting on rough ground :

Diomedes: 'Pinsit,' according to the third conjugation . . . —

They bruise their knees on the ground.[b]

---

[a] This is one of several lines where E. apparently allowed the first syllable of a hexameter to begin with ⌣⌣ instead of –

[b] Cp. *cubitis pinsibant humum*, p. 376. The expression is too strong to be applied to supplication by envoys or the like.

ENNIUS

343-4

Nonius, 370, 19: 'Passum,' extensum, patens; unde et
'passus' dicimus: quod gressibus mutuis pedes patescunt
. . . —

Aegro corde † comis †

          passis late palmis pater

passis ait palmis patentibus et extensis.

345

Donatus, ad Ter., *Phorm.*, II, 1, 57: 'Columen vero
familiae.' Columen culmen an columen columna? . . . —

'Regni versatam iam summovere columnam.

LIBER XI

346

Festus, 340, 22: 'Quippe' significare 'quidni' testimonio
est Ennius lib. XI—

Quippe solent reges omnes in rebus secundis

343-4 *sic cdd.* aegro corde comis passis *et alter. fr.* passis
late p. p. V. *alii alia cf. St., p.* 188, *quae* aegro | Corde
pater passis late palmis <lacrumatus> *coni.*   aegro c.
comis . . . passis late palmis 'pater . . . Linds. *fortasse*
a. | c. c. p. l. < et > p. p.
345 versatam iam summovere S   versatum summam
vero *cdd.*   venere Ilberg *prob.* V

  ᵃ Doubtful. Cf. St., 188-9, V., 62.
  ᵇ Or, joy of Greeks at Philip's defeat ?—V., CXCV.

ANNALS

343-4

*Demetrius, younger son of Philip, taken by Rome as a hostage ;
the parting with Philip ? :*

Nonius : ' Passum,' stretched out, spread open : whence
we also say ' passus,' step ; because the feet spread open, as
they step apart, each from the other . . . —

Sick at heart and with hands flung wide, the
father . . .[a]

By ' passis ' as applied to ' palmis ' he means open wide
and outstretched.

345

Lament of Philip on the exile of Demetrius ? :[b]

Donatus, on ' Indeed the " columen " of his household ' in
Terence : ' Columen ' in the sense of summit or ' columen '
in the sense of pillar ? . . . —

' They have now overturned and moved away the
pillar of the realm.

BOOK XI

FROM THE PEACE MADE IN 196 TO THE OPENING OF THE
WAR WITH ANTIOCHUS III (192-1); CATO IN
ROME AND IN SPAIN

346

Greece after Philip's defeat :

Festus : That ' quippe ' means ' quidni ' Ennius is a
witness in the eleventh book—

Surely are all kings wont in times of good
fortune . . .[c]

[c] Possibly a part of Flamininus' speech at the Isthmus, like
the next fr.

ENNIUS

347-8

Festus, 428, 11 : ' Sos ' pro eos . . . —

' Contendunt Graecos, Graios memorere solent sos

⟨li⟩ngua longos per† . . .

Cp. Fest., 400, 19 . . . † s appellat Enn † . . . † os Grai memo † . . .—

349-50

Macrobius, *S.*, VI, 1, 60 : ' Num capti potuere capi ? Num incensa cremavit | Troia viros ? (*Aen.*, VII, 295) Ennius in undecimo cum de Pergamis loqueretur—

' quae neque Dardaniis campis potuere perire
nec cum capta capi nec cum combusta cremari.'

351

Festus, 250, 12 : ' Petrarum ' genera sunt duo, quorum alterum naturale saxum prominens in mare . . . —

alte delata petrisque ingentibus tecta.

352

Nonius, 483, 1 : ' Lacte ' nominativo casu . . . —

' et simul erubuit ceu lacte et purpura mixta.

[347] Graecos Graios V   graios grecos *Fest.*, 428   † os grai *Fest.*, 400
[348] per < temporis tractus > Ursinus   *fortasse scribendum* annos *in fin. vers.*
[349] *fortasse* <Pergama Troiae> quae n. D.
Non. 483 lib. X *Par.* 7666 *Bamb. Lu. XI rell.*   essi (et si *Par.*) mulier erubuit *cdd.*   et simul erubuit Gulielmus

---

[a] Or, ' compare the Greeks.' The fragment seems to deal with a name given by Ennius to the Romans; cf. St., p. 191.

ANNALS

347-8

Flamininus proclaims 'The Freedom of Hellas'; he points to the relation of the Romans to the Greeks :

Festus : 'Sos' for 'eos' . . . —

'They maintain [a] that the Greeks—men are wont to speak of them as Grai— . . . language through long . . .

349-50

Brachyllas [b] (?) warns the Greeks against the power of Rome :

Macrobius, quoting Virgil : 'When captured, could they be in truth captured? No. And did Troy burning burn her warriors? No.' Ennius, when he was speaking about Pergama in the eleventh book, wrote—

'Troy's citadel, which on the plains of Dardanus could not perish or be captive when captured or when burnt become ashes.'

351

a place in Greece :

Festus : 'Rocks'; of these there are two kinds, of which one is natural stone jutting out into the sea . . . —

a cliff deep-falling, covered by mighty crags.

352

Cato [c] on the one-time modesty of women :

Nonius : 'Lacte' in the nominative case . . . —

'and she blushed [d] withal like milk and crimson mingled.

[b] A Greek strongly in favour of Macedonian supremacy in Greece.
[c] Opposing in vain, during his consulship of 195 B.C., the repeal of the Lex Oppia of 215.
[d] The tense suggests a definite occasion, possibly the refusal of the woman to take gifts from Pyrrhus in 280 B.C.

129

ENNIUS

353

Nonius, 149, 27 : ' Peniculamentum ' a veteribus pars
vestis dicitur . . . —

' pendent peniculamenta unum ad quemque pediclum.

354-5

Nonius, 195, 10 : ' Crux ' generis . . . masculini . . . —

' malo cruce ' fatur ' uti des,
Iuppiter !

356

Priscianus, ap. *G.L.*, II, 445, 7 K : ' Sono,' sonas et sonis
. . . —

Tum clipei resonunt et ferri stridit acumen ;

357

Priscianus, ap. *G.L.*, II, 419, 16 K : A ' strido ' alii ' stridi '
protulerunt . . . —

missaque per pectus dum transit striderat hasta.

358

Charisius, ap. *G.L.*, I, 200, 22 K : ' Hispane ' Ennius Annalium libro * —

Hispane non Romane memoretis loqui me.'

Cp. Fest., 400, 22.

[353] lib. XI (XII *Lu.* 1) annalis pendent *cdd.*   Annalium
splendent Mr.   pediclum B   peditum *coni.* Linds.   ad
quodque pedule S   pedum nunc *coni.* V   pedum *cdd.*
peniculamenta u. a. q. pedum dependent Ilberg, Hug
     [354] crucei Linds.
     [358] *fortasse scripsit Charis.* annalium libro XI Hispane
trib. lib. XI Hug, *VII* Norden

353

and contrasts the luxury of his own day :

Nonius : ' Peniculamentum '; a term which old writers use for part of a dress. . . . —

skirts hang low down to every little foot.[a]

354-5

He curses the ' moderns ' :

Nonius : ' Crux ' of the masculine gender . . . —

Says he, ' Give them destruction, Jupiter, with utter hell!

356

Cato in Spain, 195 B.C.; battle with the rebels :

Priscianus : ' Sono ' goes on both ' sonas ' and ' sonis ' . . . —

Then the round shields resounded, and the iron spear-points whizzed ;

357

Priscianus : From ' strido ' some have conjugated . . . stridi.'—

and the spear, shot into his breast, whizzed as it sped through.

358

A Spanish chief parleys with a Roman embassy ? :

Charisius : ' Hispane ' is a form used by Ennius in a book[b] of the *Annals*—

' Report you : it is the Spanish that I speak, and not the Roman tongue.'

[a] So *pediculum*; ' to every sole,' if we read *pedule*. Cf. V., 64 and CXCV.
[b] Probably the eleventh because : (*a*) in Fest., 400, 22, a mutilated form of this quotation comes just after the quotation about *Graecos, Graios* (p. 128); (*b*) I suggest that XI stood in Charisius' text, was copied into something like N, and then omitted as though it were a dittography of the H in Hispane.

ENNIUS

359

Paulus, ex F., 383, 16 : ' Rimari ' est valde quaerere ut in rimis quoque.

Fest., 382, 16 . . . † . . . Ennius lib. X † . . . —

⟨rimantur⟩ utrique.

LIBER XII

360-62

Cicero, *de Off.*, I, 24, 84 : Quanto Q. Maximus melius de quo Q. Ennius—

Unus homo nobis cunctando restituit rem.
Noenum rumores ponebat ante salutem;
ergo postque magisque viri nunc gloria claret.

Cp. Macrob., *S.*, VI, 1, 23 : ' Unus qui nobis cunctando restituit rem (*Aen.*, VI, 846). Ennius in XII : ' Unus . . . rem. Serv., *ad Aen.*, VI, 845; Cic., *de Senect.*, 4, 10; *ad Att.*, II, 19, 2; Senec., *de Benef.*, IV, 27, 2; Seren. Sammon., *de Med.*, 1092; Sueton., *Tib.*, 21; Liv., XXX, 26, 7; Ov., *Fast.*, II, 240-42 : Polyb., III, 105, 8; Sil., VI, 613 *s.*

363-5

Priscianus, ap. *G.L.*, II, 152, 17 K : ' Acer ' et ' alacer ' et ' saluber ' et ' celeber ' . . . in utraque . . . terminatione communis etiam generis inveniuntur prolata . . . (153, 11 K) . . . —

Omnes mortales victores, cordibus imis
laetantes, vino curatos, somnus repente
in campo passim mollissimus perculit acris.

Cp. Prisc., ap. *G.L.*, II, 230, 5 K.

³⁵⁹ ⟨rimantur⟩ B

³⁶¹ noenum L   non enim *cdd. prob.* V   *trib. lib. IX* Hug *VIII* Merula

³⁶³ imis Fruter *prob.* Havet   huius *cdd.* Par., R., Sang., Halb. vivis *rell.* 153   vivis *cdd.* 230

132

359

Unplaced fragment :

Paulus says : ' Rimari ' means to search thoroughly, as it were in the very ' rimae ' crannies. Festus says : . . . Ennius in the eleventh book—

both parties pried.[a]

BOOK XII

See under title of Book XI

360–62

A reminiscence of Fabius Maximus Cunctator : [b]

Cicero : How much better was the behaviour of Quintus Maximus of whom Ennius says—

One man by his delays restored the state ;
Hearsay he would not put before our safety ;
Hence to this day the warrior's glory shines—
In after time, and all the more for that.

363–5

Rejoicing after victory ? : [c]

Priscianus : ' Acer ' and ' alacer ' and ' saluber ' and ' celeber ' are found inflected in both *-er* and *-is* in both genders . . . —

Yes, all those victors, every single soul,
Contented from the bottom of their hearts—
Sleep on a sudden, over all the plain,
Most soft thrilled tingling through them, tended well
By wine.

[a] Hopelessly mutilated, but the fr. seems to have contained *rimari* in some form or other. Cp. our ' peer into every hole and corner.'

[b] We must keep the fr. in the book to which Macrobius assigns it. Cf. V., *Abh. B. Akad.*, 1886, 6 ff. and *Enn.*, CXCVI–CXCVII; St., pp. 193–4; contrast Skutsch, *Pauly*, s.v. Ennius, 2608.

[c] It is not possible to assign the fr. to any occasion; cf. St., 194; V., CXCV–CXCVI.

ENNIUS

Gellius, XVII, 21, 43: Ennium . . . M. Varro . . . scripsit, . . . cum septimum et sexagesimum annum haberet, duodecimum Annalem scripsisse idque ipsum Ennium in eodem libro dicere.

NOTE ON

Only two extant fragments are definitely assigned to this book, and two others can be with probability added to these. The context of all of them must remain uncertain; but the book probably described the war with Antiochus to the departure of the two Scipios for Asia in 190. The following seems to me to be the most probable arrangement of the fragments. Lines 366–8 give us the only tradition which represents Hannibal as a would-be peacemaker between Rome and Antiochus. We cannot connect it very well with Gellius, V, 5, where Hannibal shows a veiled contempt of the army which Antiochus had gathered together before the battle of Magnesia; the tale looks like a fiction Now in 193 Hannibal had a chance interview with the Roman commissioner P. Villius at Ephesus. Nothing vital was discussed, but the incident caused Antiochus to cast suspicion on all

LIBER XIII

366-8

Gellius, VI, 2, 3 : ' "Cor" masculino genere, ut multa alia, enuntiavit Ennius; nam in XIII Annali " quem cor " dixit.' Ascripsit deinde versus Ennii duo. . . . Antiochus est qui hoc dixit Asiae rex . . . sed aliud longe Ennius. Nam tres

---

Gell., XVII, 21, *post vocabula* annum haberet * $^{mu}_{XII}$ *Voss.* (*eraso* X) XII *Pet.* XVIII Merula XVII Mr.

---

[a] 172 B.C. On this passage of Gellius, cf. V., *Abh. B. Ak.,* 1886, 3 ff.
[b] See above. [c] Nonius, 195, 20 made the same mistake.

134

ANNALS

Ennius mentions his age :

Gellius: Marcus Varro has recorded that Ennius, in his sixty-seventh year,[a] wrote the twelfth book of the *Annals*; and that Ennius himself mentions this very fact in the same book.

Book XIII

that Hannibal did (Livy, XXXV, 14). In the same year Antiochus held a council of war to which Hannibal was not invited (Livy, XXXV, 17 ff.). Hence lines 366–8 may well belong to a soliloquy of Antiochus, or a speech of his delivered at the council. In Livy, XXXV, 19 we have a warlike counterblast of Hannibal which he gave when he first discovered why he was out of favour with the king. It implies that the king suspected Hannibal of being at least pacific if not pro-Roman. Line 369 seems to belong to a narrative of fears felt at Rome and elsewhere in 192 lest Antiochus should cross into Europe like another Xerxes (V., CXCVIII). Line 370 suggests Antiochus in defeat, and since it is attributed by Gellius to Book XIII, would allude to the defeat of the king at Thermopylae in 191. Line 371 might well refer to the seige of Pergamum by Seleucus IV in 190 B.C.

BOOK XIII

The War with Antiochus perhaps to the departure of Lucius Scipio and Publius Scipio Africanus for the East in 190 B.C.

366–8

Antiochus suspects Hannibal (193 B.C.) : [b]

Gellius: 'Ennius used "cor," *said Caesellius*,[c] as he did many other similar nouns, in the masculine gender; for in the thirteenth book of *Annals* he wrote "quem cor."' He then added two lines of Ennius.' . . . Antiochus, King of Asia, is the speaker of these words. . . . But what Ennius meant was something different by far. For there are three lines, not

versus sunt, non duo, ad hanc Ennii sententiam pertinentes,
ex quibus tertium versum Caesellius non respexit—

' Hannibal audaci dum pectore de me hortatur
ne bellum faciam, quem credidit esse meum cor
suasorem summum et studiosum robore belli.

Cp. Non., 195, 19.

369

Varro, *L.L.*, VII, 21 : ' Quasi Hellespontum et claustra '
quod Xerxes quondam eum locum clausit ; nam ut Ennius
ait—

Isque Hellesponto pontem contendit in alto.

370

Gellius, XVIII, 2, 16 : Nemo . . . tum commeminerat
dictum esse a Q. Ennio id verbum ('verant') in tertio
decimo Annalium . . .—

' satin vates verant aetate in agunda ?

371

Servius auctus, ad *Georg.*, I, 18 : ' Favere ' veteres etiam
' velle ' dixerunt. Ennius—

Matronae moeros complent spectare faventes.

Cp. Serv. auct. ad *Georg.*, IV, 230 . . . Ennius in XIII—

Gell., VI, 2, 5 : cum pectore   *VI*, 2, 9 dum pectore
Annibal laudacium pectore *Non.*, 195
  Serv. auct. ad G., IV, 230 : XIII Ursinus   XVI *cdd.*

two, which go to complete this sentence of Ennius; of these
Caesellius overlooked the third—

'while Hannibal with bold breast exhorts [a] me
not to make war—he whom my heart believed to
be a most mighty counsellor, yea one devoted in
war's ruggedness.

369

*Reminiscence (192 B.C.) of Xerxes crossing from Asia to
Europe (480 B.C.):* [b]

Varro: The phrase 'As it were the Hellespont and its
barriers' comes from the fact that Xerxes at one time made a
'barrier' in that region. For, as Ennius says—

and he stretched a bridge over deep Hellespont.

370

*Antiochus laments his defeat at Thermopylae in 191 B.C.
by Glabrio:*

Gellius: No one on that occasion remembered that the
verb 'verant' was used by Ennius in the thirteenth book of
the *Annals* . . .—

'Do seers, in all their life's course, tell much of
truth?

371

Siege of Pergamum by Seleucus IV in 190 B.C.?: [c]

Servius (supplemented): 'Favere.' The old writers used
it even in the sense of 'velle.' Ennius—

The matrons crowded the walls, eager to look on.

[a] *de me hortatur,* tmesis for *me dehortatur.* The construction *studiosum robore belli* is strange; but it means that
Antiochus believed Hannibal to be a zealous supporter of a
warlike policy.

[b] Ennius seems to make a pun on *Hellesponto* and *pontem:*
'And he pontoons stretched o'er deep Hellespont.'

[c] Livy, XXXVII, 20 *fin.* (spectaverunt enim e moenibus
. . feminae . . .).

ENNIUS

LIBER XIV

372–3

Gellius, II, 26, 21 : Fecistique ut intellegerem verba illa
ex Annali quarto decimo Ennii amoenissima . . . —

Verrunt extemplo placide mare marmore flavo ;
caeruleum spumat sale conferta rate pulsum.

Cp. Priscian., ap. *G.L.*, II, 171, 11 K (caeruleum *e. q. s.*).

374

Macrobius, *S.*, VI, 1, 51 : ' Labitur uncta vadis abies '
(*Aen.*, VIII, 91). Ennius in XIV—

Labitur uncta carina, volat super impetus undas.

Cp. Verg., *Aen.*, IV, 398, natat u. c.

375–6

Macrobius, *S.*, VI, 5, 10 : ' Despiciens mare velivolum '
(*Aen.*, I, 224). . . . Ennius in XIV—

Quom procul aspiciunt hostes accedere ventis
navibus velivolis,

Cp. Serv., ad *Aen.*, I, 224.

---

[372] placidum *Parrhasius*
Prisc., ap. *G.L.*, *II*, 171, 11 *K* : *post* pulsum *vocabula* per
mare *trib.* Enn. Krehl

138

ANNALS

BOOK XIV

372-3

*Defeat of Polyxenidas by Aemilius Regillus at Myonnesus,
190 B.C.; departure of the Roman fleet :*

Gellius : You made me understand those very charming
words from Ennius' fourteenth book of *Annals* . . .—

Forthwith they gently swept a sea of yellow
marble ; green foamed the brine [a] beaten by the
thronging ships.

374

The rapid advance : [b]

Macrobius, quoting Virgil : 'Smooth glides the well-
greased fir-wood through the waters.' Ennius in the fourteenth book—

Smooth glided the well-greased keel and skimmed
over the waves with a rush.

375-6

They sight the enemy near Myonnesus :

Macrobius, quoting Virgil : 'Looking down on the sail-
fluttering sea.' . . . Ennius in the fourteenth book—

When they saw far off the enemy coming towards
them with the breeze in sail-fluttering ships,

[a] *sale* is nominative. *Caeruleum* might be taken with *mare*
—'swept the sea grey.' But cp. Priscianus' quotation,
which gives the second line only. *Flavus* is yellowish-green,
caeruleus bluish or greyish green.

[b] V., CCXVIII. Possibly the fr. refers to the swift ships
of the Rhodians—St., p. 196. Cp. fr. 442, p. 164.

ENNIUS

377

Priscianus, ap. *G.L.*, II, 473, 22 K : Haec . . . ipsa et secundum tertiam vetustissimi protulisse inveniuntur coniugationem . . . —

Litora lata sonunt

378–9

Priscianus, ap. *G.L.*, II, 501, 10 K : ' Orior ' et ' morior ' tam secundum tertiam quam secundum quartam coniugationem declinaverunt auctores . . . —

' Nunc est ille dies quom gloria maxima sese
nobis ostendat, si vivimus sive morimur.'

380

Macrobius, *S.*, VI, 4, 6 : ' Tum ferreus hastis | horret ager ' (*Aen.*, XI, 601). ' Horret ' mire se habet, sed et Ennius in quarto decimo—

Horrescit telis exercitus asper utrimque.

. . . sed et ante omnes Homerus (*Il.*, XIII, 339) : ἔφριξεν δὲ μάχη φθισίμβροτος ἐγχείῃσι

Cp. Verg., *Aen.*, VII, 526, XII, 663.

381–2

Priscianus, ap. *G.L.*, II, 518, 13 K : Vetustissimi tamen tam producebant quam corripiebant supradicti verbi, id est tutudi, paenultimam . . . —

Infit, ' O cives, quae me fortuna fero sic
contudit indignum bello, confecit acerbo,

[381] fero sic *cdd.*   ferox sic Colonna   ferocis V ferocem D (l.)
[382] indignum Maehly   indigno *cdd.*   indigne et bello Colonna (*fortasse* bello et confecit)

---

[a] Or the fr. may describe the shores echoing to the noise of battle.

140

ANNALS

377

The Scipios cross the Hellespont, 190 B.C. : [a]

Priscianus : These same verbs are found, in the oldest writers, inflected according to the third conjugation also . . . —

The broad beaches sound

378–9

Speech before the battle of Magnesia, 190 B.C. :

Priscianus : ' Orior ' and ' morior ' are found to have been inflected by authors according to both the third and the fourth conjugation. . . . —

' Now is the day when glory passing great
Shows itself to us, whether we live or die.'

380

Beginning of the battle :

Macrobius, quoting Virgil : ' Then the battle-field, all iron, bristles with lances.' ' Bristles ' is strange here. But Ennius too in the fourteenth book has—

On both sides the host bristles rough with javelins.[b]

. . . But again earlier than all writers Homer said : ' The battle, man-destroying, bristled with long spears.'

· 381–2

Antiochus in his defeat :

Priscianus : Still, the oldest writers pronounced both long and short the penultimate syllable of the above-mentioned word (that is ' *tutudi* ') . . . —

He began to speak—' O my countrymen, fortune who has thus bruised me—and I deserved it not— and has destroyed me in fierce, in bitter war,

[b] Near this fragment Ennius probably mentioned *rumpiae* (long lances) which were carried by the Thracians in the Roman army; for Gellius (X, 25, 4) notes this word from Ennius' XIVth book.

ENNIUS

383

Festus, 236, 5 : ' Ob ' . . . pro ' ad ' . . . —

Omnes occisi, obcensique in nocte serena.

LIBER XV

384

Nonius, 114, 5 : ' Falae ' turres sunt ligneae . . . —

Malos diffindunt, fiunt tabulata falaeque

385–6

Priscianus, ap. *G.L.*, II, 280, 7 K : Ennius in XV Annali—

Occumbunt multi letum ferroque lapique
aut intra muros aut extra praecipe casu.

Cp. Prisc., ap. *G.L.*, II, 250, 9 K.

387

Priscianus, ap. *G.L.*, II, 259, 5 K : ' Arcus ' . . . invenitur
. . . apud veteres etiam feminini generis . . . —

Arcus subspiciunt mortalibus quae perhibentur . . .

[384] diffindunt Merula   defindunt *cdd.*   defigunt *coni.*
V
[387] subspiciunt V   ubi aspiciunt *cdd.*   aspicitur Colonna   arquum ubi adspiciunt Merula   *fortasse* arcus
quom aspiciunt   perhibetur *Halb.*   perhibentur *rell.*

ANNALS

383

Burning of the dead after the battle :

Festus : ' Ob ' instead of ' ad ' . . . —

All butchered, and burnt in the clear calm night.

BOOK XV

THE AETOLIAN WAR, 189 B.C., AND THE ACHIEVEMENT
OF M. FULVIUS NOBILIOR, WHOM ENNIUS CELE-
BRATED ELSEWHERE IN A SEPARATE WORK (PP.
358 ff.). THE ORIGINAL CONCLUSION OF THE ANNALS

384

The siege of Ambracia by Fulvius Nobilior, 189 B.C. :

Nonius : ' Falae ' are wooden towers . . . —

They cleft the corner-beams; floors and siege-
towers were built

385–6

Priscianus : Ennius in the fifteenth book of the *Annals*—

Many were laid low by death with sword and stone
in headlong fall within or without the walls.

387

Priscianus : ' Arcus ' . . . is found even in the feminine
gender in old writers . . . —

They look up at the bows (?), which are said by
mortals . . . [a]

[a] Or ' They look up at what men call " The Arches " '

ENNIUS

Macrobius, *S.*, VI, 2, 30 : Sunt alii loci plurimorum versuum quos Maro in opus suum cum paucorum immutatione verborum a veteribus transtulit . . . de Pandaro et Bitia aperientibus portas locus (*Aen.*, IX, 672 ff.) acceptus est ex libro quinto decimo Ennii qui induxit Histros duos in obsidione erupisse porta et stragem de obsidente hoste fecisse.

Cf. Virg., *Aen.*, IX, 672–687; *Il.*, XII, 127 ff.

388–9

Cicero, *de Senect.*, 5, 14 : Sua enim vitia insipientes et suam culpam in senectutem conferunt, quod non faciebat is cuius modo mentionem feci Ennius—

Sicut fortis equus spatio qui saepe supremo
vicit Olympia, nunc senio confectus quiescit,

Equi fortis et victoris senectuti comparat suam.

Cp. Ὀλύμπια νικᾶν (Thuc., I, 126; *al.*).

NOTE ON

That Ennius described the Istrian War is certain, provided that the episode about Aelius (see p. 154) is rightly interpreted. But Ennius must also have sketched the somewhat scattered events between 188 and 178, such as the march of Manlius through Thrace, the wars in Spain and Liguria, the

---

388–9 *trib. lib. XV* St.   *XII* V   *XVIII* Merula.

---

[a] Doubtless the Romans besieging Ambracia—V., CXCIX. The original of Ennius' and Virgil's passages is *Il.*, XII, 127 ff.

ANNALS

A sortie :

Macrobius : There are other passages (*in Virgil*), consisting of several lines, which Maro, with the alteration of a few words, transferred from the old poets to his own work. . . . The passage about Pandarus and Bitias opening the gates is taken from the fifteenth book of Ennius, who introduced the tale of how two Histrians during a siege burst out of the gate and caused a slaughter among the besieging enemy.[a]

388–9

Ennius' original ending to his Annals ; his old age :

Cicero : For it is their own blemishes and their own sins that fools lay to the charge of old age, a thing which he, of whom I made mention just now, was not wont to do, Ennius—[b]

Just as a valiant steed, who has often won victories at the Olympic games in the last lap, now at length, worn out by old age, takes rest,

He is comparing his old age to that of a valiant and victorious horse.

Book XVI

affairs of Italy, the trial of the Scipios, the deaths of Scipio Africanus and of Hannibal, and the censorship of Cato. Nearly all the extant fragments seem to belong either to the Prologue of the book or to the Istrian War.

Cp. St., pp. 199 ff.; Livy, XLI; Valmaggi, pp. 112 ff.

---

[b] *envoi*. St., p. 198, is probably right in taking this fr. as part of Ennius' original scheme, which ended with this book (see p. 147). But if Book XVIII was finished when Ennius died, it should be put there. Yet cf. V., *Abh. B. Akad.*, 1886, 9.

LIBER XVI

390

Festus, 340, 21 : ' Quippe ' significare quidni testimonio est
Ennius . . . lib. XVI—

Quippe vetusta virum non est satis bella moveri ?

391

Nonius, 219, 14 : ' Pigret ' . . .—

post aetate pigret subferre laborem.

392

Gellius, IX, 14, 5 : ' Dies ' pro ' diei '—

postremo longinque dies quod fregerit aetas . . .

Plinius, VII, 101 : Q. Ennius T. Aelium Teucrum fratremque cius praccipue miratus propter eos sextum decimum
adiecit Annalem.

393–4

Macrobius, S., VI, 1, 17 : ' Summa nituntur opum vi '
(Aen., XII, 552). Ennius . . . in XVI—

Reges per regnum statuasque sepulchraque quae-
    runt ;
aedificant nomen, summa nituntur opum vi.

[391] post <exacta> coni. V   subferre cdd.   scribendi
ferre B
[392] quod fregerit Valmaggi   quod fecerit vel confecerit
cdd.
Plin., VII, 101 : Aelium Bergk   Caecilium Plin.

ᵃ Pliny has Caecilius, and this may be right. But the man
referred to seems to be the brother of the gallant tribune of
fr. 409–16; see note on p. 154.

ANNALS

BOOK XVI

390

Prologue ; past work ; growing age :

Festus : That 'quippe' means 'quidni' Ennius is a witness . . . in the sixteenth book—

Surely it is enough that the old-time wars of warriors were undertaken!

391

Nonius : 'Pigret' . . . —

I am loth to take up the task late in ageing life.

392

Gellius : 'Dies' instead of 'diei' . . . —

Lastly, that which the long age of my days has crushed. . . .

But the heroism of two brothers re-inspires him :

Pliny : Quintus Ennius had a particular admiration for Titus Aelius [a] Teucrus and his brother, and on their account added to his *Annals* the sixteenth book.

393–4

A general remark [b] on this period of Roman History ? :

Macrobius, quoting Virgil : 'They strain with all their might and main' : Ennius . . . in the sixteenth book—

Kings throughout their kingship are in quest of statues and sepulchres ; they build up a name and strain with all their might and main.

[b] Possibly a part of the prologue ; whatever kings may do, my fame shall rest on my poetry—St., p. 200.

ENNIUS

395

Priscianus, ap. *G.L.*, II, 152, 17 K : ' Acer ' . . . (153, 9 K) . . . —

Aestatem autumnus sequitur, post acer hiems it.

Cp. Serv., ad *Aen.*, VI, 685; *explanat. in Donat.*, ap. *G.L.*, IV, 491, 26 K.

Cicero, *de Prov. Consul.*, 9, 20 : An vero M. ille Lepidus, qui bis consul et pontifex maximus fuit, non solum memoriae testimonio sed etiam Annalium litteris et summi poetae voce laudatus est quod cum M. Fulvio collega, quo die censor est factus, homine inimicissimo, in campo statim rediit in gratiam ?

396

Festus, 386, 4 : ' Regimen ' pro regimento . . . —

Primus senex bradys in regimen belloque peritus

397

Festus, 490, 29 : ' Spicit ' quoque sine praepositione dixerunt antiqui . . . ' spexit.' Ennius lib. XVI—

Quos ubi rex Epulo spexit de cautibus celsis,

Cp. Varro, *L.L.*, VI, 82.

---

[395] it *Car. Sang. Mon.* sit *rell.* fit Fabricius *coll.* Serv., ad *Aen.*, VI, 685
[396] bradys Mr. bradyn *cd.*
[397] Epulo Bergk / / / / ɔulo *Fest.* epulo *Varro* (Apulo *Flor., I*, 26 ; Aepulo *Liv.*, *XLI*, 11, 1 ; *at cf. Verg., Aen., XIII*, 459 Epŭlo) populos *olim* V cautibus *olim* V cotibus Bergk *nunc prob.* V montibus Laetus contibus *cd.*

ANNALS

395

The turning years :

Priscianus : ' Acer.' . . . —

Autumn follows on summer; after it comes keen
winter.

*Censorship of Marcus Aemilius Lepidus and Marcus Fulvius
Nobilior,* 179 B.C. :

Cicero : But is it not true that our famous Marcus Lepidus,
who was twice consul and also pontifex maximus, is praised,
not only by the record of tradition but also in the written
evidence of *Annals* and by the greatest of our poets,[a] because
with his colleague Marcus Fulvius, a great enemy of his, on
the day when he was made censor, he at once made a recon-
ciliation in the Campus ?

396

An ageing Roman ? [b]

Festus : ' Regimen ' for ' regimentum ' . . . —

First the aged man, tardy in his ruling, skilled in
war

397

The Istrian War, 178–7 B.C. [c]

King Epulo sees the Romans move on Lake Timavus :

Festus : ' Spicit ' is likewise used by archaic writers without
a preposition prefixed. . . . Ennius in the sixteenth book
has ' spexit '—

When King Epulo [d] spied them from the top of
high crags,

[a] There can be no doubt that Ennius is meant, and that the
attribution to this book is right. Cf. Livy, XL, 45, 6 ff.

[b] This may be a case of an appeal to the example of Fabius
Cunctator (cf. St., 205–6, especially on *bradys*).

[c] Valmaggi, pp. 114–15; Havet, in *Bibl. de l'école des
hautes ét.,* fasc. XXXV, 32 ff. Vahlen is doubtful—*Abh. B.
Ak.,* 1886, 28 ff.

[d] Bergk., *Opp.,* I, 252 ff.

ENNIUS

398

Festus, 220, 25 : ' Obstipum,' obliquum . . .—

montibus obstipis obstantibus unde oritur nox.

399

Priscianus, ap. *G.L.* II, 278, 12 K : ' Frux ' ἀπὸ τοῦ φρύγω . . .—

' Si luci si nox si mox si iam data sit frux.

400

Festus, 344, 32 : <Quando . . .> —

' Nox quando mediis signis praecincta volabit,

401–2

Macrobius, *S.*, VI, 4, 19 : . . . 'Nec lucidus aethra | siderea polus ' (*Aen.*, III, 585). Ennius prior dixerat in XVI—

interea fax
occidit oceanumque rubra tractim obruit aethra.

403–4

Servius (auctus) ad *Georg.*, IV, 230 : ' Ore fave,' cum religione ac silentio accede; in XVI Ennius—

Hic insidiantes vigilant, partim requiescunt
contecti gladiis, sub scutis ore faventes.

Cp. Serv. (auct.) ad *Georg.*, I, 18.

---

[401] *fortasse* <lunae> interea
[404] contecti Merula   protecti Colonna   tecti cum B
requiescunt tecti gladiis *cdd.*

ANNALS

398

The Istrians from behind a hill keep watch over the Roman camp by the Lacus Timavus, 178 B.C. : [a]

Festus : ' Obstipum,' slanting . . . —

Slanting mountains standing in the way, whence rises up the night.

399

The Istrians are well prepared :

Priscianus : ' Frux ' . . . derived from φρύγω . . .

' If by daylight, if at night, if soon, if now we be given success.

400

The Istrian plan of attack on the Romans :

Festus : ' Quando ' . . . —

' When night shall fly girt up by constellations in her midst,

401–2

Dawn comes :

Macrobius, quoting Virgil : ' Nor was there a clear and star-lit heaven.' Ennius had said before in his sixteenth book—

Meanwhile the torch [b] dies out and pink trailing dawnlight covers the Ocean.

403–4

The Romans on the watch :

Servius (supplemented), reading ' ore fave ' in Virgil : ' Come close with the silence of worship ' : in the sixteenth book Ennius—

Here in ambush they keep watch, while some of them take rest, guarded by their swords, keeping a shut mouth under their shields.

[a] Livy XLI, 11.   [b] Perhaps the light of the moon.

ENNIUS

405

Festus, 171, fin.: ' Navus,' celer ac strenuus . . . —

' Navorum imperium servare est induperantum.

406

Festus, 476, 28 : Idem (*sc. Ennius*) cum ait sapsam pro ipsa nec alia, ponit in lib. XVI—

' quo res sapsa loco sese ostentatque iubetque.

Cp. Paul., 477, 6.

407

Festus, 492, 5 : 'Speres' antiqui pluraliter dicebant . . . —

' Spero, si speres quicquam prodesse potis sunt,

408

Festus, 284, 30 : ' Prodit ' . . . perdit . . . —

Non in sperando cupide rem prodere summam

Cp. Paul., ex F., 285, 14.

409–16

Macrobius, *S.*, VI, 3, 1 : Sunt quaedam apud Vergilium quae ab Homero creditur transtulisse ; sed ea docebo a nostris auctoribus sumpta, qui priores haec ab Homero in carmina sua transtulerant . . . Homerus de Aiacis forti pugna ait (*Il.*, XVI, 102)—

Macrob., *VI*, **3, 3**   Ennius in XVI Bergk   XVIII
Ritter   XII *Par.* in quinto decimo *vulgo prob.* V   XII
Merula   C. Aelii Merula   cęlij *Par.*   celii *rell.*

405

*The tribune Aelius reminds the consul (A. Manlius Vulso)
of his duty :* [a]

Festus : ' Navus ' swift and strenuous . . .—

' It is the part of commanders who are men of
deeds, to keep discipline.

406

Aelius says he will stand his ground :

Festus : The same (*i.e.* Ennius), when he says ' sapsa '
instead of ' ipsa nec alia,' writes in the sixteenth book—

' in the place where my very duty displays itself
and commands me.

407

The hopes of Aelius :

Festus : The archaic writers used a plural ' speres ' . . . —

' I hope—if hopes can help at all,

408

Possibly from the consul's reply to Aelius :

Festus : ' Prodit,' . . . ruins . . .—

' Not to ruin the State by hoping eagerly

409–16

Aelius stands fast against violent attacks :

Macrobius : Virgil has certain passages which he is believed
to have transferred from Homer ; but I shall show that they
are passages which were taken from authors of ours who, earlier
than Virgil, had transferred these passages from Homer to
their own poetic works. . . . Homer on a fierce fight fought
by Ajax has—

---

[a] On this and the next two frs., cf. Livy, XLI, 2, and notes
on pp. 154–5.

ENNIUS

Αἴας δ' οὐκέτ' ἔμιμνε· βιάζετο γὰρ βελέεσσιν.
δάμνα μιν Ζηνός τε νόος καὶ Τρῶες ἀγαυοὶ
βάλλοντες· δεινὴν δὲ περὶ κροτάφοισι φαεινὴ
πήληξ βαλλομένη καναχὴν ἔχε· βάλλετο δ' αἰεὶ
κὰπ φάλαρ' εὐποίηθ'· ὁ δ' ἀριστερὸν ὦμον ἔκαμνεν
ἔμπεδον αἰὲν ἔχων σάκος αἰόλον, οὐδ' ἐδύναντο
ἀμφ' αὐτῷ πελεμίξαι ἐρείδοντες βελέεσσιν·
αἰεὶ δ' ἀργαλέῳ ἔχετ' ἄσματι κὰδ δέ οἱ ἱδρὼς
πάντοθεν ἐκ μελέων ῥέεν ἄσπετος, οὐδέ πη εἶχεν
ἀμπνεῦσαι, πάντη δὲ κακὸν κακῷ ἐστήρικτο.

Hunc locum Ennius in XVI ad pugnam C. Aelii tribuni his
versibus transfert—

Undique conveniunt velut imber tela tribuno :
configunt parmam, tinnit hastilibus umbo
aerato sonitu galeae, sed nec pote quisquam
undique nitendo corpus discerpere ferro ;
semper abundantes hastas frangitque quatitque ;
totum sudor habet corpus multumque laborat,
nec respirandi fit copia ; praepete ferro   1415
Histri tela manu iacientes sollicitabant.

Hinc Vergilius eundem locum de incluso Turno gratia
elegantiore composuit (*Aen.*, IX, 803-811)—

Ergo nec clipeo iuvenis subsistere tantum
nec dextra valet, obiectis sic undique telis
obruitur, strepit adsiduo cava tempora circum
tinnitu galea et saxis solida aera fatiscunt

Macrob. VI, 3, 3 : *vide p.* 152, *fin.*
411 *fortasse* et galea aerato sonitu   *excidisse versumconi.* V

ᵃ Bergk's attribution of this fr. to Book XVI must be
accepted. In the tradition the name of the brave tribune
was confused with that of another in the same legion. Pliny
has T. Caecilius Teucrus, which Bergk corrected to T. Aelius
Teucrus ; Macrobius has Caelius (or C. Aelius) ; Livy (XLI,
2, 9) has M. Licinius Strabo ; but in XLI, 1, 7, and 4, 3 he
mentions two brothers, both tribunes—T. and C. Aelius who
correspond with T. Caecilius Teucrus and his brother in Pliny.
Steuart suggests some falsification by the annalist C. Licinius

ANNALS

But Aias could no longer stand his ground; for distressed was he by spears. Yea, the will of Zeus overmastered him, the Trojans too who pelted him; dread was the rattle which his shining helmet thus pelted kept around his brows, for pelted was it again and again over its fair-wrought cheek-pieces. Weary was he too in his shoulder—the left where he firm and constant held his motley shield, nor could they by lunging all around him with their javelins so dash him off. And ever was he gripped in cruel gasping, while sweat unquenched poured down off his limbs from every point, nor could he in any wise draw breath; but on all sides heaped was hurt on hurt.

This passage Ennius [a] in the sixteenth book transferred to the fight of the tribune C. Aelius, in the following lines—

From all sides the javelins like a rain-storm showered in upon the tribune, and pierced his buckler; then jangled the embossment under spears, the helmets too with brassy clang; but not one of them, though strain they did from every side, could rend apart his body with the iron. Every time he shakes and breaks the waves of lances; sweat covers all his body; he is hard distressed; to breathe he has not a chance. The iron came flying as the Histrians cast the spears from their hands to harass him.

By the use of this as an example [b] Virgil, on the subject of Turnus hemmed in, has rendered the same passage with a more elegant grace—

Thus neither by the strength of his shield nor of his right hand can the young warrior withstand an onset so great, so overwhelmed is he by javelins cast at him from all sides: again and again his helmet jingles and jangles round the hollows of his temples, the firm plates of brass gave way under the

---

Macer. For another view cf. Vahlen, *Abh. B. Akad.*, 1886, 18 ff. Cf. also Havet in *Bibl. de l'école des hautes ét.*, XXXV, 35 ff.

[b] It looks, however, as though Virgil took his idea directly from Homer.

discussaeque iubae capiti nec sufficit umbo
ictibus; ingeminant hastis et Troes et ipse
fulmineus Mnestheus; tum toto corpore sudor
liquitur et piceum, nec respirare potestas,
flumen agit, fessos quatit aeger anhelitus artus.

417

Macrobius, *S.*, VI, 1, 24: 'Corruit in vulnus; sonitum
super arma dedere' (*Aen.*, X, 488). Ennius in XVI—

concidit et sonitum simul insuper arma dederunt.

Hom., *Il.*, IV, 504 δούπησεν δὲ πεσών, ἀράβησε δὲ τεύχε' ἐπ'
αὐτῷ

418

Diomedes, ap. *G.L.* I, 382, 21 K : 'Hortatur' . . . 'horitur' dixerunt . . .—

prandere iubet horiturque.

419–20

Servius (auctus) ad *Aen.*, XI, 19: Alii 'vellere' movere
accipiunt. Ennius—

Rex deinde citatus
convellit sese.

421

Varro, *L.L.*, VII, 103 : Multa ab animalium vocibus tralata
in homines . . . Ennii . . . ab haedo—

Clamor ad caelum volvendus per aethera vagit.

421 clamos L

---

a Cf. Livy, XLI, 2, 12.   *b* Livy, XLI, 4, 7.

stones, and his horse-hair crest was struck from his head;
the embossment could not bear the blows; the Trojans,
yea and Mnestheus too like a thunder-bolt, redoubled the
thrusts of their spears. Then over all his body sweat trickled
and flowed in a dark stream; no power had he to draw his
breath; a sick sore gasping shook his wearied limbs.

417

The death of Aelius ? :

Macrobius : ' He fell forward upon the wound; his weapons
dinned over him.' Ennius in the sixteenth book—

He tumbled and withal his armour dinned over him.

418

The Istrians prevailed; they feast a *in the Roman camp at
the order of the king :*

Diomedes : ' Horitur ' was used for ' hortatur ' . . . —

He orders and encourages them to break their
fast.

419-20

*The Romans recover their camp; King Epulo, half-drunk,
escapes :*

Servius (supplemented) : Others take ' vellere ' to mean
' to move.' Ennius—

Then the king, full roused, pulled himself up.b

421

The siege of Nesactum c *by C. Claudius Pulcher,* 177 B.C. ? :

Varro : There are many sounds which though belonging
to animals have been used figuratively of men . . . Ennius . . .
transferred from the goat—

The clamour rolling skyward bleated through the
air.

c Or the slaughter of the Istrians by the Romans; cf. Livy,
XLI, 11, 3. The attribution to this book is suggested by the
next fragment.

ENNIUS

422

Festus, 570, 8 : ' Vagorem ' pro vagitu . . . —

qui clamos oppugnantes vagore volanti

423

Priscianus, ap. *G.L.*, II, 518, 13 K (p. 140) : Ennius .   . in XVI—

Ingenio forti dextrum latus pertudit hasta.

424

Macrobius, *S.*, VI, 1, 50 : ' Tum gelidus toto manabat corpore sudor ' (*Aen.*, III, 175). Ennius in XVI—

Tunc timido manat ex omni corpore sudor.

425-6

Macrobius, *S.*, VI, 1, 53 : ' Apicem tamen incita summum hasta tulit (*Aen.*, XII, 492). Ennius in XVI—

       tamen induvolans secum abstulit hasta · insigne.

LIBER XVII

427

Festus, 510, 28 : ' Specus ' feminino genere . . . Ennius—

Tum cava sub monte late specus intus patebat.

Cp. Non., 223, 1 ; Priscian., ap. *G.L.* II, 260, 2 K (Ennius in XVII Annalium) ; Serv., ad *Aen.*, VII, 568.

---

[423] dextrum Merula   dextra *Prisc.*
[427] tum cava *Prisc.*   concava *Non.*   tum causa *Fest.*
cum *coni.* V   monte *Prisc.*, *Fest.*   montis *Non.*   montem Colonna   montei O. Mueller   montis latere Fruter.

---

[a] So I conclude from fr. 429. The book would include, *e.g.*, Lex Claudia ejecting socii (177 B.C.); subjugation of the Sardinians by Tib. Gracchus (177); embassies between Greece and Rome, especially in 173; trouble between Massi-

ANNALS

422

Festus : ' Vagor ' instead of ' vagitus ' . . . —

this clamour . . . the besiegers . . . with winged
bleating

423

From scenes of battle :
Priscianus on ' tutudi ' : . . . E. in the sixteenth book—

The lance of sturdy mettle punched through his
right side.

424

Macrobius, quoting Virgil : ' Then a cold sweat came flowing
down all my body.'   Ennius in the sixteenth book—

Then sweat flowed from all his fear-filled body.

425-6

Macrobius, quoting Virgil : ' Still the darting lance took
away the helmet top.'   Ennius in the sixteenth book—

Still the lance flying at him carried away with it
the badge.

BOOK XVII

PROBABLY FROM THE END OF THE ISTRIAN WAR TO THE
DEFEAT OF P. LICINIUS CRASSUS AT CALLINICUS,[a]
171 B.C., DURING THE THIRD MACEDONIAN WAR

427

Perseus of Macedon fortifies the passes of Tempe, 171 B.C. ? [b]
Festus : ' Specus ' in the feminine gender . . . Ennius—

Then a hollow cavern opened widely inwards
under the mountain.

nissa and Carthage; Perseus and his rupture with Rome,
172 B.C.   The extant frs., all of doubtful context, seem to
refer to the year 171.
   [b] At any rate the fr. describes a piece of Greek scenery.
Priscian quotes the fr. from Book XVII.

ENNIUS

428

Priscianus, ap. *G.L.*, II, 198, 6 K : Genetivum etiam in *as* (199, 4 K) . . . —

. . . dux ipse vias

429

Macrobius, *S.*, VI, 1, 22 : ' Quadrupedante putrem sonitu quatit ungula campum ' (*Aen.*, VIII, 596). Ennius . . . in XVII—

It eques et plausu cava concutit ungula terram.

430–32

Macrobius, *S.*, VI, 2, 28 : ' Diversi magno ceu quondam turbine venti confligunt zephyrusque notusque et laetus Eois | eurus equis (*Aen.*, II, 416). Ennius in XVII—

Concurrunt veluti venti quom spiritus Austri
imbricitor Aquiloque suo cum flamine contra
indu mari magno fluctus extollere certant.

Homer, *Il.*, IX, 4 :

ὡς δ' ἄνεμοι δύο πόντον ὀρίνετον ἰχθυόεντα
Βορέης καὶ Ζέφυρος, τώ τε Θρῄκηθεν ἄητον
ἐλθόντ' ἐξαπίνης· ἄμυδις δέ τε κῦμα κελαινὸν
κορθύεται,

433

Macrobius, *S.*, VI, 1, 21 : ' Tollitur in caelum clamor, cunctique Latini ' (*Aen.*, XI, 745). Ennius in XVII—

Tollitur in caelum clamor exortus utrimque.

[433] utrimque Merula   utrisque *Macrob.*

ANNALS

428

Perseus watches Crassus from Mount Ossa ? :

Priscianus : Genitive even in -as . . .—

himself the leader of the way

429

Defeat[a] of P. Licinius Crassus in a cavalry-battle at Callinicus,
171 B.C. :

Macrobius, quoting Virgil : ' The four-footed beat of the
hoof shakes the crumbling plain.' Ennius . . . in the
seventeenth book—

The horsemen charged, and the beating of their
hollow hoofs shook the ground.

430-32

The clash :

Macrobius, quoting Virgil : ' As from time to time with a
great whirlwind gales set against each other meet in conflict—
the west wind and the south, and the east happy in his horses
of the dawn.' Ennius in the seventeenth book—

They rushed together as when the breath of the
showery Wind of the South and the Wind of the
North with his counterblast strive to upheave
billows on the mighty main.

Homer : As when two winds, the Northern and the Western,
stir up the fishy sea; they come on a sudden, blowing from
Thrace, and forthwith the black billow rises to a head,

433

Macrobius, quoting Virgil : ' Uproars to heaven a shout and
the Latins, one and all,' . . . Ennius in the seventeenth
book—

Uproars to heaven the shout that rose from either
side.

[a] Or possibly the charge of the Thracians under Cotys at
Larissa earlier in the year—St., p. 206.

434-5

Servius (auctus), ad *Georg.*, IV, 188 : 'Mussant' hic 'murmurant'; quae vox ponitur et in tacendi significatione . . .

' Noenu decet mussare bonos qui facta labore
nixi militiae peperere.

Cp. Serv. ad *Aen.*, XII. 657; Paulus, ex F., 127, 7.

436-8

Nonius, 134, 19 : 'Longiscere,' longum fiefi vel frangi . . . —

neque corpora firma
longiscunt quicquam.

idem—

quom soles eadem facient longiscere longe.

LIBER XVIII

439

Nonius, 63, 4 : Est autem gruma mensura quaedam qua
fixa viae ad lineam deriguntur . . . Ennius lib. XVIII gruma
derigere dixit—

degrumare forum

434 noenu decet V non decet hic Merula non decet
Paul. non possunt *Serv. auct.* bonos *Paul.* boni
Serv. auct. facta D (I.) factam *Serv. auct.*
435 nixi militiae D (I.) enixi militiam *Serv. auct.*
438 soles V sol acstate diem B *prob.* St. soles terras
Hug cum soles tandem *olim* V cum sola est eadem
cdd. facient *cdd.* faciens Bergk
439 degrumare forum V degrumari ferrum *cdd.* *for-*
tasse degrumare forum ferro

---

a ' mumbling ' or ' grumbling ' without distinct words—
cf. 68, 122, 253, 378.

ANNALS

434–5

Slackness of discipline in the Roman army ? :

Servius (supplemented): 'Mussant' here means 'murmurant'; it is a term which is also used with a sense of not speaking ᵃ . . .—

No, it is not meet that good warriors should mumble; warriors who, straining in the toil of battle-fields, have given birth to deeds.

436–8

Unplaced fragments :

Nonius: 'Longiscere,' to become long, or to be broken . . . —

nor do their firm bodies languish ᵇ at all.

The same ᶜ poet—

when the sunny days shall make them lengthen long.

BOOK XVIII

FURTHER EVENTS OF THE YEAR 171 ? ᵈ

439

Making a camp :

Nonius: The 'gruma' is a certain measuring-instrument; by means of this, when it is fixed in position, roads are built in a truly straight line. . . . Ennius in the eighteenth book, for 'to mark out with the measuring rod,' uses the phrase—

to level off the meeting-place ᵉ

ᵇ 'Nor do even firm bodies last at all (?).' If Nonius is right, the meaning may be 'stretch' (so as to grow weaker by the strain); see also next note.

ᶜ Probably in the same book; if this and the last fr. come from the same context, then *corpora* in the last may refer to the trunk, stem, or sap of plants; cf. line 240.

ᵈ In all probability this book was unfinished at the time when Ennius died in 169 B.C.

ᵉ *forum,* 'parade-ground.' But we ought perhaps to read *degrumari ferro.*

ENNIUS

440

Gellius, XIII, 21, 14: Contra vero idem Ennius in Annali XVIII—

aere fulva

dixit, non fulvo, non ob id solum quod Homerus ἠέρα βαθεῖαν (*Il.*, XX. 446, XXI, 6) dicit, sed quod hic sonus opinor vocabilior est visus et amoenior.

Cp. Gell., II, 26, 11.

Ex Libro VIII aut IX?

The six following fragments, to judge from the probable parallelisms in Virgil, come from a description of a sham naval fight or of a fleet in training; the racing ships are compared with racing chariots and horses. Cf. V., 87–8; H. A. Koch, *Exercit. Crit.*, 11; Norden, 165–7. The scene may be the sham display by Scipio at New Carthage in 210 B.C. (Livy,

441

Festus 550, 22: ' Termonem ' Ennius Graeca consuetudine dixit . . .—

hortatore bono prius quam iam finibus termo

Cp. Paul., 551, 2.
Vergilius, *Aen.*, V, 129–130, 139–141.

442

Isidorus, *Orig.*, XIX, 1, 22: ' Celoces ' quas Graeci κέληταs vocant, id est veloces biremes vel triremes agiles et ad ministerium classis aptae. Ennius—

Labitur uncta carina per aequora cana celocis.

Vergilius, *Aen.*, V, 142–3.

ANNALS

440

the indecisive battle at Phalanna ? :

Gellius : But on the other hand Ennius again in the eighteenth book of *Annals* writes—

a tawny mist

' fulva ' not ' fulvo,' not only because Homer says ἠέρα βαθεῖαν but, I think, because he believed the former sound *a* to be more musical and pleasant.

From Book VIII or IX?

XXVI, 51; Polyb., X, 20, 1, 6); or at Syracuse in 204 B.C. (Livy, XXIX, 22); or possibly the frs. describe the training of Scipio's fleet in 205 (Livy, XXVIII, 45-6); or even the activities of the Spartan Nabis at Gytheion in 192 B.C. (Livy, XXXV, 25 ff.).

441

Festus : ' Termo ' is, as used by Ennius, a Graecism [a] ... —

. . . a good prompter before the boundary-post at the limits is reached. . . .

[Virgil describes a boat-race round a post set up by Aeneas.]

442

Isidorus : 'Celoces' are what the Greeks call κέλητες, that is, swift biremes or triremes fitted for the service of a fleet. Ennius has—

The cutter

Smooth o'er the white o' the waves on a keel very greasy she glided.[b]

[Virgil goes on to describe the racing ships.]

---

[a] In fact, however, the form is old Latin. Festus is thinking of the Greek τέρμων; but -o in Latin does not represent -ων in Greek.

[b] Cp. Bk. XIV, fr. 374. Ennius' rhythm is intentional.

ENNIUS

443-4

Schol. Bern., in *Georg.*, I, 512 (Ut cum carceribus sese effudere quadrigae) 'Carceribus,' ianuis. Ennius ait—

quom a carcere fusi
currus cum sonitu magno permittere certant,

445

Charisius ap. *G.L.*, I, 272, 22 K : Quemadmodum in navi auriga dici potest, ita et in curru gubernator, ut—

quomque gubernator magna contorsit equos vi,

Cp. Diomed., ap. *G.L.*, VI, 457, 29 K : Quintil., VIII, 6, 9; Mar. Plot. Sac., ap. *G.L.*, VI, 466, 29 K.
Vergilius, *Aen.*, V, 144-147; Hom., *Od.*, XIII, 81 ff.

446

Festus, 394, 32 : ' Restat ' pro distat ait. . . . Ennium ponere cum is dicat—

Impetus haud longe mediis regionibus restat.

Cp. Paul., 395, 7.
Vergilius, *Aen.*, V, 218 : illam fert impetus ipse volantem.

447

Festus, 550, 22 : ' Termonem ' Ennius Graeca consuetudine dixit. . . . —

Ingenti vadit cursu qua redditus termo est.

Cp. Paul., 551, 2.
Vergilius, *Aen.*, V, 241-243 (manu magna *ex altero E. loco*, *fr.* 541).

---

[443] a *cd.* (*cp. Varr., Menipp.*, 488 a carcere) e Hagen
[445] cumque *Charis., Diomed.*   atque *Mar. Plot.*   *trib.* *Enn.* Gesner *prob.* V

ANNALS

443-4

A scholiast, on Virgil's ' even as when teams of four pour out from the barriers ' : ' Barriers,' doors. Ennius says—

When pouring from the barriers the chariots with a mighty clatter strive to move headlong,[a]

445

Charisius : As in the case of a ship we can speak of a driver, so in the same way we can speak of a steersman in the case of a chariot, for example— [b]

and when the steersman has turned his horses with a mighty pull,

[Virgil likewise compares the racing ships to racing chariots, and imitates Homer.]

446

Festus : ' Restat.' Ennius is stated to use this word for ' distat ' [c] when he says—

Its rush not far off keeps steady in the course.

Virgil has : her own speed bears her flying on.

447

Festus : ' Termo ' is, as used by Ennius, a Graecism [d] ... —

with giant speed it overruns the place where the boundary-post is set.

---

[a] Nonius (162, 1) explains the word as *mittere, incitare, vel praecipitare*; the reflexive is not included in the fr.
[b] Attribution to Ennius is doubtful but probable. *Auriga, gubernator*—Cp. ' man at the wheel.'
[c] But I take ' restat ' as meaning ' remains firm.' Or it might mean ' comes to a standstill ' (of a ship which as it were ' breaks down ' in the race). If, however, *restat* really means *distat* here, Ennius describes a ship or ships not far behind other ships.
[d] See n. on fr. 441.

ENNIUS

Ex Aliis Annalium Incertis Libris

448

Cicero, *de Nat. Deor.*, II, 2, 4 : Illum vero et Iovem (*invocant*) et dominatorem rerum et omnia nutu regentem et, ut . . . Ennius—

patrem divumque hominumque

Cp. Cic., id., 25, 64.
Il., V, 425, 1 *al.* : πατὴρ ἀνδρῶν τε θεῶν τε.

449

Varro, *L.L.*, V, 65 : Ennius . . . eundem (*sc. Iovem*) appellans dicit—

divumque hominumque pater rex

Cp. Enn., *Ann.*, 207-8.

450-51

Vergilius, *Aen.*, I, 254-6 :

Olli subridens hominum sator atque deorum
vultu, quo caelum tempestatesque serenat,
oscula libavit natae.

Servius, ad 254 : ' Subridens.' Laetum ostendit Iovem et talem qualis esse solet cum facit serenum : . . . *Servius auctus ad loc.* Ennius—

Iuppiter hic risit, tempestatesque serenae

riserunt omnes risu Iovis omnipotentis.

Homerus, *Il.*, V, 426 : ὣς φάτο, μείδησεν δὲ πατὴρ ἀνδρῶν τε θεῶν τε.

168

ANNALS

(A) The gods :

448

Cicero : Yes, men call upon him not only as Jupiter but
also as lord of the universe, and ruler of all things by his nod,
and, as Ennius says—

father of gods and men

449

Varro : Ennius . . . calling upon the same god, says—

father and monarch of gods and men

450–51

Virgil says :

The begetter of gods and men, with a gentle smile for her in
his look, with which he calms the sky and the weather, gently
kissed his daughter.

Servius, on ' subridens ' : ' With a gentle smile.' He
represents Jupiter as happy and such as he is wont to be when
he brings calm weather. . . . *An augmenter of Servius adds*:
Ennius has—

Here Jupiter smiled, and with [a] the almighty's smile
Smiled clear and calm all weathers.

Homer says : So spake and smiled the father of men and
gods.

---

[a] Here Ennius expands Homer.

ENNIUS

452-3

Servius (auctus) ad *Aen.*, I, 31 : ' Arcebat,' prohibebat.
Significat autem et continet.   Ennius—

qui fulmine claro

omnia per sonitus arcet,

Cp. Prob. (ad Verg. *Ecl.*, VI, 31): Plane trinam esse mundi
originem et Lucretius confitetur dicens. . . . ' Omnia per
sonitus arcet, terram mare caelum.'
Cp. Lucret., VI, 400.

454

Cicero, *de Div.*, II, 39, 82 : Ad nostri augurii consuetudinem
dixit Ennius—

Tum tonuit laevum bene tempestate serena.

Cp. Varr., ap. Non., 408, 3; Vergil., *Aen.*, IX, 627 de parte
serena | intonuit laevum; II, 693.

455

Priscianus, ap. *G.L.*, II, 334, 19 K: 'Celerissimus' pro
' celerrimus.' . . . E. in Annalibus—

Exin per terras postquam celerissimus rumor

456

Serv., ad *Aen.*, XII, 709 : ' Inter se coisse viros et cernere
ferro '; vera et antiqua est haec lectio.   Nam E. secutus est
. . .—

Olli cernebant magnis de rebus agentes.

Cp. Lucret., V, 393 : Magnis inter se de rebus cernere
certant.

---

[453] omnia personitans arcet terram mare caelum Bernays
coll. Prob. ad Ecl., VI, 31

170

ANNALS

452-3

Servius (supplemented): ' Arcebat,' kept off. It means also ' contains.' Ennius—

who with bright thunderbolt
Encloses all things in a burst of sound,[a]

454

Cicero : It was with reference to our system of augury that Ennius wrote—

Then on the left, in weather clear and calm,
He thundered a good omen.

(B) *Affairs of State.*

455

Priscianus : ' Celerissimus ' for ' celerrimus.' . . . Ennius in the *Annals*—

' And then after most swiftest rumour had spread through the lands,

456

Servius, on Virgil's ' making decision with the sword ' : This reading is old and the true one. For he followed Ennius . . . —

Busied with great affairs they were making a decision.

---

[a] Probus quotes a whole line *Omnia p.s.a. terram mare caelum* and gives the author as Lucretius, though our extant MSS. do not contain the line. Cf. Lachmann, on Lucret., IV, 126; Munro, *Lucret.*, Vol. I, 163–4.

ENNIUS

457

Servius, ad *Georg.*, II, 424: . . . ' cum ' abundat. . . . Ennius—

Effudit voces proprio cum pectore sancto;

id est proprio pectore, nam ' cum ' vacat.

458–9

Charisius, ap. *G.L.*, I, 201, 15 K : ' In mundo ' pro ' palam ' et ' in expedito ' ac ' cito.' . . . Ennius—

' tibi vita
seu mors in mundo est '

460

Servius (auctus) ad *Aen.*, I, 69: ' Incute vim ventis.' . . . Ennius—

dictis Romanis incutit iram

461

Cicero, *ad Att.*, VI, 2, 8 : Ain tandem, Attice, laudator integritatis et elegantiae nostrae—

Ausus es hoc ex ore tuo . . . ?

inquit Ennius, ut equites Scaptio ad pecuniam cogendam darem, me rogare ?

462

Varro, *L.L.*, VII, 12 : ' Tueri ' duo significat, unum ab aspectu . . . unde est Ennii . . . —

' Quis pater aut cognatus volet vos contra tueri ?

462 vos Iun.   nos *Varro*

---

[a] A mistake of Servius. In Virgil's passage *cum* is temporal.

ANNALS

457

Servius, on ' cum vŏmĕre ' in Virgil : ' Cum ' is redundant [a] . . . Ennius—

From his own hallowed heart he poured forth
speech ;

that is, ' *proprio pectore*,' for ' *cum* ' has no force here.

458-9

Charisius : ' In mundo ' for ' palam ' and ' in expedito '
and ' cito ' . . . Ennius—

' Whether it is life or death is now in readiness for
you '

460

Servius (supplemented), on ' Strike strength into the
winds ' in Virgil : . . . Ennius— [b]

By his words he struck wrath into the Romans

461

Cicero : You don't say so, Atticus ! You, who praised
the nice honour of my conduct—

' Durst you thus out of your own mouth . . .

(says Ennius), ask me to give Scaptius some cavalry to collect
his debts with ?

462

Varro : ' Tueri ' has two meanings, one derived from the
idea of looking at, whence comes Ennius' use of it . . .—

' What man, father or kinsman, will wish to look
you all in the face ? [c]

[b] Vahlen suggests relating this fr. to fr. 510. He compares
Virg., *Aen.*, X, 367–8, and Homer, *Il.*, XI, 291.
[c] This and the next fr. seem to belong to the same context
(V, 83–4). They may be words of Scipio to those who opposed
his African schemes. That 462 is a hexameter need not be
doubted, since Ennius certainly shortened the second syllable
of ' contra ' (cf. pp. 436–7).

ENNIUS

463

Nonius, 230, 10 : ' Vultus ' . . . neutro. . . . Ennius—

' Aversabuntur semper vos vostraque vulta

464–6

Varro, *L.L.*, VII, 103 : Multa ab animalium vocibus tralata in homines . . . perspicua ut Ennii—

> animus quom pectore latrat

. . . minus aperta ut. . . . Enii a vitulo . . . ciusdem a bove—

> clamore bovantes

eiusdem a leone—

> pausam fecere fremendi.

Cp. Paul., ex Fest., 87, 9 : 'latrare' Ennius pro poscere posuit. Homer., *Od.*, XX, 13 : κραδίη δέ οἱ ἔνδον ὑλάκτει, *Il.*, II, 142 : θυμὸν ἐνὶ στήθεσσιν ὄρινεν. *et al.* ; Verg., *Aen.*, V, 363 : animusque in pectore.

467

Augustinus, *De Civ. Dei*, II, 21 : Sicut etiam ipse Tullius non Scipionis nec cuiusquam alterius sed suo sermone loquens in principio quinti libri (*de Re Publica*) commemorato prius Ennii poetae versu quo dixerat—

Moribus antiquis res stat Romana virisque.

---

[463] aversabuntur Quich.   avorsabuntur S   adversabantur *cdd.*

[464] animus cum *Varro*   animusque in S *coll. Od., XX,* 1

---

[a] But *adversabantur* may be right, ' were set against me.'

ANNALS

463

Nonius : 'Vultus' . . . in the neuter. . . . Ennius—

' You and your faces will be ever turned away [a]

464–6

Varro : Many animal sounds have been used figuratively of human beings; . . . of quite clear cases there is, for example, Ennius'—

when his heart in his breast barks his wants [b]

. . . and of less obvious cases there is for example . . .

. . . Ennius' usage drawn from the calf . . . and the same poet's usage drawn from the cow—

clamorously mooing

and also his usage drawn from the lion—

they put a stop to their roaring.

467

Augustine : Just as Tully himself declared, speaking not in Scipio's nor anyone else's words but in his own person at the beginning of his fifth book (*sc. On the Republic*), having first quoted the line of Ennius where that poet had written—

On manners and on men of olden time
Stands firm the Roman State.

[b] Paulus says : Ennius used *latrare* in the sense of *poscere*. These frs. should possibly be attributed to the *Satires*. In fr. 464 we should perhaps write *cum* (preposition), as Varro does, instead of *quom* which is the spelling used by Ennius for temporal *cum*.

ENNIUS

468-9

Varro, *R.R.*, III, 1, 2 : In hoc nunc denique est ut dici possit, non cum Ennius scripsit—

Septingenti sunt paulo plus aut minus anni
augusto augurio postquam incluta condita Roma est

Cp. Suet., *August.*, 7.

470

Nonius, 197, 2 : ' Caelum ' . . . masculino. . . . Ennius—

Fortes Romani sunt tamquam caelus profundus

Cp. Charis., ap. *G.L.*, I, 72, 16 K ; Vergil., *Aen.*, I, 58 : caelumque profundum.

471-2

Porphyrio, ad Hor., *S.*, I, 2, 37 : ' Audire est operae pretium procedere recte | qui moechis non vultis ut omni parte laborent.' Urbane abutitur Ennianis versibus—

' Audire est operae pretium procedere recte
qui rem Romanam Latiumque augescere vultis.'

Cp. Acr., ad loc. ; Varr., ap. Non., 478, 16.

473

Servius, ad *Aen.*, XI, 27 :—

           quem non virtutis egentem,

Ennii versus est.

474

Ekkehart, ad Oros., III, 9, 5 (Anno autem post hunc— sc. *A.U.C. CCCCVIX*—subsequenti) : Ennius—

quom nihil horridius unquam lex ulla iuberet.

[470] sunt *suppl.* Merula   tamquam B   quamquam *Non.*

---

[a] It is unknown what caused Ennius to date the foundation of Rome in the ninth century. This fr. may be a rough-and-ready remark from a speech (cf. St., pp. 222-23 ; V., CLIV ff.)

ANNALS

468-9

Varro: With regard to this matter, only now could it be said, and not when Ennius wrote, that—

Seven hundred years it is,[a] a little more or less, since renowned Rome was founded by august augury

470

Nonius: 'Caelum' . . . in the masculine. . . . Ennius—

Brave are the Romans as the sky 's profound

471-2

Porphyrio, on Horace's words: 'It's worth your while, all you who wish no successful path for adulterers, to hear how they are burdened on all sides': He wittily perverts lines of Ennius—

'To hear is worth your while, all you who wish the Roman State to tread a successful path and Latium to increase.'

473

Servius, on Virgil's—

whom, lacking not of valour,

says: This is a line of Ennius.

474

Over a passage of Orosius, in a *codex Sangallensis*, mentioning the punishment of Minucia a vestal virgin in 343 B.C., Ekkehart wrote: Ennius—

since nothing more horrible could any law ever demand.

The most attractive theory is that of Soltau (*Philol.*, N.F., XXV, 317 ff.), who, calculating that Ennius dated the foundation of Rome *c.* 1100, suggests that these words are spoken by Camillus on the occasion of the invasion of the Gauls (390 or 387 B.C.). In Livy, V, 54 Camillus speaks of the 365th year of Rome's existence—this, of course, follows the system by which 753 was the date of Rome's foundation.

ENNIUS

475

Nonius, 64, 29 : ' Propages ' est series et adfixio continuo vel longe ducta. . . . Ennius—

nobis unde forent fructus vitaeque propagmen.

Cp. Non., 221, 12.

476

Priscianus, ap. *G.L.*, II, 470, 21 K : Proprie necatus ferro, nectus vero alia vi peremptus dicitur. Ennius—

Hos pestis necuit, pars occidit illa duellis.

477

Cassiodorius, ap. *G.L.*, VII, 207, 1 K : ' Cum ' praepositio per c scribenda est, ' quum ' adverbium temporis, quod significat ' quando,' per q scribendum est discretionis causa, ut apud Ennium—

Cum legionibus quom proficiscitur induperator,

478

Nonius, 214, 7 : ' Metus ' . . . feminino. . . . Ennius—

Nec metus ulla tenet; freti virtute quiescunt.

Cp. Fest., 402, 15 (. . . Ennius . . . ' nulla metus '); *Il.*, XI, 9 : ἠνορέῃ πίσυνοι.

479

Festus, 510, 17 : ' Sultis ' si vultis significat. . . . Ennius—

' Pandite sultis genas et corde relinquite somnum.'

Cp. Paul., ex F., 66, 37 (15): genas Ennius palpebras putat cum dicit. . . .

---

[475] *trib. lib. IV* V
[478] nec Mercier   ni *cdd.*   freti Mercier   rite *cdd.* (tennet riae *Lu.*)   virtutem, rite V

ANNALS

475

Nonius : 'Propages' is a connected series drawn out without a break, or at great length. . . . Ennius—

Whence there might be crops and prolonging of life for us.

476

Priscianus : 'Necatus' is the proper term to use of a man killed by the sword, but 'nectus' of a man killed by some other violence. Ennius—

Some a plague did kill; others of them fell in wars.

(C) War.

477

Cassiodorius : 'Cum' as a preposition must be written with a c; 'quum' as an adverb of time meaning 'quando,' with a q for the sake of distinction, for example in Ennius— [a]

When the commander sets forth with his hosts,

478

Nonius : 'Metus' . . . in the feminine. . . . Ennius—

Nor any fear holds them; trusting in their valiance, they rest.

479

Festus : 'Sultis' means 'si vultis'; . . . Ennius—

'Open your eyelids,[b] will you all, and leave behind the sleep in your hearts.'

---

[a] He describes probably the *votorum nuncupatio* on the Capitol.

[b] Paulus says that Ennius uses *genae* in the sense of eyelids.

ENNIUS

480

' Lactantius ' ad Stat., *Theb.*, VI, 27 : ' et cornu fugiebat somnus inani ' . . . sic a pictoribus simulatur, ut liquidum somnum ex cornu super dormientes videatur effundere. Sic Ennius—

Quom sese exsiccat somno Romana iuventus.

481-2

Nonius, 134, 29 : ' Latrocinari,' militare mercede. . . . Ennius—

> . . . fortunasque suas coepere latrones inter se memorare.

483

Nonius, 223, 33 : ' Sagum ' . . . Masculini. Ennius—

> tergus igitur sagus pinguis opertat

484

Festus, 400, 29 : Ennius . . .—

> . . . surum unum unus ferre, tamen defendere
> posset. . . .

Suri autem sunt fustes, et ὑποκοριστικῶς surculi.
Cp. Fest., 424, 7, Paul., ex F., 425, 1.

485

Vergilius, *Aen.*, XI, 307 : Nec victi possunt absistere ferro. *Servius auctus* : Ennius—

Qui vicit non est victor nisi victus fatetur '

Varro et ceteri invictos dicunt Troianos quia per insidias oppressi sunt ; illos enim vinci adfirmant qui se dedunt hostibus.

---

[481] suas Mercier   quas *cdd.*
[484] surum unum unus V   *alii alia*   unũ usurũ surus
Fest., 400 * * * urus surum * * *Fest.*, 424   unus surus
surum ferret *Paul.*

ANNALS

480

'Lactantius,' on 'And sleep fled away, his horn empty' in Statius: Sleep is represented by painters so as to appear to pour out over slumberers liquid sleep from a horn. So Ennius has—

When the young warriors of Rome dry themselves from sleep.

481–2

Nonius: 'Latrocinari' to serve as a soldier for pay. . . . Ennius—

and the hired warriors began to talk among themselves of their fortunes

483

Nonius: 'Sagum' . . . Masculine form. Ennius—

Therefore a thick cloak covers his back

484

Festus: Ennius . . . —

. . . Still could one bring one stake, still could he defend . . . [a]

'suri' are stakes; the diminutive is 'surculi.'

485

Virgil: Not when conquered can they have done with the sword. *An augmenter of Servius adds*: Ennius— [b]

'He who has conquered is not conqueror
Unless the conquered one confesses it'

Varro and the rest speak of the Trojans as 'unconquered' because they were overthrown by trickery; they affirm that only those who surrender themselves are conquered.

---

[a] This fr. is almost hopeless, but it seems to refer to stakes of which each legionary carried one for the fortification of the camp. V., 95.

[b] If the augmenter, in 'Varro and the rest,' includes Ennius, then the context is probably the same as the frs. about Troy not being really captured—see pp. 128-9.

ENNIUS

486

Festus, 434, 30 : ' Superescit ' significat supererit. Ennius—

' Dum quidem unus homo Romanus toga superescit,

Cp. Paul., ex F., 435, 8.

487

Varro, *L.L.*, VII, 46 : Apud Ennium—

Iam cata signa fere sonitum dare voce parabant,

' cata ' acuta; hoc enim verbo dicunt Sabini.

488

Paulus, ex F., 83, 16 (26) : ' Lituus ' appellatus quod litis sit testis. . . . Ennius—

Inde loci lituus sonitus effudit acutos

489

Donatus, ad Ter., *Phorm.* III, 1, 1 : . . . ' cum istoc animo. . . . Ennius—

Optima cum pulchris animis Romana iuventus

490

Paulus, ex F., 37, 24 (16) : ' Cracentes,' graciles. Ennius—

Succincti gladiis media regione cracentes.

---

[486] *fortasse* super escit
[487] fere Laetus   fera O. Mr.   ferae ferę (*Varro*)

ANNALS

486

Festus : ' Superescit ' means ' supererit.'   Ennius—

' Yes, so long as one gowned man of Rome is left
alive,

487

Varro : In a passage of Ennius—

Just then the shrill watchwords were making ready
to give sound in a call,

' cata ' means sharp; for this is the word used by the Sabines
for ' acuta.'

488

Paulus : ' Lituus ' is so called on the ground that it is a
witness of ' lis ' [a] (strife) . . . Ennius—

Thereupon the war-horn poured forth sharp sounds

489

Donatus, on ' With such faint spirit as that ' in Terence :
Ennius—

The best youth of Rome with fine spirit

490

Paulus : ' Cracentes,' [b] slender.   Ennius—

Sword-girt and slender round the waist.

---

[a] In fact *lituus* originally meant crooked and was perhaps
an Etruscan word.
[b] This word occurs here only; *crac-* is obviously kindred
with *grac-*.

ENNIUS

491

Servius, ad *Aen.*, IX, 675: 'Armati ferro'; aut bene instructi armis aut, ut Asper dicit, ferrea corda habentes, id est dura et cruenta cogitantes, ut Ennium sit secutus qui ait—

> succincti corda machaeris.

492

Servius (auctus) ad *Aen.*, V, 37: 'in iaculis.' In hastis Ennius—

> levesque sequuntur in hastis.

493

Paulus, ex F., 500, 18 (20): 'Siciles,' hastarum spicula lata. Ennius—

> Incedit veles vulgo sicilibus latis.

494

Nonius, 555, 14: 'Falarica,' telum maximum. . . . Ennius—

> . . . quae valide veniunt; falarica missa

Cp. Virgil., *Aen.*, IX, 702: contorta falarica venit.

495

Schol. Bern., ad Luc., *Phars.*, I, 6: Infestisque obvia signis | signa, pares aquilas et pila minantia pilis'; Ennii versus—

> Pila retunduntur venientibus obvia pilis

---

[491] *trib. lib. XV V.*
[494] q. v. v. <velut alta> f. m. *coni.* V   q. valido venit contorta falarica missu *mg. Iunian.* (vibrata *coni. olim* V) quae valide venit falarica missa *coni.* Linds.

ANNALS

491

Servius, on 'Armed in iron' in Virgil: Either 'well equipped with arms' or, according to the statement of Asper, 'having hearts of iron,' that is, 'thinking hard and bloody thoughts'; this makes him follow Ennius, who says—

girt round their hearts with broadswords.

492

Servius (supplemented), on 'In the midst of spears' in Virgil: Ennius has 'in the midst of lances'—

and the light-armed followed in the midst of lances.

493

Paulus: 'Siciles,' broad points of lances. Ennius—

The skirmishers, holding broad cutting-spears, advanced in a body.

494

Nonius: 'Falarica,' a very large javelin. . . . Ennius—

. . . which come sturdily; the fire-spear was hurled [a]

495

A Scholiast on Lucan's 'How standards faced enemy standards, eagles were matched one with another, and spears threatened spears': A line of Ennius—

Blunted back were spears that clashed against oncoming spears

[a] The quotation is defective. Vahlen thinks Ennius compares *fulmina* with missiles (V., in *Sitz.-Ber. B. Akad.*, 1896, 727); the comparison, however, might well be of missiles with *fulmina*.

ENNIUS

496

Servius (auctus) ad *Aen.*, XII, 294: 'teloque orantem multa trabali (. . . ferit)'; Ennius—

teloque trabali

497

Paulus, ex F., 353, 1: 'Runa' genus teli significat. Ennius—

runata recedit

id est proeliata. Cp. Fest., 352, 1.

498

Festus, 490, 15: 'Spira' dicitur . . . basis columnae. . . . Ennius quidem hominum multitudinem ita appellat cum dicit—

spiras legionibus nexit.

Cp. Paul., ex F., 491, 1.

499–500

'Lactantius,' ad Stat., *Theb.*, XI, 56 (. . . iam gelida ora tacent; carmen tuba sola peregit): Ennius—

Quomque caput caderet, carmen tuba sola peregit
et pereunte viro raucus sonus aere cucurrit.

Cp. Sil. Ital., IV, 169 ff.

---

a But it probably means simply 'armed with the runa,' just as *pilatus*, as used by Virgil and Martial, means 'armed with the pilum.' The subject would be *turba* or the like.

ANNALS

496

Servius (supplemented) on 'and with a spear stout as a beam he smote him praying many a prayer' in Virgil: Ennius—

and with a spear stout as a beam

497

Paulus: 'Runa' means a kind of spear.   Ennius—

armed with spear, gave way

'runata,' that is, 'having given battle.' [a]

498

Festus: 'Spira' is a term applied to the base of a pillar. . . . But Ennius gives the name to a multitude [b] of men when he says—

coils wove he with his hosts.

499–500

'Lactantius,' on Statius . . . 'then his chill mouth fell silent; the trumpet finished alone its tune': Ennius— [c]

And when his head was falling, the trumpet finished alone its tune; and even as the warrior did perish, a hoarse blare sped from the brass.

[b] This suggests not spira (a twisted rope or the like) but a transliteration of σπεῖρα (which Polybius uses for *manipulus*).
[c] There is another imitation of Ennius' passage in Statius (IV, 169 ff.) where he is narrating the battle at the Ticinus. But Ennius' own context is not known.

ENNIUS

501-2

Servius, ad *Aen.*, X, 396 (395-6): Te decisa suum, Laride, dextera quaerit, | semianimesque micant digiti ferrumque retractant.' Ennii est, ut—

Oscitat in campis caput a cervice revulsum
semianimesque micant oculi lucemque requirunt.

Cp. Sil. Ital., VI, 10; Vergil., *Aen.*, IV, 691.

503

Porphyrio, ad Hor., *C.*, I, 9, 1 : Vides ut alta stet nive candidum (Soracte). . . . 'Stet' autem 'plenum sit' significat, ut Ennius—

stant pulvere campi

et Vergilius (*Aen.*, XII, 408): Iam pulvere caelum | stare vides.

504-5

Servius (auctus) ad *Aen.*, I, 81 (82 cavum conversa cuspide montem | impulit in latus) : . . . Ennius—

' nam me gravis impetus Orci
percutit in latus.

506

Charisius, ap. *G.L.*, I, 240, 6 K : . . . Ennius quoque in Annalium libro—

Euax ! Aquast aspersa Latinis.

505 pertudit *coni.* V *coll. fr.* 423
euax
  r
506 liber aquas istas pensa lituus *exc. Cauch.*   annalium libro aquast aspersa latinis *Charis.*

ANNALS

501–2

Servius, on Virgil's ' You, Larides, your severed right hand seeks—you—its master; and your fingers half alive lie twitching, and clench at the sword ' : The idea is Ennius', thus—

On the plains gaped his head torn out from the neck, and his eyes half alive lay twitching, and were fain to see the light.

503

Porphyrio, on Horace's ' Do you see how Soracte stands white in deep snow . . . ? ' . . . : ' Stet ' means ' is laden,' as Ennius has it—

The plains stand thick with dust

and Virgil : ' And now you see the sky stand thick with dust.'

504–5

Servius (supplemented), on Virgil's ' With inturned spear he struck into the hollow mountain's side ' : Ennius—

' for a heavy onset of Death strikes into my side.

506

Charisius : . . . Ennius also in a book of the *Annals*—

Bravo ! The Latins were refreshed.[a]

[a] The text is doubtful; *ăquast*, three syllables. *Aspergere aquam* means to revive.

ENNIUS

507–8

auctor, Bell. Hisp., XXXI, 6 : Ita cum clamor esset intermixtus gemitu gladiorumque crepitus auribus oblatus, imperitorum mentes timore praepediebat. Ut ait Ennius—

. . . ⟨hic⟩ pede pes premitur, armisque teruntur
arma . . . . ⟨viro vir⟩.

Cp. Fur. Bibac., ap. Macrob., *S.,* VI, 3 : 'pressatur pede pes, mucro mucrone, viro vir.' Vergil., *Aen.,* X, 361 : Haeret pede pes densusque viro vir. Homer., *Il.,* XIII, 130 *s.* (cp. XVI, 214 ff.) : φράξαντες δόρυ δουρί, σάκος σάκεϊ προθελύμνῳ. Ἀσπὶς ἄρ' ἀσπίδ' ἔρειδε, κόρυς κόρυν, ἀνέρα δ' ἀνήρ·

509 ·

auctor, Bell. Hisp., XXIII, 2 : Hic dum in opere nostri distenti essent, complures ex superiore loco adversariorum decucurrerunt nec detinentibus nostris multis telis iniectis complures vulneribus affecere ; ut ait Ennius—

Hic tum nostri cessere parumper.

510

Servius (auctus), ad *Aen.,* IX, 327 : 'Temere' . . . significat et subito. Ennius—

'quo tam temere itis?

511

Varro, *L.L.,* VII, 100 : Apud Ennium—

Decretum est stare ⟨et fossari⟩ corpora telis.

Hoc verbum Ennii dictum a fodiendo, a quo fossa.

[507-8] hic p. p. e. q. s. W   hic p. p. p. hic armis arma teruntur B pes premitur pede et armis arma teruntur V (*seclud.* hic) ⟨viro vir⟩ *suppl.* Norden   hic, ut ait Ennius, pes pede premitur armis teruntur arma *auct. Bell. Hisp.*

[509] hic tum ut ait Ennius *Auct.*   h. t. *seclud.* V

[511] et fossari *suppl.* Bergk   decretum est fossari Colonna decretum fossari O. Mr.

ANNALS

507-8

The author of *The Spanish War :* Thus since shouts were mingled with groans, and a clattering of swords struck upon the ear, the din confused the minds of the raw levies. As Ennius says—

Hereupon foot pressed foot and weapons weapons rubbed, and warrior warrior thronged.[a]

509

The same author : At this point, while our men were busied at the work, a number of our adversaries ran down from a higher level and by casting many spears wounded a number of our men who were unable to hold them back. As Ennius says—

Here now our men gave way a little while.[b]

510

Servius (supplemented) on Virgil : 'Temere' . . . also means 'suddenly.' Ennius—

'Whither go you all so rashly ?

511

Varro : In a passage of Ennius—

Order was given to stand and delve into their bodies with spears.

This word 'fossari' in Ennius is derived from 'fodio,' whence comes the word 'fossa.'

---

[a] Restorations of Ennius' words are all doubtful. That they include *viro vir* is likely, if we judge from other imitations (quoted opposite) of the Homeric original. V., 105; Norden, 159.
[b] Cp. Livy, XXVI, 44, *Romani parumper cessere.*

ENNIUS

512

Isidorus, *Orig.*, X, 270 : ' Taeterrimus ' pro fero nimium
. . . Ennius—

taetros elephantos

Cp. Placid., ap. *C.G.L.*, V, 157, 21 : excerpt. ex cod. Cassin.,
ap. *C.G.L.*, 581, 14 (. . . tetros elephantos † ad inguinem †).

513

Servius, ad *Aen.*, IV, 404 :—

It nigrum campis agmen

Hemistichium Ennii de elephantis dictum, quo ante Accius
est usus de Indis.

514-15

Priscianus, ap. *G.L.*, II, 518, 13 K : ' Tutudi ' . . . Ennius
in Annalibus—

viresque valentes
contudit crudelis hiems

Hic produxit paenultimam.

516

Nonius, 211, 10 : ' Lapides ' et feminino genere dici possunt
ut apud Ennium—

Tanto sublatae sunt agmine tunc lapides,

ad Homeri similitudinem qui genere feminino lapides posuit.

Il., XII, 287 : ὡς τῶν ἀμφοτέρωσε λίθοι πωτῶντο θαμειαί.
Cp. *Od.*, XIX, 494.

---

⁵¹² tetros (tetrosque *dett.*) elefantos (elephantes *dett.*) cdd.
Isid. Placid.   elephantos ad inguinem *exc. cd. Cassin.*
elephantos anguimanus *coni.* V (*Sitzungs.-Ber. B. Akad.*,
1896, 725 ff. *coll. Lucret. V*, 1302 : inde boves lucas turrito
corpore, taetras | anguimanus)
⁵¹⁶ augmine Wakefield   lapides <vi> *coni.* V
<his> *coni.* Mr.   tanto sunt sublatae a. t. l. (*pentam.*)
coni. St.   *fortasse* t. s. s. | a. t. l.

ANNALS

512

Isidorus : 'Taeterrimus' for very savage. . . . Ennius—

foul elephants [a]

513

Servius, on—

goes a black column upon the plains

in Virgil [b]: a half-line of Ennius used of elephants. Accius used it earlier (*sc.* than Virgil) of Indians.

514-15

Priscianus : 'Tutudi' . . . Ennius . . . in the *Annals*—

and their sturdy strength cruel winter crushed

Here he has scanned the penultimate long.

516

Nonius : 'Lapides.' This term can be used even in the feminine gender; for example, Ennius—

With so great a column were stones then upraised,

This is after the manner of Homer, who used his word for ' stones ' in the feminine gender.

---

[a] Vahlen's attractive conjecture *anguimanus* for *ad inguinem* in the *Exc. ex cod. Cass.* is apparently not right—cf. Goetz, in *C.G.L.*, VII, 330. This and the next fr. obviously come from some narrative about Pyrrhus or the Second Punic War, or warfare in Greece or Asia.

[b] Who used the phrase in describing ants.

ENNIUS

517-21

Macrobius, *S.*, VI, 3, 7 : Homerica descriptio est equi fugientis in haec verba (*Il.*, VI, 506 ff.)

ὡς δ' ὅτε τις στατὸς ἵππος ἀκοστήσας ἐπὶ φάτνῃ
δεσμὸν ἀπορρήξας θείῃ πεδίοιο κροαίνων,
εἰωθὼς λούεσθαι ἐϋρρεῖος ποταμοῖο,
κυδιόων· ὑψοῦ δὲ κάρη ἔχει, ἀμφὶ δὲ χαῖται
ὤμοις ἀΐσσονται· ὁ δ' ἀγλαΐηφι πεποιθώς,
ῥίμφα ἑ γοῦνα φέρει μετά τ' ἤθεα καὶ νομὸν ἵππων,

Ennius hinc traxit—

Et tum sicut equus qui de praesepibus fartus
vincla suis magnis animis abrupit et inde
fert sese campi per caerula laetaque prata
.celso pectore ; saepe iubam quassat simul altam ;
spiritus ex anima calida spumas agit albas,

Vergilius ' qualis ubi abruptis fugit praesepia vinclis ' et cetera.

[Vergilius, *Aen.*, XI, 492 ff.
Qualis ubi abruptis fugit praesepia vinclis
tandem liber equus, campoque potitur aperto :
aut ille in pastus armentaque tendit equarum
aut assuetus aquae perfundi flumine noto
emicat arrectisque fremit cervicibus alte
luxurians ; luduntque iubae per colla per armos.]

522

Charisius, ap. *G.L.*, I, 83, 22 K : Quod Ennius ait—

It equitatus uti celerissimus,

barbarismus est.

---

522 *sic* Havet, *Rev. de Phil.*, *XIV*, 27   equitatus iit
c. B   equitum celerissimus *ed. princ.*   equitatus | ut
celerissimus V *fortasse recte*   Ennius ait equitatus ut
celerrimus *Charis.*

ANNALS

517–21

Macrobius : There is in Homer a description of a horse in flight, in these words :

Even as when a stalled horse full fed at the manger breaks his tether and gallops clattering over the plain, being wont to bathe himself in a fair-flowing river, glorying therein, high holds he his head, and round his shoulders floats his mane; and he trusting in his glory—swiftly do his limbs bring him to the haunts and pastures of mares,

From this Ennius derived the following—

And then just as a horse which, full fattened from the stalls, bursts his tether in his high fettle, and away with breast uplifted bears himself over the rich grey-green meadows of the plain; and withal again and again tosses his mane on high; and his breath born of his hot temper flings out white froth,

and Virgil : ' As when, tether burst, has fled his stalls,' and the rest.

[Virgil (speaking of Turnus) has :

As when, tether burst, has fled his stalls a horse, free at last and possessed of the open plain; maybe he makes for the pastures and herds of mares, or, accustomed to bathe in the water of a river known to him, flashes forth and neighs and lifting high his neck goes glorying; and his mane plays over his neck and shoulders.]

522

Charisius : When Ennius says ' celerissimus '—

goes like the most swiftest cavalry,

it is a barbarism.

ENNIUS

523

Servius, ad *Aen.*, IX, 37 (38 : Hostis adest. Eia ! ingenti clamore per omnes | condunt se Teucri portas) : ‘ Hostis adest ’ ; hic distinguendum, ut heia militum sit properantium clamor. Et est Ennianum qui ait—

Heia machaeras !

Ergo heia ingenti clamore dicentes ad portas ruebant. Alii ‘ hostis adest, heia ’ legunt.

524

Priscianus, ap. *G.L.*, II, 482, 34 H : ‘ Detondeo ’ . . . detotondi. Ennius in Annalibus—

deque totondit agros laetos atque oppida cepit.

525

Servius, ad *Aen.*, X, 6 : ‘ Quianam.’ Cur. Quare. Ennianus sermo est. *Servius auctus* :—

‘ Quianam legiones caedimus ferro ?

526-8

Gellius, XVI, 10, 1 : Legebatur in consessu forte complurium Ennii liber ex Annalibus. In eo libro versus hi fuerunt—

Proletarius publicitus scutisque feroque
ornatur ferro, muros urbemque forumque
excubiis curant.

Cp. Non., 155, 21.

---

[524] deque totondit Merula   detondit *Bamb. m.* 2
detotondit *cdd.*
[525] *trib. lib. II* Merula
[526-8] *trib. lib. VI* V

196

ANNALS

523

Servius, on ' The enemy is here, Hi ! With a great clamour
the Teucri betook themselves through all the gates,' in Virgil:
' The enemy is here.' At this point we must punctuate so
as to make ' hi ! ' a clamour of hastening soldiers. The idea
belongs to Ennius, who says—

Hi, your swords !

Thus Virgil means :—shouting ' hi ' with a great clamour
they rushed at the gates. Others read ' the enemy is here,
hi ! '

524

Priscianus : ' Detondeo ' . . . ' detotondi.' Ennius in the
Annals—

Bare also stripped he the joyful fields, and he took
the cities.

525

Servius, on ' quianam ' in Virgil : ' Quianam,' ' why ? '
' for what reason ? ' The expression is Ennian. *An augmenter of Servius adds*—

' For why do we*a* cut down the hosts with the
sword ?

526-8

Gellius : At a sitting where a good many were present, it
happened that a book chosen from Ennius' *Annals* was being
read. In that book occurred these lines—

The lowest breeders *b* at the country's cost were
armed with shield and savage steel; it was they
with sentries guarded the city and its walls and
mart.

---

a Perhaps mutinous soldiery (at the beginning of the Second
Macedonian war ?) (St., 220). Others (Mr., Valmaggi, V.,
after Merula) believe the fr. to have come from the story of
the Horatii and the Curiatii.
b *proletarii* were the lowest class who served the state merely
by breeding children (*proles*).

ENNIUS

529

Gellius, X, 29, 2: 'Atque' particula . . . si gemina fiat auget incenditque rem de qua agitur, ut animadvertimus in Q. Ennii Annalibus, nisi memoria in hoc versu labor—

atque atque accedit muros Romana iuventus.

Cp. Non., 530, 3. Cp. *Il.*, XXII, 221: προπροκυλινδόμενος. *Od.*, XVII, 525: προπρό Apoll. Rh., III, 453.

530

Paulus, ex Fest., 559, 7: 'Trifax' telum longitudinis trium cubitorum quod catapulta mittitur. Ennius—

aut permarceret paries percussa trifaci

531

Festus, 140, 21: 'Metonymia' est tropos, cum . . . significatur . . . a superiore re inferior, ut Ennius—

Cum magno strepitu Volcanum ventus vegebat.

532

Schol. Bembin., in Ter., *Heaut.*, II, 3, 16: 'Interea loci.' Loci parhelcon . . . Ennius—

Flamma loci postquam concussa est turbine saevo,

[530] permarceret *G*   permaceret *ML Par.*   permaneret T   perluceret O. Mr.   permaceat *olim* V   percussu ' O. Mr.   percussa *cdd*.
[532] rogi Umpfenbach   concursat t. Umpf.   conclusa Faern   concussa e B   concussa preturbine *cd*. concussa praeorbine Victorin.

ANNALS

529

Gellius: The particle 'atque' . . ., should it be doubled, increases and intensifies the action with which it is connected, as we notice in the *Annals* of Quintus Ennius (unless, in giving this line, my memory is at fault)—

and then and then approached the walls young warriors of Rome.

530

Paulus: 'Trifax,' a javelin three ells in length; it is shot from a catapult. Ennius—

or the party-wall pelted by long spears might crumble away [a]

531

Festus: 'Metonymia' (change of names) is a trope which comes about when . . . a lesser thing is given its meaning from a greater one; for example, Ennius has—

With a great crackle the breeze blew big the Fire-God's blaze.

532

A scholiast, on 'interea loci' in Terence: 'loci' is redundant; . . . Ennius—

The flame there,[b] when it had been tossed about in a fierce whirl,

[a] *Permarceret* seems to be right—cp. *luxuriae rictu Martis marcent moenia*—Petron., *Cena*, 55; V., 97; St., p. 209.
[b] The force of *loci* here is not clear. At any rate it does not go with *postquam*. Probably the scholiast is wrong and *loci* may mean simply ' of the place.'

ENNIUS

533

Isidorus, *Orig.*, XIX, 2, 4: 'Agea' viae sunt, loca in navi per qua ad remiges hortator accedit; de qua Ennius—

Multa foro ponit et agea longa repletur.

534–5

Servius (auctus) ad *Georg.*, I, 12: Cui prima frementem | fudit equum (. . . tellus).' Nonnulli vero . . . 'cui prima frementem | fudit aquam' legunt, quod veteres murmura aquae fremitum dicebant. Ennius . . . —

ratibusque fremebat

imber Neptuni.

Cp. Serv. auct., ad *Aen.*, XI, 299.

536

Servius ad *Aen.*, VI, 705 (Lethaeumque domos placidas qui praenatat amnem): 'Praenatat,' praeterfluit. . . . Ennium igitur secutus est qui ait—

fluctusque natantes

537

Servius (auctus), ad *Aen.*, IX, 327: 'Temere' significat sine causa. Ennius—

' Haud temere est quod tu tristi cum corde gubernas.

Cp. *Aen.*, VI, 185 tristi cum corde volutat.

538

Isidorus, *Orig.*, XIX, 2, 12: 'Clavus' est quo regitur gubernaculum; de quo Ennius—

' dum clavum rectum teneam navemque gubernem.

Cp. Quintil., II, 17, 24.

---

[533] ponit Colonna   ponet et *cdd. pler.*   ponit et Caesenas agoeae longa replentur Valmaggi   agiavia longa repletur *Isid.*   et longa repletur agea *coni. olim* V

ANNALS

(D) Naval affairs.

533

Isidorus: 'Agea' means the footways, the spaces in a ship along which the boatswain approaches the rowers; on this Ennius has—

Many wares he put in the gangway; and the long passage was filled full.[a]

534-5

Servius (supplemented), on 'At whose bidding the Earth first gave birth to the neighing horse' in Virgil: . . . But some read 'cui prima frementem | fudit aquam,' because old writers used the term 'fremitus' for the murmuring of water. Ennius . . .—

and Neptune's water roared with ships.

536

Servius, on 'and the river of Lethe which floats in front of the peaceful dwellings' in Virgil: 'Praenatat,' flows by. Thus it was Ennius whom he followed, who says—

and floating billows

537

Servius (supplemented): 'Temere' means without cause. Ennius— [b]

'No chance is it that you steer sad at heart.

538

Isidorus: 'Clavus' is that by which a rudder is guided; on this Ennius has—

'so long as I hold tiller straight and steer the ship.

---

[a] Uncertain (St., pp. 216–17). Whatever the correct form of 'agea' may be, we can begin a new line with *longa*; or supply *ibi* after *agea*; or read (as Vahlen once suggested) *longa r.a.* Or possibly we can scan āgēā because of the liquid consonant which follows.

[b] Norden, 164.

ENNIUS

539

Isidorus, *Orig.*, XIX, 2, 14: 'Tonsilla' uncinus ferreus vel ligneus ad quem in litore defixum funes navium illigantur, de quo Ennius—

Tonsillas apiunt configunt litus aduncas.

540

Servius, ad *Aen.*, VI, 545: 'Explebo numerum' . . . 'explebo' est 'minuam.' Nam ait Ennius—

navibus explebant sese terrasque replebant.

541

Schol. Veron., ad *Aen.*, V, 241 (Et pater ipse manu magna Portunus euntem | impulit): Ennius—

atque manu magna Romanos inpulit amnis.

Homer., *Il.*, XV, 694–5: τὸν δὲ Ζεὺς ὦσεν ὄπισθε | χειρὶ μάλα μεγάλῃ.

542

Gellius, VII, 6, 2: Cur autem non Q. quoque Ennium reprehendit (*Iulius Hyginus*) qui in Annalibus non pennas Daedali sed longe diversius—

Brundisium pulchro praecinctum praepete portu

Cp. Gell., IX, 4, 1.

543

Porphyrio, ad Hor., *S.*, I, 10, 30 : 'Canusini more (bilinguis). Bilinguis dicitur quoniam utraque lingua usi sunt. . . . Ideo ergo et Ennius et Lucilius—

Bruttace bilingui

dixerunt. Cp. Paul., ex F. 25, 21.

---

[539] tonsillas apiunt *vel sim. cdd.*   t. rapiunt *edd. fortasse* aduncas | t. a. c. l.

[540] *trib. lib. IX* Hug

[542] Braundisium (*vel* Brundisium) quid pulcro *cdd.* inquit p. *coni. olim* V   portus *Vat., al.*   portust *olim* V

ANNALS

539

Isidorus: 'Tonsilla,' an iron or wooden hook to which, when it is fixed on the shore, ships' hawsers are tied; on this Ennius has—

They transpierced the beach and tied up the hooked [a] mooring-stakes.

540

Servius: 'Explebo numerum.' . . . 'Explebo' means I will diminish,[b] for Ennius says—

They unfilled themselves from the ships and filled up the land.

541

A Scholiast, on Virgil's 'And father Portunus himself with mighty hand drove him on his way': Ennius—

and with mighty hand the river drove the Romans on.

542

Gellius: Furthermore, why does he (*Julius Hyginus*) not call to task Quintus Ennius also, who in the *Annals* uses 'praepes' not of the wings of Daedalus, but of something quite different—

Brundisium belted by a beautiful fair haven [c]

543

Porphyrio, on 'speaking two tongues like a man of Canusium' in Horace: 'Bilinguis' is the term used because the Canusians used both languages (*Greek and Latin*). . . . On that account therefore both Ennius and Lucilius write—

a Bruttian speaking two languages

[a] *aduncas* is certainly right, though it is awkwardly placed. By *apiunt* is meant they tie the cables to the stakes.
[b] Servius blunders; Virgil means 'I will complete the number.'
[c] *praepes*, often used of a favourable bird-omen, here seems to be simply 'good, useful.'

ENNIUS

544

Festus, 400, 29 : . . . Ennius iocatus videtur . . . et alibi—

Inde Parum⟨ . . . . ul⟩ulabant.

545

Consentius, ap. *G.L.*, V, 400, 4 K : Poetae faciunt metaplasmos cum ipsi iam scripturam relinquunt corruptam. . . . Ennius—

huic statuam statui maiorum obatus Athenis ;

. . . per metaplasmum dempsit litteram r.

546

Cicero, *Tusc. Disp.*, I, 20, 45 : Etenim si nunc aliquid adsequi se putant, qui ostium Ponti viderunt et eas angustias per quas penetravit ea quae est nominata Argo. . . . (Enn. *Med.*, 257–8) aut ii qui Oceani freta illa viderunt—

Europam Libyamque rapax ubi dividit unda.

quod tandem spectaculum fore putamus cum totam terram contueri licebit ?

Cp. Cic., *de Nat. Deor.*, III, 10, 24.

---

⁵⁴⁴ ⟨circum quam caerula salsa ul⟩ *suppl.* Ilberg ⟨cui caerula vi valida assultabant O. Mr.

⁵⁴⁵ m. o. A. M (et *alt. m. superscript.*) maiorum abitratu (= arbitratu) Buttmann   maiorem horto (= hortor) auream ahenis L   magis mansuram auguro ahenis Ilberg   obatus (*fortasse* maiorem obatus) W

ANNALS

544

Festus: . . . Ennius seems to have jested . . . and elsewhere— [a]

Thence . . . Paros . . . were wailing.

545

Consentius: Poets make metaplasms when they of set
purpose leave a wrong spelling uncorrected. . . . Ennius— [b]

To him of my forefathers did I raise in my bereave-
ment a statue at Athens;

. . . by a metaplasm he has taken away (from *orbatus?*) the
letter *r*.

546

Cicero: For if now men who have seen the gate of the
Black Sea and the narrows through which passed the ship
which was called Argo . . . (Ennius, *Medea*) . . . or those
who saw the familiar straits of the Ocean—

where the greedy wave parts Europe and Libya,[c]

think they have achieved something, whatever kind of
spectacle think we it will be when we shall be allowed to gaze
on the whole earth?

---

[a] Probably in a book later than the ninth. That Paros
island is meant is shown by the continuation of the mutilated
notice in Festus.

[b] If the readings are uncertain, the suggested changes are
more so. If *obatus* is *orbatus*, it may go with *maiorum*, but
there is no example of the use of *orbo* with the genitive instead
of the ablative.

[c] Almost certainly from Ennius. If so, it may belong to
Scipio or to *Annals*, Book IX (V., CXCCI); the reference is
clearly to the Straits of Gibraltar.

ENNIUS

547-8

Vergilius, *Georg.*, II, 42-44—

Non ego cuncta meis amplecti versibus opto,
non mihi si linguae centum sint oraque centum,
ferrea vox.

Schol. Bern. ad 43: 'Non mihi' et reliqua. Homericus
sensus; sic nam et Ennius—

Non si, lingua loqui saperet quibus, ora decem sint,
innumerum, ferro cor sit pectusque revinctum,

Il., II, 487-9 :

πληθὺν δ' οὐκ ἂν ἐγὼ μυθήσομαι οὐδ' ὀνομήνω,
οὐδ' εἴ μοι δέκα μὲν γλῶσσαι δέκα δὲ στόματ' εἶεν
φωνὴ δ' ἄρρηκτος, χάλκεον δέ μοι ἦτορ ἐνείη,

Cp. Host., ap. Macrob., *S.*, VI, 3, 6; Ov., *Met.*, VIII, 533;
Fast., II, 119; *Trist.*, I, 5, 53; Sil., IV, 525 ff.; Vergil.,
Aen., VI, 625, *al.*

549

Augustin., *Ep.*, 231, 3 : Ego autem quod ait Ennius—

Omnes mortales sese laudarier optant

partim puto approbandum partim cavendum.

Cp. Augustin., *de Trin.*, XIII, 3, 6.

550

Servius, ad *Aen.*, XII, 499 (Saevam nullo discrimine caedem |
suscitat irarumque omnes effundit habenas). ' Irarum habenas '
. . . hic moderate locutus est, nam Ennius ait—

irarum effunde quadrigas.

[547] Non si Mommsen   monstra si sibi B   mons *cd.*
quibus (*i.e.* qb) V (*Herm.*, XV, 265) at *cd.*
[548] innumerum V   in metrum *cd.*   pectus Momm.
pecus *cd.*

ANNALS

547-8

Virgil says :

Not all of it do I ask to embrace in my verses; not if I were to have a hundred tongues and a hundred mouths and a voice of iron.

A scholiast on this passage : ' not if I ' and the rest; the idea is taken from Homer. And thus also writes Ennius—

Not if I were to have ten mouths with which my tongue could have skill to speak words without number,[a] and my heart and breast were fast bound in iron,

Homer has :

The common sort I could not number or name; no, not even if I were to have ten tongues and ten mouths and a voice that none might break, and a heart of bronze within me,

549

Augustine : But for my part I think that the remark of Ennius—

All mortal men long to be themselves acclaimed

should be partly approved of and partly avoided.

550

Servius, on Virgil's ' He wakened cruel slaughter that spared none, and let loose all the reins of wrath '; ' The reins of wrath ' . . . here he used a moderate expression, for Ennius says—

Let chariots of wrathfulness loose like a flood.

[a] *Innumerum*, used ' adverbially ' like *multum*, is probably right. But it is just possible that *in metrum* is a gloss which has ousted *in numeris* or even *in numerum*.

ENNIUS

551

'Macrobius,' ap. *G.L.*, V, 651, 35 K : 'Eructo' . . . est a verbo erugit. Ennius—

Contempsit fontes quibus exerugit aquae vis.

Cp. *op. cit.*, 626, 21.

552

Servius, ad *Aen.*, IX, 163—

vertunt crateras ahenos;

potantes exhauriunt; et est hemistichium Ennianum.

553

Gellius, III, 14, 4 : Varro . . . disserit ac dividit subtilissime, quid dimidium dimidiato intersit, et Q. Ennium scienter hoc in Annalibus dixisse ait—

Sicuti si quis ferat vas vini dimidiatum,

Pars quae deest ei vaso non 'dimidiata' dicenda est sed 'dimidia.'

554

Festus, 574, 1 : (*de veneno*) * * * cuius color inficiendo mutatur, ut Ennius cum ait—

. . . quom illud 'quo iam semel est imbuta veneno' . . .

555

Festus, 426, 33 : 'Solum,' terram. Ennius . . . —

sed sola terrarum postquam permensa parumper,

Cp. Varr., *L.L.*, V, 22.

---

[551] *trib. lib. XIII* V   *fortasse scribend.* a verbo erugo. Erugit Ennius
[553] sicuti *vell.* .   sicut *edd.*
[554] cur *aut* cumque *coni.* V   cupa illud O. Mr. imbutu ' *olim* V

ANNALS

551

Macrobius : ' Eructo ' . . . is derived from a verb ' erugo.'
Ennius—

He scorned the springs whence spirts out a rush of
water.[a]

552

Servius, on a passage in Virgil :—

They tilted up the brazen bowls ;

' they drained at a draught ' ; it is also a half-line of Ennius.

553

Gellius : Varro . . . discusses and distinguishes most
acutely the difference between ' a half ' and ' halved ' ; and
he says that Quintus Ennius in the *Annals* was wise when he
wrote—

Just as if a man were to bring a halved beaker of
wine,

The missing part of that beaker should be spoken of as
' half,' not ' halved.'

554

Festus (*on poison*) : . . . whose colour is changed by
adulteration, for example Ennius when he says—

When that proverb ' by the poison with which it
is imbued ' . . .

555

Festus : ' Solum,' earth. Ennius . . . —

But when she had passed swiftly over the fields of
Earth,[b]

---

[a] Possibly from a speech of Hannibal to Antiochus (Justin,
XXXI, 5, 7.

[b] Unless we take *permensa* in a passive sense (neuter plural),
we are tempted to make this fr. precede (directly, if we read
postquam est) lines 72–4 in Book I—*Indotuetur ibi lupus femina
conspicit omnis.* But *sola terrarum* suggests that Ennius means
' the world.'

ENNIUS

556

Charisius, ap. *G.L.*, I, 141, 24 K : ' Partum ' . . . Ennius—

iamque fere quattuor partum . . .

557

Isidorus, *de Nat. Rer.*, XII, 3 : Partes autem eius (*sc.* caeli) haec sunt : cohus axis cardines convexa poli hemisphaeria. ' Cohus ' quod caelum continet. Unde Ennius—

vix solum complere cohum terroribus caeli.

558

Isidorus, *Orig.*, XVIII, 36, 3 : Ideo rotis quadrigas currere dicunt sive quia mundus iste circuli sui celeritate transcurrit sive propter solem quia volubili ambitu rotat, sicut ait Ennius—

Inde patefecit radiis rota candida caelum.

Serv., ad *Aen.*, VI, 748 (mille) rotam volvere per annos . . . est autem sermo Ennii.

559

Priscianus, ap. *G.L.*, II, 170, 6 K : ' Iubar ' quoque tam masculinum quam neutrum proferebant. Ennius in Annalibus—

Interea fugit albus iubar Hyperionis cursum.

---

556 quattor Ritschl
557 solidum Ilberg, *fortasse recte* (*vel* soldum) pilam vix | sol mediam complere S   *fortasse* vis soldum

---

a Possibly describing the *vigiliae*, the four night-watches.
b Reading and meaning uncertain. I take *cohus* or *chous* to be, like *caelum*, akin to the Sanskrit *çva*, be hollow.

ANNALS

556

Charisius says: ' Partum ' . . . Ennius— [a]

and by then almost of four parts . . .

557

Isidorus : And the parts of the sky are the hollow, the axis, the hinges, the vaults, the poles, and the hemispheres; ' hollow ' is so called because it ' holds ' the sky. Whence Ennius—

hardly to fill with terrors the hollow alone of the sky. [b]

558

Isidorus : They say that teams of four ' run ' on ' wheels ' because this our universe ' runs ' out its course through the swiftness of its orbit, or because of the sun, since it ' wheels ' in a circular revolution; thus Ennius says—

Then the white wheel laid open the sky with its rays. [c]

Servius, on Virgil's ' when they have rolled the wheel through a thousand years ' : . . . and further this expression is Ennian.

559

Priscianus : ' Iubar ' also they used to inflect both as a masculine and as a neuter noun. Ennius in the *Annals*—

Meanwhile the white brilliance of Hyperion sped away on its course. [d]

---

[c] 'The line describes the return of spring' (St., p. 214). Surely it describes sunrise. '*Candida*': bringing fair weather' (St.). Surely it means ' bright white.'

[d] Possibly *albus iubar* is the moon; it flees before the sun's brightness.

ENNIUS

560

Servius, ad *Aen.*, XII, 115 : (116 lucemque elatis naribus efflant) . . . Ennianus versus est ordine commutato. Ille enim ait—

> funduntque elatis naribus lucem.

Cp. Mar. Victorin., ap. *G.L.*, VI, 28, 7 K (efflantque), Sil., V, 56.

561

Servius, ad *Aen.*, I, 51 (Loca feta furentibus austris): 'Austris.' Figura est celebrata apud Vergilium et est species pro genere. Legerat apud Ennium—

> furentibus ventis

562

Osbern, ap. Mai, *Class Auct.*, VIII, 332 : 'Hoc momen, -nis' pro momento. Unde Ennius—

> vestro sine momine, venti.

Cp. Vergil., *Aen.*, I, 133 : meo sine numine, venti.

563

Servius, ad *Georg.*, III, 76 (Pecus generosi pullus in arvis | altius ingreditur et mollia crura reponit). 'Altius ingreditur,' cum exultatione quadam incedit. 'Mollia crura reponit ': Ennius de gruibus—

> perque fabam repunt et mollia crura reponunt.

564

Charisius, ap. *G.L.*, I, 18, 17 K : 'Aulai medio' Vergilius (*Aen.*, III, 354);—

> terrai frugiferai

Ennius in Annalibus.

Cp. Martial., XI, 90, 5; Mar. Plot. Sac., ap. *G.L.*, VI, 449, 2 K; *etc.*

---

560 *addend. fortasse* <solis equi>

ANNALS

560

Servius on Virgil's : ' And from uplifted nostrils they send out breaths of light ' : This is a line of Ennius with a change in the order of words. For that poet says—

And they pour out a flood of light from nostrils uplifted.

561

Servius, on Virgil's ' a place teeming with furious Southerlies ' : ' Southerlies.' This is a figure of speech, namely, the particular for the general, which is frequent in Virgil. He had read in Ennius—

with raging winds

562

Osbern : ' Hoc momen,' gen. ' mominis,' for ' momentum.' Whence Ennius—

without impulse of yours, o you winds.

563

Servius, on Virgil's ' A foal of high-bred stud lifts a high pace in the fields and places a pliant leg ' : ' lifts a high pace,' advances with a kind of prancing. ' Places a pliant leg ' : Ennius on cranes—

and they creep through the beanfield, placing a pliant leg.

564

Charisius : Virgil has ' aulai medio,' [a] and Ennius in the *Annals* has—

of the fruite-bearing earthe

[a] Virgil, *Aen.*, III, 354. Priscianus says both genitive and dative singular could have this ending.

ENNIUS

565

Gellius, XIII, 21, 13 : Ennius autem ' rectos cupressos ' dixit contra receptum vocabuli genus hoc versu—

Capitibus nutantes pinos rectosque cupressos

Cp. Non., 195, 23.

---

[565] capitibus *Gell.*, *Non.*, *prob.* V captibus Schneider *prob.* Valmaggi cautibus Stowasser capite (*vers. Sotad.*) Mr. vertice Onions comptibus Damsté nutantis *Gell.* (nutantibus *Voss. min.* 1) nutantibus *Non.* capitibus nutantibus | ibi p. r. c. *olim* V

ANNALS

565

Gellius : Ennius too wrote ' rectos cupressos ' against the accepted gender of the word, in this line—

pines with nodding heads,[a] and straight cypresses

[a] Whether *capitibus* can be right is doubtful. Cf. St., p. 210, and the critical note given here on the Latin text. Did Gellius write *vertice* which was ousted by a gloss *capitibus* before Nonius copied Gellius? For other examples of hexameters beginning with ‿ ‿, see *Annals*, 339, and *Hedyphagetica*, 3 and 9.

PLAYS :
TRAGEDIES

FABULAE:
TRAGOEDIAE

ACHILLES

SIVE

ACHILLES ARISTARCHI

There seems to be no need to believe, as some do (R. 118), that Ennius wrote two plays in which Achilles played the leading part. It is more probable that our authorities cite two different titles of the same play (V. CCI), as they do also in, *e.g.*, the case of *Andromache* (see pp. 244 ff.). As in *The Ransom of Hector* (pp. 272 ff.), the material for *Achilles* was

1-3

Hom., *Il.*, IX, 10-11 : φοίτα κηρύκεσσι λιγυφθόγγοισι κελεύων | κλήδην εἰς ἀγορὴν κικλήσκειν ἄνδρα ἕκαστον.

Plautus, *Poen.*, prol. 1-2, 11, 3-4 :

1. Achillem Aristarchi mihi commentari lubet ;
2. inde mi principium capiam ex ea tragoedia—

Agamemno

11. Exsurge, praeco ; fac populo audientiam.

---

^a We must change the order of the dialogue as used by Plautus. Jahn, *H.*, III, 191, arguing that the play included

218

PLAYS :
TRAGEDIES

ACHILLES

OR

ACHILLES AFTER ARISTARCHUS

drawn from Homer, but here Ennius' model was Aristarchus of Tegea, who wrote tragedies at Athens in the time of Euripides (Suidas, *s.v.* 'Αρίσταρχος, Euseb., *Chron.*). The play deals chiefly if not wholly with the πρεσβεία πρὸς 'Αχιλλέα. (*Iliad,* IX.) At the head of the text of each Latin item I have put the probable Homeric source of the fragment.

A. Place of assembly in the Greek camp.

1–3

Agamemnon calls a meeting of the army :

Plautus : I want to imitate *Achilles after Aristarchus*; so I will take my beginning from that tragedy *ᵃ*—

Agamemnon

Up, herald ; get you a hearing for the troops.

Thersites' death, gives the words *silete e. q. s.* to Achilles calming the excited soldiery; the passage of Plautus rules this theory out.

ENNIUS

Praeco

3. Sileteque et tacete atque animum adveitite;
4. Audire iubet vos imperator

histricus.

4–5

Il., IX, 31 *s.*?

Nonius, 147, 18 : ' Obvarare,' pervertere, depravare, dictum a varis. Ennius Achille—

           nam consiliis obvarant quibus
iam concedit hic ordo.

6

Il., IX, 250–1 : ἀλλὰ πολὺ πρὶν | φράζευ ὅπως Δαναοῖσιν
ἀλεξήσεις κακὸν ἦμαρ.

Cp. Aesch., *Myrmid.*, 132 N (60 Smyth).

Nonius, 277, 24 : ' Defendere ' . . . depellere . . . —

Serva cives, defende hostes, cum potes defendere.

7–9

Il., IX, 313 : ὅς χ' ἕτερον μὲν κεύθῃ ἐνὶ φρεσίν, ἄλλο δὲ εἴπῃ.

Gellius, XIX, 8, 6 : ' Inimicitiam ' autem Q. Ennius in illo memoratissimo libro . . . —

Achilles

           eo ego ingenio natus sum ;
amicitiam atque inimicitiam in frontem gero
promptam.

   ⁵ iam Ribb.   tam *cdd.*
   ⁷⁻⁹ *senar. constit.* W   *pentametr. troch.* V, 120, 139–40
promptam gero *Gell.*

TRAGEDIES

Herald

Oyez! Be still, and turn your minds to me.
Silence! This is the order of your general

of stage-players.

4-5

Agamemnon advised a retreat from Troy; then Diomedes [a]
sharply rebuked him :

Nonius : ' Obvarare,' to turn crooked, to make corrupt, a
term derived from ' varus ' (awry). Ennius in *Achilles—*

For such men cross us by advice to which
This gathering of rank already yields.

B. Achilles' tent.

6

On Nestor's advice, Phoenix, Ajax, Ulysses and Eurybates go
to appeal to Achilles. From Ulysses' speech to him ? :

Nonius : ' Defendere ' . . . to push back . . . —

Save you your men and drive you back the foe,
While drive them back you can.

7-9

From Achilles' answer : [b]

Gellius : Furthermore, Quintus Ennius, in that most famous
book of his, used the term ' inimicitia ' . . . —

Achilles

Here is the nature which is mine from birth—
Friendliness and unfriendliness alike
Do I bear plain to see upon my brow.[c]

[a] So I take the passage; cf. *Iliad*, IX, 29 ff. R., 116
suggests that the speaker is Helenus, or some deity who
disapproves of resistance on the Trojans' part to Patroclus'
deeds. *Hic ordo*, i.e. *hic conventus principum* (V., 118).

[b] *Il.*, IX, 307 ff.

[c] V., 120 takes *promptam* with *frontem*.

ENNIUS

10-12

Il., IX, 604–5: εἰ δέ κ' ἄτερ δώρων πόλεμον φθισήνορα δύῃς |
οὐκέθ' ὁμῶς τιμῆις ἔσεαι, πόλεμόν περ ἀλαλκών.

Isidorus, *de Diff. Verb.*, 218, p. 29 A : ' Gloria ' . . .
virtutum est, fama vero vitiorum . . . —

Phoenix

Summam tu tibi pro mala
Vita famam extolles et pro bona paratam gloriam.
Male volentes famam tollunt, bene volentes gloriam.

13

Nonius, 472, 26 : ' Proeliant ' . . . —

. . . ita mortales inter sese pugnant proeliant.

Aesch. *Myrmid.*, 131 (59 Smyth) ?: τάδε μὲν λεύσσεις, φαίδιμ'
'Αχιλλεῦ | δοριλυμάντους Δαναῶν μόχθους | οὓς προπεπωκὼς εἴσω
κλισίας (θάσσεις).

14-15

Il., IX, 624 s. *suaserat Aias hoc modo*: διογενὲς Λαερτιάδη
πολυμήχαν' 'Οδυσσεῦ, | ἴομεν· οὐ γάρ μοι δοκέει μύθοιο τελευτὴ |
τῇδέ γ' ὁδῷ κρανέεσθαι.

Nonius, 166, 20 : ' Regredere,' revocare. . . . —

Ulixes

Quo nunc incerta re atque inorata gradum
regredere conare ?

12 malevolentes enim *Isid.*
13 ita *Harl. Par.* 7667 *Escor.*   inta *rell.*   interea
Klussmann *cum* L *prob.* V

222

TRAGEDIES

10-12

Achilles was not persuaded ; then Phoenix tries his powers. The following comes perhaps from his speech :

Isidore : ' Gloria ' is used of virtues, but ' fama ' is used of vices . . . —

Phoenix

For a coward's life you will raise up unto yourself the direst bad name, for a brave life, a ready store of glory ; when men are evil wishers, they do raise up a bad name ; but men who are well-wishers, they raise up glory.

13

Perhaps the following are also words of Phoenix :

Nonius : ' Proeliant ' . . . —

In such wise are mortal men justling and tussling one with another.

14-15

Achilles would not be moved ; Ajax advised Ulysses that they should give up and go ;[a] the following words are probably spoken by Ulysses in reply to Ajax :

Nonius : ' Regredere,' to retrace. . . . —

Ulysses

Wherefore now try you to restep your steps,
Our cause yet undecided and unpleaded ?

[a] *Il.*, IX, 622 ff. R. 113 (he suggests Ulysses or Phoenix. But Ajax's advice was addressed to Ulysses).

ENNIUS

16-17

Gellius, IV, 17, 13 : Ennius in tragoedia quae Achilles inscribitur ' subices ' pro aere alto ponit qui caelo subiectus est . . . —

per ego deum sublimas subices umidas,
unde oritur imber sonitu saevo et spiritu,

Cp. Fest., 436, 23 ; Non., 169, 2.

18

Il., IX, 6-7 : ἄμυδις δέ τε κῦμα κελαινὸν | κορθύεται.

Cicero, *in Verr.*, Act. II, Lib. I, 18, 46 : Tum subito tempestates coortae sunt maximae, iudices, ut non modo proficisci cum cuperet Dollabella non posset, sed vix in oppido consisteret—

ita magni fluctus eiciebantur.

Schol. Gronov., p. 403, 7, Or., *ad loc.* : Enniano hemistichio usus est ex ea tragoedia quae Achilles inscribitur.

19

Il., VII, 224.

Festus, 314, 22 :—

prolato aere astitit

Ennius in Achille Aristarchi cum ait significat clipeo ante se protento.

Cp. Paul., ex F., 315, 11 (4).

16-17 sublimas subiices | u. L
17 spiritu *Fest.* strepitu *Gell.*

16–17

Possibly words of Achilles in final [a] refusal :

Gellius : Ennius, in the tragedy which is entitled *Achilles*, puts ' subices ' (' underlayers ') for the upper air which ' underlies ' the sky—

> By heaven's god-haunted underlayers [b] on high,
> Whence springs the storm with savage shriek and
> swirl,

18

from a simile ? :

Cicero : Then suddenly, gentlemen of the jury, great storms gathered, so that Dolabella was not only unable to set out when he wished, but could hardly stay in the town—

> Such mighty billows were tossed and tossed
> again.

A scholiast on this passage : He made use of a half-line of Ennius, taken from the tragedy which is entitled *Achilles*.

19

from a battle-scene :

Festus : When Ennius, in *Achilles after Aristarchus*, says—

> Stood by with bronze held forward

he means ' with his shield spread in front of himself.'

---

[a] *Il.*, IX, 652 ff., where, however, there is nothing at all like Ennius' words.
[b] Festus, 436, 23 says Ennius means clouds.

ENNIUS

ΑΙΑΧ

The four extant lines from Ennius' *Ajax* do not allow us to say with certainty whether his model was Sophocles' Aἴας or not. It is probable that the action covered the events from

20

Nonius, 393, 7 : ' Statim ' producta prima syllaba a stando perseveranter et aequaliter significat. . . . Ennius Aiace—

. . . qui rem cum Achivis gesserunt statim.

21

Varro, *L.L.*, VII, 76 :

Aiax

Aliquod lumen—iubarne ?—in caelo cerno

' Iubar ' dicitur stella Lucifer . . . Huius ortus significat circiter esse extremam noctem.

Cp. Varro, *L.L.*, VI, 6. . . . Ennianus Aiax ' lumen e. q. s.; *ib.*, VI, 81.

22

Festus, 484, 10 : Salmacis nomine nympha Caeli et Terrae filia fertur causa fontis Halicarnasi aquae appellandae fuisse Salmacidis, quam qui bibisset vitio inpudicitiae mollesceret. . . . Ennius—

Salmacida spolia sine sudore et sanguine

Cp. Cic., *de Off.*, I, 18, 61.

Soph., *Ai.*, 1411–1413 : ἔτι γὰρ θερμαὶ | σύριγγες ἄνω φυσῶσι μέλαν | μένος. *vel oratio Tecmessae* 918–19 : φυσῶντ' ἄνω πρὸς ῥῖνας ἔκ τε φοινίας | πληγῆς μελανθὲν αἷμ' ἀπ' οἰκείας σφαγῆς. Cp. 898.

---

a V., CCI ; R., 132.
b Nonius is wrong here.

AJAX

the rivalry of Ajax and Ulysses over the arms of Achilles to
the death of Ajax by his own hand.[a]

20

from the prologue ? :

Nonius: 'Statim,' when the first syllable is pronounced
long,[b] as derived from 'stare' means perseveringly and uni-
formly. . . . Ennius in *Ajax*—

who warred with the Achaeans steadfastly.

21

Varro[c] :—

Ajax

Some glow—the star-light ?—in the heavens I see

By 'iubar' is meant the star (*Venus*) which is called
'Light-bringer.' Its rise indicates that the end of the night
is near.

22

*Outburst of Ajax in which he sneers at the spoils won by
Ulysses ? :[d]*

Festus : A nymph named Salmacis, a daughter of Sky and
Earth, is said to be the origin of the name 'Salmacis' given to
the water of a spring at Halicarnassus ; he who had drunk this
water became unmanned in the vice of lewdness.   Ennius—

Spoils of Salmacis, gained without sweat and spilt
blood.

[a] In *L.L.*, VI, 6, Varro shows that the words are spoken by
Ajax in Ennius' play of that name. Cf. V., 121–2; id.,
Enn., prooem., 1880, p. 14; R., 132, n.; 144. The light seen
by Ajax may have been Athena, who came to show him to
Ulysses (Soph., *Aj.*, 73 ff.).
[d] R., 132. His attribution is not certain.

ENNIUS

23

Festus, 530 fin. : 'Tullios' alii dixerunt esse silanos, alii rivos, alii vehementes proiectiones sanguinis arcuatim fluentis, quales sunt Tiburi in Aniene . . . —

Teucer?

. . . misso sanguine tepido tullii efflantes volant.

Cp. Paulus, ex F., 533.

ALCMEO

All the fragments of this play are words from the latter part of it spoken by Alcmaeon; they, together with Cic., *Ac., Pr.*, II, 28, 29, '*cum virginis fidem implorat*' (see p. 223), make it fairly certain that the action corresponded with the plot given by Hyginus, 73, which we can expand a little from Apollodorus' '*Library.*' Passages from both sources are

---

Hyginus, *Fab.*, 73 : Amphiaraus Oeclei et Hypermnestrae Thestii filiae filius augur qui sciret si ad Thebas oppugnatum isset se inde non rediturum, itaque celavit se conscia Eriphyle coniuge sua Talai filia. Adrastus autem ut eum investigaret monile aureum ex gemmis fecit et muneri dedit sorori suae Eriphylae, quae doni cupida coniugem prodidit. Amphiaraus Alcmeoni filio suo praecepit ut post suam mortem poenas a matre exsequeretur. Qui postquam apud Thebas terra est devoratus, Alcmeon memor patris praecepti Eriphylen matrem suam interfecit; quem postea furiae exagitarunt.

Apollodorus, *Bibl.*, III, 7, 5: χρήσαντος Ἀπόλλωνος αὐτῷ τὴν μητέρα ἀπέκτεινεν . . . Ἀλκμαίωνα δὲ μετῆλθεν ἐρινύς τοῦ μητροῴν φόνου καὶ μεμηνὼς πρῶτον μὲν εἰς Ἀρκαδίαν πρὸς Ὀικλέα παραγίνεται, ἐκεῖθεν δὲ εἰς Ψωφῖδα πρὸς Φηγέα.

---

[23] Ennius in Aiace Aiax misso *Fest. fortasse recte*

---

[a] So in Soph., *Aj.*, 1411–13. But the words may be from the speech of a messenger describing Ajax lying in his blood (R., 131); or the model may be Tecmessa's words in Soph., *Aj.*, 918–19.

TRAGEDIES

23

Teucer [a] *is about to carry away self-slain Ajax :*

Festus : Some have said that ' tullii ' are jets, others that they are streams, others that they are strong spurts of blood gushing in an arc, like the spurts in the waters of the Anio at Tibur . . . —

Teucer ?

with gush of warm blood fly the spouting jets.

ALCMAEON

included here. In at least one other case (*Alexander*, see pp. 234 ff.) Hyginus can be shown to have gone to Ennius for his plot.[b] The original may have been Theodectes' 'Αλκμαίων, but more probably it was Euripides' 'Αλκμαίων διὰ Ψωφῖδος (not his 'A. διὰ Κορίνθου).[c]

Hyginus : Amphiaraus the seer, son of Oecleus and Hypermnestra, a daughter of Thestius, because he knew that if he joined in the attack on Thebes he was destined not to return thence, went accordingly into hiding, his accomplice being his wife, Eriphyle, a daughter of Talaus. But Adrastus, that he might track him down, offered a golden necklace set with gems as a present to Eriphyle, who was his sister; and she, eager for the gift, betrayed her husband. Amphiaraus bade his son Alcmaeon exact retribution from his mother after his father's death. After the latter was engulfed by the earth [d] at Thebes, Alcmaeon, mindful of his father's bidding, slew Eriphyle his mother. Afterwards the Furies harassed him.

Apollodorus : Apollo spoke an oracle to him, and he slew his mother. . . . And Alcmaeon was pursued by the Fury of his mother's murder, and seized with madness he came first to Oecleus in Arcadia, and thence to Phegeus in Psophis.

---

[b] It must be noted, however, that in Hyginus the title of this plot is *Amphiaraus Eriphyle et Alcmeon.*

[c] V., CCI–CCII; R., 197 ff.

[d] Zeus opened a chasm to save him from death in battle.

ENNIUS

24

Nonius, 127, 13 : ' Iam diu ' pro olim. . . . Ennius Alcmeone—

Alcmeo

Factum est iam diu.

25–9

Cicero, *de Orat.*, III, 58, 218 : Aliud vocis genus iracundia sibi sumat . . . aliud metus, demissum et haesitans et abiectum—

Multis sum modis circumventus, morbo exilio atque
    inopia ;
tum pavor sapientiam omnem mi exanimato
    expectorat ;
mater terribilem minatur vitae cruciatum et necem,
quae nemo est tam firmo ingenio et tanta confidentia
quin refugiat timido sanguen atque exalbescat metu.

Cp. id., *de Fin.*, IV, 23, 62 (. . . ut enim Alcmeo . . .);
V, 11, 31; *et al.*

30–36

Cicero, *Ac. Pr.*, II, 28, 89: Quid ipse Alcmeo tuus, qui negat ' cor sibi cum oculis consentire ' (fr. 37) nonne ibidem incitato furore—

---

[27] mater Ribb. ultor *coni.* V   alter *cdd.*

---

[a] I take *quae* an ' accusative in apposition.' Cic., *de Fin.*,
IV, 23, 62 shows that the fragment comes from Ennius'
Alcmaeon. If *mater* is the right reading in line 27, then I
take it that what is meant is ἐρινὺς μητρῴου φόνου as
Apollodorus has it (see above).

230

TRAGEDIES

24

Scene: Psophis in Arcadia where Phegeus was king. Alcmaeon looks back on his deed:

Nonius: 'Iam diu' for once upon a time. . . . Ennius in *Alcmaeon*—

Alcmaeon

. . . 'Tis long since it was done.

25-9

He is haunted by the horrors of his deed and fate:

Cicero: Let wrath claim one kind of voice . . . fear claim another,—lowered, broken, and downcast—

Beset am I in sundry ways—by sickness, banishment and want; yes, and dread disheartens me wholly out of my wits, even to death; mother threatens my life with butchery and torture terrible, horrors at which *a* there is none so steadfast in spirit, none endowed with such firm trust that his blood would not flee him in his fright and turn white with fear.

30-36

Madness comes upon him: [b]

Cicero: Once more, your Alcmaeon himself, who denies that his mind sees alike with his eyes—(fr. 37) does he not shout at the very moment when his raving is quickened—

---

[b] From Cic., *Ac., Pr.,* II, 27, 88 we can be sure that Cicero quotes from Ennius' *Alcmaeon.*

ENNIUS

Alcmeo

Unde haec flamma oritur?

et illa deinceps—

Incede, incede, adsunt, me expetunt.

Quid cum virginis fidem implorat—

Fer mi auxilium, pestem abige a me, flammiferam
  hanc vim quae me excruciat.
Caerulea incinctae angui incedunt, circumstant cum
  ardentibus taedis.

Num dubitas quin sibi haec videre videatur? itemque
cetera—
    Intendit crinitus Apollo
arcum auratum laeva innixus;
Diana facem iacit a luna.

37

Cicero, *Ac. Pr.*, II, 17, 52 : Quod idem contigit insanis
ut . . . cum relaxentur sentiant atque illa dicant Alcmeonis—

sed mihi ne utiquam cor consentit cum oculorum
  aspectu.

Apollodor., *Bibl.*, III, 7, 5 : καθαρθεὶς δὲ ὑπ᾽ αὐτοῦ (Φηγέως)
᾽Αρσινόην γαμεῖ τὴν τούτου θυγατέρα.

---

³⁵⁻⁶ laeva . . . luna, *Anon. ap. Reid, Acad. Cic.*, p. 285
luna . . . laeva *Cic.*

---

^a He sees first one, then several fiery Furies. Cf. V.,
prooem., 1887–8, p. 7.
^b Sc. Arsinoe's. She is also called Alphesiboea.

232

TRAGEDIES

Alcmaeon

Whence rises this flame?

and then comes the famous outcry—

Come on, come on! Ah! They're here. 'Tis I
they seek! [a]

And again, when he implores a maiden's [b] protection—

Help me! Thrust away this plague from me, this
flaming blast which racks me to death! They come
on, girdled with snakes of colour blue, they stand
around me with blazing brands.

Surely you do not doubt that he thinks he sees all this?
Now for the rest—

Apollo never-shorn straining with his left hand
bends his gilded bow; Diana shoots her brand from
the moon.[c]

37

His madness begins to abate :

Cicero : The same thing happens to people who are mad,
so that . . . when the madness in them slackens, they feel
and say, in the famous words of Alcmaeon—

but in no wise sees my mind alike with the sight
of my eyes.

His marriage with Arsinoe ? :

Apollodorus : Purified by him (Phegeus) he married that
same king's daughter.[d]

---

[c] I assume that in the Latin *laeva* and *luna* have changed
places. Of course such a transposition might be intentional,
to express the madness of Alcmaeon.
[d] That this marriage was included in Ennius' play is
probable (R. 199).

ENNIUS

ALEXANDER

We can be certain that the ' fabula ' with the title ' *Alexander Paris* ' in Hyginus is an outline made directly from Ennius' play (see notes on lines 39, 52), which, as Varro, *L.L.*, VII, 82

Hyginus, *Fab.*, 91 : Priamus Laomedontis filius, cum complures liberos ex concubitu Hecubae, Cissei sive Dymantis filiae, uxor eius praegnans in quiete vidit se facem ardentem parere ex qua serpentes plurimos exisse. Id visum omnibus coniectoribus cum narratum esset, imperant quidquid pareret necaret ne id patriae exitio foret.

38–49

Cicero, *de Div.*, I, 21, 42 : Haec etiam si ficta sunt a poeta non absunt tamen a consuetudine somniorum. Sit sane etiam illud commenticium quo Priamus est conturbatus, quia—

Cassandra

Mater gravida parere se ardentem facem
visa est in somnis Hecuba, quo facto pater
rex ipse Priamus somnio mentis metu   40
perculsus, curis sumptus suspirantibus
exsacrificabat hostiis balantibus.
Tum coniecturam postulat pacem petens
ut se edoceret obsecrans Apollinem
quo sese vertant tantae sortes somnium.   45
Ibi ex oraclo voce divina edidit
Apollo puerum primus Priamo qui foret
postilla natus temperaret tollere ;
eum esse exitium Troiae, pestem Pergamo.

[38] quia mater *Cic. fortasse add.* mea   *trib. Enn. Alex.* Hartung

234

TRAGEDIES

ALEXANDER

shows, was based on Euripides' 'Αλέξανδρος. Thus we can give not only fragments, but also the plot of Ennius' tragedy.

Prologue spoken by Cassandra :

Hyginus : Priam, son of Laomedon, had several children in wedlock with Hecuba, daughter of Cisseus or Dymas; she, his queen, being with child, saw herself in sleep giving birth to a burning firebrand, out of which came many snakes. When this vision was told to all the interpreters, they enjoined that, whatever she gave birth to, she should slaughter it, so that it should not mean mischief to the country.

38-49

Cicero : Even if all this is fiction on the poet's part, still it is not different from the usual manner of dreams. I grant you by all means that the following also was some make-believe, by which Priamus was harassed, because

Cassandra

My mother Hecuba, heavy with child, in a dream
thought she gave birth to a burning brand [a]; on this
my father king Priam himself, daunted with fear of
mind at the dream, gripped by sighing cares, made
atoning sacrifice with bleating victims. Then in
search of peace he begged from Apollo an interpretation, beseeching him to teach him truly whither
dreams of such mighty omen would turn. Then from
his oracle Apollo with foretelling voice gave forth
that Priam should forbear to take up the first boy
who should be born to him after that ; that the boy
would be a ruin to Troy, a plague to Pergamum.

[a] The correspondence of Hyginus' words (quoted above) is close, so that the attribution of this fr. to Ennius' *Alexander* need not be doubted. V., 125; R. 82-3 (he suggests Venus as the speaker).

235

ENNIUS

Hyginus, *Fab.*, 91 : Postquam Hecuba peperit Alexandrum datur interficiendus, quem satellites misericordia exposuerunt. Eum pastores pro suo filio repertum expositum educarunt eumque Parim nominaverunt. Is cum ad puberem aetatem pervenisset, habuit taurum in deliciis.

50–51

Varro, *L.L.*, 6, 83 : ' Aures ' ab ' aveo ' quod his avemus discere semper, quod Ennius videtur ἔτυμον ostendere velle in Alexandro . . . —

Priamus

Iamdudum ab ludis animus atque aures avent avide exspectantes nuntium.

52

Hyginus, *Fab.*, 91 : Quo cum satellites missi a Priamo ut taurum aliquis adduceret venissent qui in athlo funebri quod ei fiebat poneretur, coeperunt Paridis taurum abducere. Qui persecutus est eos et inquisivit quo eum ducerent : illi indicant se eum ad Priamum adducere qui vicisset ludis funebribus Alexandri.

Festus, 460, 12 : ' Stolidus,' stultus . . . —

Nuntius

Hominem appellat: ' Quid lascivis, stolide ? ' Non intellegit.

[52] intellegit *cdd.*   intellegis V

***

[a] R., 84.
[b] The nature of the next fragment of Ennius (line 52) seems to me to suggest that Hyginus used a long speech of a

236

TRAGEDIES

Hyginus: After Hecuba had given birth to Alexander, he was given up to be killed; but the servants in pity exposed him. Some shepherds found him exposed and brought him up as a son of their own, and named him Paris. When he reached the years of manhood, he had a bull as a pet.

50–51

Meanwhile Priam had established yearly games in honour of Alexander, whom he thought to be dead. He awaits news of the games ? : [a]

Varro: 'Aures' is a term derived from 'aveo,' for with these we are on all occasions 'avid' to learn. Ennius, it seems, wishes to show in this a true root of speech in *Alexander* . . . —

Priamus

For long now my mind and my ears have been waiting eager with eagerness to hear the messenger from the games.

52

The messenger tells his strange story : [b]

Hyginus: When servants, sent by Priam in order that one of them might bring along a bull to be put up as a prize in the graveside sports which were held according to custom in his honour, came to his haunts, they began to lead away Paris' bull. He followed them up, and inquired whither they were leading it. They made known to him that they were leading it to Priam for the man who might be the winner at the graveside sports in honour of Alexander.

Paris protests against the seizure of his bull :

Festus: 'Stolidus' silly . . . —

Messenger

He calls to the fellow, 'What's this frolic, blockhead ? '

He understands not.

messenger in Ennius' play for that part of his fabula which I give here and below.

237

ENNIUS

53

Macrobius, *S.*, VI, 1, 61 : 'Multi praeterea quos fama obscura recondit ' (*Aen.*, V, 302). Ennius in Alexandro—

Nuntius

Multi alii adventant, paupertas quorum obscurat nomina.

Hyginus, *Fab.*, 91 : Ille amore incensus tauri sui descendit in certamen, et omnia vicit, fratres quoque suos superavit. Indignans Deiphobus gladium ad eum strinxit; at ille in aram Iovis Hercei insiluit.

Cp. Hygin., *Fab.*, 273.

54

Festus, 548, 19 : 'Taenias' Graecam vocem sic interpretatur Verrius ut dicat ornamentum esse laneum capitis honorati . . . —

Nuntius ?

volans de caelo cum corona et taeniis

55

Paulus, 561, 21 (12): 'Vitulans,' laetans gaudio, ut pastu vitulus. Ennius—

Nuntius ?

' is habet coronam vitulans victoria.'

[54-75] *trib. Enn. Alex.* Colonna
[55] *trib. Alex.* Hartung

---

[a] of Ζεὺς ἑρκεῖος, the most sacred spot in a house.
[b] R., 86 suggests Eros coming near the end of the play to settle all disagreements; V., 126 says either Victoria or Venus is meant (Varro, *L.L.*, V., 62). But the next fragment (if it is rightly placed) suggests that here also it is Victoria who appears.

TRAGEDIES

53

The messenger tells Priam about the spectators at the games:

Macrobius, on 'Many besides whose obscure fame hides away' in Virgil: Ennius in *Alexander*—

Messenger

And many others came, whose poverty
Rendered their names unknown.

Hyginus: He (Paris) inflamed with fondness for his bull, went down into the lists and won all the bouts; among those whom he worsted were his brothers. Deiphobus in high dudgeon unsheathed his sword against him; but he leapt to the altar of Jupiter [a] of the Courtyard.

54

The messenger tells of Paris' victories:

Festus: Verrius interprets the Greek word 'taenia' by saying that it is a woollen ornament for the head of a person of rank . . . —

Messenger?

With garlands and with ribbons wreathed, from
        heaven
As she [b] flew down,

55

he reports comments of the losers, possibly of Deiphobus,[c] a brother of Paris:

Paulus: 'Vitulans,' [d] rejoicing in gladness, like a 'vitulus,' (calf) at pasture. Ennius—

Messenger?

' He has the garland, trippling there in triumph.'

[c] Or of Hector—Serv., ad *Aen.*, V, 370.
[d] ' vitulans,' as a pun on vitulus, would be a very suitable term to apply to the strange cowman (cp. *lascivis* in line 52).

ENNIUS

56

Varro, *L.L.*, VII, 82 : Apud Ennium . . . —

Nuntius

quapropter Parim pastores nunc Alexandrum vocant.

Imitari dum voluit Euripidem et ponere ἔτυμον est lapsus, nam Euripides quod Graeca posuit ἔτυμα sunt aperta. . . .

Hyginus, *Fab.*,, 91 : Quod cum Cassandra vaticinaretur eum fratrem esse Priamus eum agnovit regiaque recepit.

57–72

Cicero, *de Div.*, I, 31, 66 : Inest igitur in amimis praesagitio extrinsecus iniecta atque inclusa divinitus. Ea si exarsit acrius, furor appellatur, cum a corpore animus abstractus divino instinctu concitatur—

Hecuba

Sed quid oculis rapere visa est derepente ardentibus ; aut ubi illa paullo ante sapiens virginali modestia ?

Cassandra

Mater optumarum multo mulier melior mulierum, missa sum superstitiosis hariolationibus,   60
neque me Apollo fatis fandis dementem invitam ciet.
Virgines vereor aequalis, patris mei meum factum
  pudet

[57] rabere . . . es Muret *fortasse recte* (*non prob.* V)
[58] <aut> L
[59] optumarum Porson optuma tu V optuma tum *vel sim cdd.*

TRAGEDIES

56

He tells how the strange victor is called Alexander :

Varro: In a passage Ennius we have . . . —

Messenger

Wherefore the shepherds now call this Paris
' Alexander.' [a]

While wishing to copy Euripides and give an example of true
roots of speech, Ennius made a slip, for, because Euripides
wrote Greek true roots of speech, *his* are obvious.

Hyginus : But when Cassandra prophesied that he was
her brother, Priam recognised him and gave him a place in
his palace.

57–72

*Cassandra, filled with prophetic frenzy, foresees the evil that
Alexander will bring upon Troy :*

Cicero : There is therefore in souls a power of boding put
in from outside and shut in by divine communication. If
it burns up very strongly, it is called raving, when the mind
withdrawn from the body is stirred up by divine inspiration—

Hecuba

But what did she seem on a sudden to catch sight
of with burning eyes? Yes, and where is she who
not long back was in her right mind, she of maidenly
modesty?

Cassandra

Mother, woman wiser far than the best of women,
driven was I by superstitious soothsayings, and
Apollo by foretellings told stirs me to madness—not
against my wish. Yet I shrink from maidens of my
own age, and my father, best of men, is ashamed of

---

[a] This was because he had kept off robbers from the cattle
and had been an averter (ἀλεξήσας Apollod.) for the herds and
so came to be called ' Alexander ' or ' Averter of men.'—
Apollod., *Bibl.*, III, 130 (12, 5, 5).

241

optumi viri.   Mea mater, tui me miseret, mei piget.
Optumam progeniem Priamo peperisti extra me ; hoc
    dolet.
Med obesse, illos prodesse, me obstare, illos obsequi !
. . . . Hecuba hoc dolet pudet piget !   66

O poema tenerum et moratum atque molle. Sed hoc
minus ad rem . . . —

Adest adest fax obvoluta sanguine atque incendio ;
multos annos latuit. Cives, ferte opem et restinguite !

Deus inclusus corpore humano, iam non Cassandra loquitur.—

Iamque mari magno classis cita
texitur, exitium examen rapit ;   70
adveniet fera velivolantibus
navibus complebit manus litora.

Tragoedias loqui videor et fabulas.

Cp. Cic., de Orat., 46, 155; de Div., II, 115, 112; ad Att.,
VIII, 11, 3; Non., 112, 22; 328, 28.

73–5

Cicero, de Div., I, 50, 114 : Furibunda mens videt ante
multo quae sint futura; quo de genere illa sunt—

Cassandra

Eheu videte ;
iudicavit inclitum iudicium inter deas tres aliquis,
quo iudicio Lacedaemonia mulier furiarum una
    adveniet.

[66] Hecuba h. d. p. p. add. ex Quintil., IX, 3, 77, trib. Enn.
Alex. R
[67] involuta Non., 112, 328

what I do. Mother mine, I pity you, I grieve for
me; to Priam you have born blessed bairns—apart
from me. That 's painful. Ah! That I should be
a hindrance, those brothers a help! That I should
stand against you, they stand with you! . . .
Hecuba,[a] That 's painful, pitiful, sorrowful!

What gentle soft poetry, fitting the characters! yet this is
but little to the point . . . —

'Tis here, the brand wreathed in blood and fire.
Many a year hath it lain hidden. Citizens! Bring ye
help and quench it!

By now not Cassandra, but a god, shut up in a human
body, is speaking.—

And now upon the mighty main a fast fleet is
built; it carries a crowd of deaths; a wild horde will
come and cover the shores with sail-fluttering ships.

It seems my talk is all tragedies and tales.

73-5

Cicero: The raving mind sees long beforehand things that
are to come; to this kind belongs the famous passage—

Cassandra

Ha! See ye! Someone hath judged a judgment widely known between three goddesses; and
out of this judgment will come to us a woman of
Lacedaemon, one of the Furies.

[a] Added from Quintilian, IX, 3, 77: 'ὁμοιοτέλευτον, when
two or more sentences have the same ending . . . it comes
about even with single words—Hecuba . . .' (V., 128;
R., 90-91; Incert. Fab., X). The attribution is conjectural
but probable.

ENNIUS

76-9

Macrobius, *S.*, VI, 2, 18 : ' O lux Dardaniae, spes o fidissima Teucrum,' et reliqua. (*Aen.*, II, 281). Ennius in Alexandro—

O lux Troiae, germane Hector,
quid ita cum tuo lacerato corpore
miser es aut qui te sic respectantibus
tractavere nobis?

80-81

Macrobius, *S.*, VI, 2, 25 : ' Cum fatilis equus *e. q. s.* (Aen. VI, 515).' Ennius in Alexandro—

Nam maximo saltu superavit gravidus armatis equus
qui suo partu ardua perdat Pergama.

Cp. id., *S.*, III, 13, 13.

82

Festus, 270, 16 : <' Putum . . . pro puro dixisse> antiquos <. . . Ennius>—in Alexandro . . . —

a medio purus putus

Cp. Gell., VII, 5, 10 (' purum putum.' . . . Ennii tragoedia quae inscribitur Alexander).

ANDROMACHA sive ANDROMACHA AECHMALOTIS

One thing certain about the plot [b] of this play is, that although its origin was Euripides (Varro, *L.L.*, VII, 82), it was not taken from that poet's Ἀνδρομάχη, since the action falls sooner after the capture of Troy. Some of the material is to be found in his Ἑκάβη and in his Τρῳάδες. The model

---

[77-8] cum . . . es V., *Rh. Mus.*, *XIV*, 567; *H.*, *XII*, 400, *XV*, 262 *s.*   miser aut *Macrob.*
[80] superavit *cdd.*   superabit Voss *prob.* V
[82] a medio W   * * amidio *cd.*

244

TRAGEDIES

76-9

Macrobius, on ' O light of Dardania, O surest hope of the Trojans ' in Virgil : And so on.   Ennius in *Alexander*—

O my own brother, Hector, you light of Troy, how is it you are thus made pitiful with your torn body ? And who are they who have thus dragged you before our very eyes ?

80-81

Macrobius, on ' when the fatal horse ' *etc.* . . . . in Virgil : Ennius in *Alexander*—

For with mighty leap the horse heavy with armed men has passed over, that he may by his brood bring bane to high-builded Pergama.

82

Unplaced fragment :

Festus says :   ' Putus '   for ' purus ' : . . . Ennius [a] in *Alexander*—

pure and clean from the middle

ANDROMACHE or ANDROMACHE CAPTIVE

may have been a play unknown to us (V., CCIII title : —'Ανδρ. αἰχμάλωτος or αἰχμαλωτίς); or Ennius may have ' contamin- ated ' several plays.   Quotations are given under two titles, but come from the same play.

---

[a] Ennius as in *Alexander*, as Gell., VII, 10 shows.
[b] V., CCII–CCIII; R., 135 ff.

ENNIUS

83-4

Eur., *Troad.*, 19 *s.*, μένουσι δὲ | πρύμνηθεν οὖρον, ὡς δεκα-
σπόρω χρόνω | ἀλόχους τε καὶ τέκν' εἰσίδωσιν . . . Cp. 1263–
1264.

Nonius, 401, 37: 'Summum,' gloriosum, laudabile. . . .
Ennius Andromache Aechmaloto—

Neptunus ?

annos multos longinque ab domo
bellum gerentes summum summa industria.

85

Eur., *Troad.*, 75 *s.*; *Iphig. Taur.*, 1379, 1394 ?

Macrobius, *S.*, VI, 6, 10: 'despiciens mare velivolum '
(*Aen.*, I, 224); Ennius . . . in Andromache—

Chorus ?

Rapit ex alto naves velivolas

86-7

Nonius, 515, 24: ' Rarenter ' . . . —

Nuntius ?

sed quasi aut ferrum aut lapis
durat, rarenter gemitum conatu trahens,

---

[86] aut f. a. *Lu. al.*, f. a. *G.*
[87] conatu trahens Lips, Fruter   conatur trabem *cdd.*
pentametrum trochaicum constit. V

TRAGEDIES

83-4

The Greeks prepare to return from Troy :

Nonius : ' Summum,' glorious, praiseworthy. . . . Ennius
in *Andromache Captive*—

Neptune ? [a]

Fighting for many a year and far from home
With glorious labour in a glorious war.

85

A storm keeps them back :

Macrobius, on ' looking down on the sail-fluttering sea '
in Virgil : Ennius . . . in *Andromache*—

Chorus ? [b]

From the high sea it sweeps sail-fluttering ships

86-7

*Grief of Hecuba (?) [c] when baby Astyanax is washed for
burial :*

Nonius : ' Rarenter ' . . . —

Messenger ?

But like unto stiff strength of iron or stone
She strained to draw sobs fitfully,

[a] Cf. Eur., *Tr.*, 19 (Poseidon speaks). Contrast R., 139.
[b] Perhaps of sailors or warriors ? Or the speaker may be
Cassandra. R., 140.
[c] V., 134 and CCIII thinks the fr. describes Andromache;
but she was not present.

ENNIUS

88-9

Eur., *Troad.*, 1133 *s.*, 1156 *s.*, 1193, 1220-1223, 1228 *s.*

Nonius, 504, 18 : ' Lavere ' etiam inde manavit . . . —

Nuntius ?

nam ubi introducta est puerumque ut laverent
   locant
in clipeo,

90

Nonius, 292, 7 : ' Exanclare ' etiam significat perpeti . . . —

Andromacha

Quantis cum aerumnis illum exanclavi diem!

91-2

Eur., *Androm.*, 399-400 : ἥτις σφαγὰς μὲν Ἕκτορος τροχηλά-
τους | κατεῖδον. Cp. 107-108, 8-9.

Cicero, *Tusc. Disp.*, 1, 44, 105 : Hic ulciscitur, ut quidem
sibi videtur; at illa sicut acerbissimam rem maeret—

Vidi videre quod me passa aegerrume
Hectorem curru quadriiugo raptarier.

Quem Hectorem, aut quam diu ille erit Hector? Melius
Accius. . . .

93

Eur., *Androm.*, 9-10 : ἐσεῖδον, παῖδά θ' ὀντίκτω πόσει |
ῥιφθέντα πύργων . . .

Varro, *L. L.*, V., 70 : Dicebant ut quaestorem praetorem sic
Hectorem Nestorem. Ennius ait—

Hectoris natum de moero iactarier

[93] de moero iactarier S   e L   de Troiano muro iactari
cdd.

---

[a] Hector's shield. V., 131 rightly I think takes the fr.
 as referring to Hecuba; but cf. R., 138.

TRAGEDIES

88-9

Nonius: 'Lavere' is another form derived from this verb . . . —

Messenger ?

for when she was led in, and they put the boy into the shield [a] that they might wash him,

90

Andromache begins to tell of her grief and loneliness :

Nonius: 'Exanclare' means also to bear to the end . . . —

Andromache

In what dread hardships did I on that day
Serve a full term!

91-2

Cicero: Achilles avenges himself, or so he thinks at least. But she grieves as it were over a most bitter woe—

I saw what I could hardly bear to see—
Hector by four-horsed chariot dragged along.

Hector Indeed! Or how long will he be Hector? Accius is better. . . .

93

Varro: People used to pronounce 'Hectorem' and 'Nestorem' like 'quaestorem' and 'praetorem.' Thus Ennius writes—

. . . Hector's child hurled from the wall [b]

[b] I follow Scaliger; V. (130–1 and CCIII, n.) thinks someone describes the intention of the Achaeans to hurl Astyanax down; he cites Eur., *Tr.*, 725, ῥῖψαι δὲ πύργων δεῖν σφε Τρωικῶν ἄπο (told by Talthybius), and compares Serv. auct., in *Aen.*, III, 489.

ENNIUS

94–100

Eur., *Tr.*, 587, 590 (cp. *Androm.*, 523–5): μόλοις ὦ πόσις μοι
. . . σᾶς δάμαρτος ἄλκαρ.

Cicero, *Tusc. Disp.*, III, 19, 44 : Quaerendum igitur quem
ad modum aegritudine privemus eum qui ita dicat (*Thyest.*,
363–5). . . . Ecce tibi ex altera parte ab eodem poeta—

ex opibus summis opis egens Hector tuae

Huic subvenire debemus; quaerit enim auxilium—

Quid petam praesidi aut exequar, quove nunc
auxilio exili aut fuga freta sim?
arce et urbe orba sum.   Quo accidam, quo applicem,
cui nec arae patriae domi stant, fractae et disiectae
    iacent,
fana flamma deflagrata, tosti alti stant parietes
deformati atque abiete crispa. . . .

101–8

Eur., *Androm.*, 394: ὦ τάλαιν' ἐμὴ πατρίς . . . 400 . . .
κατεῖδον, οἰκτρῶς τ' Ἴλιον πυρούμενον.

Cicero, *l.c.* : Scitis quae sequantur, et illa in primis—

O pater o patria o Priami domus!
saeptum altisono cardine templum ;
vidi ego te, adstante ope barbarica,
tectis caelatis laqueatis
auro ebore instructam regifice.   105

  O poetam egregium, quamquam ab his cantoribus Euphor-
ionis contemnitur. Sentit omnia repentina et necopinata
esse graviora. Exaggeratis igitur regiis opibus quae vide-
bantur sempiternae fore, quid adiungit ?—

---

103 adstante *Cic.*, *Tusc. Disp.*, *I.*, 35, 85   adstantem
Tusc. Disp., *III*, 19, 44, *prob.* V

TRAGEDIES

94–100

Cicero : We must inquire therefore in what manner we are to free from his distress him who thus speaks (*see Thyest.*, 363-5). . . . Here you have something on the other side from the same poet—

Once mighty in resources, now resource
Needing from you, my Hector

Her we ought to go and help, for she seeks our aid—

What succour should I seek and follow? What help in retreat or what escape could I rely on now? Bereft am I of citadel and city; where can I kneel, where can I appeal—I for whom at home no country's altars stand—they lie broken, torn apart; the holy places are burnt down by fire, the high walls stand scorched and misshapen, and with fir-wood crinkled up . . .

101–8

Cicero continues : You all know what follows, and especially these famous lines—

O father, O fatherland, O house of Priam, you temple close-fixed by high-creaking hinge, I have seen you, with barbaric throng [a] at hand, furnished in kingly fashion with gold and ivory, with ceilings chiselled and fretted.

Truly an excellent poet, in spite of the fact that he is despised by your warblers of Euphorion's [b] melodies. He feels that all that is sudden and unlooked for comes the heavier. Well then, following on that heightened account of royal riches which seemed to be everlasting, what does he say ?—

---

[a] Cp. Virgil, *Aen.*, VIII, 685 : *ope barbarica* in this sense.
[b] A grammarian and poet of Chalcis in Euboea, born about 275 B.C.

ENNIUS

Haec omnia vidi inflammari,
Priamo vi vitam evitari,
Iovis aram sanguine turpari.

Praeclarum carmen; est enim et rebus et verbis et modis lugubre.

Cp. Cic., *de Orat.*, III, 26, 102; 47, 183; Rufin., ap. *G.L.*, VI, 569, 13 K; Cic., *de Orat.*, 27, 93 (. . . dixit Ennius ' arce e. q. s.'); III, 58, 217; 26, 102; *pro Ses.*, 57, 121; Serv., ad *Aen.*, II, 241 (101 versus Ennianus) *al.*

109

Eur., *Tr.*, 658 *s.* ? (663, 667–8); cp. 38.

Varro, *L.L.*, VII, 82 : Apud Ennium—

Andromachae nomen qui indidit recte ei indidit. . . .

. . . Ille ait ideo nomen additum Andromachae quod ἀνδρὶ μάχεται. Hoc Enni quis potest intellegere versum significare . . .?

110

Eur., *Hec.*, 116 ff. : πολλῆς δ' ἔριδος συνέπαισε κλύδων . . .

Nonius, 76, 1 : ' Augificat,' auget . . . —

Quid fit? Seditio tabetne an numeros augificat suos?

111

Festus, 424, 27 : ' Summussi ' dicebantur <mur-muratores> . . . —

di⟨cere . . . . summussi . . . .⟩

---

a This is Vahlen's interpretation; cf. V., CCIII, 134. Ennius followed Euripides, but there is no extant parallel in Greek.

TRAGEDIES

All this I saw with flame devoured, Priam's living force by force unlifed, Jupiter's altar with blood befouled.

A glorious monody indeed; mournful it is in subject, words, and rhythms.

109

Someone refers to Andromache's refusal to think of marrying again after the death of Hector : [a]

Varro : In a passage of Ennius we have—

He who ' Man-fighter ' named her, named her well.

. . . Euripides says that Andromache was given this name because ἀνδρὶ μάχεται (she fights against man). Who can be aware that this is what is meant by Ennius' line. . .?

110

Discord caused by the demand made by the shade of Achilles for Polyxena's blood ? :

Nonius : ' Augificat,' increases . . . —

What's happening? Wanes riot, or swells its numbers? [b]

111

Festus : ' Summussi,' a term once used for murmurers . . . —

the mumblers . . . say . . . [c]

[b] R., 139. He suggests that Neoptolemus or Nestor inquires from Ulysses or a herald how goes the voting in the camp.

[c] The passage in Festus is mutilated, but *summussi* (cp. *mussare*) implies discontent. Therefore I have put the fragment here.

ENNIUS

112

Eur., *Hec.*, 299-300 : ΟΔ. 'Εκάβη διδάσκου, μηδὲ τῷ θυμου-μένῳ | τὸν εὖ λέγοντα δυσμενῆ ποιοῦ φρενί.

Nonius, 505, 11 : 'Sonunt' etiam inde manavit . . .—

nam neque irati neque blandi quicquam sincere sonunt.

113-16

Eur., *Hec.*, 367-8, 435 (*Polyx. loqu.*), 414; *Androm.*, 414, 503 (*Androm. loqu.*).

Cicero, *Tusc. Disp.*, I, 21, 48 : Quae est anus tam delira quae timeat ista quae vos videlicet si physica non didicissetis, timeretis ?—

Acherusia templa alta Orci
salvete infera
pallida leti nubila tenebris
loca !

ANDROMEDA

Model : Euripides' play of the same name. The following summary is based on Hygin., *Fab.*, 64, with Apollodor., *Bibl.*, II, 4, 3.

Because Cassiope (Cassiepeia), wife of King Cepheus of Ethiopia, claimed that her beauty (or that of her daughter

117-18

Aristoph., *Thesm.*, 1065 *s.* (ex Eurip.) : ὦ νὺξ ἱερὰ ὡς μακρὸν ἵππευμα διώκεις ἀστεροειδέα νῶτα διφρεύουσ' αἰθέρος ἱρᾶς τοῦ σεμνοτάτου δι' 'Ολύμπου (Eur., *Andromeda*, fr. 114 N.)

Varro, *L.L.*, 5, 19 : Omnino magis puto a chao choum et hinc caelum . . . itaque Andromeda nocti—

---

[114] salvete infera *add. ex* Varr., *L.L.*, *VII*, 6

---

[a] R., 139. But V., 134, CCIII makes Andromache the speaker.

254

TRAGEDIES

112

Ulysses addresses Andromache ? :

Nonius : ' Sonunt ' is another form derived from this word . . . —

for neither the angry nor the courteous utter anything without guile.*a*

113–16

Polyzena *b* *is about to die :*

Cicero : What old crone is there so crazy as to fear what you, I would have you know, would fear if you had not learnt nature's laws ?—

Hail, you tall temples of Orcus and Acheron below, you wan places of death, clouded in everlasting ebon darkness !

ANDROMEDA

Andromeda ?) was greater than the beauty of Nereus' daughters, Neptune sent floods and a sea-monster to plague the land. Relief could come only if Andromeda were given to the beast to be devoured. So she was chained to a seaside rock.

117–18

Opening of the play. *At the mercy of the monster, Andromeda longs for daybreak :*

Varro : I am altogether more of the belief that from ' chaos ' comes ' chous ' *c* and from this comes ' caelum ' . . . and thus Andromeda says to the night—

---

b R., 139: or Andromache, when death threatens her together with Molottus (her son by Neoptolemus)—V., 135 ' *salvete infera* ' are supplied from Varro, *L.L.*, VII, 6, who shows that the words come from this play of Ennius.

c On this word see line 557 of the *Annals.*

ENNIUS

Andromeda

⟨Sacra nox⟩ quae cava caeli
signitenentibus conficis bigis,

Cp. Cael. Aurel., *Morb. Chron.*, I, 4, 50 (. . . velut tragicus
poeta sacram noctem, h. e. magnam appellavit).

119

Festus, 570, 28 : ' Urvat ' Ennius in Andromeda significat
circumdat, ab eo sulco qui fit in urbe condenda urvo
aratri . . . —

Nuntius

Circum sese urvat ad pedes a terra quadringentos
caput,

120

Nonius, 169, 25 : ' Scabres ' pro ' scabra es ' . . . —

scrupeo investita saxo, atque ostreis squamae
scabrent.

Cp. Fest. 494, 13.

121

Nonius, 20, 18 : ' Corporare ' est interficere et quasi
corpus solum sine anima relinquere . . . —

Corpus contemplatur unde corporaret vulnere.

---

117 Sacra nox *suppl.* Buecheler
119 ad *fortasse secludendum*
120 *si suppleas* fera, *fortasse coniungendum est hoc fr. cum*
119   squamae scabrent Mercier   squamis s. Onions
quam excrabrent *cdd.*

256

TRAGEDIES

Andromeda

O hallowed night, you who pass over all the hollow
of the heaven with your star-spangled chariot and
team of two,

119

Perseus fights the beast ; it turns its head :

Festus : ' Urvat.' By this, Ennius in *Andromeda* means
draws round; it is derived from the making of a furrow with
the ' urvum ' (ploughtail) when a city is being founded . . . —

Messenger

        Ploughs [a] the head around itself
A line well nigh four hundred feet from earth,

120

The monster's skin :

Nonius : ' Scabres ' for ' scabra es.' . . . —

Enwrapped with scraggy stones; its scales were
    scurfed
With mussels.[b]

121

Perseus seeks a vital spot :

Nonius : ' Corporare ' means to kill, and as it were to leave
the body only, without life . . . —

He scanned the carcass seeking whence he might
Make it indeed a carcass with a wound.

[a] This seems to me to be the meaning; V., 137 thinks the
killing of the beast is described.
[b] Possibly this line describes the beast when turned to
stone by Perseus, and so should be put later. Nonius gives
this Ennian example with *scabrent* before his example from
Pacuvius with *scabres*.

ENNIUS

122

Nonius, 165, 8 : ' Reciproca ' . . . —

    . . . rursus prorsus reciprocat fluctus feram.

Cp. Non., 385, 1.

123-4

Nonius, 183, 17 : ' Visceratim ' . . . —

    alia fluctus differt dissupat
visceratim membra, maria salsa spumant sanguine.

125

Priscianus, ap. *G.L.*, II, 293, 10 *s.* : ' His natabus filiabus.
. . .' Et ' filiis ' tamen in eodem genere dictum est . . . —

Andromeda

Filiis propter te obiecta sum innocens Nerei.

126

Festus, 346, 14 : ' Quaesere ' ponitur ab antiquis pro
quaerere . . . —

Andromeda

liberum quaesendum causa familiae matrem tuae.

Cp. Paulus, 347, 3.

Eur., *Andromeda*, 133 N : ἄγου δέ μ' ὦ ξεῖν' εἴτε πρόσπολον
θέλεις εἴτ' ἄλοχον εἴτε δμωΐδα.

---

[122] fluctus feram *cdd.* 385   fructus feram *cdd.* 165
fluctus fera Bergk   fluctus, feram . . . *coni.* V
[123] *fortasse scribend.* alio
[125] *fortasse* - ⌣ - ⌣ filiis *e. q. s.* | Nerei

---

  [a] Or according to the interpretation of R., 168-9 (he reads
fera, after Bergk)—' in and out the beast belched the billows.'
But Nonius has *feram*—in two passages; yet the copy used
by him may have had *feram* wrongly. V., 136 takes *reciprocat*
as intransitive and *feram* as dependent on a verb not quoted
by Non. or Varro.

TRAGEDIES

122

The beast is harassed by wounds and waves :
Nonius : ' Reciproca ' . . . —
A wave drove back the beast and back again.[a]

123–4

Nonius : ' Visceratim ' . . . —
A wave shattered and scattered other limbs
Piecemeal; the salt seas spewed a bloody spray.

125

Andromeda will go with Perseus to Argos [b]: she addresses her mother :
Priscianus : Dat. and abl. : ' natabus filiabus ' : . . . But in the same gender the form ' filiis ' was also used . . . —

Andromeda

For your sake was I, who had done no hurt,
Cast out,[c] for Nereus' daughters.

126

Andromeda declares [d] to Perseus her willingness to be the mother of children by him :
Festus : ' Quaesere ' is used by archaic writers for ' quaerere '
. . . —

Andromeda

Mother of thy household, for the sake
Of getting children.

[b] Hygin., *Fab.*, 64, Eratosth., *Catast.*, 17, p. 118 R.
[c] Either Ennius joined *obiecta* with *filiis*, by implication from the fact that A. was *obiecta ferae*, or else *filiis* is ' to satisfy the daughters,' *obiecta* going with *ferae* not quoted (V., 138).
[d] Or, wishes Perseus to confirm his own desire to have children by her—V., 137.

ENNIUS

127

Varro, *L.L.*, VII, 16: Ennius—

Perseus

Ut tibi Titanis Trivia dederit stirpem liberum.

Titanis Trivia Diana est. . . .

ATHAMAS

Athamas, a Thessalian king, in the belief that his wife Ino was dead, married Themisto, only to learn that Ino was still alive on Parnassus, whither she had come on account of the Bacchic celebrations there. He took her back without telling her or Themisto who Ino was; but Themisto, knowing that Ino was alive somewhere, planned to murder Ino's two sons, unknowingly choosing Ino herself to help her. Ino was to

128–32

Charisius, ap. *G.L.*, I, 241, 3 ff. K: 'euhoe' Maro VII. . . . Ennius in Athamante—

Nuntius ?

His erat in ore Bromius, his Bacchus pater;
illis Lyaeus vitis inventor sacrae.
Tum pariter Euhan euhoe euhoe Euhium
ignotus iuvenum coetus alterna vice
inibat alacris Bacchico insultans modo.

---

[130] <euhoe euhoe> Fabricius

---

[a] V., 137–8. But some (R., 156) would add this fr. to Ennius' *Medea*.

TRAGEDIES

127

Perseus assures her that she shall have her wish :

Varro : Ennius has—

Perseus

As Trivia, Titan's daughter, will grant you off
spring of children.[a]

Titan's daughter Trivia is Diana. . . .

ATHAMAS

dress her sons in black, and Themisto's two children in white;
but she did the reverse, and Themisto having killed her own
children by mistake, killed herself also. Ennius' model is
not known, but it may have been Euripides' Ἰνώ (R., 204–5;
Hygin., *Fab.*, 4). In the single surviving fragment it seems
that a messenger tells of the Bacchic crowd in which Ino was
apparently found.

128–32

Charisius : Maro in Book VII (389) has ' euhoe ' . . .
Ennius in *Athamas*—

Messenger ?

Some ' God of Noise ' were mouthing, others ' Father
Bacchus,' others again ' The Loosener,
Discoverer of the all-hallowed vine ' !
Then group by group the gathering of girls,
Beyond our ken,[b] in concert striking up,
Sang ' Euhan euhoe euhoe Euhium,'
Upleaping in a brisk and Bacchic measure.

---

[b] V., 139 seeing no sense in *ignotus*, suggests *unosus*, i.e.
universus (cf. V., *H.*, XII, 399 ff.). But might not *ignotus*
be right and mean ' distant,' as it does in Tib., I, 3, 3 ? We
might even take the word as meaning ' having no knowledge,'
sc. *iuvenum*, of young men.

ENNIUS

CRESPHONTES

The original of this play is unknown, but the only other play of this name is the lost Κρησφόντης of Euripides (V., CCIV and *prooem*. 1888–9, 17 ff., from whom I differ materially; R., 186 ff. is not convincing). Polyphontes of Messenia slew Cresphontes (who in the division of the Peloponnese by the Heracleidae had gained Messenia by a trick), took his kingdom and married his widow Merope; a surviving son of Cresphontes

133

Nonius, 471, 2 : 'Sortirent' pro sortirentur. . . . Ennius Cresphonte—

. . . an inter sese sortiunt urbem atque agros?

134–5

Macrobius, *S.*, VI, 2, 21 : 'Nec te tua funera mater | produxi pressive oculos aut vulnera lavi' (*Aen.*, IX, 484). Ennius in Cresphonte—

Merope

Neque terram iniieere, neque cruenta convestire
    corpora
mihi licuit, neque miserae lavere lacrimae salsum
    sanguinem.

136

Festus, 346, 1 : 'Quaesere' . . . pro quaerere . . . —

Ducit me uxorem liberorum sibi quaesendum gratia.

---

[133] sese Voss.   se *cdd.*
[134-5] corpora mihi Bothe   mihi corpora *Macrob.*

TRAGEDIES

CRESPHONTES

with the same name Cresphontes (thus Euripides; Telephontes
or Aegyptus in other versions) was brought up in Aetolia;
and wishing to avenge his father's death, came to Polyphontes' court, told him that he had killed the survivor,
and demanded the blood-money promised by Polyphontes.
Cresphontes killed Polyphontes at a sacrifice and became
master of the kingdom.

133

Someone questions Merope about her father's history ? :

Nonius: ' Sortirent ' for ' sortirentur.' . . . Ennius in
Cresphontes—

Or did they share among themselves by lot
The city and its territory?

134-5

Merope bewails the fate of Cresphontes and his sons :

Macrobius, on Virgil's ' Nor did I your mother lead you,
yes, your dead body, to burial, or close your eyes, or cleanse
yours wounds ' : Ennius in Cresphontes—

Merope

Nor did they let me shroud their blood-stained bodies.
Nor throw earth over them; nor could a tear
Of grief bathe salt their blood.

136

Merope describes her forced marriage with Polyphontes [a] :

Festus: ' Quaesere ' . . . for ' quaerere ' . . .—

He took me to wife for to get children of his own.

[a] Or perhaps she alludes to her earlier marriage with the
now dead Cresphontes.—R., 189.

ENNIUS

137

Festus, 370, 21 : ' Redhostire,' referre gratiam . . .

Audi atque auditis hostimentum adiungito.

138

Gellius, VII, 16, 10 : . . . Ennius in Cresphonte—

Ego meae quom vitae parcam letum inimico deprecer ?

139

Nonius, 144, 12 : ' Nitidant,' abluunt, dictum a nitore . . . —

† opie † Eam secum advocant, eunt ad fontem, nitidant corpora.

ERECHTHEUS

Lycurgus, κατὰ Λεωκράτους, 98–99 : φασὶ γὰρ Εὔμολπον τὸν Ποσειδῶνος καὶ Χιόνης μετὰ Θρᾳκῶν ἐλθεῖν τῆς χώρας ταύτης ἀμφισβητοῦντα, τυχεῖν δὲ κατ' ἐκείνους τοὺς χρόνους βασιλεύοντα Ἐρεχθέα γυναῖκα ἔχοντα Πραξιθέαν τὴν Κηφισοῦ θυγατέρα. Μεγάλου δὲ στρατοπέδου μέλλοντος αὐτοῖς εἰσβάλλειν εἰς τὴν χώραν, εἰς Δελφοὺς ἰὼν ἠρώτα τὸν θεόν, τί ποιῶν ἂν νίκην λάβοι παρὰ τῶν πολεμίων. Χρήσαντος δὲ αὐτῷ τοῦ θεοῦ τὴν θυγατέρα εἰ θύσειε πρὸ τοῦ συμβάλλειν τὼ στρατοπέδω κρατήσειν τῶν πολεμίων, ὁ δὲ τῷ θεῷ πειθόμενος τοῦτ' ἔπραξε καὶ τοὺς ἐπιστρατευομένους ἐκ τῆς χώρας ἐξέβαλε.

---

[137] audi S   audis cd.
[138] cum meae Gell.
[139] opie eam cdd. opie corrupt. ex Meropen quasi gloss. seclud. W Meropam secum abducunt Mr.   Pelopiae eam s. avocant coni. Linds.

TRAGEDIES

137

Polyphontes entertained the younger Cresphontes (? Tele-phontes) until his story might be proved true :

Festus : ' Redhostire,' to render thanks . . . —

Hear and make requital follow on what you hear.

138

Cresphontes (?) the younger is determined to kill Polyphontes :

Gellius on ' deprecor ' : . . . Ennius in *Cresphontes*—

What, though I be merciful to my own life, must I forbear death to a foe ?

139

The sacrifice at which Cresphontes (?) killed Polyphontes :

Nonius : ' Nitidant,' they wash clean, a term derived from ' nitor.' . . .—

They call to her [a] to come with them, they go to the spring ; and they cleanse their bodies.

ERECHTHEUS

There can be no doubt that Ennius followed Euripides' Ἐρεχθεύς, of which Lycurgus gives us the plot as follows :

Lycurgus : For they say that Eumolpus, a son of Poseidon and Chione, came with a body of Thracians to lay claim to this land of Attica, and that the king at that time happened to be Erechtheus, who had Praxithea, Cephisus' daughter, as his wife. He, when the great army was about to make an invasion into their land, went to Delphi, and asked the god what he should do to gain the victory over his foes. When the god had answered him that he would get the mastery over his foes if he were to sacrifice his daughter before the two armies came to blows, he obediently did this, and expelled the attacking host from the land.

---

[a] I take it that *opie* in Non. is a corruption of a gloss on *eam* sc. Meropen.

ENNIUS

140-41

Eur., *Erechth.*, 362, 14-15 N: ἔπειτα τέκνα τοῦδ' ἕκατι τίκτο-
μεν | ὡς θεῶν τε βωμοὺς πατρίδα τε ῥυώμεθα.

Servius auctus, ad *Aen.*, II, 62 : ' Occumbere morti ' novae
locutionis figura et penitus remota. Ennius—

ut nos nostri liberi
defendant pro nostra vita morti occumbant obviam.

142-3

Nonius, 290, 15 : ' Deprecor ' . . . propulso . . .—

Praxithea

cui nunc aerumna mea libertatem paro,
quibus servitutem mea miseria deprecor.

Cp. Gellius, VII, 16, 9.

Cf. Eur., *Erechth*, 362, 50-3 N : χρῆσθ' ὦ πολῖται τοῖς ἐμοῖς
λοχεύμασιν | σῴζεσθε, νικᾶτ', ἀντὶ γὰρ ψυχῆς μιᾶς | οὐκ ἔσθ' ὅπως
νῦν τήνδ' ἐγὼ οὐ σώσω πόλιν.

144

Festus, 160, 3 : <' Neminis ' . . . Enni>us Erechtheo—

Lapideo sunt corde multi quos non miseret neminis.

Cp. Paul., ex Fest., 161, fin.

145-6

Macrob., *S.*, VI, 4, 6 : ' Tum ferreus hastis | horret ager '
(*Aen.*, XI, 601). ' Horret ' mire se habet; sed et Ennius . . .
in Erechtheo—

arma arrigunt,
horrescunt tela.

[140-1] nos nostri . . . nostra Ribb.   vos vestri . . . vostra
cdd. (vos nostri *cd. Cass.*)
[142] cui *cdd. Non.* qui *cdd. Gell. fortasse recte*   quis Mercier
266

TRAGEDIES

140-41

*Erechtheus and Praxithea debate as to whether they shall
sacrifice their daughter :*

Servius (supplemented), on ' occumbere morti ' in Virgil :
This is a figure of speech of a strange kind and quite out
of the way.   Ennius—

>   . . . that our children shield us,
> And fall in death's way for our own lives' sake.[a]

142-3

Nonius : ' Deprecor,' . . . I thrust away . . . —

Praxithea

For which [b] I now through my distress do win
Freedom, for whom I pray God to forbear
Slavery through my woe.

144

Festus : ' Neminis ' . . . Ennius in *Erechtheus*—

>   Stony-hearted are there many,
> Who have no pity, no, for nobody.

145-6

The battle :

Macrobius, quoting Virgil : ' Then the steely earth bristled
with spears.'   ' Bristles ' is here a strange expression.   But
Ennius also . . . in *Erechtheus*—

Weapons they raised ; then bristled up the spears.

---

[a] R., 185.
[b] *cui* would refer to *patria*, understood, *quibus* to *cives*.
But if we read *qui* (Gell.), the speaker must be Erechtheus.

ENNIUS

EUMENIDES

Aesch., *Eumen.*, 276-9 : OP. ἐγὼ διδαχθεὶς ἐν κακοῖς ἐπίσταμαι | πολλοὺς καθαρμούς, καὶ λέγειν ὅπου δίκη | σιγᾶν θ' ὁμοίως. ἐν δὲ τῷδε πράγματι | φωνεῖν ἐτάχθην πρὸσ σοφοῦ διδασκάλου.

147-8

Nonius, 474, 34 : 'Opino' pro opinor. . . . Ennius Eumenidibus—

Orestes

Tacere opino esse optumum et pro viribus
sapere atque fabulari tute noveris.

149

Aesch., *Eumen.*, 463-467 : [OP.] ἔκτεινα τὴν τεκοῦσαν, οὐκ ἀρνήσομαι, | ἀντικτόνοις ποιναῖσι φιλτάτου πατρός. | καὶ τῶνδε κοινῇ Λοξίας ἐπαίτιος, | ἄλγη προφωνῶν ἀντίκεντρα καρδίᾳ | εἰ μή τι τῶνδ' ἔρξαιμι τοὺς ἐπαιτίους·

Nonius, 292, 18 : ' Exanclare,' effundere . . . —

Orestes

nisi patrem materno sanguine exanclando ulciscerem.

150-53

Aesch., *Eumen.*, 614-618 : 'ΑΠ. λέξω πρὸς ὑμᾶς τόνδ' Ἀθηναίας μέγαν | θεσμὸν δικαίως, μάντις ὢν δ' οὐ ψεύσομαι. | οὐ πώποτ' εἶπον μαντικοῖσιν ἐν θρόνοις | οὐκ ἀνδρὸς οὐ γυναικὸς οὐ πόλεως πέρι | ὃ μὴ κελεῦσαι Ζεὺς 'Ολυμπίων πατήρ.

Cicero, *de Orat.*, I, 45, 199 : Quid est enim praeclarius quam honoribus et rei publicae muneribus perfunctum senem posse suo iure dicere idem quod apud Ennium dicat ille Pythius Apollo, se esse eum—

TRAGEDIES

EUMENIDES

This play was modelled, if freely, upon Εὐμενίδες of Aeschylus, and thus the order of the fragments is in most cases certain.

147–8

Orestes before the temple of Athene Polias at Athens replies to the attack of pursuers :

Nonius : ' Opino ' for ' opinor.' . . . Ennius in *Eumenides*

Orestes

Best silence keep, I think; and you will know
How to be wise with all your powers, how talk
When talking 's safe.[a]

149

Orestes tells his case to Minerva :
Nonius : ' Exanclare,' to pour out . . . —

Orestes

Unless by spilling out my mother's blood
My father I avenged.

150–53

Apollo defends Orestes [b] at the Areopagus :

Cicero : For what is more honourable than that an old man who has discharged offices and duties of state should be able to say, with justice on his side, what your Pythian Apollo says in Ennius, that he is the one—

---

[a] *noveris* may be corrupt.
[b] If V., 142 is right in comparing Aesch., *Eumen.*, 177 ff., then Ennius described the oracle at greater length than Aeschylus did. But R., 147–8 would compare the fr. with Aesch., *Eumen.*, 64 ff. where Apollo is giving evidence.

ENNIUS

Apollo

unde sibi populi et reges consilium expetunt
suarum rerum incerti quos ego ope mea
ex incertis certos compotesque consili
dimitto, ut ne res temere tractent turbidas.

Est enim sine dubio domus iuris consulti totius oraculum
civitatis.

154

Aesch., *Eumen.*, 657 : ΑΠ. καὶ τοῦτο λέξω καὶ μάθ' ὡς ὀρθῶς
ἐρῶ.

Nonius, 505, 16 : ' Expedibo' pro expediam . . . —

Apollo

– ᴗ id ego aecum ac ius fecisse expedibo atque
eloquar.

155

Aesch., *Eumen.*, 742-3 : ΑΘ. ἀνὴρ ὅδ' ἐκπέφευγεν αἵματος
δίκην· | ἴσον γάρ ἐστι τἀρίθμημα τῶν πάλων.

Nonius, 306, 26 : ' Facessere' significat recedere . . . —

Minerva

Edico vicisse Oresten—Vos ab hoc facessite.

[150] expetant *Cic.*   *trib. Eumen.* S
[154] ius atque aecum V
[155] edico Mr.   ego dico Auratus   dico ego S   dico
cdd.

---

[a] Ennius has altered the sense of the Greek.

TRAGEDIES

Apollo

from whom for themselves peoples and kings seek
counsel when they are unsure about their affairs,
whom I in my helpfulness send away partakers of
my counsel and sure instead of unsure so that they
may not treat rashly things that are troublous.

For without doubt the lawyer's house is the whole city's
oracle.

154

*Apollo expounds the precedence of a father's rights over a
mother's :*

Nonius : ' Expedibo ' for expediam . . . —

Apollo

That he was fair and just in doing it
I will unfold and tell.[a]

155

Acquittal of Orestes : [b]

Nonius : ' Facessere ' means to withdraw . . . —

Minerva

I proclaim Orestes has prevailed—
Get you away from there.

[b] Ennius has made the scene more vivid by making Minerva
interrupt her announcement with an order to ' stand back.'
If in line 156 we read *quid d. ? quam p. ?* these words are
spoken by Orestes—Aesch., *Eum.,* 744 : πῶς ἀγὼν κριθήσεται;

ENNIUS

156

Varro, *L.L.*, VII, 19: Enni—

- ∪ - Areopagitae quia dedere aequam pilam.

Areopagitae ab Areopago : is locus Athenis.

157-61

Aesch., *Eumen.*, 902 *s.* : XO. τί οὖν μ' ἄνωγας τῆδ' ἐφυμνῆσαι χθονί; | ΑΘ. ὁποῖα νίκης μὴ κακῆς ἐπίσκοπα, | καὶ ταῦτα γῆθεν ἔκ τε ποντίας δρόσου | ἐξ οὐρανοῦ τε κἀνέμων ἀήματα | εὐηλίως πνεόντ' ἐπιστείχειν χθόνα· | καρπόν τε γαίας καὶ βοτῶν ἐπίρρυτον | ἀστοῖσιν εὐθενοῦντα μὴ κάμνειν χρόνῳ, | καὶ τῶν βροτείων σπερμάτων σωτηρίαν. Cp. 938 *s.*

Cicero, *Tusc. Disp.*, I, 28, 69: Hic autem ubi habitamus non intermittit suo tempore—

Minerva

Caelum nitescere, arbores frondescere,
vites laetificae pampinis pubescere,
rami bacarum ubertate incurvescere,
segetes largiri fruges, florere omnia,
fontes scatere, herbis prata convestirier.

Cp. Cic., *de Orat.*, 38, 154; Non., 122, 17.

HECTORIS LYTRA

This play offers several problems which cannot be discussed here (R., 188 ff., V., CCV–CCVII), but the following points have a degree of probability which justifies their mention : —
(*a*) that Hyginus, in Plot 106, entitled *The Ransom of Hector*, carelessly sketched Ennius' play, so that we may assume that Ennius covered events from the sulking of Achilles (and its cause, told in a prologue ?) to the delivery of the dead Hector to Priam and the burial of Hector; (*b*) that Aeschylus wrote

---

[156] quia Ribb.   quid *cdd.* (qui *Vind.*)   aequam Ribb. quam *cdd.*   pilam Ribb.   palam (parum) L   tubam *coni.* V   pudam *cdd.*   *trib. Eumen.* S

TRAGEDIES

156

Varro: Of Ennius we have—

Because the judges of the hill of Ares
Have cast an equal ballot.

'Areopagitae' is from Areopagus; this is a place at Athens.

157–61

Minerva enjoins the Furies to bless Attica :

Cicero: But here where we dwell there cease not each in
its season—

Minerva

The sky to shine, the trees to put forth leaves,
Joy-making vines to sprout with fresh young shoots,
Their branches to bend down with grapes abundant,
The growing cornfields to bestow their harvests,
All things to bloom, the springs to bubble, meads
To be o'erclothed with grasses.

THE RANSOM OF HECTOR

a trilogy (' *The Myrmidons*,' ' *The Daughters of Nereus*,'
' *The Phrygians* ' or ' *The Ransom of Hector* ') which extended
from the sending out of Patroclus by Achilles to the delivery
of the dead Hector; (c) that Ennius pressed these three plays
into one, shaped it to fit the Homeric story, added further
details from Homer, and gave it the title of the third play of
the trilogy. (R., 124, 126–7; V., *l.c.*); (d) that the main
action begins with the events of the *Iliad*, Bk. XI.

---

¹⁵⁷ <suo non intermittat tempore> caelum Hermann
qui trib. Enn. Eumenid.

ENNIUS

Hyginus, *Fab.*, 106 : Agamemnon Briseidam, Brisei sacerdotis filiam ex Mysia captivam, propter formae dignitatem quam Achilles ceperat, ab Achille abduxit eo tempore quo Chryseida Chrysi sacerdoti Apollinis Zminthei reddidit. . . . Quam ob iram Achilles in proelium non prodibat sed cithara in tabernaculo se exercebat. Quod cum Argivi ab Hectore fugarentur, . . .

Il., I, 182 *s.*, IX, 185 *s.*

162

Nonius, 489, 29 : ' Tumulti.' Ennius Hectoris Lytris—

Agamemno

Quid hoc hic clamoris, quid tumulti est ? nomen qui

usurpat meum ?

163

Il., XI, 1 *s.*; 10 *s.* ?

Nonius, 490, 6 : ' Strepiti ' pro strepitus . . . —

Quid in castris strepitist ?

164-5

XI, 56 *s.*

Nonius, 355, 4 : ' Occupare ' est proprie praevenire . . . —

Nuntius

Hector vei summa armatos educit foras

castrisque castra ultro iam conferre occupat.

---

[162] *numeros constit.* Bothe
[164] haectorci *cdd.* (-ii *Lu* 1)   vi Mercier
[165] conferre Voss.   inferre Mercier   *alii alia*

TRAGEDIES

Hyginus : Agamemnon, at the time when he gave back Chryseis to Chryses the priest of Apollo Zmintheus, took away from Achilles Briseis daughter of the priest Briseus, whom Achilles had brought from Mysia on account of her comely beauty. . . . Through this wrath of his, Achilles would not go out to battle, but sat in his tent amusing himself with a lute.[a] And when the Argives were in full flight under Hector's attacks. . . .

162

Agamemnon [b] hears an uproar as he prepares for battle :

Nonius : 'Tumulti.' Ennius in *The Ransom of Hector*

Agamemnon

What is this shouting here? What means this
    hubbub?
Who is it makes free with my name?

163

Nonius : 'Strepiti' for 'strepitus' . . . —

What means this clatter in the camp?

164–5

He is told of an attack made by Hector and Polydamas :

Nonius : 'Occupare' means properly to outstrip . . . —

Messenger

Hector leads out his armed men in full force,
And pitting camp 'gainst camp e'en now outstrips us.

---

[a] The words *Agamemnon . . . reddidit* may be a summary of a prologue; while the imperfects *prodibat, exercebat* suggest to me a scene where Achilles is in his tent; possibly, therefore, the play began with a prologue spoken by Achilles. After *reddidit* something was dropped out unless we alter *iram* to *rem*.

[b] So V., 144.

ENNIUS

166

XI, 459 *s.*

Diomedes, ap. *G.L.*, I, 387, 10 K. : 'Nomus' pro eo quod est novimus . . . Ennius in Lustris—

Menelaus

Nos quiescere aequum est? Nomus ambo Ulixem.

167

XI, 658 *s.* (*Nestor loqu.*); cp. 825–6; XVI, 23 *s.*

Schol. Gronov., ad Cic., *pro Rosc. Amer.*, 32, 89 ('quis ibi non est vulneratus ferro Brugio') : 'Ferro Brugio.' In Ennio haec fabula inducitur Achilles quo tempore propter Briseidam cum Graecis pugnare noluit, quo etiam tempore Hector classem eorum incendit. In hac pugna Ulixes vulneratus inducitur et fugiens ad Achillem venit. Cum interrogaretur ab Aiace cur fugisset, ille ut celaret dedecus . . . —

Ulixes

Quis ibi non est vulneratus ferro Brugio?

168

Servius auctus, ad *Aen.*, III, 241 : 'Foedare,' cruentare. Ennius—

ferro foedati iacent.

[166] Ulixem *cdd.* Ulixeum Buecheler, Fleckeisen *qui constit. senar.*

[167] *trib Hect. Lytr.* Ribb.; *Achill.* Bergk

---

a At least he is the speaker in the parallel passage in the *Iliad*.

TRAGEDIES

166

Ulysses, hard pressed by the Trojans, shouted thrice for help;
Menelaus ᵃ hears and addresses Ajax :

Diomedes the grammarian: ' Nomus ' for the form
' novimus ' . . . Ennius in *The Ransom*—

Menelaus

Is it right for us to be sluggards ?   We both know
Ulysses' voice.

167

Ulysses wounded talks with Ajax :

A scholiast, on ' Who was not wounded, etc.' (*see below*) in
Cicero : This incident is staged in Ennius at the time
when Achilles,ᵇ on account of Briseis, chose not to join with
the Greeks in fighting; representing the time too when
Hector set fire to their fleet.   In this fight Ulysses is brought
on to the stage wounded, and in the course of his flight he
comes to Achilles.   When he is asked ᶜ by Ajax why he has
fled, he, in order to cloak his dishonour, says—

Ulysses

Who was not wounded there by Brugian ᵈ blade?

168

Servius (supplemented), on ' foedare ' in Virgil : To stain
with blood.   Ennius— ᵉ

From sword-thrusts fouled with blood they lie.

ᵇ The reading is not certain; if *Achillis* is right, then
the fr. might belong to Ennius' *Achilles.* But cf. V., 147.
  ᶜ Possibly before he met Achilles.
  ᵈ On ' Brugian ' for ' Phrygian ' see fr. 183.
  ᵉ Attribution to this play is admittedly uncertain, but it
fits well with *Il.*, XI, 658–9.

ENNIUS

169–81

XI, 581 s., XVI, 27–8; XI, 842 s.

Cicero, *Tusc. Disp.*, II, 16, 38: Quin etiam videmus ex
acie efferri saepe saucios et quidem rudem illum et inexer-
citatum quamvis levi ictu ploratus turpissimos edere. At
vero ille exercitatus et vetus ob eamque rem fortior medicum
modo requirens a quo obligetur—

Eurypylus

O Patricoles, ad vos adveniens auxilium et vestras
    manus
peto priusquam oppeto malam pestem mandatam
    hostili manu—
neque sanguis ullo potis est pacto profluens con-
    sistere—
si qui sapientia magis vestra mors devitari potest;
namque Aesculapi liberorum saucii opplent porticus,
non potest accedi.
. . . . . .

Patricoles

Certe Eurypylus hic quidem est; hominem exercitum!

Ubi tantum luctus continuatur, vide quam non flebiliter
respondeat, rationem etiam adferat cur aequo animo sibi
ferendum sit—

Eurypylus

           qui alteri exitium parat,   76
cum scire oportet sibi paratum pestem ut participet
    parem.

[169] Patricoles inquit *Cic.*
[169–81] *trib. Hect. Lytr.* Ribb.; *Achill.* Bergk (*et olim* Ribb.)

278

TRAGEDIES

169–81

Eurypylus wounded by Alexander goes for help to Patroclus, and tells him news of the fighting : [a]

Cicero : Why, we even see many a time wounded soldiers carried away from the battle-line, and moreover your raw and untrained recruit groaning most shamefully even at a very light thrust; but your seasoned veteran, and all the braver for being that, asking for a surgeon merely, and no more, to bind him up, says he—

Eurypylus

O Patroclus, I come to all of you, and ask to meet help of your hands before I meet death and destruction bestowed by the hand of an enemy—ah no! the flowing blood can in no wise be staunched—to see if death can be evaded by your wisdom above others'; for the colonnades of Aesculapius' sons are filled full with wounded—none can go near . . . —

Patroclus

Surely it is Eurypylus, no other. A troubled toiler he !

While this great distress goes on continuously,[b] see how he makes reply without weeping, and even tells why and wherefore it must be borne with a calm mind—

Eurypylus

He who plans death for his foe should know well that a like death is planned for himself to share in.

---

[a] The attribution to this play is not certain, but it is most probable. As will be seen on reference to the relevant passages of the *Iliad*, Ennius dealt freely with his original, as he often did; the order of the dialogue is changed; this may be due to Aeschylus. After *exercitum* (line 175) Cicero omits several lines which Ennius gave to Patroclus.

[b] Here probably Cicero skips a few lines.

279

ENNIUS

Abducet Patricoles credo ut conlocet in cubili ut vulnus obliget; si quidem homo esset, sed nihil vidi minus. Quaerit enim quid actum sit—

Patricoles

Eloquere eloquere, res Argivum proelio ut se sustinet.

Eurypylus

Non potest ecfari tantum dictis quantum factis suppetit.

Patricoles

Laberis; quiesce

Eurypylus

Et volnus alliga.   180

Etiam si Eurypylus posset, non posset Aesopus—

Eurypylus

Ubi fortuna Hectoris nostram acrem aciem incli-natam⟨dedit⟩,

et cetera explicat in dolore.

Cp. Cic., *de Orat.*, 46, 155.

182

XII, 49 *s.*; XIII, 123 (*Nept. loqu.*); XII, 35 *s.*; 127 *s. al.*

Festus, 234, 19 : ' Obsidionem ' potius dicendum esse quam obsidium adiuvat nos testimonio suo Ennius . . . item alio loco—

Hector qui haud cessat obsidionem obducere,

---

¹⁸⁰ laberis Bentley   laboris *cdd. prob.* V   laberis . . . adliga *trib. Enn.* Bentley   quiesce igitur *Cic.*
¹⁸¹ ⟨dedit⟩ *suppl.* Ribb. *prob.* V

ᵃ As he does in Homer; not so in Ennius.

TRAGEDIES

Patroclus will lead him away, I suppose, that he may lay him
down on a bed and bind up his wound [a]—at least he would
if he were a man. But I never saw anything less like one.
For he asks what has happened—

Patroclus

Speak out, speak out—
Come, tell me how the fortune of the Argives
Maintains itself in battle.

Eurypylus

I cannot tell you of it all in words
To fit the deeds that have been done.

Patroclus

You sink;

Lie quiet.

Eurypylus

And tightly bind the wound.

Even if Eurypylus could do this, Aesopus [b] could not—

Eurypylus

When Hector's fortune
Made our brave battle-line give way,
and while [c] still in pain he recounts the rest.

182

Further news of Hector's attack on the ramparts :

Festus : In thinking that the term 'obsidio' should be
used rather than obsidium, we are supported by the testimony
of Ennius . . . and in another place— [d]

Hector who 's not slow in drawing round a blockade,

[b] Who clearly acted the part of Eurypylus in Cicero's
time. He could not have borne real pain as Eurypylus did.
[c] *i.e.* he does not wait to be bound up first.
[d] The attribution to this play is probably right.

ENNIUS

183

XII, 445 *s.*; XIII, 90 *s.*; 123–4 (*Nept. loqu.*).

Cicero, *de Orat.*, 48, 160 : ' Burrum ' semper Ennius, numquam ' Pyrrhum '—

> vi patefecerunt Bruges . . .

non ' Phryges '; ipsius antiqui declarant libri.

XII–XIII; XVI, 40 *s.*, 276 *s.*, 490–4.

Hyginus, *Fab.* 106 : Quod cum Argivi ab Hectore fugarentur, Achilles obiurgatus a Patroclo arma sua ei tradidit
quibus ille Troianos fugavit aestimantes Achillem esse,
Sarpedonemque Iovis et Europae filium occidit.

184–6

XVI, 145 *s.*

Nonius, 407, 24 : ' Tenacia ' est perseverantia et
duritia . . . —

Patricoles

> . . . duc et quadrupedum iugo; invitum doma
> infrena et iunge valida ⟨equorum . . . robora⟩
> . . . . . .   quorum tenacia infrenari minis,

187–8

XVI, 233 *s.*

Nonius, 111, 7 : ' Fuam,' sim vel fiam . . . —

Achilles ?

> at ego omnipotens
> ted exposco ut hoc consilium Achivis auxilio fuat.

Non. 407 Hectoris Lystris
[184] *fortasse* Xanthum et Balium duces (*Il.* XVI, 149)
[185-6] valida quorum tenacia infrenari minis *Non.; locus
desperatus ;* cf. *Linds.*, *ed. Non.* < equorum . . . robora >
supplevi et fragm. septenar. constituo
[187] ego o. < Iuppiter Ribb.
[188] auxilio Voss. auxilii *cdd.*

TRAGEDIES

183

News that Hector has broken open the gates :

Cicero : ' Burrus ' is the form always used by Ennius, never ' Pyrrhus '—

The Brugians by force have broken open . . .

Not ' Phrygians.' The old manuscripts of the author himself make this quite clear.

Hyginus : And when the Argives were in full flight under Hector's attacks, Achilles, scolded by Patroclus, gave up to him his weapons, with which Patroclus put to flight the Trojans, who believed him to be Achilles, and slew Sarpedon son of Jupiter and Europa.

184–6

Patroclus orders Automedon to harness the horses Xanthos and Balios for battle :

Nonius : ' Tenacia ' means perseverance and sturdiness . . . —

Patroclus

And lead them in a gallopers' collar; break, bridle, and harness the horses' brawny strength though they wish it not; . . . whose stubbornness . . . to be bridled with threats,[a]

187–8

Achilles is about to send Patroclus (in Achilles' armour) into battle :

Nonius : ' Fuam,' the same as ' sim ' or ' fiam ' . . . —

Achilles ?

But yet I beg of thee, almighty god, That this plan be of help to the Achivi.[b]

[a] This fr. is corrupt. I suggest that *valida equorum . . . quorum* caused a copyist to omit all between *valida* and *quorum.*

[b] V., CCVI thinks Patroclus speaks after the prayers of Achilles in *Il.*, XVI, 233 ff.

ENNIUS

Hyginus, *Fab.*, 106 : Postea ipse Patroclus ab Hectore interficitur armaque ei sunt detracta.

189

XVI, 818 *s.*

? XVI, 777; cp. XVII, 685 *s.*; XVIII, 2.

Diomedes, ap. *G.L.*, I, 345, 3 K : ' Halare ' et ' halitare.' Ennius in Lytris—

Antilochus

sublime iter quadrupedantes flammam halitantes

190

XVI, 856 (vel XXIII, 74; vel XXII, 482).

Nonius, 222, 25 : ' Specus ' genere masculino . . . —

inferum vastos specus

XVIII, 112 *s.*; XIX, 35, 65, 140 *s.*; 245–265; XVIII, 614 *s.*

Hyginus, *Fab.*, 106 : Patroclo omisso Achilles cum Agamemnone redit in gratiam Briseidamque ei reddidit. Tum contra Hectorem cum inermis prodisset, Thetis mater a Vulcano arma ei impetravit quae Nereides per mare attulerunt.

191

XVIII, 188, 192; Aesch., *Myrmid.*, fr. 140.

Nonius, 469, 25 : ' Cunctant ' pro ' cunctantur ' . . . —

Achilles

qui cupiant dare arma Achilli ut ipsei cunctent

[191] ipsei Linds.   ipse *cdd.*

---

[a] The context cannot be fixed with certainty. R., 126 refers this to Achilles' horses, but probably the sun is meant. I take it that the speaker is Antilochus, who describes its rising on the day on which Patroclus was killed.

TRAGEDIES

Hyginus : Later on Patroclus himself was killed by Hector, and the weapons were taken from his corpse.

189

the sun :

Diomedes the grammarian : ' Halare ' and ' halitare.' Ennius in *The Ransom*—

Antilochus

Gallopers puffing fire . . . their lofty course on high [a]

190

Antilochus? tells Achilles of the death of Patroclus? :

Nonius : ' Specus ' in the masculine gender . . . —

Wide roomy caverns of the realms below

Hyginus : After Patroclus was lost, Achilles was reconciled to Agamemnon and gave Briseis back to him. Then when he had gone forth against Hector unarmed, Thetis his mother obtained weapons for him from Vulcan, and these the Nereids brought to him across the sea.[b]

191

Achilles wonders where he can get new weapons :

Nonius : ' Cunctant ' for ' cunctantur ' . . . —

Achilles

Who might desire their weapons to surrender
To Achilles so that they themselves become
As dawdlers [c]

[b] In this Ennius followed Aeschylus, not Homer.

[c] V., *prooem.*, 1888-9, 5 ff. R., 123 thinks the speaker is one of the Myrmidons who dare not give up their arms and so seem to be cowardly; if this is right, then the model here was Aeschylus, not Homer.

ENNIUS

192

XIX, 364 *s.*; 372, 387.

Festus, 370, 21 : ' Redhostire ' referre gratiam . . . —

Achilles

Quae mea comminus machaera atque hasta hostibitis
manu,

193

XXII, 131 *s.*; 395 *s.*

Hyginus, *Fab.*, 106 : Quibus armis ille Hectorem occidit
astrictumque ad currum traxit circa muros Troianorum.

Nonius, 510, 32 : ' Saeviter ' pro saeve . . . (511, 11)—

Nuntius

Saeviter fortunam ferro cernunt de victoria.

194–5

XX, 441 *s.*, *al.*

Nonius, 518, 3 : ' Derepente ' . . . —

Nuntius

Ecce autem caligo oborta est, omnem prospectum
abstulit ;
derepente contulit sese in pedes.

---

192 hostibitis manu V   hostibit (hostivit) e manu S
hostibis *coni.* Linds.   hospius manu *cd.*
193 fortunam Ribb.   fortuna *cdd.*
194-5 *post* abstulit *lacun. stat.* Ribb.   abstulit. <Con-
stitit : tum> derepente *coni.* V

---

^a Thus R., 125 (V., 148 prefers to make Achilles speak these
words when giving his old weapons to Patroclus).

286

192

Achilles, possessed of new armour ª through Thetis, addresses his sword and his spear :

Festus : ' Redhostire,' to return a favour . . . —

Achilles

O you my sword and you my spear—you weapons
Who in close fight some favours ᵇ will return
From my own hand,

193

A messenger tells of the exploits of Achilles :

Hyginus : With these weapons Achilles slew Hector and then dragged him, tied to a chariot, round the walls of Troy.

Nonius : ' Saeviter ' for ' saeve ' . . . —

Messenger

Right savagely they settle with the sword
Their chance of victory.

194-5

Nonius : ' Derepente ' . . . —

Messenger

But see, a mist rose over him, and hid him from all view ; on a sudden he gathered himself upon his feet.ᶜ

ᵇ There may be a pun : hostire, ' to requite,' hostire, ' to strike ' (Paul., ex Fest., 102) ; as it were ' bury the hatchet.'
ᶜ This may refer to the death of Patroclus (*Il.*, XVI, 790 ff.), but it more probably tells of Achilles' attack on Hector (*Il.*, XX, 441) ; less probably of Ajax (XVII, 644) or of Achilles' fight with Aeneas (XX, 321, 341).

196

XX, 455 *s.*, 493 *s.*

Nonius, 504, 30 : ' Sonit ' pro sonat . . . —

Nuntius

Aes sonit franguntur hastae terra sudat sanguine.

197

XXI, 15–16; 218–220, 234 *s.*

Nonius, 467, 31 : ' Vagas ' pro vagaris . . . —

Nuntius

Constitit credo Scamander, arbores vento vacant.

XXII, 416 *s.*; XXIV, 136 *s.*, 440 *s.*

Hyginus, *Fab.*, 106 : Quem sepeliendum cum patri nollet dare, Priamus Iovis iussu duce Mercurio in castra Danaorum venit.

198

XXIV, 488 ff. (486 Achill. alloqu.), 503, 680.

Nonius, 472, 21 : ' Commiserescimus ' . . . —

Priamus

Per vos et vostrum imperium et fidem, Myrmidonum
vigiles, conmiserescite !

199

XXIV, 483; 518.

Varro, *L.L.*, VII, 12 : ' Tueri ' duo significat, unum ab aspectu . . . unde est Enni illud—

---

[197] cerno Mr.   vacant Colonna *prob.* V   vagant *cdd.*

288

TRAGEDIES

196

Nonius: ' Sonit ' for ' sonat ' . . . —

Messenger

Bronze clatters, spears are snapped, Earth sweats
with blood.

197

Nonius: ' Vagas ' for ' vagaris ' . . . —

Messenger

Stood still, it seems, Scamander, and the trees
Of wind were emptied.[a]

Hyginus: When Achilles was not willing to give Hector
to his father to be buried, Priam at the command of Jupiter
entered, under Mercury's guidance, the camp of the Danai.

198

*Priam implores the pity of the Myrmidons who are keeping
watch at Achilles' tent :*

Nonius: ' Commiserescimus ' . . . —

Priam

You watchmen Myrmidons, I pray you all
Have pity, by your sacred trust and duties!

199

Varro: ' Tueor ' has two meanings, one from the act of
looking. . . . Whence comes that phrase of Ennius—

---

[a] *vacant* is right; Nonius has blundered. In any case,
Ennius adds a detail not in Homer. Cp. p. 394. Whether
credo is right I am not sure.

ENNIUS

Achilles

tueor te senex? Pro Iuppiter!

Cp. Donat., in Ter., *Adelph.*, I, 2, 31.

Hyginus, *Fab.*, 106: (Priamus) . . . filii corpus auro repensum accepit; quem sepulturae tradidit.

200–1

XXIV, 596 *s.*, 786 *s.*

Nonius, 399, 8 : ' Spernere ' rursum segregare . . . —

Priamus

Melius est virtute ius, nam saepe virtutem mali nanciscuntur; ius atque aecum se a malis spernit procul.

Cf. Aesch., fr. ~~259 N.~~ 266 N. (!!)

HECUBA

Eurip., *Hec.*, 3: Πολύδωρος Ἑκάβης παῖς γεγὼς τῆς Κισσέως.

Servius, ad *Aen.*, VII, 320: Cisseis. Regina Hecuba secundum Euripidem quem Ennius Pacuvius et Vergilius sequuntur.

202

Hec., 26–27 : καὶ κτανὼν ἐς οἶδμ' ἁλὸς | μετῆχ' ἵν' αὐτὸς χρυσὸν ἐν δόμοις ἔχῃ | (vel 28 ἄλλοτ' ἐν πόντου σάλῳ, cp. 701 πόντου νιν ἐξήνεγκε πελάγιος κλύδων).

Nonius, 223, 24 : ' Salum ' neutri generis . . . Masculini Ennius Hecuba—

Polydori Umbra

undantem salum

202 <in> u. s. <demisit> *coni.* V

---

a R., 129–130; V., 151. Perhaps Ennius follows Aeschylus closely here, as R. thinks.

TRAGEDIES

Achilles

Is it you I see, O aged man? Ah, heavens!

Hyginus: Priam took back the dead body of his son for a ransom of gold, and committed him to burial.

200–1

Priam, with Polyxena, Andromache and others discussed long with Achilles ; the following words are spoken probably by Priam : [a]

Nonius: 'Spernere' again means to set apart . . . —

Priam

A better thing than bravery is justice;
For bravery the wicked oft attain;
But justice and the fair deed thrust themselves
Far from the wicked.

HECUBA

Model : Euripides' Ἑκάβη.

The ghost of Polydorus speaks the prologue :

Servius, on Cisseis (daughter of Cisseus) in Virgil: Queen Hecuba, according to Euripides, who is followed by Ennius, Pacuvius, and Virgil.

202

He tells of the misdeed of Polymestor :

Nonius: 'Salum' is of the neuter gender. . . . Ennius has it in the masculine in *Hecuba*—

Ghost of Polydorus

the surging sea [b]

Or, 'billowing brine': but *salum* or *salus* (σάλος), 'open sea,' is apparently not connected with *sal*.

ENNIUS

203

Hec., 68 : ὦ στεροπὰ Διός, ὦ σκοτία νύξ.

Varro, *L.L.*, VII, 6 : In caelo templum dicitur ut in Hecuba—

Hecuba

O magna templa caelitum conmixta stellis splendidis,

204-5

Hec., 166–169: ὦ κάκ' ἐνεγκοῦσαι | Τρωάδες, ὦ κάκ' ἐνεγκοῦσαι | πήματ' ἀπολέσατ' ὠλέσατ'· οὐκέτι μοι βίος | ἀγαστὸς ἐν φάει.

Nonius, 474, 32 : ' Miserete ' . . . —

Hecuba

Miserete anuis
date ferrum qui me anima privem.

206-8

Gellius, XI, 4, 1 : Euripidis versus sunt in Hecuba (293–5), verbis sententia brevitate insignes inlustresque. Hecuba est ad Ulixen dicens.

> τόδ' ἀξίωμα κἂν κακῶς λέγῃς τὸ σὸν
> πείσει· λόγος γὰρ ἔκ τ' ἀδοξούντων ἰὼν
> κἀκ τῶν δοκούντων αὐτὸς οὐ ταὐτὸν σθένει.

Hos versus Quintus Ennius cum eam tragoediam verteret non sane incommode aemulatus est. Versus totidem Enniani hi sunt—

Hecuba

Haec tu etsi perverse dices facile Achivos flexeris,
namque opulenti quom loquuntur pariter atque
  ignobiles,
eadem dicta eademque oratio aequa non aeque valet.

---

[204] anuis S   manu Mr.   manus *cdd.* prob. V
Gell., XI, 4: κακὸς Gell.   κακῶς *cdd. Eur.*   νικᾷ *Gell.*
πείθει *vel* πείσει *cdd. Eur.*
[207] namque opulenti cum S   nam opulenti cum *cdd.*

292

TRAGEDIES

203

Hecuba is about to tell her dream :

Varro: Men speak of a ' templum ' in the sky, as in *Hecuba*—

Hecuba

You mighty precincts of all those who dwell
In heaven, commingled with the shining stars,

204–5

Hecuba has heard news that Polyxena is to be slain :

Nonius: ' Miserete ' . . . —

Hecuba

Pity me an aged woman; give me a sword that I
may reave me of life.

206–8

Hecuba tries to persuade Ulysses to make the Achivi change their minds :

Gellius: There are lines of Euripides in *Hecuba* remarkable and famous for their diction, thought and terseness. Hecuba is in the course of a speech addressed to Ulysses.[a] ' But your influence, though you speak on the wrong side, will prevail. For speech issuing from those held in no repute, though it be the same as speech from the reputable, has not the same power.' These lines Quintus Ennius, when he was translating that tragedy, rivalled in no unsuitable way, I can assure you. The lines of Ennius are the same in number, as follows—

Hecuba

Although this message you will give is crooked,
An easy task you'll find to sway the Achivi;
For when the well-to-do and lowly born
Speak in like purport, yet their words and speech,
Though equal and alike, have not like weight.

[a] I give the quotation as our texts of Euripides have it. See opposite.

ENNIUS

209

Hcc., 438 : ? οἵ 'γώ· προλείπω· λύεται δέ μου μέλη. | ὦ
θύγατερ, ἅψαι μητρός, ἔκτεινον χέρα, | δός· μὴ λίπῃς μ' ἄπαιδ'·
ἀπωλόμην, φίλαι.

Nonius, 224, 6 : ‘Sanguis masculino genere . . . neutro
Ennius Hecuba—

Hecuba

Heu me miseram interii; pergunt lavere sanguen
sanguine !

Cp. Non., 466, 27; 504, 6.

210-11

Hcc., 497-8 :

> φεῦ φεῦ γέρων μέν εἰμ', ὅμως δέ μοι θανεῖν |
> εἴη πρὶν αἰσχρᾷ περιπεσεῖν τύχῃ τινί |

Troad., 415 : καὶ πένης μέν εἰμ' ἐγώ.

Nonius, 494, 3 : ‘ Pauperies ’ pro paupertate . . .—

Talthybius

Senex sum; utinam mortem obpetam prius quam
evenat

quod in pauperie mea senex graviter gemam.

Cp. Non., 507, 18.

212

Hcc., 627-8 : κεῖνος ὀλβιώτατος | ὅτῳ κατ' ἦμαρ τυγχάνει
μηδὲν κακόν.

Cicero, *de Fin.*, II, 13, 41 : Non . . . si malum est dolor,
carere eo malo satis est ad bene vivendum. Hoc dixerit
potius Ennius—

Hecuba

Nimium boni est ⟨huic⟩ cui nihil est mali ⟨in diem⟩.

Nos beatam vitam non depulsione mali sed adeptione boni
iudicemus.

---

²¹² ⟨huic⟩ *suppl.* W   nimium boni est cui nil mali est
Muret *alii alia*   ⟨in diem⟩ *add. ex Eur., Hec.,* 628   *trib.*
Hcc. Muret

294

TRAGEDIES

209

Hecuba despairs of saving Polyxena :

Nonius : ' Sanguis ' . . . in the masculine gender . . .
Ennius in *Hecuba* has it in the neuter—

Hecuba

Ah! Woe is me! I am undone; on they go,
to bathe blood in blood! [a]

210–11

Talthybius has found Hecuba lying in a swoon :

Nonius : ' Pauperies ' for ' paupertas ' . . . —

Talthybius

I am an old man; would that I could meet
My death before a thing should come to pass
Which in my poverty [b] and age I should
Loudly bewail.

212

From Hecuba's speech after she has heard of the death of
Polyxena :

Cicero : Even if pain is an evil, to be without that evil
is not enough to make a good life. Let Ennius, if he prefers,
say that—

Hecuba

A passing good thing has the man who suffers
No ill for one day.

But let us reckon a happy life not by the repulse of evil but
by the attainment of good.

---

[a] There is no close parallel in Euripides.
[b] It is curious to note that ' *in pauperie mea* ' are words
suggested by a speech of Talthybius in Euripides' Τρῳάδες
(415).

ENNIUS

213

Hec., 760 : ὁρᾷς νέκρον τόνδ' οὗ καταστάζω δάκρυ;

Nonius, 155, 28 : ' Guttatim ' . . .—

Hecuba

Vide hunc meae in quem lacrumae guttatim cadunt.

214

Hec., 826 *s.* : πρὸς σοῖσι πλευροῖς παῖς ἐμὴ κοιμίζεται. . . .

Nonius, 342, 24 : ' Modicum ' veteres moderatum et com-
modum dici volunt . . .—

Hecuba

quae tibi in concubio verecunde et modice morem
gerit.

215

Hec., 836–7 : εἴ μοι γένοιτο φθόγγος ἐν βραχίοσι | καὶ χερσὶ
καὶ κόμαισι καὶ ποδῶν βάσει. . . .

Cicero, *Orat.*, 45, 153 : Sine vocalibus saepe brevitatis
causa contrahebant ut ita dicerent ' multi modis ' ' et vas
argenteis '—

Hecuba

palm et crinibus
' tecti fractis.'

216

Hec., 1226–7 : ἐν τοῖς κακοῖς γὰρ ἀγαθοὶ σαφέστατοι | φίλοι.

Cicero, *de Amicit.*, 17, 64 : Quam graves quam difficiles
plerisque videntur calamitatum societates; ad quas non est
facile inventu qui descendat; quamquam Ennius recte—

---

[216] *trib. Hec.* Hartung

TRAGEDIES

213

Hecuba shows Agamemnon the corpse of Polydorus :

Nonius : ' Guttatim ' . . . —

Hecuba

See him on whom my tears fall drop by drop.

214

Hecuba implores Agamemnon in the name of Cassandra, who shares his bed, to help her to avenge her son :

Nonius : ' Modicum ' is a term which the old writers would use for moderated and fitting . . . —

Hecuba

A woman who as bed-mate grants your wishes
With shyness and restraint.

215

Hecuba wishes that her very body could speak :

Cicero : They often used to contract for brevity's sake, quite apart from vowels, so as to use expressions like ' multi modis,' ' et vas argenteis,' ' palm et crinibus '—

Hecuba

              with hand and hair

' tecti fractis.' [a]

216

Hecuba on true friendship :

Cicero : How heavy and hard do most people find it to be someone's companion in disasters ! It is not easy to find anyone who could condescend to such fellowships. Yet Ennius is right when he says—

---

[a] R., 145 : V., 154. The attribution to Ennius is doubtful; Leo, *Quaest. Plaut.*, 299; Birt, *Rh. Mus.*, LI, 248.

ENNIUS

Hecuba

Amicus certus in re incerta cernitur.

217–18

Hec., 1247–8 : τάχ' οὖν παρ' ὑμῖν ῥᾴδιον ξενοκτονεῖν· | ἡμῖν δέ
γ' αἰσχρὸν τοῖσιν Ἕλλησιν τόδε (cp. 803–4).

Nonius, 153, 22 : ' Perbitere,' perire . . . —

Agamemno

Set numquam scripstis qui parentem aut hospitem
necasset quo quis cruciatu perbiteret.

219

Hec., 1258 : οὐ γάρ με χαίρειν χρή σε τιμωρουμένην;

Nonius, 116, 31 : ' Gratulari,' gratias agere . . . —

Hecuba

Iuppiter tibi summe tandem male re gesta gratulor.

IPHIGENIA

Eurip., *Iph. A.*, 1–3 :

    ΑΓ. Ὦ πρέσβυ δόμων τῶνδε πάροιθεν
      στεῖχε. ΠΡ. στείχω. τί δὲ καινουργεῖς
      Ἀγάμεμνον ἄναξ.
    ΑΓ. πεύσει.
        ΠΡ. σπεύδω.

  138–9. ἀλλ' ἴθ' ἐρέσσων σὸν πόδα γήρᾳ
    μηδὲν ὑπείκων.

TRAGEDIES

Hecuba

A friend in need is a friend indeed.[a]

217–18

Agamemnon tells Polymestor of his disapproval of Polymestor's crime :

Nonius : ' Perbitere,' to perish . . . —

Agamemnon

But you have never made a written law
Establishing the pains whereby should perish
The murderer of parent or of guest.

219

Hecuba gives thanks for the success of her vengeance on Polymestor :

Nonius : ' Gratulari,' to give thanks . . . —

Hecuba

All-Highest Jupiter, the ill deed done,
To thee I render thanks at last.

IPHIGENIA

That Ennius followed Euripides' Ἰφιγένεια ἡ ἐν Αὐλίδι is certain; but instead of a chorus of maidens, Ennius most fittingly makes his chorus of warriors. This like certain other divergences may have been based on a Sophoclean version (R., 494 ff.).

---

[a] Hartung's attribution to this play is very likely right.

---

[218] quo quis cruciatu Iun.   quos quis cruciatur *cdd.*
cruciatus Mr.   is quo Pontanus

ENNIUS

220–1

Festus, 324, 24 : ' Pedum ' est quidem baculum incurvum quo pastores utuntur ad comprehendendas oves aut capras, a pedibus; cuius meminit etiam Vergilius in Bucolicis (V., 88). . . . Sed in eo versu qui est in Iphigenia Enni—

Agamemno

Procede, gradum proferre pedum
nitere, cessas o fide

id ipsum baculum significari cum ait Verrius .mirari satis non possum, cum sit . . . significatio aperta.

Cp. Schol. Veron., ad Verg., *Ecl.*, V., 88.

222–5

Iph. A., 6–10 :

ΑΓ. τίς ποτ' ἄρ' ἀστὴρ ὅδε πορθμεύει ; | ΠΡ. Σείριος ἐγγὺς τῆς ἑπταπόρου | Πλειάδος ἄσσων ἔτι μεσσήρης | ΑΓ. οὔκουν φθόγγος γ' οὔτ' ὀρνίθων | οὔτε θαλάσσης.

Varro, *L.L.*, VII, 73 :—

Agamemno

Quid noctis videtur in altisono
caeli clipeo ?

Senex

Temo superat
stellas sublime agitans etiam atque
etiam noctis iter.

Hic multam noctem ostendere volt a temonis motu.

Cp. id., V, 19; Fest., 504, 9 (. . . Ennius superat . . .). Apulei., *de deo Socr.*, 2, 6 (mundi . . . clipeo).

---

²²¹ o fide *add. ex Schol. Veron. ad Verg., Ecl., V.*, 88
o fide <senex> Bergk
²²²⁻⁸ *trib. Iph.* Colonna
²²⁴ agitans V   agens *Varro*   sublimen Buecheler
²²⁵⁻⁶ *arte coniungenda ; sed desunt nonnulla post* ite

TRAGEDIES

220-1

Opening of the play :

Agamemnon bids an old servant hurry to him to take a letter for Clytaemnestra :

Festus: ' Pedum ' (sheep-hook) is a curved staff which shepherds use for catching hold of ewes or she-goats; it is derived from ' pedes.' Virgil among others makes mention of it in the *Bucolics* (V., 88). . . . But I cannot wonder enough when Verrius says that in that line which occurs in *Iphigenia* of Ennius—

Agamemnon

Come hither, strive to put forward the support of your steps—you loiter, O trusty one

a sheep-hook is actually meant, because . . . the real meaning is plain to see.[a]

222-5

Progress of the night :

Varro :—

Agamemnon

What is it I see upon heaven's high-sounding shield of night?

Old Servant [b]

The Wain, driving on and on through night's lofty course, surmounts the stars.

He wishes to indicate, from the movement of the Wain, a late hour of the night.

---

[a] Festus says the sense is : gradum proferre pedum cessas; nitere. Scaliger thought this fr. was taken from Eur., *Iph. A.*, 138–39; but cf. V., *prooem.*, 1888–9, 13 ff. Why should we not take ' gradum pedum ' as ' the steps of the feet ' ? Comparison with Eurip., 1–3 suggests that Ennius read or misread (for πεύσει) σπεῦδε or σπεῦσον or σπεύσεις.

[b] This division is suggested by the corresponding passage in Euripides, with which Ennius has certainly dealt freely. V., 156 and *prooem.*, 1888–9, 14 ff. gives the whole quotation to Agamemnon.

ENNIUS

226–8

Cicero, *de Div.*, II, 26, 57 : Democritus optimis verbis causam explicat cur ante lucem galli canant . . . silentio noctis ut ait Ennius—

Agamemno

Favent faucibus russis
⟨galli⟩ cantu, plausuque premunt alas.

229–30

Iph. A., 317 *s.*; cp. 327.

ΑΓ. . . . ὦ θεοὶ σῆς ἀναισχύντου φρενός

Cic., *Tusc. Disp.*, IV, 36, 77 : Ira vero . . . cuius impulsu existit etiam inter fratres tale iurgium—

Agamemno

Quis homo te   exsuperavit   usquam   gentium
    impudentia ?

Menelaus

Quis autem malitia te ?

Nosti quae sequuntur; alternis enim versibus intorquentur inter fratres gravissimae contumeliae ut facile appareat Atrei filios esse. . . .

231

Iph. A., 329, 331.

ΑΓ. Τί δέ σε τἀμὰ δεῖ φυλάσσειν; οὐκ ἀναισχύντου τόδε; | οὐχὶ δεινά; τὸν ἐμὸν οἰκεῖν οἶκον οὐκ ἐάσομαι;

Rufinianus, ap. *R.L.M.*, 41, 28 H : ᾿Αγανάκτησις indignatio, quae fit maxime pronuntiatione. Ennius in Iphigenia—

---

227 galli *suppl.* W, missis V   *fortasse* <gallique> favent

TRAGEDIES

226–8

Cicero: Democritus with very good argument explains the reasons why cockerels crow before dawn . . . in the silence of the night, in the words of Ennius—

Agamemnon

The cockerels indulge their ruddy-wattled throats in crowing and with a clap beat their wings.[a]

229–30

Quarrel between Agamemnon and Menelaus:

Cicero: Next wrath . . . under whose impulse there starts even among brothers a brawl like this—

Agamemnon

What man in all the world has surpassed you in shamelessness?

Menelaus

Or who you in spite?

You know what follows; for the brothers hurl the most crushing taunts at each other, line for line, so that you can easily see that they are Atreus' sons. . . .

231

Rufinianus: Ἀγανάκτησις is indignation, which comes about chiefly by tone of voice. Ennius in *Iphigenia*—

---

[a] V., 156–7 and *prooem.*, 1888–9, 10 ff. I have supplied *galli* after *russis*; Cicero naturally omits it since he has just said: *galli . . . qui quidem silentio noctis, ut ait Ennius.* . . .

ENNIUS

Agamemno

Menelaus me obiurgat; id meis rebus regimen
restitat.

232–4

Iph. A., 384, 388–390, 396 *s.*: ΑΓ. . . . εἶτ' ἐγὼ δίκην δῶ
σῶν κακῶν ὁ μὴ σφαλείς; . . .
Τἀμὰ δ' οὐκ ἀποκτενῶ 'γω τέκνα· κοὺ τὸ σὸν μὲν εὖ | παρὰ
δίκην ἔσται κακίστης εὔνιδος τιμωρίᾳ. Cp. id., 482 ff. (*Menel.
loqu.*).

Rufinianus, ap. *R.L.M.*, 47, 16 H : Σύγκρισις sive ἀντίθεσις
comparatio rerum atque personarum inter se contrariarum,
ut—

Agamemno

Ego proiector quod tu peccas? Tu delinquis, ego
arguor?
Pro malefactis Helena redeat, virgo pereat innocens?
Tua reconcilietur uxor, mea necetur filia?

235–6

Iph. A., 446–49 : ἡ δυσγένεια δ' ὡς ἔχει τι χρήσιμον. | καὶ
γὰρ δακρῦσαι ῥᾳδίως αὐτοῖς ἔχει | ἅπαντά τ' εἰπεῖν· τῷ δὲ γενναίῳ
φύσιν | ἄνολβα ταῦτα.

Hieronymus, *Epist.*, 60, *Epit. Nepot.*, 14 : . . . Prudenterque
Ennius . . . ait—

Agamemno

Plebes in hoc regi antistat loco : licet
lacrumare plebi, regi honeste non licet.

---

[231] restitat Bentley   restat *cdd.*
[232] proiector *cdd.*   ut ego plectar Bentley   proh
plector *coni.* Halm

TRAGEDIES

Agamemnon

Menelaus brawls at me; it is that domination of
his which stands an obstacle to my affairs.

232-4

Rufinianus : Σύγκρισις or ἀντίθεσις is to put side by side
things or persons contrary to each other, for example—

Agamemnon

Am I taunted because you do wrong? Because
you go astray, am I brought to task? For her
misdeeds should Helen come back, in her guiltless-
ness should a maiden perish? Should your wife be
brought back to favour, my daughter be butchered? [a]

235-6

*Agamemnon laments because he sees that the sacrifice of
Iphigenia will be unavoidable :*

Jerome : And wisely does Ennius write—

Agamemnon

The commoners stand better than their king
In this—the commoners may weep, the king
May not, with honour.[b]

[a] Comparison with Euripides, *Iph. A.*, 317 ff., given opposite
shows how freely Ennius has dealt with his original.
[b] Cf. V., *prooem.*, 1880, 5.

232-4 *trib. Enn. Iph.* Colonna
235-6 *trib. Iph.* Colonna

ENNIUS

237–8

Iph. A., 631–2 : ὦ σέβας ἐμοὶ μέγιστον Ἀγαμέμνων ἄναξ, ἤκομεν ἐφετμαῖς οὐκ ἀπιστοῦσαι σέθεν.

Cicero, *ad Att.*, XIII, 47, 1 :—

Clytaemnestra

Postquam abs te, Agamemno, ut venirem tetigit
    aures nuntius,
extemplo . . .

instituta omisi, ea quae in manibus habebam abieci, quod
iusseras edolavi.

239

Iph. A., 708–9 :

    ΚΛ. Θέτις δ' ἔθρεψεν ἦ πατὴρ Ἀχιλλέα ;
    ΑΓ. Χείρων, ἵν' ἤθη μὴ μάθοι κακῶν βροτῶν.
Vel 701.   ΑΓ. . . . ὁ Πηλεὺς δ' ἔσχε Νηρέως κόρην.

Varro, *L.L.*, VII, 87 : ' Lymphata ' dicta a lympha;
lympha a nympha, ut quod apud Graecos Θέτις apud Ennium—

Thelis illi mater.

240

Iph. A., 735–7 : ΑΓ. οὐ καλὸν ἐν ὄχλῳ σ' ἐξομιλεῖσθαι στρατοῦ.
    ΚΛ. καλὸν τεκοῦσαν τἀμά μ' ἐκδοῦναι τέκνα.
    ΑΓ. καὶ τάς γ' ἐν οἴκῳ μὴ μόνας εἶναι κόρας.

Servius auctus, ad *Aen.*, I, 52 : Sane ' vasto ' pro desolato
veteres ponebant . . . —

Agamemno

Quae nunc abs te viduae et vastae virgines sunt.

[237-8] non ' ut venirem ' (nam id quoque fecissem nisi
Torquatus esset) sed ut scriberem ' tetigit ' e. q. s. *Cic.
trib. Enn. Iph.* Ladewig
[238] extemplo *fortasse non Ennio tribuend., sed cp. Non.,*
263, 5
[239] *trib. Iph.* V

TRAGEDIES

237–8

Clytaemnestra, complying with a deceitful message, has come with her daughter and greets her husband :

Cicero :—

Clytaemnestra

So soon as tidings from you, that I was to come, reached my ears, Agamemnon, I forthwith . . . [a]

gave up what I had begun; I put aside what I had in hand and I wrote rough-hewn what you had asked for.[b]

239

From the dialogue where Agamemnon tells Clytaemnestra of the past life of Achilles :

Varro : 'Lymphata' is a term derived from 'lympha' (water), 'lympha' from 'nympha'; in like manner Θέτις as written by Greek authors is in a passage of Ennius— [c]

Thelis his mother.

240

Agamemnon tries in vain to persuade Clytaemnestra to return to Argos :

Servius (supplemented), on *Aen.*, I, 52 : It is a fact that the old writers used to put ' vastus ' for ' desolate ' . . . —

Agamemnon [d]

Maids who are now bereft of you and desolate.

[a] This is all that can be attributed to Ennius; but cf. Ladewig, *Anal. Scen.*, 15, R., 98.

[b] Cic. gave up work on *De Natura Deorum* and set to work on a letter to Caesar; 'edolavi' is from a satire of Ennius? (p. 437.)

[c] Vahlen's attribution to this play is probable. Varro means that just as a change of one letter makes *Thetis* into *Thelis*, so a change of one letter makes *nympha* into *lympha*.

[d] V., *prooem.*, 1888, 9 ff.

ENNIUS

241-8

Iph. A., 801 ff. (*Achill. loqu.*), 813-8, 1000-1001.

Gellius, XIX, 10, 12 (*de vocabulo praeterpropter*) : Statim proferri Iphigeniam Q. Enni iubet (Celsinus). In eius tragoediae choro inscriptos esse hos versus legimus—

Chorus

Otio qui nescit uti . . .
plus negoti habet quam cum est negotium in negotio ;
nam cui quod agat institutumst non ullo negotio
id agit, id studet, ibi mentem atque animum delectat
  suum :
otioso in otio animus nescit ⟨quid agat⟩ quid
  velit.   245
Hoc idem est ; em neque domi nunc nos nec militiae
  sumus ;
imus huc, hinc illuc ; cum illuc ventum est, ire
  illinc lubet.
Incerte errat animus, praeterpropter vitam vivitur.

. . . Petimus igitur dicas . . . quid sit ignotus huiusce versus sensus 'incerte errat animus praeterpropter vitam vivitur.'

249-51

Iph. A., 956-8 : AX. πικροὺς δὲ προχύτας χέρνιβάς τ' ἐνάρξεται
  Κάλχας ὁ μάντις· τίς δὲ μάντις ἔστ' ἀνήρ,
  ὃς ὀλίγ' ἀληθῆ πολλὰ δὲ ψευδῆ λέγει
  τυχών, ὅταν δὲ μὴ τύχῃ διοίχεται;

Cicero, *de Re Publ.*, I, 18, 30 : In ore semper erat ille de Iphigenia Achilles—

---

[243] non ullo negotio Hermann   nil nisi negotium Hertz
militi negotium Ribb.   in illis *vel* in illo *cdd.*
[244] id agit <id> Ribb.
[245] <quid agat> Dziatzko
[247] illinc *cdd. praeter Par.* (illuc)

TRAGEDIES

241-8

Impatience of the army held back in Aulis :

Gellius, on the word ' praeterpropter ' : Celsinus at once ordered a copy of Quintus Ennius' *Iphigenia* to be brought out. In a chorus of that tragedy we read the following lines—

Chorus [a]

He who knows not how to use leisure has more work than when he is awork at work. For he for whom a task is set to do, does it without any work; he attends to it; therein too he delights his mind and his thoughts. In leisurely leisure the mind knows not what it does or wants. Thus it is with us also; look you, we are now neither at home nor are we afield. We go hither and then thither; and when thither we have come, away again it pleases to go.[b] Our mind wanders unsure; our lives we live but more or less.

. . . Well then we ask you to tell us . . . what is the unknown meaning of this line, ' Our mind wanders unsure; our lives we live but more or less.'

249-51

Achilles sneers at Calchas' prophecy :

Cicero : The famous words of Achilles from *Iphigenia* were always in his mouth —

---

[a] Of warriors—see p. 299; V., in *H.*, XV, 262 ff.
[b] These poor soldiers must have felt towards Agamemnon like the soldiers of the brave old Duke of York, who had ten thousand men. The lines are very corrupt, and inelegant even where they are sound. That part of the speech of Achilles in Euripides which gave Ennius his ideas is perhaps an interpolation into Euripides' play.

ENNIUS

Achilles

astrologorum signa in caelo quid sit observationis,
cum capra aut nepa aut exoritur nomen aliquod
beluarum,
quod est ante pedes nemo spectat, caeli scrutantur
plagas.

Cp. Cic., *de Div.*, II, 13, 30 : Donat., ad Ter., *Adelph.*,
III, 3, 32; Seneca, *Apocolocynt.*, 8.

252

Iph. A., 1505–1509 : ἰώ, ἰώ | λαμπαδοῦχος ἀμέρα Δι|ός τε
φέγγος, ἕτερον ἕτερον | αἰῶνα καὶ μοῖραν οἰκήσομεν· | χαῖρέ μοι
φίλον φάος. vel 1375, κατθανεῖν μέν μοι δέδοκται.

Festus, 5 : ʻ Ob ʼ praepositione antiquos usos esse pro
ʻ ad ʼ testis est Ennius quum ait . . . in Iphigenia—

Iphigenia
Acherontem obibo ubi Mortis thesauri obiacent.

MEDEA
SIVE
MEDEA EXUL

Eur., *Med.*, 1–8 :

Εἴθ᾽ ὤφελ᾽ Ἀργοῦς μὴ διαπτάσθαι σκάφος
Κόλχων ἐς αἶαν κυανέας Συμπληγάδας,
μηδ᾽ ἐν νάπαισι Πηλίου πεσεῖν ποτὲ
τμηθεῖσα πεύκη μηδ᾽ ἐρετμῶσαι χέρας
ἀνδρῶν ἀρίστων οἳ τὸ πάγχρυσον δέρος
Πελίᾳ μετῆλθον. οὐ γὰρ ἂν δέσποιν᾽ ἐμὴ
Μήδεια πύργους γῆς ἔπλευσ᾽ Ἰωλκίας
ἔρωτι θυμὸν ἐκπλαγεῖσ᾽ Ἰάσονος. . . .

---

²⁴⁹ sit *Cic.*   fit V *fortasse recte*

ᵃ Efforts to emend these lines may be needless—V., 160
and *prooem.*, 1878, 7. *Sit* or *fit observationis* seem to govern

TRAGEDIES

Achilles

. . . what a peering there is at the star-readers'
constellations in the sky; when the She-goat or the
Scorpion rises, or some such name chosen from the
beasts, no man looks at what is before his feet; one
and all scan the stretches of the sky.[a]

252

*Agamemnon and Menelaus have yielded to the demands of
Ulysses and the army. Iphigenia is ready to be sacrificed :*

Festus : That the archaic writers used the preposition
ob for *ad* Ennius bears witness when he says . . . in *Iphigenia*—

Iphigenia

I shall go to meet Acheron, where the treasures
of Death lie in my way.

MEDEA

OR

MEDEA BANISHED

Cicero (*de Fin.*, I, 2, 4) includes Ennius' *Medea* among
plays which were translated word for word from the Greek.
That this is not really true of this play the following fragments
will show. In all the essentials, however, it was a Latin
reproduction of Euripides' Μήδεια. But Ennius extended
his play to include also the plot of Euripides' Μήδεια ἐν Αἰγεῖ,
or at least far enough to bring Medea to Athens (Schol. ad
Il., XI, 741 and other sources; V., CCVIII). It is not right
to assume a second play ' Medea Atheniensis ' (R., 157–9;
see fr. 294–5); Varro, Cicero, and Nonius knew only one
Medea of Ennius, to which the poet apparently gave the title
Medea Exul (that is, in exile at Corinth with Jason).

---

the accusative *signa* as though the sentence were e.g. *quae
observent homines signa.*

ENNIUS

253-61

Auctor, *ad Herenn.*, II, 22, 34 : Hic quod extremum dictum est satis fuit exponere ne Ennium et ceteros poetas imitemur quibus hoc modo loqui concessum est—

Nutrix

Utinam ne in nemore Pelio securibus
caesae accedissent abiegnae ad terram trabes,
neve inde navis inchoandi exordium   255
coepisset quae nunc nominatur nomine
Argo, quia Argivi in ea delecti viri
vecti petebant pellem inauratam arietis
Colchis imperio regis Peliae per dolum ;
nam numquam era errans mea domo efferret pedem
Medea animo aegro amore saevo saucia.

Nam hic satis erat dicere, si id modo quod satis esset curarent poetae ' utinam ne era errans mea domo efferret pedem Medea animo aegro amore saevo saucia.'

Cp. Prisc., *ap. G.L.*, III, 423, 36, etc., etc.

262-3

Med., 49–51 : παλαιὸν οἴκων κτῆμα δεσποίνης ἐμῆς, | τί πρὸς πύλαισι τήνδ' ἄγουσ' ἐρημίαν | ἕστηκας, αὐτὴ θρεομένη σαυτῇ κακά.

Nonius, 38, 29 : ' Eliminare,' extra limen cicere. . . . Ennius Medea exule—

Paedagogus

Antiqua erilis fida custos corporis,
quid sic te extra aedes exanimata eliminas?

Cp. Non., 292, 20.

---

[254] caesae accedissent (*vel* accidissent *vel* cecidissent) abiegnae *auct. ad Herenn., Prisc.*, III, *Cic., alii*   caesa accidisset (accedisset *Prisc. VII*) abiegna *vel sim. Varro, Prisc. VII prob.* V

TRAGEDIES

253-61

Opening of the play; prologue spoken by Medea's aged nurse:

The author of *To Herennius* says : I have deemed what I have last said to be enough by way of exposition at this point, lest we be found to be copying Ennius and the rest of the poets, who were granted the right to speak in the following way—

Nurse

Would that the firwood timbers had not fallen to earth hewn by axes in a Pelian grove ; and that thereupon no prelude had been made to begin the ship which is now known by the name of Argo, for that chosen Argive heroes were carried in it when they were seeking the golden fleece of the ram of Colchis, by trickery, at the behest of King Pelias. For thus never would my misled mistress Medea, sick at heart, smitten by savage love, have set foot outside her home.

For if the poets had a care for that only which were enough, then it was enough to say here, 'would that my mistress Medea, sick at heart, smitten by savage love, had not set foot outside her home.'

262-3

The usher to Jason's children addresses the nurse :

Nonius : ' Eliminare,' to thrust outside the ' limen ' . . . Ennius in *Medea Banished*—

Usher

You aged faithful woman, guardian of your mistress' person, wherefore bring you yourself thus outdoors, forspent outside your dwelling ?

ENNIUS

264-5

Med., 57-8 : ὥσθ' ἵμερός μ' ὑπῆλθε γῆ τε κοὐρανῷ | λέξαι
μολούσῃ δεῦρο δεσποίνης τύχας.

Cicero, *Tusc. Disp.*, III, 26, 63 : Sunt autem alii quos in
luctu cum ipsa solitudine loqui saepe delectat, ut illa apud
Ennium nutrix—

Nutrix

Cupido cepit miseram nunc me proloqui
caelo atque terrae Medeai miserias.

266-8

Med., 214-18 : Κορίνθιαι γυναῖκες, ἐξῆλθον δόμων, | μή μοί τι
μέμφησθ' οἶδα γὰρ πολλοὺς βροτῶν | σεμνοὺς γεγῶτας, τοὺς μὲν
ὀμμάτων ἄπο | τοὺς δ' ἐν θυραίοις· οἱ δ' ἀφ' ἡσύχου ποδὸς |
δύσκλειαν ἐκτήσαντο καὶ ῥαθυμίαν.

Cicero, *ad Fam.*, VII, 6, 1 : Tu modo ineptias istas et
desideria urbis et urbanitatis depone et quo consilio profectus
es id assiduitate et virtute consequere; hoc tibi tam ignos-
cemus nos amici quam ignoverunt Medeae—

Medea

Quae Corinthum arcem altam habetis matronae
opulentae optimates,

quibus illa manibus gypsatissimis persuasit ne sibi vitio
illae verterent quod abesset a patria; nam—

Multi suam rem bene gessere et publicam patria
procul,
multi qui domi aetatem agerent propterea sunt
inprobati.

Quo in numero tu certe fuisses nisi te extrusissemus.

---

²⁶⁶ habebant *Cic.*   ne mihi vos vitio vortatis a patria
quod absiem *add. ex Eur.* Elmsley
²⁶⁶⁻⁸ *trib. Enn. Med.* Politianus

314

TRAGEDIES

264–5

From the end of the nurse's reply :

Cicero : But there are others to whom in their grief it
is often a delight to hold converse with loneliness itself, for
example the well-known nurse in Ennius—

Nurse

Now has a desire taken hold of me, poor wretch,
to speak out to heaven and earth Medea's miseries.

266–8

Medea comes out of the palace and defends her moody behaviour :

Cicero writes to Trebatius : All you have to do is to lay
aside the silly fads and longings of town and town's fashions,
and follow up with zest and fortitude the plan with which
you set out. We as your friends will pardon you this as readily
as Medea was pardoned by—

Medea

You well-to-do and well-born ladies, who have for
your own the lofty stronghold Corinth,

whom she with thickly plastered hands persuaded not to call
her to task that she was away from her native land [a]; for—

Many there are who have performed well their
own and their commonweal's tasks far from the
fatherland; and many there are who because they
passed their days at home were for this held in no
honour.

Among the latter number you certainly would have been
numbered had we not pushed you out of it.

---

[a] As will be seen from the quotation opposite, Ennius
misunderstood the Greek of Euripides. That Poliziano was
right in assigning this fragment to Ennius' *Medea* is clear
from the fact that Cicero goes on to quote (without naming
the author) fr. 271 which we know from another passage
of Cicero to belong to Ennius; see below, line 271. In
gypsatissimis Cic. alludes to the whitened hands of the actor.

ENNIUS

269-70

Med., 250–51 : ὡς τρὶς ἂν παρ' ἀσπίδα
στῆναι θέλοιμ' ἂν μᾶλλον ἢ τεκεῖν ἅπαξ.

Nonius, 261, 18 : 'Cernere' rursum dimicare vel contendere . . .

Medea

. . . nam ter sub armis malim vitam cernere
quam semel modo parere.

Cp. Non., 261, 9; Varro, *L.L.*, VI, 81.

271

Med., 303–05? Cp. 381–3; 400–1.

Cicero, *ad Fam.*, VII, 6, 2 : Tu qui ceteris cavere didicisti,
in Britannia ne ab essedariis decipiaris caveto, et quoniam
Medeam coepi agere, illud semper memento—

Medea

Qui ipse si sapiens prodesse non quit, nequiquam
sapit.

Cp. Cic., *de Off.*, III, 15, 62 (ex quo Ennius e. q. s.); Cic.,
ad Fam., XIII, 15, 2 . . . vera praecepta Εὐριπίδου μισῶ
σοφιστὴν ὅστις οὐχ αὑτῷ σοφός (fr. 905 N).

272-3

Med., 352–4 : εἰ σ' ἡ 'πιοῦσα λαμπὰς ὄψεται θεοῦ | καὶ παῖδας
ἐντὸς τῆσδε τερμόνων χθονός, | θανεῖ.

Cicero, *pro Rabir.*, 11, 29 : Regum autem sunt haec
imperia . . . et illae minae—

Creon

Si te secundo lumine hic offendero,
moriere.

Quae non ut delectemur solum legere et spectare debemus,
sed ut cavere etiam et fugere discamus.

Cp. Cic., *ad Att.*, VII, 26, 1.

---

270 quam s. m. parere add. ex *Non.*, 261, 9
272-3 trib. Enn. Med. S

316

TRAGEDIES

269-70

Nonius : ' Cernere ' also means to fight or strive . . . —

Medea

for I would fain make trial of my life thrice under arms, than give birth just once.

271

Medea answering Creon who is suspicious of her :

Cicero writes to Trebatius : You who have learnt to look out on behalf of the rest of mankind, in Britain look out lest you be taken in by carters, and (since I began [a] with playing the part of Medea) remember you at all times that famous line—

Medea

He who, though wise himself, cannot help himself, is wise in vain [b]

272-3

Creon threatens Medea as he grants a day's delay before she leaves the land :

Cicero : And to kings belong these commands.[c] . . . And the famous threat—

Creon

If one day hence I do light upon you, you shall die.

Of these we ought to be readers and spectators, not that we may merely be delighted by them, but that we may learn how to beware also and to escape.

---

[a] See fr. 266–8.
[b] Wherever we place this line, we need not doubt that Ennius took the words from one of the lost plays of Euripides, not his *Medea*.
[c] Scaliger attributes to Ennius' *Medea* all of the three examples given by Cicero.

ENNIUS

274-80

Med., 364-75; 398-99.

Cicero, *de Nat. Deor.*, III, 25, 65 : Balbus 'interpellare te,' inquit ' nolo, Cotta, sed sumemus tempus aliud; efficiam profecto ut fateare. Sed . . . —

Medea

Nequaquam istuc istac ibit; magna inest certatio.
Nam ut ego illi supplicarem tanta blandiloquentia
ni ob rem?

Parumne ratiocinari videtur et sibi ipsa nefariam pestem machinari? Illud vero quam callida ratione—

Qui volt esse quod volt, ita dat se res ut operam
dabit.

Qui est versus omnium seminator malorum—

Ille traversa mente mi hodie tradidit repagula
quibus ego iram omnem recludam atque illi perniciem
dabo,
mihi maerores illi luctum, exitium illi exilium mihi.

Hanc videlicet rationem quam vos divino beneficio homini solum tributam dicitis bestiae non habent. Videsne igitur quanto munere deorum simus adfecti?

281

Med., 431-2 : σὺ δ' ἐκ μὲν οἴκων πατρῴων ἔπλευσας | μαινο-μένα κραδία . . . | 627 ff. : Ἔρωτες ὑπὲρ μὲν ἄγαν ἐλθόντες κ.τ.λ.

Nonius, 297, 16 : ' Efferre ' significat proferre. . . . Ennius Medea—

---

274 s. *trib. Enn. Med.* Osann
276 ni ob rem Mayor   *alii alia*   ni orbem *vel* obem *vel sim. cdd.*

TRAGEDIES

274–80

After the departure of Creon, Medea in a monologue ponders on her plan of revenge :

Cicero : I do not want to interrupt you, Cotta, said Balbus, so let us choose another time; I will certainly make you confess. But . . . —

Medea

In no way thither shall the business go; not on that course; great is the striving within it. What! Would I have humbled myself before him with such charm of speech were it not to my purpose?

Do you think her reasoning is at fault and that she is engineering for herself an unspeakable evil? But with what cunning reasoning does she argue in these well-known words—

Whoever has a wish that whatever he wishes shall come about, according to the trouble he will take, so turns out the event.

This is a line which is a sower of all and every ill—

Yonder wretch crooked in soul has this day given me charge of bolts and bars whereby I shall let open all my wrath and make ruin for him, yes, sorrows for me, grief for him, for me a banishment, for him a bane.

To be sure this gift of reasoning, which you say is bestowed by divine kindness on man alone, is something which the beasts have not. Do you see what a great gift of the gods we are blessed with?

281

The chorus speaking to Medea ᵃ in an ode :

Nonius : ' Efferre ' means to put forward. . . . Ennius in Medea—

ᵃ R., 154; contrast V., 170.

ENNIUS

Chorus

Utinam ne umquam Mede Colchis cupido corde
pedem extetulisses . . .

282-3

Med., 475-82 : ἐκ τῶν δὲ πρώτων πρῶτον ἄρξομαι λέγειν. |
ἐσωσά σ' . . . πεμφθέντα ταύρων πυρπνόων ἐπιστάτην | ζεύγλαισι
καὶ σπεροῦντα θανάσιμον γύην | δράκοντά θ' . . . κτείνασ' ἀνέσχον
σοὶ φάος σωτήριον.

Charisius, ap. *G.L.*, I, 284, 7 K : Fit schema dianoeas . . .
per paralipsim, cum volumus negantes aliquid indicare
tamquam—

Medea

Non commemoro quod draconis saevi sopivi impetum,
non quod domui vim taurorum et segetis armatae
manus.

Cp. *id.*, 286-7.

284-5

Med., 502-4 : νῦν ποῖ τράπωμαι: πότερα πρὸς πατρὸς δόμους |
οὓς σοὶ προδοῦσα καὶ πάτραν ἀφικόμην | ἢ πρὸς τάλαινας Πελιάδας ;

Cicero, *de Orat.*, III, 58, 217 : Aliud vocis genus iracundia
sibi sumat . . . aliud miseratio ac maeror, flexibile plenum
interruptum flebili voce—

Medea

Quo nunc me vortam ? Quod iter incipiam ingredi ?
Domum paternamne anne ad Peliae filias ?

[281] mede cordis *cdd.* Colchis Lips Medea foras
Onions Mede portis *coni.* Linds. extetulisses Buecheler
extulisses *cdd.* trochae. octon. *constit.* V *anapaest.*
Buecheler

TRAGEDIES

Chorus

O Medea of Colchis, would that you had not ever
with hankering heart set foot outside . . .

282-3

Dispute between Medea and Jason :

Charisius: A 'figure of thought' comes about . . . by
'paraleipsis' when we want to point out something while
denying that we are doing so, for example—

Medea

    . . . I say no word [a] of how I lulled
To sleep the fury of the savage snake,
Nor how I tamed the temper of the bulls,
And the stout valour of the warrior crop.

284-5

Medea stresses her loneliness :

Cicero: Let wrath claim for itself one kind of voice . . .
pity and grief another kind—wavering, full, broken by a
sobbing tone—

Medea

Whither shall I turn now? What road set out
To tread? Towards my father's home, or what?
To Pelias' daughters?

[a] V., 169. Notice how Ennius uses a device of rhetoric
thoroughly Roman; contrast the Greek.

283-4 *trib. Enn. Med.* Welcker
284-5 *trib. Enn. Med.* Colonna

ENNIUS

286

Med., 530–1 : ὡς Ἔρως σ' ἠνάγκασε | τόξοις ἀφύκτοις τοὐμὸν ἐκσῶσαι δέμας.

Cicero, *Tusc. Disp.*, IV, 32, 69 : Quid ait ex tragoedia princeps ille Argonautarum ?—

Iason

Tu me amoris magis quam honoris servavisti gratia.

Quid ergo, hic amor Medeae quanta miseriarum excitavit incendia.

287

Med., 752 : ΑΙ. ὄμνυμι Γαίας δάπεδον Ἡλίου τε φῶς. *vel* 764 : ΜΗ. ὦ Ζεῦ Δίκη τε Ζηνὸς Ἡλίου τε φῶς.

Nonius, 170, 8 : 'Sublimare,' extollere. Ennius Medea—

Sol qui candentem in caelo sublimat facem

288

Med., 773 : [ΜΗ.] λέξω· δέχου δὲ μὴ πρὸς ἡδονὴν λόγους. *vel* 132 : ΧΟ. ἔκλυον φωνὰν ἔκλυον δὲ βοάν.

Nonius, 467, 7 : 'Aucupavi,' activum positum pro passivo . . . —

fructus verborum aures aucupant.

289–90

Med., 1070–2 : δότ' ἀσπάσασθαι μητρὶ δεξιὰν χέρα. | ὦ φιλτάτη χείρ, φίλτατον δέ μοι στόμα | καὶ σχῆμα καὶ πρόσωπον εὐγενὲς τέκνων, . . .

Nonius, 84, 31 : 'Cette' significat dicite vel date ab eo quod cedo . . . —

Medea

salvete optima corpora ; cette manus vestras measque accipite.

²⁸⁶ *trib. Enn. Med.* Colonna
²⁸⁸ fructus *cdd.* fremitus Mr. *fortasse* fluctus

322

286

Jason replies to Medea :

Cicero : What says the renowned leader of the Argonauts in the tragedy ? —

Jason

You saved me more for love's sake than for
  honour's.

Well then, what a blaze of woes did this love of Medea stir up.

287

King Aegeus of Athens on making an oath, or Medea reveals her plan of taking refuge with Aegeus at Athens :

Nonius : ' Sublimare,' to lift right up. Ennius in *Medea*—

. . . The sun,
Who lifts aloft in heaven his blazing brand

288

Medea revealing her plan to the chorus ? :

Nonius : ' Aucupavi,' an active form put for the passive . . . —

a harvest of words catches the ears.

289–90

Medea takes leave of her children :

Nonius : ' Cette ' means ' tell ye ' or ' give ye,' from the word cĕdŏ . . . —

Medea

Good-bye, you dearest little things; there now!
Give me your hands and you take mine.

ENNIUS

291-3

Med., 1251-4 : ἰὼ Γᾶ τε καὶ παμφαὴς | ἀκτὶς Ἀελίου κατίδετ' ἴδετε τὰν | οὐλομέναν γυναῖκα πρὶν φοινίαν | τέκνοις προσβαλεῖν χέρ' αὐτοκτόνον· Cp. 1258-9.

Probus, ad Verg., *E.*, VI, 31 : Homerum ipso hoc loco (*Il.*, XVIII, 483) possumus probare quattuor elementorum mentionem fecisse . . . similiter et Ennius in Medea exule in his versibus—

Chorus

Iuppiter tuque adeo summe qui res omnis inspicis

quique tuo Sol lumine mare terram caelum contines,

inspice hoc facinus priusquam fiat, prohibessis scelus.

Nam et hic Iuppiter et Sol pro igni, qui mare et terram et caelum continet, ut non dubie caelum pro aere dixerit.

294-5

Nonius, 469, 34 : 'Contempla' . . . Ennius Medea—

Asta atque Athenas anticum opulentum oppidum

contempla,

Varro, *L.L.*, VII, 9 : In hoc templo faciundo arbores constitui fines apparet † et intra eas regiones qua oculi conspiciant, id est tueamur, a quo templum dictum et contemplare, ut apud Ennium in Medea ' contempla '—

et templum Cereris ad laevam aspice.

[291-2] summe qui . . . tuo Sol Havet, *Rev. de Phil.*, III, 80 summe Sol qui res omnes spicis, | quique tuo cum V summe Sol qui res omnis inspicis quique tuo lumine *cdd.*

324

TRAGEDIES

291-3

From the song sung by the chorus while Medea does her horrid work within :

Probus : We can prove that Homer also in this very passage made mention of the four elements . . . and Ennius likewise in *Medea Banished*, in the following lines—

Chorus

O Jupiter, and thou too, Sun most high,
Who lookest upon all things, and pervadest
Sea land and sky with thy light, look on this
Dread deed before 'tis done ; prevent this sin.

For here too both Jupiter and the Sun are put for fire, which pervades sea and land and sky ; so we need not doubt that he used the term 'sky' for 'air.'

294-5

Medea in flight approaches Athens ; the city is pointed out to her :

Nonius : 'Contempla,' . . . Ennius in *Medea*—

Stand there and Athens [a] contemplate. a city
Ancient and wealthy,

Varro : In making this sort of 'temple' we see that trees are established as the boundaries,[b] † and also within those regions where the eyes look forth, that is where we 'tueamur,' from which is derived 'temple' and 'contemplate,' as we read in Ennius in *Medea*—'contemplate' . . .—

and towards the left,
Look upon Ceres' temple.

---

[a] This goes beyond the plot of Euripides' *Medea*—see p. 311.
[b] A clause has dropped out of Varro's text here.

ENNIUS

MELANIPPA

Of the two plays of Euripides on the tale of Melanippe
Ennius took as his model Μελανίππη ἡ σοφή. Melanippe, in
the absence of her father King Aeolus, bore twin sons by
Poseidon; she exposed them; but they were reared by wild
kine. When her father returned, some cowherds took the
children for a monstrous brood of one of the cows, and brought

296-7

Nonius, 469, 3 : ' Auguro ' . . . Ennius Melanippa—

Certatio hic est nulla quin monstrum siet;
hoc ego tibi dico et coniectura auguro.

298

Nonius, 246, 9 : ' Auscultare ' est obsequi . . . —

Hellen

Mi ausculta, nate, pueros cremitari iube.

299-300

Nonius, 176, 2 : ' Sospitent,' salvent . . . —

Hellen ?

     regnumque nostrum ut sospitent
superstitentque.

Cp. Non., 170, 10.

---

[298] cremitari (*vel* iube cremarier) Bothe   cremari *cdd.*
[300] *om.* ut *cdd.* 176   superstitentque *cdd.* 176, 170
fortasse que *delendum*

TRAGEDIES

MELANIPPE

them as such to the king. The children were doomed to be burnt. Melanippe, who was given the duty of preparing them for the pyre, tried to prove, by Anaxagorean metaphysics, that the babes might be the natural offspring of the cattle. When Aeolus learnt the truth, he imprisoned Melanippe in a dungeon and had the babes thrown to the mercy of wild beasts.

296–7

Hellen [a] *(father of Aeolus) or a herdsman-messenger ? :*

Nonius : ' Auguro ' . . . Ennius in *Melanippe*—

Here can there be no dispute that it is a monstrous brood. This I say unto you and foretell it as from a sign.

298

Hellen advises Aeolus that the babes be burnt with brush-wood [b] *:*

Nonius : ' Auscultare ' means to obey . . . —

Hellen

Listen to me, my son ; enjoin you that the boys be burned.

299–300

Hellen (?) prays for the fortunes of the kingdom :

Nonius : ' Sospitent,' they may save . . . —

Hellen ?

and that they may save and spare our realm for long.

[a] V., 173.
[b] For by burning the monsters upon ἄγρια ξύλα ill luck would be avoided. R., 178; *Rhet. G.*, VII, 1313 W : ὁ δε τῇ τοῦ πατρὸς ῾Ελληνος γνώμῃ πεισθεὶς ὁλοκαυτοῦν τὰ βρέφη κρίνας κ.τ.λ.

ENNIUS

301

? Eurip., *Mel.*, 485–8 N: κοὐκ ἐμὸς ὁ μῦθος ἀλλ' ἐμῆς μητρὸς
πάρα, | ὡς οὐρανός τε γαῖά τ' ἦν μορφὴ μία· | ἐπεὶ δ' ἐχωρίσθησαν
ἀλλήλων δίχα | τίκτουσι πάντα κἀνέδωκαν εἰς φάος, κ.τ.λ. vel 490.

Macrobius, *S.*, VI, 4, 7 : ' Splendet tremulo sub lumine
pontus ' (*Aen.*, VII, 9). Tremulum lumen de imagine rei ipsius
expressum est : sed prior Ennius in Melanippe—

Melanippe ?

Lumine sic tremulo terra et cava caerula candent.

302

Gellius, V, 11, 11 : Media forma quaedam est . . . qualis
a Quinto Ennio in Melanippa·perquam eleganti vocabulo—

stata ⟨forma⟩

dicitur, quae neque κοινὴ futura sit neque ποινή . . .

303

Priscianus, ap. *G.L.*, II, 516, 14 K : ' Scindo scidi.' Vetustissimi tamen etiam scicidi proferebant . . . —

Aeolus ?

quum saxum sciciderit,

Cp. Gell., VI, 9, 15.

NEMEA

According to the original story, Adrastus founded the
Nemean games in honour of Opheltes (son of King Lycurgus
of Nemea); who, left unguarded by Hypsipyle while she guided
the ' Seven against Thebes ' to a spring, was killed by a snake;

301

Possibly Melanippe speaks the following words in her effort to prove that the babes are the cattle's natural offspring :

Macrobius, on 'The sea shines bright under the flickering light' in Virgil: 'Flickering light' is an expression drawn from a picture of the thing itself. But Ennius used it first in *Melanippe*—

Melanippe ?

Thus with flickering light
Do earth and heaven's blue hollows brightly glare.

302

Melanippe's moderate beauty :

Gellius: There is a kind of middling looks . . . I mean the sort to which the term—

well balanced looks

is applied in a most elegant choice of a word by Quintus Ennius in *Melanippe*: looks which are destined neither for 'common gain' nor 'private pain.'

303

Aeolus shuts Melanippe up in a dungeon :

Priscianus: 'Scindo scidi.' Nevertheless the oldest writers used to say 'scicidi' . . .—

Aeolus ?

when she has riven the rock,

NEMEA [a]

to this other details were added later. We know nothing of Ennius' play, except that its title suggests that the model was Aeschylus (R., 159 ff.).

---

[a] *i.e.* 'the Vale,' 'Grove' or 'Town Nemea'—otherwise Nonius and Priscianus would have written *Nemeis*.

ENNIUS

304

Priscianus, ap. *G.L.*, II, 171, 4 K : Hic et haec et hoc pecus. Ennius in Nemea—

Pecudi dare vivam marito.

305

Nonius, 183, 14 : ' Venor,' circumvenior. Ennius Nemea—

Tencor consipta undique venor.

Cp. Paul., ex F., 43, 37 : consiptum apud E. pro conseptum.

PHOENIX

The material for plays about Phoenix was found in the *Iliad*, IX, 447 ff., from which we can get glimpses of the plot of Ennius' play. Comparison of lines 312-13 with what we know of Euripides' Φοῖνιξ (who made his hero innocent and

306

Il., IX, 447 (*Phoen. loqu.*). . . .

'Η δ' αἰὲν ἐμὲ λισσέσκετο γούνων
παλλακίδι προμιγῆναι ἵν' ἐχθρήρειε γέροντα.
Τῇ πιθόμην καὶ ἔρεξα· πατὴρ δ' ἐμὸς αὐτίκ' ὀϊσθεὶς
πολλὰ κατηρᾶτο.

Nonius, 91, 4 : ' Cupienter,' cupidissime. . . . Ennius Phoenice—

Phoenix ?   Amyntor ?

Stultus est qui cupida mente cupiens cupienter cupit.

[305] consipta S *sec. Paul.*   concepta *G*   consepta *rell.*
[306] stultust *vel* stultast quae Linds.   siqui cupienda Bergk   qui non c. Ribb.   sicui cupido Mr.   mente *add.* V

330

304

Priscianus : ' Pecus,' all genders. Ennius in *Nemea*

To give her alive to a bull *ᵃ* as her mate.

305

Nonius : ' Venor,' I am surrounded. Ennius in *Nemea* —

I am held hedged in, on all sides am I hunted.*ᵇ*

PHOENIX

blinded by his father) suggests that Euripides was the model.
But if I have interpreted line 318 rightly, Euripides cannot
have been the pattern throughout.

306

*Amyntor's wife persuaded her son Phoenix to become the lover
of her husband's mistress. This enraged Amyntor. Either he
or Phoenix speaks the following :*

Nonius : ' Cupienter,' with much cupidity. . . . Ennius in
Phoenix—

Phoenix ?   Amyntor ?

A fool is he who lusts with lustful mind,
Lusting lustingly.

ᵃ The meaning is not known, but it might refer to Europa
and Zeus.
ᵇ These words may be from a speech by Hypsipyle in
flight after the death of little Opheltes. In one passage Paulus
(43, 37) tells us that Ennius used *consiptum* for *conseptum*;
in another (45, 15) he says *consiptum* means *clavis praefixum.*

ENNIUS

307

IX, 435–6 : μήποτε γούνασιν οἶσιν ἐφέσσεσθαι φίλον υἱὸν | ἐξ ἐμέθεν γεγαῶτα.

Cicero, *de Orat.*, 46, 155 : Itaque idem poeta qui inusitatius contraxerat . . . non dicit ' liberum ' . . . sed ut isti volunt—

Amyntor

neque tu meum umquam in gremium extollas
liberorum ex te genus.

308–11

Gellius, VI, 17, 10 (*de vocabulo ' obnoxius* ') : Iam vero illud etiam Q. Ennii quo pacto congruere tecum potest quod scribit in Phoenice in hisce versibus ?—

Phoenix

Sed virum vera virtute vivere animatum addecet
fortiterque innoxium stare adversum adversarios.
ea libertas est qui pectus purum et firmum gestitat;
aliae res obnoxiosae nocte in obscura latent.

312–13

Eur., *Phoenix*, 809 N : ἤδη δὲ πολλῶν ἡρέθην λόγων κριτής.

Nonius, 245, 30 : ' Argutari ' dicitur loquacius proloqui . . .

Amyntor

Tum tu isti crede te atque exerce linguam ut argutarier
possis.

[307] *trib. Enn. Phoen.* Bergk   meum *add.* V
[312] te Haupt   tu nec metuisti credere ? (Amyntor)
tuque exercere Ribb.

TRAGEDIES

307

Amyntor curses Phoenix :

Cicero : And so the same poet, who had somewhat
unusually contracted words, . . . does not say ' liberum '
. . . but as your purists would like it ' liberorum '—

Amyntor

And may you never lift up to my bosom any
offspring of children gotten of you.

308–11

Phoenix makes a stand against Amyntor :

Gellius (on the word ' obnoxius ') : Well now, tell me, in
what way can your argument be squared with what no less a
person than Quintus Ennius writes in *Phoenix*, in the following
lines ?—

Phoenix

But it behoves a man of virtue true
To live a life inspired, to stand steadfast
With guiltless bravery in the face of foes.
The man who bears himself both pure and staunch—
That is true liberty.   All conduct else
Lies lurking in dim darkness, fraught with guilt.[a]

312–13

Amyntor jeers at the ready speech of Phoenix ? [b] :

Nonius : ' Argutari' is an expression used in the sense of
to declaim very glibly . . .—

Amyntor

Then trust yourself to yonder fellow, and give
your tongue training, that you may be able to trick
by your prating.

[a] In *obnoxiosae* and *nocte* there is a play of words.
[b] The context is not clear; V., 176; R., 194.

ENNIUS

314

Il., IX, 458 *s.* :

τὸν μὲν ἐγὼ βούλευσα κατακτάμεν ὀξέϊ χαλκῷ,
ἀλλά τις ἀθανάτων παῦσεν χόλον ὅς ῥ' ἐνὶ θυμῷ
δήμου θῆκε φάτιν καὶ ὀνείδεα πόλλ' ἀνθρώπων . .
ὡς μὴ πατροφόνος μετ' 'Αχαιοῖσιν καλεοίμην.

Nonius, 507, 22 : ' Faxim,' fecerim . . . —

Phoenix

Plus miser sim si scelestum faxim quod dicam fore.

315

Nonius, 510, 32 : ' Saeviter ' pro saeve . . . —

saeviter suspicionem ferre falsam futtilum est.

316

IX, 464-5 :

ἦ μὲν πολλὰ ἔται καὶ ἀνεψιοὶ ἀμφὶς ἐόντες
αὐτοῦ λισσόμενοι κατερήτυον ἐν μεγάροισιν. . . .

Nonius, 512 : ' Duriter ' pro dure . . . —

Quam tibi ex ore orationem duriter dictis dedit!

Cp. Charis., ap. *G.L.*, I, 197, 27 K.

317

Nonius, 514, 12 : ' Futtile,' futtiliter . . . —

Ut quod factum est futtile amici vos feratis fortiter.

318

IX, 478 *s.* ?

Nonius, 518, 4 : ' Derepente ' . . . —

Nuntius ?

Ibi tum derepente ex alto in altum despexit mare.

---

[a] This fr. certainly suggests that in this play Phoenix is innocent of any association with his father's mistress, and here laments that his father suspects him of it.

TRAGEDIES

314

Phoenix was tempted to kill his father, but some god held him back lest he should be called a parricide by the Achaeans :

Nonius : ' Faxim,' the same as ' fecerim ' . . . —

Phoenix

More wretched would I be should I perform
What I would come to call a villainy.

315

Nonius : ' Saeviter ' for ' saeve ' . . . —

It is the part of shallow-wits to bear
A false mistrust with passion.[a]

316

Phoenix desired to leave his father's house but was kept back forcibly by his friends and kinsmen ; a friend [b] *speaks ? :*

Nonius : ' Duriter ' for ' dure ' . . . —

How hard were the words of his mouth which he
mouthed unto you!

317

Nonius : ' Futtile,' the same as ' futtiliter ' . . . —

My friends, see to it that you bravely bear
What has been vainly done.

318

Phoenix escaped and fled to Peleus in Phthia :

Nonius : ' Derepente ' . . . —

Messenger ?

Then and there he suddenly looked down from a
height onto the high sea.[c]

[b] V., 176.
I attribute this fr. to some speech coming near the end
of the play and reporting the escape of Phoenix.

ENNIUS

TELAMO

319–22

Cicero, *Tusc. Disp.*, III, 13, 28 : Videntur . . . omnia repentina graviora; ex hoc et illa iure laudantur—

Telamo
⟨liberos⟩
ego cum genui tum morituros scivi et ei rei sustuli :
praeterea ad Troiam cum misi ob defendendam
    Graeciam,
scibam me in mortiferum bellum non in epulas
    mittere.

Cp., 24, 58 (atque hoc idem et Telamo ille declarat ' ego cum genui.' . . .) Fronto, *de b. Parth.*, 217; Seneca, *de Consolat.*, 11, 12.

323

Nonius, 172, 19 : ' Squalam ' pro squalidam. Ennius Telamone—

Telamo ?

strata terrae lavere lacrumis vestem squalam et
    sordidam.

Id., 504, 4 (terra *cd. Harl.*).

324

Nonius, 505, 35 : ' Audibo ' pro ' audiam.' . . . —

Telamo

More antiquo audibo atque auris tibi contra utendas
    dabo.

336

TRAGEDIES

TELAMON

The original of this play is unknown; nor has any probable theory been put forward (R., 133 ff.; V., CCIX; Hermann, *Opusc.*, VII, 378 ff.).

319-22

Telamon in Salamis bears bravely the loss of Ajax :

Cicero : All disasters which are sudden seem to come the heavier. Hence it is that the following lines are rightly praised—

Telamon

When children I begat, I knew that they
Must die, and for that end I took them up;
Moreover, when I sent them out to Troy
That they might Greece defend, I did but know
That I was sending them not to a banquet
But to death-dealing war.

323

Grief of Eriboea [a] for her son Ajax :

Nonius : 'Squalam' is used by Ennius in *Telamon* for 'squalidam '—

Telamon ?

              Stretched on the ground
She bathed with tears her dingy dress of mourning.

324

Telamon to his bastard son Teucer (by Hesione) :

Nonius : 'Audibo ' for ' audiam.' . . .—

Telamon

By age-long custom will I hear in turn,
Lending to you my ears to use.

[a] It might be a fr. referring to the grief of Hesione for Teucer, who was at first thought to be dead. R., 134.

ENNIUS

325-6

Nonius, 85, 23 : ' Claret,' clara est . . . —

Teucer

Nam ita mihi Telamonis patris atque Aeaci et proavi
Iovis
† gratia ea est † atque hoc lumen candidum claret
mihi,

327

Festus, 234, 19 : ' Obsidionem ' potius dicendum . . . quam
obsidium . . . —

Telamo

Scibas natum ingenuum Aiacem cui tu obsidionem
paras.

328-9

Cicero, *de Div.*, II, 50, 104 : Si sunt di benefici in homines
sunt. Quis hoc vobis dabit ? . . . An noster Ennius ? Qui
magno plausu loquitur adsentiente populo—

Telamo

Ego deum genus esse semper dixi et dicam caelitum,
sed eos non curare opinor quid agat humanum genus ;

Et quidem cur sic opinetur rationem subicit.

---

[326] gratia ea est *cdd.*   gratia extet (est) Ribb.   astet
vel adsit Buecheler   gratia esse est V., *Abh. B. Ak.* 1888,
38 *s.*

TRAGEDIES

325-6

Teucer having told his story protests his innocence in the matter of Ajax's death :

Nonius : 'Claret,' 'is clear' . . . —

Teucer

As this bright light
Shines on me, so stands sure regard in me
For Telamon my father, for Aeacus,
For Jupiter my great-grandfather,[a]

327

Telamon accuses Teucer :

Festus : 'Obsidio' should be used rather than 'obsidium'
. . . —

Telamon

You knew that Ajax, of whom you, yes you,
The assailant stand, was in true wedlock born.

328-9

Teucer seems to have told how the seer Calchas represented Ajax's death as divine justice. Telamon in reply [b] :

Cicero : If there are gods, then they are kindly towards mortal men. Who will grant you this? . . . Can our Ennius do it? But he, with great applause from the crowd who thinks alike with him, speaks thus—

Telamon

For my part I have always said, will say,
There is a race of gods in heaven; and yet
They take no thought, it seems, how fares mankind;

And indeed he goes on to give the reason why he thinks so.

---

[a] The reading is not certain, but it is clear that Teucer is making a solemn statement that he is innocent.
[b] V., 179, R., 134.

ENNIUS

330

Cicero, *de Nat. Deor.*, III, 32, 79 : Telamo . . . uno versu locum totum conficit, cur di homines neglegant—

nam si curent, bene bonis sit, male malis; quod nunc abest.

331

Soph., *Ai.*, 746 *s.*; 950 *s.*; 1036; *al.*

Cicero, *de Div.*, I, 40, 88 : Atque etiam ante hos Amphiaraus et Tiresias, non humiles et obscuri neque eorûm similes ut apud Ennium est—

qui sui quaestus causa fictas suscitant sententias,

sed clari et praestantes viri.

332-6

Cicero, *de Div.*, I, 58, 132 : Non habeo . . . nauci Marsum augurem, non vicanos haruspices, non de circo astrologos, non Isiacos coniectores, non interpretes somniorum. Non enim sunt hi aut scientia aut arte divini sed—

. . . superstitiosi vates inpudentesque harioli,
aut inertes aut insani aut quibus egestas imperat;
qui sibi semitam non sapiunt, alteri monstrant
    viam;
quibus divitias pollicentur, ab iis drachumam ipsi
    petunt.
De his divitiis sibi deducant drachumam, reddant
    cetera.

Atque haec quidem Ennius qui paucis ante versibus esse deos censet sed eos non curare opinatur quid agat humanum genus (*vide* 328-9).

---

[332] *fortasse* <sunt> superstitiosi
[336] *fortasse non Enni*

TRAGEDIES

330

Cicero : Telamo sums up in one line the whole topic why the gods trouble not about mankind—

for if they did care, it would go well with well-doers, and ill with ill-doers; but this, as things are, is not to be seen.

331

Cicero : And even before these Amphiaraus and Tiresias, men not lowly or obscure or like those, we find in a passage of Ennius—[a]

Who for the sake of their own gain call up
Thoughts that are false,

but illustrious and outstanding.

332–6

Cicero : I care not a fig for your Marsian diviner, nor your village-trotting gut-gazers, nor your star-readers from the circus, nor your guessers of Isis, nor your interpreters of dreams. For it is not by knowledge or skill that they are prophetic, but they are—

soothsaying prophets, shameless gut-gazers, clumsy or crazy, or obedient to the behests of want; men who know not their own path yet point the way for another, and seek a shilling from the very persons to whom they promise riches. From these riches let them take out a shilling for themselves, and hand over the rest.

All these are words, if you please, of Ennius, who a few lines before believes that there are gods, but thinks that they take no thought how fares mankind.

---

[a] The attribution to this play is probably right—R., 96, V., 195.

ENNIUS

337

Nonius, 475, 20 : 'Partiret' pro 'partiretur' . . . —

Teucer

Eandem me in suspicionem sceleris partivit pater.

338

Nonius, 160, 5 : 'Porcet' significat prohibet . . . —

Teucer

Deum me sancit facere pietas, civium porcet pudor.

TELEPHUS

From Euripides' Τήλεφος. Reconstruction must be largely guesswork. Telephus, heir of Teuthras' realm in Mysia, wounded in battle by Achilles, was told by Apollo that only

339

Eurip., *Tel.*, 698 N : πτώχ' ἀμφίβλητα σώματος λαβὼν ῥάκη | ἀλκτήρια τύχης.

Nonius, 537, 23 : 'Stolam' veteres non honestam vestem solum sed omnem quae corpus tegeret. Ennius Telepho—

Telephus

Caedem caveo hoc cum vestitu squalida saeptus
    stola.

Cp. Fest., 486, 34.

---

[337] in me Delrio
[338] sancit Bergk   sinit id Buecheler   sentit *cdd. prob.*
V (*Il.*, *XV*, 260), Linds.

TRAGEDIES

337

Teucer is troubled about his father's suspicions :

Nonius : ' Partiret ' for ' partiretur ' . . . —

Teucer

My father in that very same [a] misgiving
Has made me share—that I'm a miscreant.

338

Teucer, banished, will not retaliate :

Nonius : ' Porcet ' means prevents . . . —

Teucer

My loyalty [b] towards the gods ordains that I do
this, respect for my townsmen hinders me from it.

TELEPHUS

the thing which had wounded him could cure him. Hearing
that Achilles was in Argos, where Agamemnon held sway,
Telephus went thither.

339

Telephus in Argos tells why he has left his native land :

Nonius : ' Stola ' is a term used by the old writers not only
for a respectable garment but also any garment which covers
the body. Ennius in *Telephus*—

Telephus

Slaughter avoid I by this garb, wrapped up
In a mean shabby coat.

[a] *i.e.* the same suspicion as Agamemnon and Odysseus
incurred in the matter of Ajax's death. V., 179, 180.
[b] *pietas* here may mean obedience to Apollo, on whose
advice Teucer acted.

---

[339] caedem caveo h. c. v. Geel　　　cedo et abeo Madvig
sorde et scabie Mr.　　convestitus Colonna　　cedo et caveo
cum vestitus *cdd.*　　quam ve <. . . *Fest.*

ENNIUS

340

Tel., 703 N : μή μοι φθονήσητ' ἄνδρες Ἑλλήνων ἄκροι
εἰ πτωχὸς ὢν τέτληκ' ἐν ἐσθλοῖσιν λέγειν.

Festus, 124, 12 : ' Muttire,' loqui . . . —

Telephus

Palam muttire plebeio piaculum est.

Cp. Paul., ex F., 125, 14.

341

Cp. *Tel.*, 699 N : δεῖ γάρ με δόξαι πτωχὸν. vel 698 (*v. supra*).

Nonius, 537, 23 : ' Stolam ' . . . idem in eadem—

Telephus

Regnum reliqui saeptus mendici stola.

342

Tel., 720 N : κακῶς ὀλοίατ·' ἄξιον γὰρ Ἑλλάδι.

Nonius, 342, 6 : ' Mactare ' malo adficere significat . . . —

Agamemno

Qui illum di deaeque magno mactassint malo !

343

Tel., 723 N : ὦ πόλις Ἄργους κλύεθ' οἷα λέγει. 713 N :
ἅπασαν ἡμῶν τὴν πόλιν κακορροθεῖ.

Nonius, 429, 1 : Urbs est aedificia, civitas incolae . . . —

et civitatem video Argivum incendere.

[343] telefus et *vel* telefo et *cdd.* Telepho set Mr. sed
Linds. (*qui* incedere *coni. pro* incendere)

344

TRAGEDIES

340

Telephus addresses the Greek leaders at Argos, keeping up his part of a low-born fugitive :

Festus : ' Muttire,' to speak . . . —

Telephus

It is a sin for commoner to mutter
A word in open gathering.

341

Telephus reveals himself to Clytaemnestra ? :

Nonius : ' Stola ' . . . the same poet in the same play—

Telephus

Wrapped up in beggar's coat I left my kingdom.

342

Agamemnon [a] to Telephus as he seizes the babe Orestes ? :

Nonius : ' Mactare ' means to afflict with evil . . . —

Agamemnon

What ! May the gods and goddesses doom him
To dire damnation !

343

Dissension caused by Telephus' boldness ? :

Nonius : A ' town ' consists of buildings, a ' state ' consists of inhabitants . . . —

And I see he sets the Argives' town ablaze.

[a] This seems to me to be likely. Cf. Hyginus, *Fab.*, 101, monitu Clytaemnestrae Orestem . . . rapuit.

ENNIUS

344

Nonius, 490, 10 : 'Itiner' pro iter . . . —

deumque de consilio hoc itiner credo conatum
    modo.

345-6

Nonius, 232, 17 : 'Advorsum' rursum apud significat . . . —

Te ipsum hoc oportet profiteri et proloqui

advorsum illam mihi.

347-8

Nonius, 15, 3 : 'Enoda' significat explana . . . —

            Verum quorum liberi leto dati
sunt in bello, non lubenter haec enodari audiunt.

THYESTES

What models Ennius used for his *Thyestes* (his last play—
Cic., *Brut.*, 20, 78) we do not know; and the stories about
Thyestes were various. There are traces of a Euripidean
origin. My reconstruction is based on the belief that the play
had two scenes—one at the court of Atreus, the other at
the court of Thesprotus; it appears that Ennius made a

---

[344] *fortasse* te   de *cdd.*
[346] advorsus Mr.

TRAGEDIES

344

*Agamemnon (?) tells Telephus that he understands that T.
had come by divine will to be a guide against Troy :*

Nonius : ' Itiner ' for *iter* . . . —

I think too, 'twas by counsel of the gods
That you did lately venture on this journey.

345-6

*Telephus ª demands that Agamemnon shall assure him safety ;
Clytaemnestra must hear his assurance :*

Nonius : ' Advorsum ' also means ' in the presence of ' . . . —

Yourself must in her presence thus avow,
I pray you, and affirm this.

347-8

Chorus in a commentary on the course of events ? :

Nonius : ' Enoda ' means explain . . . —

But those whose children have been given up to
death do not willingly hear such riddles unknotted.

THYESTES

greater impression with the second part of his play. Hyginus,
Fab., 88, provides us with a sketch of the action.
  Atreus, King of Mycenae, wishing to take vengeance on
his brother Thyestes, pretended to be reconciled to him and
welcomed him at his court.

ª R., 111; or possibly Agamemnon, who demands from
Telephus that he will not harm the baby Orestes.

ENNIUS

349

Nonius, 369, 29 : ' Putare,' animo disputare. . . . Ennius Thyeste—

Ibi quid agat secum cogitat curat putat.

350

Nonius, 261, 13 : ' Cernere,' iudicare . . . —

Impetrem facile ab animo meo ut cernat vitale brabium.

351

Probus, ad Verg., *Ecl.*, VI, 31 (de quattuor elementis). Principem habuerunt Empedoclem Agrigentinum qui de his ita scripsit :

τέσσαρα δὴ πάντων ῥιζώματα πρῶτον ἔασιν,
Ζεὺς ἀργὴς . . . .

ut accipiamus Ζεὺς ἀργὴς ignem qui sit ζέων et candens, quod ignis est proprium, de quo Euripides :

ὁρᾶς τὸν ὑψοῦ τόνδ᾽ ἄπειρον αἰθέρα
καὶ γῆν πέριξ ἔχονθ᾽ ὑγραῖς ἐν ἀγκάλαις ;
τοῦτον νόμιζε Ζῆνα, τόνδ᾽ ἡγοῦ θεόν (935 N).

et Ennius—

Aspice hoc sublime candens quem invocant omnes Iovem.

Cp. Fest., 442, 16 (. . . Ennius in Thyeste); Cic., *de Nat. Deor.*, II, 2, 4, etc.

Cp. Eur., 869 N : αἰθήρ . . . Ζεὺς ὃς ἀνθρώποις ὀνομάζεται.

---

[349] curat Studemund   parat *cdd.*
[350] meo *suppl.* Quich.   babium *cdd.*   habitum V
(*II.*, *XII*, 254)   viam Buecheler   abigeum Ribb.
vitale brabium Linds.
[351] sublime *Cic.*, *Apulei.*, *Prob.*   sublimen *epit.* Fest.,
Ritschl (*Opp.*, *II*, 462 *ff.*) *non prob.* Klotz, Heraeus (*Philol.*,
LV, 197 *s.*)   vocant *Fest.*, *Prob.*   invocant *rell. vide Eur.*,
935 N.

TRAGEDIES

349

Prologue ? Evil plans of Atreus :

Nonius : ' Putare,' to debate in the mind. . . . Ennius
in *Thyestes*—

Thereon he muses, ponders, and considers
In his own mind what he should do.

350

Atreus forms his plan ? :

Nonius : ' Cernere,' to judge . . .—

May I with ease cause him to adjudge the vital
prize [a] to my liking.

351

*When Atreus served Thyestes his own sons at a feast, the
very sun turned aside his chariot :* [b]

Probus, on the four elements : Their chief expounder was
Empedocles of Acragas, who writes about them thus : ' Firstly,
four roots there are of all things; White Zeus, etc.' So we
may take ' White Zeus ' as fire which is ζέων and glowing
white, a peculiar property of fire, of which Euripides says :
See you this ether on high, boundless, embracing earth in
pliant arms? This you shall believe is Zeus : this shall you
think is a god.' And Ennius—

Look you on this that glows white aloft : all men
call on it as ' Iupiter.'

[a] I accept Lindsay's reading *brabium*, i.e. βραβεῖον, a prize
won in athletic contests. But we do not know how the word
is used here.

[b] I base this interpretation on Hygin., *Fab.*, 88 *ob id
scelus etiam sol currum avertit.* In Ennius, *sublime candens*
is the sky, but I suggest that the occasion is the sun's horror
which someone points out. Other views—R., 201-2; V.,
CCX, CCXIX, 185.

ENNIUS

352

Nonius, 268, 9 : ' Contingere,' evenire . . .

Thyestes

Quam mihi maxime hic hodie contigerit malum.

353

Nonius, 97, 29 : ' Delectare,' illicere, attrahere . . . —
et me Apollo ipse delectat ductat Delphicus.

354

Nonius, 255, 25 : ' Crepare,' ferire . . . —
sed sonitus auris meas pedum pulsu increpat.

355

Cicero, *Orat.*, 55, 184 : Similia sunt quaedam etiam apud
nostros, velut ille in Thyeste—

Chorus

Quemnam te esse dicam qui tarda in senectute . . .

et quae sequuntur; quae nisi cum tibicen accessit, orationis
sunt solutae simillima.

---

[352] mihi m. *cdd.*   maxime mihi Bothe
[353] et *cdd.*   set Mercier *prob.* V

TRAGEDIES

352

Thyestes bewails his fate :

Nonius : ' Contingere,' to turn out . . . —

Thyestes

How utterly has ruin befallen me
Here on this day.

353

and plans to consult Apollo about vengeance on Atreus :

Nonius : ' Delectare,' to entice, attract . . . —

and Apollo himself of Delphi charms and draws me
on.

354

*Thyestes fled to Thesprotus King of Epirus.   One of the
Epirotes (chorus-leader ?)   hears the approach of Thyestes ? :*

Nonius : ' Crepare,' to beat . . . —

But beats upon my ears a sound of footsteps.

355

He addresses Thyestes :

Cicero : There are some examples like this even in works of
our own poets; take the speaker in *Thyestes* [a]—

Chorus

And who pray shall I say you are, who thus
With aged lagging steps . . .

and the words which follow.   Except where a flute-player
accompanies them, they are much like prose.

---

[a] Probably not Pacuvius' *Thyestes.*

ENNIUS

356-60

Cicero, *Tusc. Disp.*, III, 11, 25 : Nunc aegritudinem si possumus depellamus . . . taetra enim res est, misera . . . fugienda; qualis enim tibi ille videtur ?—

Thyestes

Tantalo prognatus Pelope natus qui quondam a
    socru

Oenomao rege Hippodameam raptis nanctus nuptiis,

Iovis iste quidem pronepos. Tamne ergo abiectus tamque fractus ?—

Nolite hospites ad me adire, ilico istic!

Ne contagio mea bonis umbrave obsit.

Meo tanta vis sceleris in corpore haeret!

Tu te Thyesta damnabis orbabisque luce propter vim sceleris alieni ?

361

Cicero, *de Orat.*, III, 41, 164 : Nolo esse verbum angustius id quod translatum sit quam fuisset illud proprium ac suum—

Chorus

Quidnam est obsecro quod te adiri abnutas ?

Melius esset ' vetas ' ' prohibes ' ' absterres,' quoniam ille dixerat ' ilico. . . .

---

[356] socru Bentley socero *cdd.*
[357] *post* nuptiis *trib. Ennio verba* Iovis i. q. p. Bentley
[358] Nolite inquit hospites *Cic.*   istim Wolf
[360] meo *add.* Bentley *alii alia*

TRAGEDIES

356-60

Thyestes tells who he is ; he ^a warns them not to touch him :

Cicero : Well now, let us thrust distress away if we can . . . for it is a loathsome, wretched thing . . . to be avoided. What think you of the well-known hero ?—

Thyestes

I, sprung from Tantalus, begotten of Pelops,
Who having once gained Hippodamea,
A ravished wife from King Oenomaus,
The father of my bride,

Well, *he* was a great-grandson of Jupiter ! And then was he so downcast, so broken ? Says he—

Strangers, draw you not near to me ! Back there, back ! Lest a tainted touch from me, lest my very shadow harm you that are sound. Oh, such a deadly violence of sin clings to my body !

What, will you, Thyestes, utter your own doom, and rob yourself of the light of day, because of the ' violence ' of another's sin ?

361

Cicero : I do not want a word which is figurative to have a narrower meaning than the same would have had in its own proper sense—

Chorus

Why then is it, I pray you, that you nod me back from approaching you ?

' Do you forbid ' or ' debar ' or ' scare away ' would be better, since the other speaker had said just before : ' Back there. . . .' (line 358)

---

^a With a sudden change of movement comes a change of metre. No doubt can be felt that Cicero quotes from Ennius' *Thyestes.*

353

ENNIUS

362

Nonius, 90, 13 : ' Conglomerare,' involvere, superaddere.
. . . —

Thyestes

Eheu mea fortuna ut omnia in me conglomeras
mala !

363-5

Cicero, *Tusc. Disp.*, III, 19, 44 : Quaerendum igitur quem
ad modum aegritudine privemus eum qui ita dicat—

. . . Pol mihi fortuna magis nunc defit quam genus.
Namque regnum suppetebat mi, ut scias quanto e
loco
Quantis opibus quibus de rebus lapsa fortuna accidat.

Quid ? Huic calix mulsi impingendus est ut plorare desinat,
aut aliquid eius modi ?

366-70

Cicero, *Tusc. Disp.*, I, 44, 107 : Exsecratur luculentis sane
versibus apud Ennium Thyestes, primum—

Ut naufragio pereat Atreus !

Durum hoc sane; talis enim interitus non est sine gravi
sensu; illa inania—

Ipse summis saxis fixus asperis evisceratus,
latere pendens saxa spargens tabo sanie et sanguine
atro,

362 eheu L   heu *cdd.*
363-5 *trib. Thyest.* Ribb.
366 *fortasse* ut n. p. A. *Ennii sententiam non verba indicant ;*
ut n. p. A. *trib. Enn. Schol. Basilic.*

354

TRAGEDIES

362

Thyestes goes on to tell of his misfortunes :

Nonius : ' Conglomerare,' to roll upon, to add over and above . . . —

Thyestes

Alas, my fortune, how dost thou roll all
And every ill upon me!

363–5

Cicero : We must inquire, therefore, in what way we are to free from distress him who thus speaks—

And now i' faith my fortune more than birth
Fails me; that you may know from what great
    pride
Of place, what wealth, what worldly goods my
    fortune
Has slipped and fallen—I once did have a kingdom.

Well? Must we tip him a cup of mead to make him stop wailing, or something of that kind?

366–70

Thyestes curses Atreus :

Cicero : In a play of Ennius Thyestes utters curses in lines admittedly magnificent; first comes—

May Atreus perish by shipwreck!

Admittedly a cruel prayer, for such a death does not come without great suffering. The following lines are meaningless—

He, set disbowelled on sharp steep rugged rocks,
Hanging by his own flank and spattering
The rocks with gore, with mess of black-hued blood,[a]

[a] Lucilius quoted these two lines; see *Remains, etc.*, Vol. III.

ENNIUS

Non ipsa saxa magis sensu omni vacabunt quam ille 'latere pendens,' cui se hic cruciatum censet optare. Quae erant dura si sentiret; nulla sunt sine sensu. Illud vero perquam inane—

Neque sepulchrum quo recipiat habeat portum corporis
ubi remissa humana vita corpus requiescat malis.

Vides quanto haec in errore versentur; portum esse corporis et requiescere in sepulchro putat mortuum, magna culpa Pelopis qui non erudierit filium nec docuerit quatenus esset quidque curandum.

Cp. Cic., *in Pison.*, 19, 43; Non., 405, 3.

371-2

auctor, *ad Herenn.*, II, 25, 39 : Item vitiosum est cum id pro certo sumitur quod . . . etiam nunc in controversia est, hoc modo—

Thesprotus

Eho tu di quibus est potestas motus superum atque inferum,
pacem inter sese conciliant conferunt concordiam.

Nam ita pro suo iure hoc exemplo utentem Thesprotum Ennius induxit quasi iam satis certis rationibus ita esse demonstasset.

Cp. Cic., *de Inv.*, I, 49, 91.

373

Nonius, 110, 11 : ' Flaccet,' languet, deficit . . .—

Thesprotus

Sin flaccebunt condiciones repudiato et reddito.

[373] sin Guilielmus   in *cdd.*

---

[a] This was after Thyestes had left. During a famine at Mycenae, Atreus was ordered to restore Thyestes.
[b] It is not certain whether or not *Cresphontem* should be read here. Cf. V., CCX, 184 and *prooem.*, 1888-9, 17, which I accept.
[c] I suspect that the scene is where Atreus, having obtained the hand of Pelopia, possibly has suspicions of her; she had

The very stones will not be freer of pain than he 'hanging by his flank,' for whom Thyestes thinks he is desiring torments. These would be heavy pains if he felt them; they are nothing without feeling. Then the following is utterly meaningless—

And may he have no tomb where he may find
A haven for his carcase, where that carcase,
The mortal life let out, may rest from trouble.

You see how great is the error in which all this is involved; he believes there is a 'haven' for the body, and that a dead man 'rests' in a tomb, to the great discredit of Pelops, in that he did not school his son or teach him how far everything should be a cause for anxiety.

371–2

Atreus[a] has come to Thesprotus' court ; Thesprotus believes the brothers will be reconciled ? :

The author of *To Herennius* : There is again a fault when something is taken as decided, which is still a matter of dispute, in this way—

Thesprotus

Ho! See you, the gods who guide the power and busy bustle of beings that dwell above and below, they make a friendly peace among themselves and talk together of agreement.

For in this manner does Ennius stage Thesprotus [b] as making use of this example on his own authority, as though he had already proved it by really convincing arguments.

373

Thesprotus makes an agreement with Atreus about Pelopia :

Nonius : 'Flaccet,' pines, weakens . . . —

Thesprotus

But if our terms go lax, then cast her off
And give her back.[c]

been ravished by her father Thyestes (who did not know she was his daughter) and was already with child (who was afterwards Aegisthus)—Hygin., *Fab.*, 88.

357

ALIAE FABULAE

AMBRACIA

Ennius accompanied Marcus Fulvius Nobilior on his appointment to a command against the Aetolians, and shared in the campaign which Fulvius conducted there in 189 B.C. (Cic., *Tusc. Disp.*, I, 2, 3; *Brut.*, 20, 79; cp. *pro. Arch.*, 11, 27). That Ennius' work entitled *Ambracia* was a

374

Nonius, 183, 11 : ' Veget ' pro vegetat vel erigit vel vegetum est. . . . Ennius Ambracia—

' et aequora salsa veges ingentibus ventis.'

375

Nonius, 471, 11 : ' Populat ' . . . —

Agros audaces depopulant servi dominorum domi.

376

Nonius, 87, 29 : ' Cluet,' nominatur. . . . —

Esse per gentes cluebat omnium miserrimus.

[375] domi Buecheler   domini Bothe   minis Ribb.   m. |
<non coerciti> *coni*. V   dominis *cdd*. *prob*. Pascal
[376] esse per gentes Guietus   per gentes Asiae Buecheler
per gentes esse *cdd*.

---

[a] R., 207–211; V., XIII–XV. The same subject was dealt with in the XVth book of the *Annals*.

OTHER PLAYS

OTHER PLAYS

AMBRACIA

' fabula praetexta ' is probable.[a] It was written with the
object of glorifying M. Fulvius with special reference to
his capture of Ambracia—*quam victoriam per se magnificam
Q. Ennius amicus eius insigni laude celebravit* (' Vict.,' *de Vir.
Illustr.*, 52 M).

374

The dangers of the Adriatic ? :

Nonius : ' Veget ' for ' vegetat,' ' lifts up ' or ' is big.' . . .
Ennius in *Ambracia*—

' and thou makest the salt seas to grow big with
mighty winds.'

375

Lawless character of the Aetolians ? :

Nonius : ' Populat.' . . . —

The naughty slaves lay waste at home [b] their
masters' fields.

376

One of the Aetolians :

Nonius : ' Cluet,' is called. . . . —

Through all the nations was he called the
wretchedest of men.

[b] In Nonius *dominis* at the end of the line has perhaps
ousted by dittography another word, possibly one in the
ablative case. But *domi* would be typical of the alliterations,
assonances and word-plays so common in old Latin verse.

ENNIUS

377-8

Nonius, 469, 25 : ' Cunctant ' pro cunctantur . . . —

> ' Bene mones ;
> tute ipse cunctato ; o vide fortem virum.

SABINAE

379-80

Iulius Victor, ap. *R.L.M.*, 402, 30 H : Ab eventu in qualitate, ut qualia sunt ea quae evenerunt aut videantur eventura, tale illud quoque existimetur ex quo evenerunt; ut Sabinis Ennius dixit—

> Cum spolia generis detraxeritis, – ‿ –
> quam inscriptionem dabitis ?

CAUPUNCULA

381

Nonius, 155, 30 : ' Propitiabilis ' <promptus> ad propitiandum. Ennius Caupuncula—

> hinc est animus propitiabilis.

---

[377] cunctato o vide V   cunctato *rel* cuncto *cdd.*
monens . . . ipse cunctat o Buecheler
[379-80] generis Iahn, Christ *prob.* V generi *cdd.*   detraxeritis
<impie> *vel* <mortuis> V   detraxeritis quam patres |
inscriptionem Mr. *prob.* Ribb.
[381] *Non.*, 155 promptus *add.* W   propitiabilis ad p. *LuG*

OTHER PLAYS

377-8

The campaign :

Nonius : ' Cunctant ' for ' cunctantur ' . . . —

' That's good advice of yours ; then you yourself
Hold back. Oh! See the valiant warrior.

THE SABINE WOMEN

Doubtless a ' fabula praetexta ' [a] on the story of the rape
of the Sabines.

379-80

Julius Victor : Again, there is argument as to quality made
from an event, so that that from which things have resulted
is deemed to be of like kind as the things which have resulted
from it or may seem likely to result : like the words of Ennius
in *The Sabine Women*—

Now that you have dragged us as spoils from our
bridegrooms, what inscription will you cut upon us ? [b]

THE LITTLE HOSTESS

A comedy; but the single fragment does not even give us
the title for certain.

381

Nonius : ' Propitiabilis,' ready to be propitiated. Ennius
in *The Little Hostess*—

Hence can the feelings be soothed.

[a] Vahlen, *Rh. Mus.*, XVI, 580. R., 205-7.
[b] As though we were dedicated spoils of war.

---

a   propitiando   *rell. prob.*   Linds.   caupuncula   Ribb.
cupuncula V   coponicula Onions   cupiuncula *cdd. Non.*

ENNIUS

PANCRATIASTES

382

Nonius, 505, 35 : 'Audibo' pro audiam.   Ennius . . . Pancratiaste—

A

Quo nunc me ducis?

B

      Ubi molarum strepitum audibis maximum.

383

Nonius, 513, 12 : 'Poterviter' . . . —

Quis est qui nostris foribus tam proterviter?

384

Nonius, 517, 10 : 'Desubito' . . . —

cum desubito me orat mulier lacrimansque ad genua accidit.

EX FABULIS INCERTIS

EX TRAGOEDIIS

385

I.

Servius, ad *Aen.*, IX, 253 : 'integer aevi,' integri aevi figurate, id est adulescens cui aetas integra superest, unde Ennius—

    deos aevi integros

UNASSIGNED FRAGMENTS

THE ALL-ROUND CHAMPION

A comedy.

382

Nonius says : ' Audibo ' for ' audiam ' . . . the same in *The All-round Champion*—

A

Where are you leading me now ?

B

Where you'll hear a mighty rumble of mills.

383

Nonius : ' Proterviter ' . . . —
Who's that so boldly at our doors ?

384

Nonius : ' Desubito ' . . . —
when on a sudden the woman takes to praying and falls weeping at my knees.

UNASSIGNED FRAGMENTS OF PLAYS

FROM TRAGEDIES

385

I. *From passages connected with gods and religious things :*

Servius, on ' integer aevi ' in Virgil : Figuratively for ' integri aevi '; that is, a young person whose life still remains unimpaired. Whence Ennius—

the gods untouched by time

ENNIUS

386

Terentius, *Eun.*, III, 5, 42 :

At quem deum ! Qui templa caeli summa—

                            sonitu concutit

Donatus, *ad loc.* : ' Sonitu concutit ' parodia de Ennio. ' Templa caeli ' sententia tragica, sed de industria non errore.

387

Cicero, *de Orat.*, III, 40, 162 : Quo in genere primum est fugienda dissimilitudo—

                    caeli ingentes fornices.

Quamvis sphaeram in scaenam ut dicitur attulerit Ennius, tamen in sphaera fornicis similitudo non potest inesse.

Cp. Varro, *L.L.*, V, 19.

388

Cicero, *de Nat. Deor.*, II, 25, 65 (de Iove) : Hunc igitur Ennius ut supra dixi nuncupat ita dicens . . . planius quam alio loco idem—

Cui quod in me est exsecrabor, hoc quod lucet, quidquid est—

389

Eur., *Med.*, 168–70 (*nutrix loqu.*) : κλύεθ' οἷα λέγει κἀπιβοᾶται | θέμιν εὐκταίαν Ζῆνά θ' ὃς ὅρκων | θνητοῖς ταμίας νενόμισται. Cp. id., 207–8.

Cicero, *de Off.*, III, 29, 104 : Est enim ius iurandum adfirmatio religiosa . . . non ad iram deorum quae nulla est sed ad iustitiam et ad fidem pertinet ; nam praeclare Ennius—

O Fides alma apta pinnis et ius iurandum Iovis !

Cp. Apulei., *de deo Socr.*, 5, 10.

---

[386] *Ter.* : qui t. c. s. *fortasse Ennio tribuenda*
[388] *trib. Melanipp.* R   qui Gulielmus
[389] *trib. Thyest. vel Med.* V

UNASSIGNED FRAGMENTS

386

Terence : And what a god ! He who heaven's highest precincts—

with thunder shakes [a]

Donatus on this line : ' With thunder shakes ' : a parody of Ennius : ' Heaven's precincts ' : an idea from tragedy, but put here on purpose, not by mistake.

387

Cicero : In dealing with a thing of this kind we must first avoid any unlikeness—

Heaven's huge arches.

Although, it is said, Ennius brought a sphere on to the stage, nevertheless you cannot possibly find a likeness between an arch and a sphere.[b]

388

Cicero : It is Jupiter, therefore, as I said above, who is named by Ennius in the words . . . more plainly too than he does in another place—

This that shines, whate'er it is, to which so far as in me lies I shall utter my curses—

389

Cicero : For sworn oath is a solemn affirmation . . . it has nothing to do with the wrath of the gods, which does not exist, but with justice and faith. For Ennius has a brilliant saying—

O Faith, kindly wing-girt goddess ; O thou oath sworn in Jupiter's name !

[a] Only these words, I think, belong to Ennius.
[b] The allusion is not known, but V. quotes a suggestive passage of Hygin., *Fab.*, 130 : Atlanti . . . caeli fornicem super humeros imposuit.

ENNIUS

390–1

Festus, 430, 6 : ' Sospes ' . . . Ennius—

parentem et pa⟨triam . . .
⟩ sospitem.

392–3

II.

Diomedes, ap *G.L.*, I, 447, 5 K : ' Homoeoteleuton ' oratio similibus clausulis terminata . . . ut apud Ennium—

Eos reduci quam reliqui, devehi quam deseri
malui.

Cp. Charis., ap. *G.L.*, I, 282, 10 K ; Donatus, ap. IV, 398, 25 K. Cp. Eur., *Iph. A.*, 370–2, 495.

394

Varro, *L.L.*, VII, 49 : Apud Ennium—

quin inde invitis sumpserint perduellibus

perduelles dicuntur hostes.

395–6

Plinius, *N.H.*, XVIII, 84 : Pulte non pane vixisse longo tempore Romanos manifestum quoniam et pulmentaria hodieque dicuntur et Ennius antiquissimus vates obsidionis famem exprimens—

Offam eripuere liberis plorantibus
patres.

commemorat.

[390-1] pa⟨triam di servate⟩ S   *trib. Erechth.* R
[392-3] *trib. Iphig.* R
[395-6] liberis pl•rantibus St.   eripuisse plorantibus liberis *Plin.*   eripuere patres pueris plorantibus offam Bergk, *Opp., I*, 258 *n.*   *alii alia*

UNASSIGNED FRAGMENTS

390-1

Festus : ' Sospes ' . . . Ennius—

Parent and native land . . . safe and sound.[a]

392-3

II. *From passages referring to warfare and fighting :*

Diomedes : ' Homoeoteleuton ' comes about when parts of
a sentence end with the same closing sound . . . for example,
in a passage of Ennius [b]—

>   I preferred
> That home they should be taken, not forsaken;
> And shipped away, not cast away.

394

Varro : In a passage of Ennius—

that they took it not thence against the will of their
foes

' perduelles ' is a term used for foes.

395-6

Pliny : It is clear that the Romans lived for a long
time on pulse, not bread, since we speak of ' pulmentaria '
even to-day, and Ennius, a very early archaic poet, to express
the hunger of a siege, uses the words—

Fathers snatched the morsel from their wailing
children.[c]

---

[a] Scaliger's restoration, which is generally accepted, does
not seem to me to fill the gap in Festus (cf. Fest., ed. Linds.).

[b] This might well come from *Iphigenia*.

[c] To transpose *plorantibus* and *liberis*, and so get a senarius
with one word over, seems to be the simplest emendation;
I therefore put this fragment among the plays.

ENNIUS

397

? *Il.*, XII, 275 *s.*; 28 *s.*

Nonius, 196, 29 : ' Caementa ' . . . feminini Ennius—

Labat, labuntur saxa, caementae cadunt.

398

? *Il.*, XII, 253 *s.*

Nonius, 205, 23 : ' Fretum ' . . . masculini. . . . Ennius—

Crassa pulvis oritur, omnem pervolat caeli fretum.

399

? *Il.*, XVI, 802-3 (*de Patrocl. interitu*).

Varro, *L.L.*, VII, 93 : ' Euax ' verbum nihil significat,
sed effutitum naturaliter est ut apud Ennium—

Hehae, ipse clipeus cecidit.

Cp. auct. ap. *G.L.*, V, 574, 24 K.

400

III.

Gellius, V, 15, 9 : Ennianum Neoptolemum probabamus
qui profecto ita ait—

Neoptolemus

Philosophari mihi necesse, paucis, nam omnino
haud placet.

Id., V, 16, 5 : eiusdemque illius Enniani Neoptolemi de quo
supra scripsimus consilio utendum est qui degustandum ex
philosophia censet, non in eam ingurgitandum.

Cf. Cic., *Tusc. Disp.* II, 1, 1.

401

Fronto, *Epp.*, Vol. I, p. 76 Haines : De Herode quod
dicis perge, oro te, ut Quintus noster ait,—

Pervince pertinaci pervicacia.

[399] *trib. Hect. Lytr.* R, *comoediae* Spengel
[400] philosophandum est paucis *Gell.*   philosophari sibi ait
necesse esse sed p. *Cic.*   *alterum versum* degustandum ex
ea non in eam ingurgitandum censeo *constit.* Ribb.

UNASSIGNED FRAGMENTS

397

Nonius: 'Caementa' . . . Ennius has it in the feminine—
It totter'd, and tottered the stones, the blocks
    fell down.

398

Nonius: 'Fretum' . . . in the masculine . . . Ennius—
Thick rose the dust and soared over the sea of
heaven.

399

Varro: The word 'euax' means nothing, but is a natural
exclamation, like the one in a passage in Ennius—
Aha! His very shield fell.

400

III. *Philosophic and moral precepts :*

Gellius: I agreed with Neoptolemus in Ennius; he speaks
as follows—

Neoptolemus

 I must needs be a philosopher—in a few things;
for in all ways—that displeases me.

Gellius: And we must follow the counsel of that very same
Neoptolemus in Ennius, of whom I wrote above: he says,
'A man should take a taste of philosophy, and not rush to
swallow her.'

401

Marcus Aurelius, in Fronto's correspondence: About
Herodes, I pray you go on with what you say, and, in the
words of our Quintus [a]—
Conquer with sturdy staunchness.

       [a] Probably Quintus Ennius.

---

     [401] *trib. Enn.* R

ENNIUS

402–3

Cicero, *de Off.*, I, 8, 26 : Apud Ennium—

                 Nulla regni sancta societas
nec fides est.

Cp. Cic., *de re publ.*, I, 32, 49.

404

Fronto, *Epp.*, Vol. I, p. 136 Haines : . . . a⸍lfinitate
sociatum neque tutelae subditum, praeterea in ea fortuna
constitutum in qua ut Q. Ennius ait—

Omnes dant consilium vanum atque ad voluptatem
    omnia.

405–6

Cicero, *de Orat.*, II, 54, 221 : Est hominibus facetis et
dicacibus difficillimum, habere hominum rationem et temporum
et ea quae occurrant, cum salsissime dici possunt, tenere.
Itaque nonnulli ridiculi homines hoc ipsum non insulse
interpretantur ; dicere enim aiunt Ennium—

Flammam a sapienti facilius ore in ardente opprimi
quam bona dicta teneat ;

Haec scilicet bona dicta quae salsa sint.

407

Cicero, *Tusc. Disp.*, IV, 33, 70 : Mihi quidem haec in
Graecorum gymnasiis nata consuetudo videtur, in quibus
isti liberi et concessi sunt amores ; bene ergo Ennius—

Flagiti principium est nudare inter cives corpora.

Cp. Eur., *Androm.*, 595 ff.

---

[402] regni *fortasse reiciendum*   *trib. Thyest.* R

UNASSIGNED FRAGMENTS

402-3

Cicero : In a work of Ennius—

When one is king no partnership, no pledged word
is holy.

404

Marcus Aurelius, in Fronto's correspondence : . . . a man
allied by kinship and not entrusted to a guardian; and
moreover established in that rank of society in which, as
Quintus Ennius has it—

They all give empty counsel; all their deeds they
do with an eye to pleasing.

405-6

Cicero : The wags and wits find it hard to take proper
account of time and character, and as thoughts occur to
them, to hold them back at the moment when they can be
expressed most smartly. And so there are some jokers who
give a quite worthy turn to this also. For they declare that
Ennius says—

'Tis easier for a wise man to smother the flame of
burning speech than to hold in good words ;

that is to say, those ' good words ' which are smart.

407

Cicero : As for me, I think that this custom had its birth
in the gymnastic schools of the Greeks : in them such love-
making was free and tolerated. Rightly, therefore, does
Ennius say—

It is the beginning of disgrace to bare the body
among fellow-citizens.

ENNIUS

408-9

Cicero, *Tusc. Disp.*, III, 3, 5 : At et morbi perniciosiores pluresque sunt animi quam corporis; hoc enim ipso odiosi sunt quod ad animum pertinent eumque sollicitant, animusque aeger ut ait Ennius—

Animus aeger semper errat, neque pati neque perpeti

potis est, cupere numquam desinit.

410

Cicero, *de Off.*, II, 7, 23 : Omnium autem rerum nec aptius est quicquam ad opes tuendas ac tenendas quam diligi nec alienius quam timeri; praeclare enim Ennius—

Quem metuunt oderunt, quem quisque odit periisse expetit.

Cp. Ovid., *Am.*, II, 2, 10; Hieron., *Epist.*, 82, 3 (I, 737 Migne).

411

Paulus, ex F., 88, 31 (16) : 'Metus' feminine dicebant. Ennius—

Vivam an moriar nulla in me est metus.

412-14

Cicero, *de Off.*, I, 16, 51 : Omnium autem communia hominum videntur ea quae sunt generis eius quod ob Ennio positum in una re transferri in permultas potest—

Homo qui erranti comiter monstrat viam
quasi lumen de suo lumine accendat facit;
nihilo minus ipsi lucet cum illi accenderit.

Cp. id., III, 13, 54 ; *pro Balbo*, 16, 36.

---

[408] animusque aeger ut ait Ennius semper e. q. s. *Cic.* poti (potiri) Ribb. *fortasse recte*
[409] potis est Ribb.   potest *Cic.*

UNASSIGNED FRAGMENTS

408-9

Cicero : But the diseases too of the soul are more deadly and more numerous than those of the body. For they are loathsome through the very fact that they have to do with the soul, and trouble it, and, as Ennius says—

A sick soul is always wandering; it can neither bear troubles nor bear with them; it never ceases longing.

410

Cicero : But in all the world there is nothing better fitted for guarding and keeping one's power than to be loved, nothing more remote from this than to be feared. For brilliantly does Ennius put it—

Whom men fear they hate; whom anyone hates he desires to be dead.

411

Paulus : Writers used to use 'metus' in the feminine. Ennius—

Should I live or die—there is no fear in me.

412-14

Cicero : But all men, it seems, have in common goods of the kind which, applied to one example only in Ennius, can be transferred so as to apply to very many—

The man who kindly points the way to a wanderer, does as though he kindle a light from the light that is his; it shines none the less for himself when he has kindled it for his fellow.

412-14 *trib. Teleph.* R   suae lumine accendit facis Hartman, *Mnemos.*, *XXI*, 382 *fortasse recte*

ENNIUS

415

Varro, *L.L.*, VII, 89 : Apud Ennium—

Si voles advortere animum comiter monstrabitur.

comiter hilare ac lubenter.

416

Cicero, *de Off.*, II, 18, 62 : In iis qui se adiuvare volent . . . restricti omnino esse nullo modo debemus sed in deligendis idoneis iudicium et diligentiam adhibere. Nam praeclare Ennius—

Benefacta male locata malefacta arbitror.

417
IV.

Rutilius Lupus, ap. *R.L.M.*, 8, 14 H : διαφορά. Hoc schema cum verbum iteratum aliam sententiam significat ac significavit primo dictum. Id est huiusmodi . . . item in Ennii versu—

mulierem; quid potius dicam aut verius quam mulierem?

Cp. Eur., *Hec.*, 1178; *Stheneb.*, 607 N.

418

Nonius, 197, 28 : ' Quis ' et generi feminino attribui posse veterum auctoritas voluit . . . Ennius—

. . . Et quis illaec est quae lugubri succincta est stola ?

419

Servius ad *Aen.*, I, 4 : ' Saevae.' . . . Saevam dicebant veteres magnam. Sic Ennius—

induta fuit saeva stola

[415] *trib. Teleph.* R
Rutil.: in Enni versu Meinecke   universum *cdd.*
[418] *trib. Andromedae* R   et quis *cdd.*   set quis Ribb.

UNASSIGNED FRAGMENTS

415

Varro : In a passage of Ennius—

If you will deign to turn your mind to me, kindly shall it be shown to you.

' comiter ' means cheerfully and willingly.

416

Cicero : In dealing with persons who will want help given them . . . we ought by no means to be niggards towards all of them; but yet we ought to bring judgment and diligence to bear in picking out the worthy. For brilliantly does Ennius put it—

Good deeds ill placed I think are ill deeds.

417

IV. *Various :*

Rutilius Lupus : Diaphora. This is a figure of speech which comes about when a word by repetition takes a meaning different from that which it had at the first utterance. This is the kind of thing . . . again in Ennius' line—

a woman; what better or truer term could I use than ' woman '? [a]

418

Nonius : The old writers held it possible to assign the word ' quis ' to the feminine gender also. . . . Ennius—

and who is she girt up in a gown of mourning?

419

Servius, on ' saevae ' in Virgil : The old writers [b] used the term ' saeva ' for ' big.' Thus Ennius—.

Clothed she was in a huge gown

[a] This might well come from *Hecuba* : V., 198. The second utterance of the word ' woman ' is scornful.
[b] Certainly not Virgil in *Aen.*, I, 4.

ENNIUS

420

Festus, 548, 3 : At antiqui tam etiam pro tamen usi sunt,
ut . . . Ennius—

ille meae tam potis pacis potiri.

421

Varro, *L.L.*, V, 23 : ' Terra ' ut putant eadem et humus ;
ideo Ennium in terram cadentis dicere—

cubitis pinsibant humum

422

Festus, 538, 14 : ' Tesca ' sunt loca augurio designata . . .
aspera, difficilia aditu . . . —

⟨lo⟩ca aspera, saxa tesca tuor

423

Servius auctus, ad Verg., *Georg.*, I, 12–13 (Vol. III, p. 134,
T.) : Nonnulli vero ob hoc ' cui prima frementem fudit
aquam ' legunt quod veteres murmura aquae fremitum
dicebant. Ennius—

ager oppletus imbrium fremitu.

424-5

Varro, *L.L.*, V, 14 : ' Locatum ' veteres id (*collocatum*)
dicere solitos apparet apud . . . Ennium—

O terra Thraeca ubi Liberi fanum inclutum
Maro locavit,

Cp. Eur., *Hec.*, 1088.

426

Acro, ad Hor., *C.*, III, 11, 18 : 'Muniant angues caput
eius ' . . . ut ait Ennius—

anguivillosi canis.

---

[422] *trib. Andromedae* R, *cf. V.*, 203
[424-5] *trib. Erechth. vel Hec.* V   inclutum Gulielmus
inciviū *cd.*   locavi *Varro*
[426] anguivillosi *coni.* V   angue villosi canis *Acro*

376

UNASSIGNED FRAGMENTS

420

Festus: But the archaic writers used 'tam' even for 'tamen': for example . . . Ennius—

Still he can get my good will.

421

Varro: 'Terra,' it is thought, is the same as 'humus'; and that therefore Ennius with the words—

They did bruise their elbows on the ground

speaks of persons falling.[a]

422

Festus: 'Tesca' is a term used of places which are marked out for augury . . . rough, and not easy to approach . . .—

I see rough places and high ragged rocks

423

Servius (supplemented) on a passage in Virgil: But there are some who read 'cui prima frementem fudit aquam' (*instead of equum*) because the old writers were wont to use 'fremitus' for the murmuring of water. Ennius—

The land was filled with the roar of waters.

424–5

Varro: That the old writers were wont to use 'locatum' for 'collocatum' appears in . . . Ennius—

O land of Thrace, where Maro[b] did place a renowned temple of Liber,

426

Acro, on 'Though snakes fortify his head' . . . in Horace:

of the snake-shaggy dog.[c]

[a] As they stand the words suggest an assembly of people lying on the ground and listening to a speaker; cp. *pinsunt terram genibus* in *Annals*, fr. 342.

[b] Maro, a companion of Bacchus, who founded the Thracian town Maronea.

[c] *i.e.* Cerberus.

ENNIUS

EX COMOEDIIS

427

Cicero, *de Div.*, II, 62, 127 : Iam vero quis dicere audeat
vera omnia esse somnia—

◡ Aliquot somnia vera ⟨sunt⟩

inquit Ennius—

               sed omnia non necesse est.

428

Festus, 170, 6 : ' Naucum ' ait Ateius philologus poni pro
nugis. . . . Ennius—

– ◡ – ◡ Illic est nugator, nil, non nauci homo.

429

Varro, *L.L.*, VII, 101 : Apud Ennium—

Vocibus concide ; fac iam musset obrutus.

Mussare dictum quod muti non amplius quam μῦ dicunt.

430

Diomedes, ap. *G.L.*, I, 400, 15 ff. K : Moro . . . crebro
moror dicimus. . . . Ennius—

An aliquid quod illi dono moraret ? Non, sed accipit.

[427] sunt *add.* W   *alii alia*   non ~~nunc~~ necesse est
Voss. B   nonnunc haec cēt *Voss. A Vind.*
[428] *sic constituo.*   nihili Ursinus   nihil *cdd.*   nauci
< est > V
[429] fac iam musset Zander   facito musset Mr.   faxis
musset Ribb.   facimus et obrutus (obrutum *Flor.*
facimus musset *cd. Turn.*)
[430] Ennius an aliquid quod dono illi morare sed accipite
demolio *cdd.*   Ennius añali Stowasser   do nil morares ?
accipe V   accipe. item demolio *coni.* Keil   illi dono
moraret ? non sed accipit W

378

UNASSIGNED FRAGMENTS

FROM COMEDIES^a

427

Cicero: Well now, who would dare to say that all dreams are true.   Says Ennius—

Some dreams are true; but it does not follow that all are so.^b

428

Festus: Ateius the philologist says that 'naucus' is a term put for nonsense. . . . Ennius—

That fellow there is a noodle, a nobody, a good-for-nothing.

429

Varro: In a passage of Ennius—

Split him with shouts; reduce him to mumbles at once, all smothered.^c

'Mumble' is used because the dumb say no more than 'mum.'

430

Diomedes: 'Moro' we frequently use in the form 'moror.' . . . Ennius—

Would he delay to take any gift I offer him? No, but he takes it.^d

^a We can judge these (doubtfully at best) only by the general tone of the words quoted.
^b It is uncertain in what metre Ennius wrote this saying. By adding *sunt*, I make an *iambic septenarius* (*tetram. catal.*), a metre found chiefly in Plautus and Terence (cp. Catullus, XXV) and so suggesting a comedy.
^c All restorations are doubtful.
^d A very corrupt fragment.

ENNIUS

431

Varro, *L.L.*, VII, 93 : Apud Ennium—

Heu mea puella ipse quidem id succenset tibi!

432

auctor *ad Herenn.*, IV, 12, 18 : Vitabimus eiusdem litterae nimiam adsiduitatem cui vitio versus hic erit exemplo . . . et hic eiusdem poetae—

Quicquam quisquam cuiquam quemque quisque conveniat neget.

INCERTA

433

Varro, *L.L.*, VII, 12 : A tuendo et templa et tesca dicta cum discrimine eo quod dixi; etiam indidem illud Ennii—

Extemplo acceptum me necato et filium.

Extemplo enim est continuo, quod omne templum esse debet continuo septum nec plus unum introitum habere.

434

Diomedes, ap. *G.L.*, I, 345, 1 K : Item ' adeo adis '; hoc iteramus ' adito aditas ' dictitantes, ut Ennius—

Ad eum aditavere.

435

Servius, ad *Aen.*, VI, 686 : ' Genis,' palpebris. Ennius de dormiente—

imprimitque genae genam.

431 ipse quidem L   e spe quidem id successit Ribb. (*sec.* O. Mueller)   puella spe q. i. succenset *cdd.*
432 *cf. V.*, p. 201

UNASSIGNED FRAGMENTS

431

Varro (on exclamations) : In a passage of Ennius—

Oh dear, my girl, that very man is in a heat of rage at you for that!

432

The author of *To Herennius* : We will avoid too frequent repetition of the same letter; for which blemish the following line will be an example . . . and this line of the same poet—

Let anyone deny anyone anything, whoever meets whomever.

THE FOLLOWING MIGHT COME EITHER FROM TRAGEDIES OR FROM COMEDIES

433

Varro : Both 'templa' and 'tesca' are derived from 'tueor' with the difference which I have spoken of. From the same derivation comes also the following by Ennius—

Forthwith take and slay me and my son.

For 'extemplo' means 'without a break,' because [a] every 'temple' must be fenced round 'without a break' and have no more than one entrance.

434

Diomedes : Again, 'adeo, adis'; we get the frequentative form of this verb by saying 'adito,' 'aditas,'; for example, Ennius—

They kept going up to him.

435

Servius on 'genis' in Virgil [b] : 'Genis,' eyelids. Ennius describes a person sleeping—

and he presses eyelid to eyelid.

[a] This is, of course, fanciful.
[b] *Aen.*, VI, 686 where *genis* could mean ' on his cheeks.'

436

Servius (auctus), ad *Aen.*, IX, 399 : ' Pulchram properet per vulnera mortem '; aut deest adire aut deest ad . . . aut certe antique properet mortem ut . . . Ennius—

festivum festinant diem

Cp. Serv. auct., ad Verg., *Georg.*, IV, 170.

437

Festus, 532, 4 : ' Topper' significare ait Artorius cito, fortasse, celeriter, temere. . . . Sinnius vero sic : topper fortasse valet in Enni et Pacuvi scriptis; apud Ennium est—

Topper quam nemo melius scit

SATURAE

It is a matter of doubt whether Ennius wrote four or six books of Satires; nor is it known whether any or all of Ennius' minor works under other titles should be included in them. With regard to the number of books, Porphyrio, ad Hor., *S.*, I, 10, 46, says that Ennius left four books of Satires. But Donatus, ad Ter. *Phorm.*, II, 2, 25, seems to quote from a sixth book. In Porphyrio, UII was perhaps written or misread as IIII, and even the name Ennius is not there clearly recorded; or in Donatus IV was read or miscopied as VI. With regard to certain minor works, it is possible that the work *Scipio* cited by several authors (see below) is the title of the third book of the Satires, to which the frs. of *Scipio*

---

a The fragment might be from the *Annals*, but Festus in this passage seems to be quoting from plays only.

SATIRES

436

Servius (supplemented) on 'Hastens death' in Virgil:
We must supply 'adest' or 'ad' . . . or at any rate 'pro-
peret mortem' is put in archaic style as we find in . . .
Ennius—

They hurry the merry-making of the day

437

Festus: Artorius says that 'topper' means quickly,
perhaps, swiftly, rashly. . . . But Sinnius writes thus:
'topper' in the writings of Ennius and Pacuvius has the force
of 'perhaps'; we find in a passage of Ennius *a*—

Whom perhaps no one *b* knows better

SATIRES

would thus belong. I would point out that only Nonius quotes
from *Satires* Bk. III, and he never quotes from *Scipio*. But
in view of Gellius, VI, 9, 1, *etc.*, and IV, 7, 2 (quoted below),
we must separate *Scipio* from the *Satires*. We can see that
the Satires were written in a variety of metres; that they
included dialogues and fables; that some of them had a
direct and censorious bearing on public morals and politics;
and that Ennius claimed to write in a free conversational and
light-hearted manner. It seems that, the old native drama
satura having been replaced by Greek plays, Ennius invented
here a new form of literature which preserved some of the
essential spirit of the earlier type.

---

b Yet *topper* seems to be simply *toto opere*, ' with all speed '
or ' diligence.'

ENNIUS

Liber I

1

Nonius, 474, 22 : 'Convivant' pro convivantur. . . .
Ennius Satyrarum lib. I—

Malo hercle magno suo convivat sine modo![1]

2

Nonius, 510, 7 : 'Celere' pro celeriter . . . —

Dum quidquid des celere.

Liber II

3-4

Servius (auctus), ad Aen., XII, 121 : 'Pilata,' fixa et
stabilia. . . . Ennius Saturarum II—

                         Contemplor
inde loci liquidas pilatasque aetheris oras,

cum firmas et stabiles significaret quasi pilis fultas.

5

Nonius, 147, 8 : 'Obstringillare,' obstare . . . —

Restitant occurrunt obstant obstringillant obagitant.

[1] magno suo Bothe   suo m. *Non.*   convivat.   Sine
modo Bothe, *Rh. Mus.*, *V.*, 266 *fortasse recte*

SATIRES

Book I

1

a glutton :

Nonius : ' Convivant ' for ' convivantur.' . . . Ennius in Book I of the *Satires*—

He's one of the guzzlers without limit, and, by god, may he be utterly damned for it !

2

giving :

Nonius : ' Celere ' for ' celeriter ' . . . —

So long as whatever you give it is done quickly.

Book II

3-4

Servius (supplemented), on ' pilata ' in Virgil : ' Pilata,' fixed and standing steady. . . . Ennius in Book II of the *Satires*—

From that place I gaze on the piled spaces of the ether,

where he meant ' firm and standing steady,' as it were supported by ' pilae.'

5

busybodies :

Nonius : ' Obstringillare,' to stand in the way. . . —

They loiter and run to meet you, they hinder and hamper and harass you.

ENNIUS

LIBER III

6-7

Nonius, 33, 4 : ' Propinare ' a Graeco tractum, post potum tradere. . . . Ennius Satyrarum lib. III—

Enni poeta salve qui mortalibus
versus propinas flammeos medullitus!

Cp. Non., 139, 15.

8-9

Nonius, 470, 19 : ' Criminat ' . . . —

Nam is non bene vult tibi qui falso criminat
aput te.

10-11

Nonius, 66, 18 : ' Politiones ' agrorum cultus diligentes, ut polita omnia dicimus exculta et ad nitorem deducta . . . —

Testes sunt
lati campi quos gerit Africa terra politos.

LIBER IV

12-13

Macrobius, S., VI, 5, 5 : ' Tristis ' pro amaro translatio decens est, ut ' tristisque lupini.' Et ita Ennius in libro Saturarum quarto—

neque ille triste quaeritat sinapi
neque caepe maestum.

Cp. Serv., auct. ad Verg., Georg., I, 75.

---

[8] namque is *olim* V (*Rh. Mus. XIV*, 567)

SATIRES

Book III

6–7

Nonius : ' Propinare ' is derived from the Greek; it means to hand on after drinking. . . . Ennius in Book III of the *Satires*—

Your health, poet Ennius, who pass to mortal men a cup of flaming verses drawn from your very marrow !

8–9

Nonius : ' Criminat ' . . . —

For no well-wisher of yours is he who spreads slanders in your family.

10–11

Benefits conferred by Scipio ? : [a]

Nonius : ' Politiones ' means zealous cultivation of fields; even so we call ' polita ' all things that are carefully worked and brought up to brilliance . . . —

The broad plains which the land of Africa bears in neat tillage are witnesses.

Book IV

12–13

Habits of the refined ? :

Macrobius : ' Tristis ' is a neat figure of speech for ' amarus,' like ' harsh lupine ' (Virg., *G.*, I, 75). And so also Ennius in the fourth book of the *Satires*—

He seeks and yearns neither for harsh mustard nor for the weepy onion.

[a] A great store of corn brought by Scipio from Africa in 201 B.C. was distributed among the people (cf. Livy, XXXI, 4).

387

c c 2

ENNIUS

Ex Libris Incertis

14-19

Donatus, ad Ter., *Phorm.*, II, 2, 25 : ' Tene asymbolum venire . . . (ille ringitur tu rideas).' Haec non ab Apollodoro sed e IV (?) Satyrarum Ennii . . . —

Quippe sine cura laetus lautus cum advenis
inferctis malis expedito bracchio,
alacer celsus, lupino expectans impetu—
mox cum tu alterius abligurias bona
quid censes domino esse animi? Pro divum fidem
is tristest dum cibum servat, tu ridens voras.

Gellius, II, 29, 1 *s.*: fabula de avicula ' cassita.'

20

Festus, 444, 2 : ' Subulo ' Tusce ·tibicen dicitur; itaque Ennius—

Subulo quondam marinas propter astabat plagas.

Cp. Varro, *L.L.*, VII, 35.

Donat. sed de sexto salis *cdd. Leid. Dresd. cf. V., p.* 206, *vide supra, p.* 382.
[16] expectans i. Muret   i. e. *cdd.*
[17] mox cum *cdd.*   Quam mox Muret   abligurias *Leid.* obligurias *Vat.*   tu *addidi*
[18] domino Muret   dominos *cdd.*
[19] is W   tristest Plasberg   ille tristis cibum dum *vulg.* ille tristis est dum *cdd.*   voras *ed. princ.*   vorans *cdd.*

[a] From a sixth book ? V., 206-7; *prooem.*, 1880, 14 ff. But see p.
[b] This seems to be correct here; but in all other occurrences of the verb *infarcio* (*infercio*) the meaning is ' I stuff.'

SATIRES

Unplaced Fragments from the Satires

14-19

A parasite [a] :

Donatus on 'The idea of your coming scot-free' in Terence :
All this is taken not from Apollodorus but from the fourth (?)
book of Ennius' *Satires*—

Why, when you come along without a care in the
world, gaily spick and span, your cheeks unstuffed,[b]
your arm bared ready, tripping a-tip-toe, waiting
all taut like a wolf—when soon you are lapping up
another's goods, in what mind, think you, is your
host? He's down in the dumps, God's truth, while
he lays up a store of vittles and you gobble it with a
grin.

I. *In trochaic metre.*

A complete (?) *Satire on Aesop's fable ' The crested Lark and
its Chicks.'* [c] See text and translation in the Loeb edition of
Gellius.

20

*On the flute-player who tried to catch sea-fish by piping to
them.* [d]

Festus : ' Subulo ' is a Tuscan term for a flute-player ;
and so we have in Ennius—

A piper once stood near the regions of the sea.

[c] Aesop, *F.,* 210 H.; Babr., 88; Avianus, 21. There can be
no doubt, on the evidence of words and phrases of archaic
look and of trochaic metre in Gellius' reproduction, that
Vahlen is right in believing that Gellius' prose reproduces
Ennius' verse though it hides the metre almost completely—
V., CCXI–CCXII; Ribbeck, *Rh. Mus.,* X, 290 ff. (an attempt
at restoring Ennius' verses).

[d] Herod., I, 141; V., CCXIII–CCXIV.

ENNIUS

21

Priscianus, ap. *G.L.*, II, 434, 6 K : Nos quoque philosophor architector poetor in usu habuimus. Ennius—

Numquam poetor nisi si podager.

22

Gellius, VI, 9 : Q. Ennius in Saturis ' memorderit' dixit per *e* litteram non momorderit—

Non est meum ac si me canis memorderit.

23

Cicero, *de Nat. Deor.*, I, 35, 97 : Ipsa vero quam nihil ad rem pertinet quae vos delectat maxime similitudo. Quid ? Canis nonne similis lupo atque ut Ennius—

Simia quam similis turpissima bestia nobis !

At mores in utroque dispares.

Cp. Seren. Sammon., *Lib. Med.*, 819.

24

Paulus, ex Fest., 41, 27 (23) : . . . Ennius . . . cum dicit—

Propter stagna ubi lanigerum genus piscibus pascit,

esse paludem demonstrat in qua nascuntur pisces similes ranunculis quos oves consectatae edunt.

---

21 si *add.* V   sim Mr.   nisi p. *cdd.*
22 non est ut *cdd. Non.*   meum inquit non est ac *cdd. Gell.*

II. *In iambic metre.*

21

Ennius and his Satires:

Priscianus: We also have had in use the verbs 'philosophor,' 'architector,' 'poetor.' Ennius—

I never indulge in poetics
Unless I am down with rheumatics.

22

His indifference:

Gellius: Quintus Ennius in the *Satires* used 'memorderit' with the letter *e*, not momorderit. He says—

It's not my way, as if a dog has bitten me.

III. *In hexameters.*

23

Cicero: But that very resemblance which takes your fancy so very much—how utterly beside the point it is! Why, does not a dog look like a wolf? And again, as Ennius has it—

That ugly beast the ape 's the very spit of us!

But in both the habits are different.

24

Beginning of a fable?:

Paulus: . . . Ennius . . . when he says—

Hard by the pools where the woolly tribe feeds on fishes,

he illustrates the existence of a swamp in which are bred fishes looking like buttercups [a] which sheep hunt out and eat.

---

[a] I take the word as meaning the flower described by Pliny, XXV, 172. Would sheep hunt things looking like little frogs or tadpoles?

ENNIUS

25–6

Varro, *L.L.*, VII, 71 : Apud Ennium—

⟨massas⟩ - ‿ decem coclites quas montibus summis
Ripaeis fodere,

ab oculo cocles ut ocles dictus, qui unum haberet oculum.

27

Festus, 490, 7 : 'Scirpus' est id quod in palustribus
locis nascitur leve et procerum unde tegetes fiunt. Inde
proverbium est in eas natum res quae nullius inpedimenti
sunt, in scirpo nodum quaerere. Ennius—

Quaerunt in scirpo soliti quod dicere nodum.

Cp. Isidor., *Orig.*, XVII, 9, 97.

28–31

Gellius, XVIII, 2, 7 : Nuper quaesita esse memini numero
septem quorum prima fuit enarratio horum versuum qui
sunt in Saturis Q. Enni uno multifariam verbo concinniter
inplicati. Quorum exemplum hoc est—

Nam qui lepide postulat alterum frustrari

quem frustratur frustra eum dicit frustra esse;

nam qui sese frustrari quem frustra sentit,

qui frustratur frustra est si non ille est frustra.

---

[25] ⟨massas⟩ L
[30] nam qui sese *cdd.*   nam si se Usener, Hosius
frustra sentit *Pet.*   frustras *rell.*
[31] ille frustra est Skutsch

SATIRES

25–6

Gold-mining of the Arimaspi in Scythia : [a]

Varro : In a passage of Ennius—

ten nuggets which the One-Eyed have mined on the
Ripaean mountain-tops,

' cocles,' as it were ' ocles,' was derived from ' oculus,' ' cocles '
meaning a man having one eye.

27

Ill-natured critics :

Festus : ' Scirpus ' is that smooth tall plant which grows
in marshy places and from which mats are made. From this
rose the proverb which is applied to things which present
no hindrance—' to look for a knot in a bulrush.' Ennius—

As the common saying goes, they are seeking a
knot in a bulrush.

IV. *In Saturnian metre.*

28–31

On cheating :

Gellius : I remember that not long ago we put questions
seven in number, of which the first was an explanation of
those lines in the *Satires* of Quintus Ennius, which are deftly
tangled up with one word used in a number of different
phrases. They read as follows—

For he who wants to be smart and trick his fellow,
is tricked when he says the other whom he tricks is
tricked. For he who is tricked into feeling that he
is tricking someone, the tricker is tricked if the other
is not tricked.

[a] Herod., III, 116; IV, 13, 14, 27. The fr. suggests a
mocking allusion to ostentatious wealth.

ENNIUS

Quintilianus, IX, 2, 36 : Sed formas quoque fingimus saepe ut . . . Mortem et Vitam quas contendentes in satura tradit Ennius.

SCIPIO

This poem (probably not to be taken either as a drama or as the third book of the *Satires* or as part of it—see p. 382) celebrated the African campaigns of Ennius' friend Scipio Africanus, in which Scipio brought the second Punic War to a

---

Suidas, s.v. Ἔννιος : ῾Ρωμαῖος ποιητὴς ὃν Αἰλιανὸς ἐπαινεῖν ἄξιόν φησιν. Σκιπίωνα γὰρ ᾄδων καὶ ἐπὶ μέγα τὸν ἄνδρα ἐξᾶραι βουλόμενός φησι μόνον ἂν Ὅμηρον ἐπαξίοις ἐπαίνους εἰπεῖν Σκιπίωνος.

1-4

Macrobius, S., VI, 2, 26 : 'Tum pater omnipotens . . . premit placida aequora pontus' (*Aen.*, X, 100 *s.*). Ennius in Scipione—

Mundus caeli vastus constitit silentio
et Neptunus saevus undis asperis pausam dedit,
sol equis iter repressit ungulis volantibus,
constitere amnes perennes, arbores vento vacant.

---

a It was probably a poem with the same idea as Novius' ' *Mortis et Vitae iudicium.*' Vahlen, CCXIII.
b I would compare Livy, XXIX, 27 (204 B.C.) ; others cite Livy, XXVIII, 17 (206 B.C.).

SCIPIO

V. *Unknown.*

A dialogue between Life and Death :

Quintilian : But we often enough personify the abstract, as Ennius does in one [a] of his *Satires* where he represents Death and Life wrangling with each other.

SCIPIO

close with the battle of Zama in 202 B.C. I have not adopted Vahlen's order, because it seems to me natural that in the poem the description of the campaign should come before the description of Scipio's reception by the Roman people.

I. *Prelude.*

Scipio is worthy of the greatest of poets :

Suidas : Ennius, a Roman poet whom Aelian states to be worthy of praise. For, in a poem of praise on Scipio, with the desire of extolling his hero he says that ' Homer alone could utter praises worthy of Scipio.'

II. *Scipio's African campaigns described in varying metres to suit either slow or rapid action.*

1–4

The calm crossing to Africa : [b]

Macrobius, on Virgil's verses about the calm caused by Jupiter speaking : Ennius in *Scipio*—

The vast firmament of heaven stood still in silence, and wild Neptune gave rest to his rough billows, Sun checked the charge of his horses' winged hoofs, the ever-flowing rivers stood still, and the trees were void of wind.

ENNIUS

5

Gellius, IV, 7, 3 : Solius Ennii versum unum ponit (Probus) ex libro qui Scipio inscribitur; eum versum quadrato numero factum subiecimus, in quo nisi tertia syllaba de Hannibalis nomine circumflexe promatur numerus clausurus est. Versus Ennii quem dixit ita est—

. . . qua propter Hannibalis copias considerat.

6

Il., XIII, 339-40: ἔφριξεν δὲ μάχη φθισίμβροτος ἐγχείῃσιν | μακρῇς.

Macrobius, *S.*, VI, 4, 6 : ' Tum ferreus hastis | horret ager.' 'Horret' mire se habet; sed et Ennius . . . in Scipione—

Sparsis hastis longis campus splendet et horret.

Cp. Serv., ad *Aen.*, XI, 601.

7

Cicero, *Orat.*, 45, 152: Nobis ne si cupiamus quidem distrahere voces conceditur. Indicant . . . omnes poetae praeter eos qui ut versum facerent saepe hiabant . . . Ennius saepe—

Scipio invicte

8–9

Paulus, ex F., 561, 32 (20): ' Vel' conligatio . . . est disiunctiva . . . earum (rerum) quae non sunt contra, e quibus quae cligatur nihil interest, ut Ennius—

' Vel tu dictator vel equorum equitumque magister esto vel consul.'

[5] qua *cdd.*   quaque Hertz   si qua Buecheler

---

[a] Some compare App., *Lib.*, 39: Σκιπίων Πάρθον . . . εἷλε καὶ πλησίον 'Αννίβου μετεστρατοπέδευεν.

[b] Or, ' wherefore he reconnoitres Hannibal's host.' In this line Hannibalis must be spoken with the third syllable long instead of short.

SCIPIO

5

Scipio pitches his camp close to Hannibal : [a]

Gellius : It is from Ennius alone that Probus cites a line,
and only one, from the book entitled *Scipio.* I have given this
line below, written in eight-footed rhythm; in this line,
unless the third syllable of the genitive of the name ' Hannibal '
is spoken with a circumflex ' Hannibālis,' the rhythm is bound
to halt. The line of Ennius which he quoted is as follows—

where near Hannibal's host he had made his
camp.[b]

6

A battle :

Macrobius, on ' the plain bristles with spears ' in Virgil :
' Horret ' is a very strange term. But Ennius also has . . .
in *Scipio*—

The plain gleams and bristles with long spears
all over it.

III. *After the victory, the Roman people offer great honours
to Scipio :*

7

Cicero : We do not allow ourselves to leave a hiatus even
if we may wish; . . . all the poets point this way to us . . .
except those who used many a time to allow a hiatus in order
to make a line . . . Ennius often does it—

O Scipio [c] unconquered

8–9

The people offer him a perpetual [d] dictatorship or consulship :

Paulus : ' Vel ' is a connecting particle which is disjunctive
. . . and parts those things which are not opposites, and of
which it does not matter which you choose; for example,
Ennius has—

' Be you dictator or master of the horse and
horsemen, or be you consul.'

[c] As Cicero shows in his next example, Ennius' phrase scans:
Scīpiŏ invicte.   [d] Livy, XXXVIII, 36.

397

ENNIUS

10–11

Trebellius Pollio in *Hist. Aug.*, *Claud.*, 7, 6: Rogo quantum
pretium est clypeus in curia tantae victoriae, quantum una
aurea statua ? Dicit Ennius de Scipione—

[Quantam statuam faciet populus Romanus
quantam columnam quae res tuas gestas loquatur ?]

12–14

Cicero, *de Fin.*, II, 32, 106 : Fluit igitur voluptas corporis,
et prima quaeque avolat saepiusque relinquit causam paeni-
tendi quam recordandi. Itaque beatior Africanus cum patria
illo modo loquens—

' Desine Roma tuos hostes

et reliqua praeclare—

' Nam tibi moenimenta mei peperere labores.

Cicero, *de Orat.*, III, 42, 167 : Ornandi causa proprium
proprio commutatum . . . —

' Testes sunt campi magni.

EPIGRAMMATA

1–2

Cicero, *Tusc. Disp.*, V, 17, 49 : Est in aliqua vita praedicabile
aliquid et gloriandum ac prae se ferendum, ut . . . Africanus—

---

¹⁰⁻¹¹ *fortasse* quantam statuam faciet quantamve colum-
nam | Romanus populus quae te et tua gesta loquatur
vel –◡◡– q. s. q. c. | R. p. faciet tua gesta loquentem,
Quam tantam statuam statuet populus Romanus | quamve
columnam quae te res gestasque loquatur L Quantam
statuam statuet p. | quamve c. | quae te et tua gesta loquatur
Röper, *de Q. E. Scip.*, 29
¹³ moenimenta Klotz munimenta Muret moni-,
monumenta *cdd.*

EPIGRAMS

10–11

They desire to set up statues of him :

Trebellius Pollio : What sort of reward for so great a victory,
I ask you, is a shield in the senate-house or a golden statue ?
Ennius says of Scipio—

What statue, what pillar, will the Roman people
make, such as will tell of your great deeds ? [a]

IV. *Scipio refuses* [b] *all these honours :*

12–14

Cicero : Well then, bodily pleasures flow away; each in
turn fades and leaves oftener cause for repentance than for
remembrance. The happier therefore was Africanus when he
was conversing with his fatherland in the following fashion—

' Rome, cease you your foes to fear

and the rest, a brilliant speech—

' since bulwarks for you have my toils begotten.

Cicero : For the sake of adornment one proper name is
exchanged for another . . . —

' The great plains are witnesses.[c]

EPIGRAMS *(Epitaphs)*

I. *On Scipio Africanus :*

1–2

(a) Cicero : In some life or other there is something worthy
to be praised and boasted of and shown in full view; for
example . . . Africanus—

---

[a] Trebellius has not given Ennius' verses. I give some
possible restorations; see the critical note.

[b] Livy, *l.c.*

[c] In this passage of Cicero this fr. is preceded by line 12,
and so it probably belongs to Ennius' *Scipio.* For the place
called Magni Campi, cf. Livy, XXX, 8.

ENNIUS

A sole exoriente supra Maeotis paludes
nemo est qui factis aequiperare queat.

3-4

Lactantius, *Div. Instit.*, I, 18, 10 : Siquis unum hominem
iugulaverit pro contaminato ac nefario habetur . . . Ille
autem qui infinita hominum milia trucidarit . . . non modo
in templum sed etiam in caelum admittitur. Apud Ennium
sic loquitur Africanus—

Si fas endo plagas caelestum ascendere cuiquam est,
mi soli caeli maxima porta patet.

Cp. Sen., *Ep.*, 108, 34.

5-6

Cicero, *de Leg.*, II, 22, 57 : (Sulla) primus e patriciis
Corneliis igni voluit cremari. Declarat enim Ennius de
Africano—

Hic est ille situs

vere, nam siti dicuntur ii qui conditi sunt.
    Seneca, *Ep.*, 108, 32 : (grammaticus) deinde Ennianos
colligit versus et in primis illos de Africano scriptos—

cui nemo civis neque hostis
quibit pro factis reddere opis pretium.

Ex eo se ait intellegere aput antiquos non tantum auxilium
significasse opem sed operam; ait enim Ennius neminem
potuisse Scipioni neque civem neque hostem reddere operae
pretium.

---

[1] *Sen.*, *Ep.*, 108, 32 Ennianos, Pintianus   inanes *cdd.*
    [6] quibit Pintianus   quivit Muret   qui vult *cdd.*
opis V   operae *cdd.*

EPIGRAMS

From the rising of the sun above the marshes
of Maeotis [a] comes no one whose deeds could balance
his.

3–4

Lactantius: If anyone has cut even one man's throat
he is held to be polluted and loathsome . . . but he who has
butchered men in thousands without end . . . is received
not only into a temple but even into heaven. In a passage of
Ennius, Africanus speaks in this way—

If it is right for anyone to go up into the
regions of heaven's dwellers, for me alone
heaven's great gate lies open.

5–6

(b) Cicero: Sulla was the first of those Cornelii who were
patricians to see fit that his corpse should be burnt. Now
Ennius has a statement about Africanus—

Here lies the man

truly so; for 'lies' is a term applied to those who have been
buried in a grave.

Seneca: And then the scholar collects verses of Ennius,
especially those written about Africanus—

to whom no one, fellow-countryman
or foeman, will be able to render for his pains a
recompense fitting his deeds.

From this the scholar states he understands that in works
of archaic writers 'ops' meant not only help but efforts;
for what Ennius means is that no one, neither countryman nor
foeman, was able to render Scipio a recompense for his efforts.[b]

---

[a] Sea of Azov.
[b] The close union of these quotations from Cic. and Sen. is
probably right, but the reading in the second line is doubtful.
Cf. V., 215–16, whom I have followed.

ENNIUS

7–10

Cicero, *Tusc. Disp.*, I, 15, 34 : 'Quid ? Poetae nonne post mortem nobilitari volunt ? Unde ergo illud —

Aspicite o cives senis Enni imaginis formam.

Hic vestrum pinxit maxima facta patrum.

Mercedem gloriae flagitat ab iis quorum patres adfecerat gloria. Idemque—

Nemo me lacrimis decoret nec funera fletu

faxit. Cur ? Volito vivus per ora virum.

Cp. id., 49, 117; *de Senect.*, 20, 73.

SOTA

Cf. Fronto, *Epp.*, Vol. I, p. 78, Haines : Sota Ennianus remissus a te et in charta puriore et volumine gratiore et littera festiviore quam antea fuerat videtur.

1

Paulus, ex F., 41, 25 (23) :—

Cyprio bovi merendam

Ennius Sotadico versu cum dixit significavit id quod solet fieri in insula Cypro, in qua boves humano stercore pascuntur.

---

⁸ pinxit *cdd.* panxit *edd.*
⁹⁻¹⁰ decoret n. f. f. faxit *add. ex Cic.*, id., 49, 117 *et de Senect.*, 20, 73

SOTAS

II. *On Ennius himself.*

7-10

(a) *For his portrait ;* (b) ᵃ *for his sepulchre :*

Cicero : Why, do not poets wish to be made famous after death ? Well then, hence arises the famous—

(*a*)   Look, ye citizens, on the portrait of Ennius in his old age. 'Twas he painted the doughtiest deeds of your fathers.

He demands a guerdon of glory from those whose fathers he had endowed with glory. And the same poet has—

(*b*)   Let none embellish me with tears,
          Or make a funeral with wailing;
          And why? Alive from lips to lips of men
             I go a-winging.

SOTAS

This title was probably one given by Ennius to some poem of Sotades (a coarse poet of the third century B.C.) which he translated. Sota would correspond with Σωτᾶς a shortened form of Σωτάδης.

1

On cattle of Cyprus :

Paulus : When Ennius in a Sotadic line used the phrase—

lunch for a bull of Cyprus

he referred to what often happens in the island of Cyprus, where the kine are pastured on human dung.

ᵃ Cicero's own way of quotation here makes it certain that these are two separate epigrams; and other passages (see opposite) show that the author of both was Ennius; cf. Jahn, *Herm.*, II, 242.

ENNIUS

2

Varro, *L.L.*, V, 62 : A vinctura dicitur vieri id est vinciri, a quo est in Sota Enni—

Ibant malaci viere Veneriam corollam!

Cp. Fest., 570, 22 : auct., *de metr.*, ap. *G.L.*, VI, 613, 15 K.

3

Festus, 538, fin. : 'Tonsam' Ennius significat remum, quod quasi tondeatur ferro, cum ait . . . in Sota—

Alius in mari vult magno tenere tonsam

4

Paulus, ex F., 539, 5 : 'Tongere' nosse est, nam Praenestini tongitionem dicunt notionem. Ennius—

alii rhetorica tongent.

Cp. Fest., 538, 12.

5

auct., *de metr.*, ap. *G.L.*, VI, 613, 16 : Ionicus a maiore—

Ille ictus retro reccidit in natem supinus.

habet vitium in tertia syllaba.

---

[4] *trib. Sot. et cum* 3 *coniunx.* S
[5] *trib. Enn. Sot.* L

SOTAS

2

Wanton living :

Varro : From ' vinctura ' is derived ' vieri' which means ' vinciri.' Hence it is we have in Ennius' *Sotas*—

They were going along to plait a little love-garland—the lechers !

3

Ambitions of men ; the would-be mariner :

Festus : By ' tonsa ' Ennius means oar, because it as it were ' tonditur ' with a knife, when he says . . . in *Sotas*—

One man wishes to hold a trimmer on the mighty main

4

Would-be orators :

Paulus : ' Tongere ' means to know, for the Praenestines use the term ' tongitio ' to express knowing. Ennius—

Others ken well the rules of rhetoric.[a]

5

A comic scene ? :

A grammarian : Ionic ' a maiore '—

Punched he fell back again square on his bum.

This line has [b] a fault in the third syllable.

---

[a] The attribution of this and the next fragment is not certain, but they probably do come from *Sotas*.

[b] Not if we elide the *s* in *ictus* and read *ille īctŭ' rĕtro*. This line is quoted closely after line 2.

ENNIUS

PROTREPTICUM
SIVE
PRAECEPTA

1-3

Priscianus, ap. *G.L.*, II, 532, 16 K : Vetustissimi tamen
etiam in simplici ' serui ' protulisse inveniuntur pro ordinavi
et pro sevi. Ennius in Praeceptis—

Ubi videt avenam lolium crescere inter triticum,
selegit secernit aufert; sedulo ubi operam addidit,
. . . quam tanto studio seruit.

HEDYPHAGETICA (?)

Cp. Athenae., III, 92 d :

Ἀρχέστρατος δ' ἐν Γαστρονομίᾳ φησί·
τοὺς μῦς Αἶνος ἔχει μεγάλους ὄστρεια δ' Ἄβυδος
τοὺς δὲ κτένας ἡ Μιτυλήνη·
πλείστους δ' Ἀμβρακία παρέχει   2-3

VII, 300 d : τὸν δ' ἔλοπ' ἔσθε μάλιστα Συρακούσαις ἐνὶ
κλειναῖς | τόν γε κρατιστεύοντα.   6

VII, 320 a : σκάρον ἐξ 'Εφέσου ζήτει. . . . καὶ σκάρον ἐν
παράλῳ Καλχηδόνι τὸν μέγαν ὅπτα.   7

VII, 318 f : πούλυποι ἔν τε Θάσῳ καὶ Καρίᾳ εἰσὶν ἄριστοι 10
καὶ Κέρκυρα τρέφει μεγάλους πολλούς τε τὸ πλῆθος.

PROTREPTICUS V, E. in Protreptico *Charis. G.L.*, I, 54
³ *lacun. post 2 stat.* W   quoniam V., *Rh. Mus.*, *XVI*, 580
quam *cdd.*

ᵃ Charisius, quoting ' pannibus ' as abl. or dat. plural for
' pannus ' (rag), says Ennius in *Protreptico*. Vahlen would

406

EXHORTATION

AN EXHORTATION

OR

RULES OF CONDUCT

Doubtless a poem of precepts based on a Greek model of which the title was Προτρεπτικόν.[a]

1–3

Priscianus : Still the oldest writers are found to have used, when conjugating, the form ' serui ' even in the non-compounds, both in the sense of ' I put together ' (i.e. *from sero, sertum*) and of ' I sowed ' (i.e. *from sero, satum*). Ennius in *Rules of Conduct*—

When he sees wild oats and darnel growing among the wheat, away he picks them, parts them, carts them; when he has further bestowed honest care [b] . . . which was sown with such ardour.

DELIKATESSEN (?)

Whether this be the true title or not, it is certain that Ennius wrote a poem on tit-bits based on a mock-heroic poem of Archestratus of Gela (fourth cent. B.C.), which is quoted under various titles. The single surviving fragment of Ennius' version is quoted by Apuleius from the part dealing with fish and other sea-animals. He quoted from memory and could remember only a few lines; the corresponding fragments of Archestratus given opposite suggest that Apuleius left out some lines. Some of the readings [c] are very uncertain, and there are irregularities in the metre.

---

make the title Προτρεπτικός, but the title (?) *Praecepta* given by Priscianus suggests that Protrepticum is right.

[b] It looks as though a whole line and one word more has dropped out here.

[c] For these cf. V., *Rh. Mus.*, XVI, 581 ff. Bergk., *Annal. Fleckeis.*, LXXXII, 621 ff.

ENNIUS

1–11

Apuleius, *Apolog.*, 39 : Q. Ennius hedyphagetica scripsit. Innumerabilia genera piscium enumerat quae scilicet curiose cognorat. Paucos versus memini; eos dicam—

Omnibus ut Clupea praestat mustela marina!
Mures sunt Aeni asperaque ostrea plurima Abydi. . .
Mitylenae est pecten crebrumque apud Ambraciae
　　oras.
Brundisii sargus bonus est, hunc magnus si erit sume.
Apriculum piscem scito primum esse Tarenti.　　　5
Surrenti tu elopem fac emas glaucumque ἀπὸ Κύμης.
Quid scarus?　Praeterii, cerebrum Iovis paene
　　supremi,
(Nestoris ad patriam hic capitur magnusque bonusque)
melanurum　　turdum　　merulamque　　umbramque
　　marinam.
Polypus Corcyrae est, calvaria pinguia, acarnae,　10
purpura, muriculi, mures, dulces quoque echini.

Apul.: Hedyphagetica Scriver　　hedesphagitica *cdd.*
[1] Clupeae T　　clipea *cd. Fl.*, 68, 2
[2] Aeni super B
[3] *fortasse* Mitylenae │ c. p. c. a. Ambraciai fines crebrum B, W　　caradrum *Fl.*, 68, 2; 29, 2　　oras W Ambracienses Casaubon　　'Αμβρακίηφιν *coni.* V.　　Ambraciae finis *Fl.*, 68, 2, 29, 2　　caradrumque apud Ambraciai Vliet　　finis *seclud.* Vliet
[4] *fin. vers. corrupt. ? latet fortasse* assum
[6] Surrenti tu B　　Surrentid Saumaise　　Surrenti face emas helopem *olim* V　　surrentia elopē fac emas *vel* surenti a telopē face emas *Fl.*, 68, 2; 29, 2 ἀπὸ Κύμης Bergk　　glaucum prope Mr.　　face Cumis B　　aput cumas *Fl.*, 68, 2; 29, 2
[7] Quid scaru' Bergk　　quid scarum *cdd.*
[9] *fortasse* et t. et merulam melanurum u. m.
[10] Corcyraest Bergk　　corcirę *cdd.*　　acarnae Saumaise acarne *cdd.　fortasse* carne
[11] murex Casaubon

DELIKATESSEN

1-11

Apuleius : Quintus Ennius wrote on delikatessen. He enumerated countless kinds of fish with which no doubt he was acquainted as a connoisseur. I remember a few lines and will give them here—

How the sea-weasel from Clupea [a] beats all others! There are sea-mice at Aenus and scaly oysters in great plenty at Abydus. . . . At Mitylene is the scallop; it's a common thing [b] along the shores of Ambracia. The sarge is fine at Brundisium—buy it if it's big. Know that the little boar-fish can be had first-rate at Tarentum. Make sure it's at Surrentum that you purchase your herring, and from Cumae [c] your blue-fish. What of the parrot-fish? I overlooked that! It's almost the very brain of all-highest Jupiter! This fellow is caught big and fine in Nestor's land. And I overlooked the black-tail, the plaice, the sea-merle, the sea-shadow. At Corcyra men catch the cuttle, fat flounders, acarnae, the purple and the little purple-fish, sea-mice and sweet urchins too.

[a] In Africa. I suggest we might read *clupeis* here as the name of tiny fresh-water fish (Pliny, IX, 44). Thus Ennius is going to tell of the greater excellence of salt-water fish over river-fish. The sea-weasel is the dog-fish.

[b] A glance at the corresponding lines of Archestratus makes one suspect that *caradrum* (which occurs here only) is wrong and *crebrum* right. For *fines* I read *oras* in the belief that it was ousted by *fines* as a gloss. Or *finis* was perhaps added to mark ' end of line '; or, if we read *Caradrum* (as a place-name) and *Ambracini*, it may have been added to fill up a supposed gap in the sense.

[c] ἀπὸ Κύμης is probably right—note, however, that there is a fish which was called *apua*.

ENNIUS

Alios etiam multis versibus decoravit, et ubi gentium quisque eorum, qualiter assus aut iusulentus optime sapiat, nec tamen ab eruditis reprehenditur.

EPICHARMUS

Ennius probably based this didactic poem on a separate work of the Greek philosopher-poet (or on one which passed for his) about nature and the four elements. Cf. V., CCXVIII ff., XXXVII ff. Epicharmus of Cos (c. 540–450 B.C.) dwelt at Syracuse and wrote two kinds of comedies:

1

Cicero, *Ac. Pr.*, II, 16, 51 : Num censes Ennium cum in hortis cum Servio Galba vicino suo ambulavisset dixisse visus sum mihi cum Galba ambulare ? At cum somniavit ita narravit . . . in Epicharmo—

Nam videbar somniare med ego esse mortuum.

2

Varro, *L.L.*, V, 60 : Quibus iunctis caelum et terra omnia ex se genuerunt, quod per hos natura—

Frigori miscet calorem atque humori aritudinem.

3

Varro, *R.R.*, I, 4, 1 : Eius principia sunt eadem quae mundi esse Ennius scribit—

aqua terra anima et sol.

Cp. Menand. ap. Stob., *Flor.*, 91 (*ad fr.* 10–14 *adscr.*).

---

[1] med ego Manutius   me ego *cdd.*
[2] *trib. Enn. Epicharm.* Colonna
[3] et sol *cdd.*   et *secl.* Politianus *prob.* V   *trib. Epicharm.* Colonna

EPICHARMUS

He honoured others also with many verses and told in what part of the world each of them is to be found, and in what condition, fried or stewed, each tastes best. And still he is not brought to task by the experts.

EPICHARMUS

mythological travesties, and plays dealing with different classes of people at Syracuse. The dramas were noted for their pithy philosophic sayings, but we have no tradition that he wrote a definite work on philosophy. For an echo of this work of Ennius in the *Annals*, see pp. 6–7.

1

Prelude :

Cicero : Surely you do not believe that Ennius, when he had walked in the gardens with his neighbour Servius Galba, said 'Methought to myself I was walking with Galba?' But when he had dreamed, he related as follows . . . in *Epicharmus*—

For I thought in a dream that I was dead.

2

Nature's working :

Varro : From a union of these (*sc.* of cold with heat and of dryness with moisture), sky and earth gave birth to all things from their own stuff, for it is through these that nature—

mingles heat with cold, and dryness with moisture.[a]

3

Beginnings of the Universe :

Varro, on tillage : The first beginnings of it are the same as those which, according to what Ennius writes, are the first beginnings of the universe—

Water, earth, air, sun.

[a] Varro in the same chapter quotes *Epicharmus* by name. The subject of this fr. further supports the attribution.

411

ENNIUS

4–6

Varro, *L.L.*, V, 64: Terra Ops, quod hic omne opus et hac opus ad vivendum; et ideo dicitur Ops mater quod terra mater. Haec enim—

Terris gentis omnis peperit et resumit denuo;

quae—

> dat cibaria,

ut ait Ennius; quae—

> quod gerit fruges, Ceres;

Antiquis enim quod nunc g'e.

7

Priscianus, ap. *G.L.*, II, 341, 19 K: Hic et haec amentis et hoc amente; nec mirum cuius simplex quoque mentis Ennius protulit in Epicharmo—

> Terra corpus est at mentis ignis est

pro mens.

8–9

Varro, *L.L.*, V, 59: . . . Epicharmus dicit de mente humana—

Istic est de sole sumptus ignis

idem de sole—

> isque totus mentis est.

EPICHARMUS

4–6

Earth :

Varro : Earth is Ops, because herein lies all ' opus,' and
there is ' opus ' (need) of this in order to live; and Ops is
named ' mother ' because earth is ' mother.' For she it is
who—

gave birth to all races on earth and takes them
back again;

who—

bestows food-stores,

as Ennius says; who is also—

Ceres, because she gets us crops;

for among the archaic writers c was put for what is now g.

7

Soul :

Priscianus : We find ' amentis' nom. masc. and fem., and
' amente' nom. sing. neut. This is not surprising, since
Ennius in *Epicharmus* uses the form ' mentis ' as the nominative, instead of ' mens,' even in the non-compound—

Body is earth, but soul is fire

8–9

Varro : Epicharmus says of the human soul—

This fire is got from the sun

and the same writer states about the sun—

and in this consists all soul.[a]

> [a] Here again ' mentis ' is nom. sing.

413

ENNIUS

10–14

Menander, ap. Stobae., *Flor.*, 91 :

ὁ μὲν Ἐπίχαρμος τοὺς θεοὺς εἶναι λέγει
ἀνέμους ὕδωρ γῆν ἥλιον πῦρ ἀστέρας.

Varro, *L.L.*, V, 65 : Idem hi dei Caelum et Terra, Iupiter
et Iuno, quod ut ait Ennius—

Istic est is Iupiter quem dico, quem Graeci vocant
aerem qui ventus est et nubes, imber postea,
atque ex imbre frigus, ventus post fit, aer denuo.
Haecce propter Iupiter sunt ista quae dico tibi,
quando mortales atque urbes beluasque omnis iuvat.

EUHEMERUS

SIVE

SACRA HISTORIA

It is certain that Ennius translated or put together in a
Latin form, probably in several books, the *Sacred Chronicle*
of Euhemerus (a man of uncertain birthplace, but born
c. 340 B.C.), by whom the old myths were given a rational
explanation in a philosophic romance ; herein the gods were
explained as men of old who were heroes and conquerors.
The two following quotations give information in addition
to that provided by Lactantius in passages given below.
Cicero, *de Nat. Deor.*, 1, 42, 119 : ' Well, those who teach
that brave or famous or powerful men have after death
attained the estate of gods ; and that these are the very beings
whom we are wont to worship and pray to and adore—are
they not strangers to all and every religious scruple ? The
man who went farthest in this line of thought was Euhemerus,
of whom our Ennius was, beyond all others, a translator and
follower ; and in Euhemerus' scheme even deaths and burials
of gods are set forth.' Lactantius, *Div. Inst.*, I, 11, 33 :
' The ancient author Euhemerus, whose birthplace was the

---

[13] haecce (haece) *olim* Spengel, L   haec propterea
Spengel   haec *Varro*
[14] quando L   quoniam O. Mr.   quia Laetus   qua *Varro*

EUHEMERUS

10-14

Air :

Varro: These same deities, Sky and Earth, are the same as
Jupiter and Juno,[a] for, according to the words of Ennius—

That is this Jupiter of whom I speak, whom the
Greeks call Aer, which is wind and clouds, and
afterwards moisture; out of wetness comes cold,
and after that wind is formed, and air once again.
That is why Jupiter is the name for all I have spoken
of, since he rejuvenates[b] all men and cities and
beasts.

EUHEMERUS

OR

THE HOLY HISTORY

state of Messene, collected the acts of Jupiter and of the rest
of those who are thought to be gods, and wove a *History*
out of the contents of the labels and holy inscriptions which
were to be found in the most archaic temples and above all
in the shrine of the Triphylian Jupiter, where the label on
a golden pillar showed that it was put up by Jupiter himself;
on the pillar he wrote out an account of all his acts, so that
it might be a monument to after-time of his achievements.
This History Ennius both translated and followed.'

All the fragments of Ennius' version (with one exception)
are given in prose by Lactantius and it is certain that this work
of Ennius was known to Lactantius in a prose version only.
It has been believed, therefore, that Ennius likewise wrote
his version in prose. But it has been pointed out (V., CCXXII ff.)
that Lactantius' quotations contain fragments if not whole

---

[a] We may note here that in *L.L.*, V. 18, Varro says that
Ennius in *Epicharmus* calls the moon Proserpina.

[b] We might say in English 'God is the name . . . since
he does good to all men. . . .' The two words God and good
are not connected in English any more than *Iupiter Iuno* and
iuvo are in Latin.

415

ENNIUS

lines of septenarian rhythm, while hardly a single phrase
occurs which could be part of a hexameter. Thus, although
any attempted reconstruction of any of Ennius' verse-contexts
would be an idle task, and although one can trace a good many
iambic and trochaic rhythms in any Latin prose just as one
can blank verse lines in English prose, still it is worth while
giving such [a] remains of rhythms as we can dimly see, without
maintaining in any instance that the words stand exactly as
Ennius wrote them.[b] I have noted the following, which are
numbered according to the lines of the full Latin text (given
on pp. 418 ff.) from which these are quoted :

1 Primus in terris imperium summum Caelus
2   id regnum una cum fratribus suis
12   uti de regno ne concedat fratri
13 qui facie deterior esset quam Saturnus
21   Tum Saturno filius qui primus natus est,
        eum necaverunt
22 Deinde posterius nati sunt gemini, Iuppiter . . .
26 dantque eum Vestae educandum, celantes
31   Pluto Latine est Dis pater, alii Orcum vocant
32 filiam Glaucam Saturno ostendunt
33 filium Plutonem celant atque abscondunt.
34 Deinde Glauca parva emoritur. Haec ut scripta
        sunt Iovis . . .
39 Deinde [c] Titan postquam rescivit Saturno filios
40 procreatos (atque) educatos esse clam se
41   ducit secum filios suos
44 eosque muro circumegit et custodiam
     his apponit
51   parentes vinculis
     exemisse, patri regnum reddidisse

[a] V. has given some—CCXXII-CCXXIV. He points out
that the quotations show signs of Ennius apart from rhythm.
[b] Particularly where an apparent septenarian allows
$- \smile - \smile - \smile \asymp$ at the end instead of $- \smile - - - \smile \asymp$.
[c] V., CCXXIII believes that the fr. *Deinde . . . apponit*
(see lines 39–45) represents four lines of Ennius' poetry.

53   Post haec deinde Saturno sortem datam
ut caveret.

59 cum iactatus esset (per) omnes terras persequentibus
armatis quos (ad eum) conprehendendum vel
     necandum Iuppiter
miserat

62   vix in Italia locum.

64 consedisse illi aquilam in capite

66 Deinde Pan eum deducit in montem
qui vocatur Caeli stela

68   ascendit contemplatus est
late terras.

74   caelo nomen indidit
idque Iuppiter quod aether

78   Iuppiter Neptuno imperium dat maris

79 quae secundum mare loca essent omnibus

81 (ea tempestate Iuppiter) in monte Olympo maximam

83   veniebant si quae res in controversia

89   humanam carnem solitos esitare

91   edicto prohibuisse ne liceret

93 Nam cum terras circumiret

94 reges principesve – ◡ populorum hospitio sibi

111   simile quiddam in Sicilia
fecit Aeneas cum conditae urbi Acestae hospitis

114   inposuit ut eam post modum
laetus ac libens Acestes

118   exemplum ceteris ad imitandum dedit.

120   omnibusque amicis atque cognatis suis

123   fecit, inmortali gloria
memoriaque adfectus sempiterna monumenta

128   curaverunt . . . decoraveruntque eum

131   eius est inscriptum antiquis litteris
Graecis ZAN KPONOY ◡ – id est Latine Iuppiter
Saturni

ENNIUS

Lactantius, *Div. Inst.*, I, 13, 14 : Ennius quidem in
Euhemero non primum dicit regnasse Saturnum sed Uranum
patrem—

Initio primus in terris imperium summum Caelus habuit; is id regnum una
cum fratribus suis sibi instituit atque
paravit.

Cp. *epit.*, 14, 4.

I, 11, 63 *s.*: . . . In Sacra Historia . . . Ennius tradit
. . . Cui ergo sacrificare Iuppiter potuit nisi Caelo avo ?—

5   quem dicit Euhemerus in Oceania
mortuum et in oppido Aulacia sepultum.

I, 14, 1 : Nunc quoniam ab his quae rettuli aliquantum
Sacra Historia dissentit, aperiamus ea quae veris litteris
continentur, ne poetarum ineptias in accusandis religionibus
sequi ac probare videamur. Haec Enni verba sunt—

Exim Saturnus uxorem duxit Opem.
Titan qui maior natu erat postulat ut
10 ipse regnaret. Ibi Vesta mater eorum
et sorores Ceres atque Ops suadent
Saturno uti de regno ne concedat fratri.
Ibi Titan qui facie deterior esset quam
Saturnus, idcirco et quod videbat matrem
15 atque sorores suas operam dare uti
Saturnus regnaret, concessit ei ut is
regnaret. Itaque pactus est cum Saturno
uti si quid liberum virile secus ei natum
esset, ne quid educaret. Id eius rei

---

[1] initio inquit primus *Lactant.*
[6] aut lacia *R*   aulatia *S*   Huracia Némethy *Euhem.*,
53, 79 *coll. Diod.*, *V*, 45, 2 : Τρακίαν . . . Ὠκεανίδα.

---

[a] *i.e.* older than Saturn.

EUHEMERUS

The rule of Caelus or Sky :

Lactantius : Ennius indeed in *Euhemerus* states that the first to hold rule was not Saturn but Uranus his father. He says—

> In the beginning Sky held highest authority in the world; he together with his brothers established and formed this kingship for himself.

The death of Sky :

In *The Holy History* . . . Ennius . . . relates . . . to whom therefore can Jupiter have sacrificed if not to Sky his grandfather ?—

> who, according to Euhemerus, died in Oceania and was buried in the town Aulacia.

Birth of Jupiter, Juno, Neptune, and Pluto ; vengeance of Titan. Triumph of Jupiter and flight of Saturn to Italy :

And now since *The Holy History* disagrees somewhat with what I have related, allow me to disclose the contents of true records, lest in calling to task religious superstitions I seem to follow and approve of the foolish sayings of the poets. Ennius' words are these—

> After that Saturn took Ops to wife. Titan who was the elder in years [a] asked that he might be king. Thereupon Vesta their mother and Ceres and Ops their sisters advised Saturn not to yield to his brother in the matter of the kingship. Thereupon Titan, because he was less handsome than Saturn and saw that the efforts of his mother and sisters were made in order that Saturn might be king, yielded to him the right to be king. Therefore he made an agreement with Saturn that if any freeborn child of the male sex should be born to him, he should not bring it up. This he did

20 causa fecit uti ad suos gnatos regnum
rediret. Tum Saturno filius qui primus
natus est eum necaverunt. Deinde
posterius nati sunt gemini Iuppiter atque
Iuno. Tum Iunonem Saturno in con-
25 spectum dedere atque Iovem clam
abscondunt dantque eum Vestae educandum celantes Saturnum. Item Neptunum
clam Saturno Ops parit eumque clanculum
abscondit. Ad eundum modum tertio
30 partu Ops parit geminos Plutonem et
Glaucam. Pluto Latine est Dis pater,
alii Orcum vocant. Ibi filiam Glaucam
Saturno ostendunt at filium Plutonem
celant atque abscondunt. Deinde Glauca
35 parva emoritur. Haec ut scripta sunt
Iovis fratrumque eius stirps atque cog-
natio; in hunc modum nobis ex sacra
scriptione traditum est.

Item paulo post haec infert—

Deinde Titan postquam rescivit
40 Saturno filios procreatos atque educatos
esse clam se, seducit secum filios suos
qui Titani vocantur, fratremque suum
Saturnum atque Opem conprehendit
eosque muro circumegit et custodiam his
45 apponit.

. . . Reliqua Historia sic contexitur—

Iovem adultum cum audisset patrem
atque matrem custodiis circumsaeptos
atque in vincula coniectos, venisse cum

³¹ Pluto . . . vocant, in hunc modum . . . traditum est
fortasse non Ennio tribuenda ; at latent ut videtur septenarii.

in order that the kingship might return to his own sons. Next they slew the first son born to Saturn. And then later on there were born twins, Jupiter and Juno. Then they allowed Saturn to see Juno, but secretly smuggled Jupiter away, and hiding him from Saturn gave him to Vesta to be brought up. Next Ops bore a son to Saturn, Neptune, unknown to him, and smuggled him away secretly. In the same way Ops in a third delivery gave birth to twins, Pluto and Glauca. (The Latin counterpart of Pluto is Dis Pater, though some call him Orcus.) Thereupon they presented the daughter Glauca to Saturn, but hid the son Pluto, and smuggled him away. Then Glauca died while still a little girl. Such according to the records are the stock and kin of Jupiter and his brothers; this is the manner of it as handed down to us out of the holy writings.

Again, a little farther on the *History* offers the following—

And then Titan, after he had learnt that sons had been born to Saturn, and had been brought up without his knowledge, took away with him his own sons who are called Titans, seized his brother Saturn and also Ops, put them behind prison-walls, and kept them under guard.

. . . The thread of what remains in the *History* on this point is as follows, that—

When Jupiter was grown up he heard that his father and mother were beset by guards and cast into bonds, and came with a great host

magna Cretensium multitudine Titan-
50 umque ac filios eius pugna vicisse,
parentes vinculis exemisse, patri regnum
· reddidisse atque ita in Cretam remeasse.
Post haec deinde Saturno sortem datam
ut caveret ne filius eum regno expelleret,
55 illum elevandae sortis atque effugiendi
periculi gratia insidiatum Iovi ut eum
necaret. Iovem cognitis insidiis regnum
sibi denuo vindicasse ac fugasse Saturnum,
qui cum iactatus esset per omnes terras
60 persequentibus armatis, quos ad eum
conprehendendum vel necandum Iuppiter
miserat, vix in Italia locum in quo lateret
invenit. . . .

Cp. *epit.*, 13, 3.

I, 11, 64 : Caesar quoque in Arato refert Aglaosthenen
dicere Iovem cum ex insula Naxo adversus Titanes pro-
ficisceretur et sacrificium faceret in litore, aquilam ei in
auspicium advolasse. . . . Sacra vero Historia etiam ante—

consedisse illi aquilam in capite atque
65 ei regnum portendisse

testatur.

I, 11, 62 (de Saturno) : Nunc dicam quo modo ubi a quo
sit hoc factum. Non enim Saturnus hoc sed Iuppiter fecit.
In Sacra Historia sic Ennius tradit—

Deinde Pan eum deducit in montem
qui vocatur Caeli Stela. Postquam eo
ascendit contemplatus est late terras

⁶⁶ Pan eum *cdd.* (pavenium *R*   pane deducit *H*)
fortasse Panchaeum *vel* Panchaeam eum
⁶⁷ Stela Ciaconius stella *cdd.*   sella Krahner *coll. Diodor.*,
V, 44, 5 *s.*

of Cretans and defeated Titan and his sons
in battle, freed his parents from their bonds,
gave back the kingship to his father, and so
went back to Crete. And then after this
an oracle was given to Saturn, saying that he
must beware lest a son of his thrust him out
of his kingship; in order to thwart the oracle,
and avoid the danger, he ambushed Jupiter
to slay him; Jupiter having found out the
ambush, claimed afresh the kingdom for
himself, and made Saturn a fugitive. He,
driven all over the world by armed pursuers,
whom Jupiter had sent to seize or slay him,
almost failed to find in Italy a place to hide
in.

Caesar also in Aratus records that Aglaosthenes says that
when Jupiter was setting out from Naxos island against the
Titans and was sacrificing on the shore, an eagle flew to him
as an omen. . . . But even before this *The Holy History* bears
witness that—

an eagle perched on his head and foretold
that he would win the kingship.

How Saturn came to be called son of Sky :

Now I will tell you how and when and by whom this was
done; for it was not done by Saturn but by Jupiter. In *The
Holy History* Ennius relates as follows—

Then Pan led him up to a mountain which is
called Sky's Pillar.[a] When he had climbed it
he gazed on the world far and wide, and then

[a] Or, if we accept *Panchaeam* (or the like) and *sella*, readings
based on the parallel account of the eastern Utopia in Diodor.
V, 44 (from Euhemerus)—' Then he led him to Panchaea . . .
Sky's Seat.'

ENNIUS

ibique in eo monte aram creat Caelo,
70 primusque in ea ara Iuppiter sacrificavit.
In eo loco suspexit in caelum quod nunc
nos nominamus, idque quod supra mundum
erat quod aether vocabatur, de sui avi
nomine caelo nomen indidit, idque
75 Iuppiter quod aether vocatur placans
primus caelum nominavit eamque hostiam
quam ibi sacrificavit totam adolevit.

I, 11, 32: Sic Neptuno maritima omnia cum insulis
obvenerunt. Quomodo id probari potest? Nimirum veteres
historiae docent. Antiquus auctor Euhemerus. . . . Historiam contexuit. . . . Hanc historiam et interpretatus est
Ennius et secutus, cuius haec verba sunt—

. . . ubi Iuppiter Neptuno imperium dat
maris ut insulis omnibus et quae secundum
80 mare loca essent omnibus regnaret.

. . . In Olympo Iovem habitasse docet eadem Historia
quae dicit—

Ea tempestate Iuppiter in monte Olympo
maximam partem vitae colebat et eo ad
eum in ius veniebant, si quae res in
controversia erant. Item si quis quid
85 novi invenerat quod ad vitam humanam ⌄
utile esset, eo veniebant atque Iovi
ostendebant.

I, 13, 2 (de Saturno): Idem sororem suam Rheam quam
Latine Opem dicimus cum haberet uxorem, responso vetitus

⁷⁴ idque Iuppiter . . . nominavit *secl.* Mr.
⁷⁹ ut *edd.* ut et Thilo et ut *coni.* Brandt et *cdd.*
(hoc est ut *S, H*)
⁸⁰ regnare Hartel

on that mountain he built an altar to Sky, and on that altar Jupiter was the first to make sacrifice. Standing at that place he looked up at what we now name the sky; and to that which was above the universe, and was called ether, Jupiter gave the name 'Sky' after his grandfather's name; and being the first to appease that which is called ether, he named it the sky; and he burnt whole the victim which he sacrificed there.

The powers given by Jupiter to Neptune ; Jupiter dwells on Olympus :

Thus to Neptune's share fell all the things of the sea and the islands in it. How can this be proved? Why, of course the old histories attest it. The ancient author Euhemerus . . . wove a *History*. . . . This *History* Ennius both translated and followed; his words are these—

. . . where Jupiter gave Neptune authority over the sea so as to be king over all the islands and all places which might be near the sea.

. . . That Jupiter dwelt on Olympus we are taught by that same *History*, which says—

In those days Jupiter was spending the greater part of his life on Mount Olympus, and thither to him men used to come to law if there were any matters in dispute. Likewise if anyone had discovered any new thing which might be useful towards the life of mankind, thither men used to come, and show it to Jupiter.

Jupiter forbids the eating of human flesh :

And Saturn again, when he had taken for his wife his sister Rhea, whom we call in Latin Ops, is said to have been forbidden

425

ENNIUS

esse dicitur mares liberos educare quod futurum esset ut a
filio pelleretur; quam rem metuens natos sibi filios non
utique devorabat ut ferunt fabulae sed necabat, quanquam
scriptum sit in Historia Sacra—

Saturnum et Opem ceterosque tunc
homines humanam carnem solitos esitare;
90 verum primum Iovem leges hominibus
moresque condentem edicto prohibuisse
ne liceret eo cibo vesci.

I, 22, 21 : Historia vero Sacra testatur ipsum Iovem
postquam rerum potitus sit in tantam venisse insolentiam
ut ipse sibi fana in multis locis constituerit—

Nam cum terras circumiret, ut in
quamque regionem venerat, reges prin-
95 cipesve populorum hospitio sibi et amicitia
copulabat et cum a quoque digrederetur
iubebat sibi fanum creari hospitis sui
nomine, quasi ut posset amicitiae et
foederis memoria conservari. Sic con-
100 stituta sunt templa Iovi Ataburio, Iovi
Labryandio, Ataburus enim et Labryandus
hospites eius atque adiutores in bello
fuerunt; item Iovi Laprio, Iovi Molioni,
Iovi Casio, et quae sunt in eundem
105 modum. Quod ille astutissime excogit-
avit, ut et sibi honorem divinum et hospiti-
bus suis perpetuum nomen adquireret
cum religione coniunctum. Gaudebant
ergo illi et huic imperio eius libenter
110 obsequebantur et nominis sui gratia ritus

426

by the answer of an oracle to bring up freeborn male children on the ground that it was fated that he would be deposed by a son. In fear of this, it is plain that he did not, as the stories go, eat up sons that were born to him, but slew them; in spite of what is written in *The Holy History* that—

Saturn and Ops and all the rest of mankind were wont to feed on human flesh. But Jupiter, the first to lay down laws and customs for men, forbade by edict that men should be allowed to eat such food.

The origin of the different cults of Jupiter :

But *The Holy History* is a witness that Jupiter himself, after he had become supreme, went to such a pitch of haughtiness that he established, himself for himself, temples in many places—

For when he was making the round of the world, the kings or chiefs of the peoples of every region, wherever he had come, bound themselves in hospitality and friendship with him; and whenever he was departing from any place, he ordered that a shrine should be built in the name of his host, so that the memory as it were of friendship and agreement should be preserved. Thus were established the temples of Jupiter Ataburius, Jupiter Labryandius, for Ataburus and Labryandus were his hosts and his helpers in war; and also to Jupiter Laprius, Jupiter Molio, Jupiter Casius, and all the other temples which are dedicated in the same manner. This was a most cunning idea of his, to get for himself divine honour and for his hosts a name for ever known and connected with religion. Thus they were glad, and willingly obeyed this authority of his and celebrated yearly rites

427

annuos et festa celebrabant. Simile
quiddam in Sicilia fecit Aeneas, cum
conditae urbi Acestae hospitis nomen
inposuit, ut eam postmodum laetus
115 ac libens Acestes diligeret augeret orna-
ret. Hoc modo religionem cultus sui
per orbem terrarum Iuppiter seminavit
et exemplum ceteris ad imitandum dedit.

Cp. *epit.*, 19, 14.

I, 11, 44 : Quare si Iovem et ex rebus gestis et ex moribus
hominem fuisse in terraque regnasse deprehendimus, superest
ut mortem quoque eius investigemus. Ennius in Sacra
Historia descriptis omnibus quae in vita sua gessit ad ultimum
sic ait—

Deinde Iuppiter postquam quinquies
120 terras circumivit omnibusque amicis atque
cognatis suis imperia divisit reliquitque
hominibus leges mores frumentaque
paravit multaque alia bona fecit, inmortali
gloria memoriaque adfectus sempiterna
125 monumenta suis reliquit. Aetate pessum
acta in Creta vitam commutavit et ad
deos abiit eumque Curetes filii sui
curaverunt decoraveruntque eum; et
sepulchrum eius est in Creta in oppido
130 Gnosso et dicitur Vesta hanc urbem
creavisse inque sepulchro eius est inscriptum antiquis litteris Graecis ZAN
KPONOY id est Latine Iuppiter Saturni.

Hoc certe non poetae tradunt sed antiquarum rerum
scriptores.

Cp. *epit.*, 13, 4.

EUHEMERUS

and holidays for their name's sake. Aeneas
achieved something like this in Sicily when
he gave to a city at its foundation the name
of Acestes his host, so that later on Acestes
should cheerfully and willingly cherish increase
and honour it. In this way did Jupiter sow the
seeds of his own religious worship throughout
the world and provide an example for all the
rest of the world to imitate.

The death of Jupiter :

Wherefore if we grasp the fact that Jupiter, to judge both
from his achievements and his character, was a man and a
king on earth, there remains for us to inquire into his death
also. In *The Holy History* Ennius, having described all the
deeds done by him during his life, says near the end—

And then Jupiter after he had gone the
round of the world five times and had made
division of authorities to all his friends and
relations, and bequeathed to mortals laws and
manners, and furnished corn and provided
many other good things, he was honoured
with deathless renown and remembrances
and bequeathed everlasting monuments to his
friends. When he was sunk in the depths of
old age, he parted with his life in Crete, and
went away to join the gods ; and the Curetes
his sons tended and decked his corpse. His
tomb exists in Crete in the town of Cnossus
(a city which Vesta is said to have set up)
and on his tomb is written in archaic Greek
letters ZAN KPONOY, that is, in Latin, Jupiter
Son of Saturn.

This at any rate is a tradition not of the poets but of writers
on antiquities.

I, 17, 9 : Quid loquar obscenitatem Veneris omnium
libidinibus prostitutae. .? . . Quae ' prima,' ut in Historia
Sacra continetur—

artem meretriciam instituit auctorque
135 mulieribus in Cypro fuit uti vulgo corpore
quaestum faceret; quod idcirco imperavit
ne sola praeter alias mulieres inpudica et
virorum adpetens videretur.

Cp. *epit.*, 9, 1.

EX INCERTIS
SCRIPTIS

EX ANNALIBUS?

1

Cicero, *Orat.*, 47, 157 : ' Isdem campus habet ' inquit Ennius
et—

in templis isdem

Servius, ad *Aen.*, II, 274 : (' Ei mihi qualis erat, quantum
mutatus ab illo Hectore ') ' Ei mihi.'   Ennii versus.

2

Servius (auctus) ad *Aen.*, IX, 744 : ' Versat,' librat, iactat;
et est Ennianum—

Versat mucronem.

Serv., *Aen.*, II, 274, *verba* qualis erat (*vel etiam totus versus*)
fortasse Ennio trib. Ann. lib. I

430

VARIA

Venus :

Why should I speak of the lewdness of Venus prostituted to the lusts of all ? . . . who, according to what we find contained in *The Holy History*, first—

established the art of the courtesan and in Cyprus founded for women the custom of getting profit out of their bodies by making them public; this she ordained so that she should not be the only one among women to appear a hussy and a gaper after men.

FRAGMENTS NOT ASSIGNED TO ANY WORK

FROM THE ANNALS?

1

Cicero : ' For them too the plains hold,' says Ennius (see p. 52), and also—

in those same temples [a]

Servius, on Virgil's ' Ah me ! In what guise he was—how changed from that Hector . . . !' : ' Ah me.' A line [b] of Ennius.

2

Servius (supplemented), on ' versat ' in Virgil : ' Versat,' he poises, brandishes; it is further an Ennian term—

Passes made he with his sword's point.

[a] The text of Cicero is not quite certain. Cf. St., 129–30; V., 86.
[b] As elsewhere, by ' versus,' Servius may not mean a whole verse. But if he does in this case, it may describe the dead body of Tarquinius Priscus (Bk. III).

431

ENNIUS

3-4

Donatus, ad Ter., *Phorm.*, V, 9, 39: ' sum mactatum.'
' Sum ' pro eo quod est eum; sic frequenter veteres. Ennius—

. . . omnes corde patrem debent animoque benigno
circum sum.

5

Paulus, ex F., 193, 7: ' Ob ' . . . pro ad, ut Ennius ' ob
Romam e. q. s. (Ann., fr. 288). Festus, 192, 21 . . . —

Ob Troiam duxit ⟨exercitum⟩

Cp. Paulus, 131, 11, (7): (. . . ' ob Troiam duxit
exercitum ').

6

Varro, *L.L.*, VII, 48: Apud Ennium—

quae cava corpore caeruleo cortina receptat

' cava cortina ' dicta quod est inter terram et caelum ad
similitudinem cortinae Apollinis. Cp. Lucret., II, 1001: id
rursum caeli rellatum templa receptant.

7

Varro, VII, 32: Dubitatur . . . utrum primum una canis
aut canes sit appellata. . . . Ennius . . . —

tantidem quasi feta canes sine dentibus latrat.

3-4 *Cf.* V., *pp.* 84-5
5 ⟨exercitum⟩ *suppl. ex Paul.*, 131   *fortasse tribuend.*
Ann. lib. I
6 q. . . . r. O. Mr.   corpore caeruleo cava quae cortina
receptat T   quaeque freto cava caeruleo S   queq in
corpore causa ceruleo felo orta nare ceptat *Varr.*   *trib. Ann.*
lib. I V

---

a Donatus' quotation from Ennius is defective and his
reading of Terence wrong; Terence wrote *sit mactatus.*

VARIA

3–4

Donatus, on a passage in Terence: 'Sum' for 'eum';
thus frequently the old writers. Ennius—[a]

All men should love their father with all their
hearts, and hold kind thoughts towards him.

5

Paulus: 'Ob' . . . for 'ad'; for example, Ennius
'*Against Rome*, etc.' (fr. 288). *Festus has* . . . —

Against Troy he led an army [b]

6

Varro: In a passage of Ennius [c]—

Which the hollow caldron takes back again within
its embodiment of heaven's blue

The term 'cava cortina' is used because it lies between
'terra' and 'caelum,' and is likened to Apollo's caldron.

7

Varro: It is a matter of doubt . . . whether the original
term for 'canis' in the feminine was 'canis' or 'canes.' . . .
Ennius [d] . . . —

meaning no more than the barking of a toothless
bitch in pup.

[b] Apparently a quotation from Ennius; if it comes from the
Annals, its place is near fr. 15 of Bk. I.
[c] The restorations of the text are probably right. V.
(CXLVIII; and p. 3) assigns the fr. to Homer's speech in
Bk. I (cf. V., *ed. I*, XXIII–XXIV); the fragment seems to
describe how (according to Empedocles) the sky or space
'takes back' as it were the four elements of which things are
made, and causes them to combine into new things.
[d] Perhaps in the *Satires*. Possibly Ennius means 'gives
a toothless bark,' 'bark with no bite.'

ENNIUS

Servius, ad *Aen.*, VII, 804 : Ennius et Lucretius (IV, 450 bina lucernarum florentia lumina flammis) florere dicunt omne quod nitidum est.

Servius, ad *Aen.*, XII, 605 : ' flavos Lavinia crines.' Antiqua lectio floros habuit, id est florulentos, pulchros, et est sermo Ennianus.

8-9

Cicero, *de Orat.*, III, 42, 168 : Sunt finitima . . . cum intellegi volumus . . . ex uno plures—

At Romanus homo, tamen et si res bene gesta est, corde suo trepidat

Servius, ad *Aen.*, VII, 691 : Ab hoc (Messapo) Ennius dicit se originem ducere.

Cp. Sil., XII, 393; Suid., s. v. Έννιος.

Gellius, XVII, 17, 1 : Quintus Ennius tria corda habere sese dicebat quod loqui Graece et Osce et Latine sciret.

10

Cicero, *de Orat.*, III, 42, 168 : Videtis profecto genus hoc totum . . . cum ex pluribus intellegitur unum—

Nos sumus Romani qui fuimus ante Rudini

Cp. Sil., XII, 393 ff.

---

[10] fuvimus *Lambinus*   fuimus *cdd.*   *trib. Enn. Ann. lib.* XVI Mr.   XII (*olim* XVIII) V

---

[a] In view of Lucretius' line, Vahlen may be right in believing that fr. 317 in Bk. IX of Ennius began with the words *Florebant flammis* (V., *Sitz.-Ber. B. Ak.*, 1896, 720).

VARIA

Servius: Ennius [a] and Lucretius ('flame-flowering lights of two lamps') used the term 'to flower' of everything that is bright.

Servius, on 'Lavinia her yellow hair' in Virgil: An old reading had 'flowery,' that is flower-like, beautiful; it is further a term taken from Ennius.

8-9

Cicero: Closely allied to this are the following . . . when we wish several to be understood by one—

But the man of Rome, though success has blest his trials, is fearful in his heart [b]

Servius, on Messapus in Virgil: From him Ennius says [c] he draws his descent.

Gellius: Quintus Ennius used to say that he had three hearts on the ground that he knew how to speak in Greek, Oscan and Latin.

10

Cicero: Of course you see all this kind of thing . . . when one is understood by several—

We who once were Rudians are now Romans [d]

[b] The metre and the thought suggest Ennius' *Annals*, and Cicero goes on to give another hexameter which at any rate refers to Ennius.

[c] Where he says it is not known. But Vahlen (CXCVII) may be right in believing that mention of Ennius' descent, origin and grant of Roman citizenship came in Bk. XII, where the poet himself stated that he wrote that book when he was sixty-seven years old.

[d] That the author of this line is Ennius is most probable. May it not belong to Bk. XVI, which included the year 184 B.C., when Ennius was granted Roman citizenship? Or it might come in Bk. I; or in either of the literary works (*Annals*, Bk. XV, or *Ambracia*, pp. 358 ff.) which celebrated Fulvius Nobilior, through whose son Ennius received the franchise.

ENNIUS

EX SATURIS?

11

Cicero, de Div., II, 54, 111 : Non esse autem illud carmen
sc. Sibyllae) furentis cum ipsum poema declarat (est enim
magis artis et diligentiae quam incitationis et motus), tum
vero quae ἀκροστιχίς dicitur, cum deinceps ex primis versus
litteris aliquid conectitur, ut in quibusdam Ennianis—

Q. Ennius fecit

Nonius, 448, 10 : ' Edolare ' fabrorum est verum verbum
cum materiarum conplanatur asperitas. . . . Varro Bimarco
' Cum Quintipor Clodius tot comoedias sine ulla fecerit Musa,
ego unum libellum non edolem ut ait Ennius ' ?
Cicero, ad Att., XIII, 47, 1 : ' Postquam e. q. s.' (Iphig., fr.
237-8) extemplo instituta omisi, ea quae in manibus habebam
abieci, quod iusseras edolavi.

12-13

Servius auctus, ad Aen., VIII, 361 : ' Carinare ' est obtrec-
tare. Ennius—
Contrā carīnantes verba aeque obscena profatus.
alibi—
– neque me decet hanc carīnantibus edere chartis.

[12] aeque Castricomius   atque cdd.   c. c. | verba atra
atque obscena olim V   et contra carinans verba aeque
Saumaise   fortasse contra, carinantia verba | atque obscena
profatus.   trib. olim lib. VI V
[13] nec me rem decet hanc Ilberg   sed neque me Saumaise
fortasse neque me decet haec   trib. Ann. VII ed. Lips.

---

[a] If Cicero really means works, they would probably be
Satires. But if he means manuscripts, he alludes to acrostics
which we may assume were attached by later writers to works
of Ennius like the acrostics attached to Plautus' plays.

[b] Cicero's remark is not assigned by him to anyone; it
follows a quotation from Ennius' Iphigenia (p. 306); it refers

VARIA

FROM THE SATIRES?

11

Cicero: And that the famous song of the Sibyl is not a product of raving is quite evident partly from the poem itself (for it is a work of art and care rather than excitement and emotion) and partly because it is written in what is called an 'acrostic,' where the first letter of each line, the lines being taken one after the other and joined in order, makes some sort of sense; for example, in some poems[a] of Ennius—

> Q. Ennius his work

Nonius: 'To hew out' is a verb used properly of joiners when they plane down the roughness of their material. . . . Varro in *Bimarcus*: While Boy Quintus Clodius has made so many comedies without taste, may I not, as Ennius has it, 'write rough-hewn one little book'?

Cicero: So soon as . . . (*Iphig.*, fr. 237-8) gave up what I had begun, I put aside what I had in hand, and I wrote rough-hewn what you had asked for.[b]

12-13

Servius augmented, on 'carinae' in Virgil: 'Carinare' means to revile. Ennius—

> against the foul-mouthed uttering words no less unclean.[c]

Elsewhere—

> nor does it befit me to publish this[d] and make these pages foul.

to a written work (in praise of Caesar); Varro suggests Ennius used '*edolavi*' of a little book. Hence I have put the passage from Cicero and the one from Nonius together here, and believe them to contain a word from Ennius' *Satires*.

[c] This and the next fr. may belong to the *Annals*; carīnare or carīnare is as it were *scarinare* (cp. *scortum*). For *contrā* cf. pp. 172-3.

[d] sc. *saturam? rem?*; or read *haec*.

ENNIUS

14

Varro, *L.L.*, VII, 103 : Multa ab animalium vocibus tralata in homines . . . Ennii a vitulo—

tibicina maximo labore mugit.

15

Festus, 124, 11 : ' Moene ' singulariter dixit Ennius—

Apud emporium in campo hostium pro moene,

16

Donatus, ad Ter., *Andr.*, III, 2, 25 : ' Mutire.' Ennius—

nec dico nec facio mu.

17

Varro, *L.L.* 7 : Apud Ennium . . . mussare dictum quod muti non amplius quam μῦ dicunt . . . —

neque ut aiunt μῦ facere audent.

Censorinus, *de Die Nat.*, 19, 2 : Philolaus annum naturalem dies habere prodidit CCCLXIIII et dimidiatum . . . at noster Ennius CCCLXVI.

VARIA INCERTAE SEDIS

18

Varro, *L.L.* VII, 41 : Cum res maior erat, orationi legabantur potissimum qui causam commodissime orare poterant. Itaque Ennius ait—

oratores doctiloqui

15 Ennius apud *Fest.*   Naevius apud O. Mr.   *trib. Ann.* B
16 mu *cdd.* Colonna   *fortasse* μῦ (*cp.* 17)
Censorin.: scripsit fortasse E. habet trecentos sexaginta sex dies | annus.

---

a Probably a Saturnian line.

VARIA

14

Varro: Many animal sounds are used figuratively of human beings . . . there is Ennius' usage drawn from the calf—

the flute-girl moos with a very great to-do.

15

Festus: ' Moene,' a singular form, was used by Ennius—

In a market on the plain before the enemy's wall,[a]

16

Donatus, on ' mutire ' in Terence :

Not a mumble do I mouth or make.

17

Varro: In a passage of Ennius . . . ' Mussare ' is a term used because mutes say no more than mu . . .

nor do they dare to make (as we say) a mumble.

Censorinus: Philolaus published the statement that the natural year has $364\frac{1}{2}$ days . . . but our own writer Ennius says 366.

VARIOUS FRAGMENTS

18

Varro: On any occasion when a case was of the more important kind, persons deputed for an oration were preferably those who could ' orate ' or plead the cause most suitably. Hence the expression of Ennius—

orators of clever speech [b]

[b] This might come from a play or from the *Annals*—probably it belongs to the *Annals*, and possibly came from Bk. VI (see p. 197) because Varro has just quoted a fr. (about an orator) which apparently came from Bk. VI and goes on to quote three that certainly belong to Bk. II (see pp. 42-3).

ENNIUS

19

Paulus, ex F., 5, 4 : ' Adgretus ' apud Ennium—

adgretus fari

pro eo quod est adgressus ponitur.

20

Diomedes, ap. *G.L.*, I, 385, 15 K : ' Possum ' . . . (29) ' potestur ' apud Ennium reperimus—

nec retrahi potestur imperiis.

21

Cicero, *de Re Publ.*, I, 2, 3 :—

Urbes magnas atque imperiosas

ut appellat Ennius, viculis et castellis praeferendas puto.

22

Charisius, ap. *G.L.*, I, 105, 18K : ' Saga ' . . . masculini . . . Ennius—

sagus caerulus

23

Servius, ad *Ecl.*, X, 10 : ' Indigno,' vel meretricio vel magno. Nam et Ennius ait—

indignas turres

24

Cic., *de Nat. Deor.*, II, 18, 49 : Epicurus . . . dum palato quid sit optimum iudicat—

caeli palatum

ut ait Ennius, non suspexit.

Cp. Augustin., *de Civ. Dei*, VII, 8.

---

[20] nec r. ◡ ◡ – ◡ potestur | imperiis V (*qui* retrahi reprimive *coni.*)

VARIA

19

Paulus : ' Adgretus ' in a passage of Ennius—

having stepped forward to speak
is put for the form ' adgressus.'

20

Diomedes : ' Possum.' . . . We find ' potestur ' in Ennius

And he is not abled to be drawn back by commands.

21

Cicero : I think that—

cities great and puissant
are to be preferred to hamlets and forts.

22

Charisius : ' Saga ' . . . of the masculine . . . Ennius—

a cloak of colour blue

23

Servius : ' Indignus,' wanton, or great.[a]   For Ennius too
thus uses indignas—

unworthy towers

24

Cicero : Epicurus . . . while he was judging what is best
for the palate, did not look up at—

the palate of the sky

as Ennius writes.

---

[a] There is no need to adopt Servius' interpretation.   Ennius
probably meant ' cruel ' or ' ugly towers.'

ENNIUS

25

auctor, de dub. nom., ap. *G.L.*, V, 584, 26 K : ' Nix ' generis feminini, ut Ennius—

hae nives

26

Nonius, 190, 20 : ' Armenta ' . . . Feminino Ennius—

ipsius ad armentas easdem.

Cp. Paul., ex F., 3, 25.

27

Servius, ad *Aen.*, I, 190 : ' Tum vulgus.' Bene vulgus ductoribus interemptis. Servius auctus : Ennius—

avium vulgus

Il., XV, 690–1 : ὀρνίθων πετεηνῶν . . . . | ἔθνος.

28

Nonius, 192, 11 : ' Araneae ' et feminini sunt generis. . . . Ennius—

bussus araneae

29

Nonius, 194, 23 : ' Buxum ' generis . . . feminini Ennius—

buxus icta taxus tonsa

30

Paulus, ex F., 457, 5 : ' Stipes ' fustis terrae defixus. *Festus*, 456, 21 . . . Ennius * * *—stip⟩ites abiegno * * * * e stipitem * * * * * mit eum qua * * * rripit.

Servius (auctus), ad *Aen.*, II, 173 : ' Salsus sudor.' . . . Hoc autem Ennius de lamis dixit.

---

[26] ipsius a. a. eosdem *cdd.*   easdem *Ald.*   ad armentas ipsius easdem S (eodem Onions)
[27] *Cf.* V, *p.* 232 *et* Thilo *ad loc.*
[28] bussus Quich.   buxus *cdd.* (buxis *Harl.* 1)   aranae *F.* 1
[29] icta Mercier   vincta Iun.   victa *cdd.*
[30] *Paul.* 457 : *fortasse* abiegno ⟨robore⟩

VARIA

25

A grammarian: 'Nix,' feminine gender; for example, Ennius—

these snowstorms

26

Nonius: 'Armenta.' . . . Ennius has it in the feminine—

to those same herds of his.[a]

27

Servius, on Virgil: 'Then the rabble.' 'Rabble' is well-chosen, since the leaders have been slain. *The augmenter of Servius adds :* Ennius—

a rabble of birds

28

Nonius: 'Araneae.' This word is used even in the feminine gender. . . . Ennius—

the gauze of the spider's web

29

Nonius: 'Buxum' . . . Ennius has it in the feminine—

the box hewn,[b] the yew shorn

30

Paulus: 'Stipes,' a stock fixed tight in the earth. *Festus* . . . Ennius . . . 'stumps of fir-wood.' . . .

Servius (supplemented) on 'Salt sweat' in Virgil.[c] . . . Ennius too uses it of marshes.

---

[a] *ipsius* may be right; or it may be corrupt or misplaced.
[b] Iunius' reading *vincta* is often accepted. But what is 'a bound box-tree'?
[c] Who refers to the Palladium.

Serv. auct. Aen., II, salsas lamas *trib. Enn. Ann.* V (*coni. olim* de lacrimis)

ENNIUS

31

Priscianus, ap. *G.L.* VIII, 383, 6 : Ennius—

adsectari se omnes cupiunt ;

adsectari passive ἀκολουθεῖσθαι.

32

Cicero, *Tusc. Disp.*, IV, 23, 52 : An est quicquam similius insaniae quam ira, quam bene Ennius—

‘ initium insaniae ’

dixit ?

Schol. ad Lucan., X, 249–52 : Ennius haec de Nilo ait, quod per aestatem sol ab inferioribus aquam supra revocet et hinc eo tempore Nilus increscat.
Servius, ad *Aen.*, I, 741 : Ennius dicit Nilum Melonem vocari, Atlantem vero Telamonem.

33

Servius (auctus) ad *Aen.*, X, 10 : Non est ‘ hos suasit ’ ne fiat σολοικοειδές, quamvis inveniatur huiusmodi figura, ut . . . Ennius—

‘ Quis te persuasit ?

34

Fronto, *Epp.*, Vol. I, p. 10 Haines : Enni sententia ‘ oratorem audacem esse debere.’

35

Varro, *L.L.*, VI, 61 : ‘ Dico ’ originem habet Graecam, quod Graeci † ΝΙΔΙΚΕ †. Hinc Ennius—

dico qui hunc dicare

Hinc iudicare quod tunc ius dicatur.

Cp. Fest., 140, 17.

444

VARIA

31

Priscianus : Ennius has—

all men long to have a following ;

' adsectari ' in a passive sense like ἀκολουθεῖσθαι.

32

Cicero : Is there anything more like madness than anger, which Ennius well calls—

' the beginning of madness ' ?

A scholiast on a passage of Lucan : Ennius says this about the Nile; for (he states) the sun during summer-time calls the waters up from the regions below, and hence it is that at that season the Nile grows in volume.

Servius : Ennius says that the Nile is called ' Melo,' and Mount Atlas ' Telamo.' [a]

33

Servius (supplemented) on a passage in Virgil : The order must not be ' hos suasit,' lest the result be something like a solecism. Nevertheless, we do come across a construction of this kind; for example . . . Ennius—

' Who persuaded you ? '

34

Fronto : An opinion of Ennius—' an orator ought to be bold.'

35

Varro : ' Dico ' has a Greek origin. . . . Hence Ennius—

I who say that he states,[b]

Hence ' iudicare ' to judge, because then ' ius dicitur,' justice is delivered.

---

[a] This word is clearly the same as telamo in Vitruv., Arch., VI, 7, 6, where it means a carved male figure (called ἄτλας by the Greeks) upholding the entablature of a temple.

[b] A very doubtful fr. The quotation is perhaps corrupt and hunc dicare may hide iudicare; but even so the sense would not be clear.

ENNIUS

36

Isodorus *Orig.*, XI, 1, 108 : Genua sunt commissiones femorum et crurum et dicta genua eo quod in utero sint genis opposita. . . . Ennius—

atque genua comprimit arta gena

SPURIA?

1

Marius Victorinus, ap. *G.L.*, VI, 101, 24 K : Herous figuram trimetri accipit, velut—

Albani muris Albam Longam cinxerunt.

Hic enim si per dipodias percutiatur, fiet trimetrus.

2

Auctor de metr., ap. *G.L.*, VI, 612, 5 K : Hexameter heroicus . . . totus ex spondiis—

Cives Romani tunc facti sunt Campani.

Cp. 616, 9.

3

Auctor *de speciebus hexam. her.*, ap. *G.L.*, VI, 634, 15 K : Genus unum est XII syllabarum ex omnibus spondeis, tamquam—

Introducuntur legati Minturnenses

Cp. Maxim. Victorin., ap. *G.L.*, VI, 211, 22.

VARIA

36

Isidorus : The knees are the junctures of the thighs and the legs, and they are called ' genua ' on the ground that in the womb they are placed over against the ' genae,' cheeks. . . . Ennius—

and the cheek compresses the knees, all close-packed.

SPURIOUS FRAGMENTS?

1

Marius Victorinus : A ' heroic ' line can take the shape of a trimeter, like— [a]

Long Alba's people ringed their town with enclosures.

For this line, if it be split up into two-footed metre, will become a trimeter.

2

An author on metres : The heroic hexameter . . . one consisting entirely of spondees—

Then the Campani were made of Rome burgesses.[b]

3

An author on *Forms of the heroic hexameter* : There is one kind which consists of twelve syllables, all of the feet being spondees, such as— [c]

Then there were brought in the envoys of Minturnae

[a] Probably an example invented by Victorinus.
[b] Invented by the grammarian ? But cf. Valmaggi, p. 46, V., CLXXIII–IV. The author has just quoted Virgil and Lucretius.
[c] Another invention ?

ENNIUS

4

Columna, p. 239 :—

perculsi pectora Poeni

Hoc fragmentum mihi e Cosentia Fabius Aquinas misit; quod a quodam suo vetustissimo Statii interprete m. s. excerpsit.

Cp. Sil., VIII, 242 : instincti pectora Poeni.

5

Pompeius, ap. *G.L.*, V, 303, 19 K : Faciebant versum in quo versu non invenies nisi omnia nomina, ut—

Marsa manus, Paeligna cohors, Vestina virum vis

Cp. Charis., ap. *G.L.*, I, 282, 6 K : *Explanat. in Donat.*, ap. IV, 565 K (de scematibus . . . Enni versus), etc.

6-7

Placidus, 79, 3 D :—

Romam ex aquilone
Rhaeti destringunt

vel conlimitant vel finibus se eius adiungunt.

8

Priscianus, ap. *G.L.*, III, 205, 20 K :—

O genitor noster Saturnie, maxime divum,

Homer., *Il.*, VIII, 31 :

ὦ πάτερ ἡμέτερε Κρονίδη, ὕπατε κρειόντων.

VARIA

4

Colonna [a] :—

The Phoenicians, stricken at heart

This fragment was sent to me from Cosenza by Fabius of Aquinum; he gleaned it from the manuscript of a certain very old interpreter of Statius which was in his possession.

5

Pompeius : They used to compose a kind of verse which you will not find to contain anything but nouns and names [b]; for example—

Marsian troop, Paelignian company, Vestinian warrior-force

6–7

Placidus [c] :—

Rome on the North is touched on by the Rhaeti

'Destringunt,' border on, or are joined directly to her boundaries.

8

Priscianus :—

O son of Saturn, O our begetter, greatest of gods, [d]

[b] Pompeius includes both nouns and names in *nomina*. Only one grammarian assigns this fr. to Ennius, but it may be genuine—cf. Polyb., II, 24; Sil. Ital., VIII, 495–515 (battle of Cannae); there is another line in Ennius of the same type—see p. 112.

[c] Probably quoting from a much later poet than Ennius; it suggests a writer of a date subsequent to the granting in 49 B.C. of the Roman franchise everywhere in Italy up to the Alps.

[d] This line is quite worthy of Ennius.

ENNIUS

9-10

Serv., ad *Aen.*, IV, 638 : Sciendum Stoicos dicere unum esse deum cui nomina variantur pro actibus et officiis, unde etiam duplicis sexus esse dicuntur. . . . Iovis oratio—

Caelicolae, mea membra, dei quos nostra potestas officiis divisa facit,

11

Varro, *L.L.*, VII, 7 : Quaqua intuiti erant oculi a tuendo primo dictum templum; quocirca caelum, qua attuimur, dictum templum sic—

Contremuit templum magnum Iovis altitonantis.

Homer., *Il.*, I, 354, *al.* : Ζεὺς ὑψιβρεμέτης.

12

Charisius, ap. *G.L.*, I, 266, 15 K : ' Soloecismus ' est oratio inconsequens. . . . (267)—

vosque Lares, tectum nostrum qui funditus curant,

13

Explanat. in Donat., ap. *G.L.*, IV, 565, K : Tmesis est unius partis orationis facta diruptio, alia scilicet interposita, ut est illud ' septem subiecta trioni ' (Verg., *G.*, III. 381). Tolle de medio subiecta et habes septemtrioni. Ennius—

saxo cere comminuit brum

Cp. Donat., ap. *G.L.*, IV, 401, 16 K : Pompei., ap. IV, 310, 4 K : Serv., ad *Aen.*, I, 412.

---

[12] *trib. Enn.* Koch
[13] et saxo *expl. in Donat.*

---

[a] Baehrens' attribution may be right.

VARIA

9–10

Servius, on ' Iovi Stygio ' in Virgil : We must note that the
Stoics say there is but one god, to whom various names are
given according to his activities and functions, whence we
have names of gods belonging to both sexes . . . a speech
of Jupiter— [a]

Dwellers of heaven, my own members, gods
made by the division of my power into its duties,

11

Varro : ' Templum ' is a term which was first used of spaces
wheresoever our eyes had held ' contemplation,' ' intuiti erant ';
it is derived from ' tueri '; hence it is that the term ' templum '
was used of the sky also, where we see it in ' contemplation,'
thus—

Trembled all the mighty precinct of high-thundering
Jupiter.[b]

12

Charisius says : A ' solecism ' is grammar which does not
follow the rule . . .—

And you, House-Gods, who make our home, from
floor to roof, their care,

13

A commentator on Donatus : ' Tmesis ' is the splitting apart
of one word, that is to say, by the interposition of another,
like the familiar example *septem subiecta trioni*. Take *subiecta*
away from the middle and you have ' *septemtrioni*.' Ennius— [c]

With a stone he his crani [d] split um

---

[b] Worthy of Ennius. But it may be a fr. of Cn. Matius or
Ninnius Crassus, who were translators of the *Iliad*.

[c] Some (*e.g.* Koch, *Exerc. Crit.*, 2; Leo, *Gesch. d. Röm. Lit.*,
182; W. Hardie, *Res Metrica*, 4–5) refuse to believe that Ennius
ever wrote such a thing, and only one source attributes it to
him. On the other hand, such a comic idea as this might have
found a place in the *Satires*.

[d] Or ' occi split put.'

ENNIUS

14

Diomedes, ap. *G.L.*, I, 499, 12 K: ' Partipedes ' sunt qui in singulis pedibus singulas orationis partis adsignant, ut—

Miscent foede flumina candida sanguine sparso.

15

Nonius, 312, 30 : ' Fundere ' prostenere, iacere. Vergilius, *Aen.*, lib. I . . . (192) et *Aen.*, lib. II : fusi sine mente ac sine ullo sensu iacerent.

16–17

auctor, Bell. Hisp., 5 : Hic † alterius † non solum morti mortem exaggerabant, sed tumulos tumulis exaequabant.

Enii versum ita restituit Woelfflin :—

Exaequant tumulis tumulos ac mortibus mortes accumulant.

18

Explanat. in Donat., ap. *G.L.*, IV, 563, 32 K : Per genera verborum fiunt soloicismi, sicut—

– spoliantur eos et corpora nuda relinquunt.

pro ' spoliant.'

Cp. Donat., ap. *G.L.*, IV, 394, 8 K; Pompei., ap. V., 291, 25 K.

Non., 312 Enn. lib. II fusi *ed. pr.*   *v.* Linds. *ad loc.*
Bell. Hisp., 5, hic ut ait Ennius Woelfflin, *Arch.*, VIII, 597 *fortasse scribend.* hic tumulos tumulis, hic mortem morti . . .

VARIA

14

Diomedes: ' Partipedes ' are lines in which to each single foot a single complete word is assigned, for example— [a]

> They with
> Bloodstains filthily spattered limpid rivulets tainted.

15

Nonius: ' Fundere,' to hurl down, to throw. Virgil in the first book of the *Aeneid* . . . and in the second book of the *Aeneid* [b]: ' sprawled they lay, out of their minds, their senses utterly gone.'

16–17

The author of *The Spanish War*: ' Hereon they not only heaped death on death . . . but piled barrows level with barrows.'

Woelfflin restores a fr. of Ennius :—

> They pile barrows by barrows; and deaths on
> deaths they heap.

18

A commentator on Donatus: ' Solecisms ' come about in misuse of the voices of verbs, like this example—

> Them they despoil and leave the bodies bare.

where ' spoliantur ' stands for ' spoliant.'

---

[a] Invented by the grammarian?
[b] Clearly the second quotation from Virgil—*fusi per moenia Teucri* has been ousted by *fusi sine mente ac sine ullo sensu iacerent* (Cic., *in Verr.*, II, 5, 28). Both these passages and also Lucretius, III, 113 may echo a phrase of Ennius (Pascal, *Riv. di fil. class.*, XXVI, 27), but it is obvious that we cannot restore a real fr. of Ennius here (Ilberg, *Symb. Philol.*, Bonn., 438).

ENNIUS

19

Marius Plotius, ap. *G.L.*, VI, 468, 6 K : Synecdoche est oratio plus minusve dicens quam necessaria postulat significatio . . . —

rex ambas ultra fossam protendere coepit.

Subauditur enim manus.

20

Porphyrio, ad Hor., *A.P.*, 403 : Per versus hexametros reddidit responsa . . . —

Phemonoe Burro! Cluo purpurei Epirotae.

21-2

Orosius, *Hist.*, IV, 1, 14 : Sed Pyrrhus atrocitatem cladis quam hoc bello exceperat dis suis hominibusque testatus est adfigens titulum in templo Tarentini Iovis, in quo haec scripsit—

[Qui antehac invicti fuere viri, pater optime Olympi, hos ego in pugna vici victusque sum ab isdem.]

Et cum a sociis increpitaretur cur se victum diceret qui vicisset, respondisse fertur : ' ne ego si iterum eodem modo vicero sine ullo milite Epirum revertar.'

Cp. Paul. Diac., *Hist.*, II, 16.

23

Festus, 570, 26 : ' Veruta pila ' dicuntur, quod ⟨velut verua⟩ habent praefixa. Ennius li. X—

       cursus quingentos saepe veruti

(Lucret., IV, 409 : vix etiam cursus quingentos saepe veruti.)

---

[20] *v.* St., *pp.* 91, 235–6.   [21] qui invicti ante fuere *Paul.*
[22] hos et ego *Paul.*

---

[a] Taken as part of the oracle given to Pyrrhus of Epirus (*Ann.*, Bk. VI, Valmaggi, pp. 50–51; Stowasser, *W. Stud.*, XIII, 325 ff.), but it is almost certainly not even poetry at all; cf. St., pp. 235–6. The name Phemonoe (priestess at Delphi) does not occur before Pliny and Lucan.

VARIA

19

Marius : ' Synecdoche ' comes about when an utterance expresses more, or less, than the minimum of meaning which necessity demands . . .

The king began to stretch both across the ditch.

Here ' hands ' is understood.

20

Porphyrio, on ' *dictae per carmina sortes* ' in Horace : Answers were made in hexameters by . . . —

Phemonoe to Burrus ! I hear the Epirote in purple clad.[a]

21-2

Orosius, on the battle of Heraclea, 280 B.C. : But as for the atrocity of the slaughter which Pyrrhus sustained in this campaign, he bore witness to it before his own gods and before mankind by fixing up in the temple of Jupiter of Tarentum a notice in which he wrote these words— [b]

Best father of Olympus, men in war
Unbeaten, beat I them, by them was beaten.

And when his allies angrily asked why he who had beaten his enemies said he was himself beaten, he is stated to have answered, ' Sure it is that if I beat them again in the same manner I shall return to Epirus without a single soldier.'

23

Festus : ' Pronged spears ' are so called because they are pointed as it were with prongs. Ennius [c] in the tenth book—

Oftentimes five hundred castings of a pronged spear.

[b] Orosius gives what is probably a prose translation which, being not far from poetry, was emended later to : *Qui invicti ante fuere viri, pater optume Olympi hos et ego in pugna vici victusque sum ab isdem* (Paul. Diac.); cf. St., pp. 236–7.

[c] But the phrase comes from Lucretius, IV, 409; all other phrases which Lucretius borrows from Ennius are in some way remarkable, but this is not.

ENNIUS

24

Diomedes, ap. *G.L.*, I, 447, 4 K : 'Parhomoeon' fit cum verba similiter incipiunt, ut—

Machina multa minax minitatur maxima muris

25

Nonius, 418, 3 : 'Urgere' est premere, cogere. . . . Varro Antiquitate Rerum Humanarum—

'Qua murum fieri voluit urgemur in unum.'

26

Glossa in *cd. Adm.*, 472, *Wien. Stud.* (J. Huemer), II, 305 : Albus est tabula ubi scribebantur nomina illorum qui ad militiam recipiebantur, et si contigisset ut aliquis eorum fuisset interemptus, apponebatur super nomen illius theta littera, quae mortem significat. . . . Ennius versificatur optimus—

O multum ante alias infelix littera theta!

Cp. Isid., *Orig.*, I, 3, 8 (. . . de qua quidam O *e. q. s.*) ; Schol., ad Pers., *S.*, IV, 13) (. . . quidam ait O *e. q. s.*).

27

Barth, ad Achill. Tat., I, 558 ('*Schol.*' ad A.T., I, 558) : 'Carbasus' navis, a velo, ut Ennius—

Carbasus alta volat pandam ductura carinam.

Cp. Vergil., *G.*, II, 445 pandas . . . carinas.

---

[24] minitatur V   minatur *cdd.*

VARIA

24

Diomedes : ' Parhomoeon ' comes about when words begin with the same letter; for example— [a]

A most mighty menacing machine menaces much the muniments.

25

Nonius : ' Urgere ' means to press, to force. . . . Varro, in *Human Antiquities*—

Where he has willed the wall to be, therein are we squeezed in a mass.[b]

26

A gloss : ' Album ' means a tablet in which were written the names of those who were recruited for military service; and if it so happened that any one of them had been killed, the letter theta was added above his name. . . . That most excellent verse-writer Ennius [c] has—

O theta, you letter unluckier far than others !

27

Barth professes to quote a scholiast : ' Carbasus,' a ship, derived from its use as a sail; for example, Ennius— [d]

High flits the flaxen sail, that will lead on the curved keel.

---

[a] Surely invented by the grammarian. It has been referred to Marcellus at Syracuse—V., in *Sitzungsber. B. Akad.*, 1899, 269 ff.

[b] Possibly from the outburst of Remus against Romulus.

[c] Possibly; but Isidore and a scholiast on Persius attribute the fr. to *quidam*. The Greek letter Θ (for Θάνατος, ' death ') occurs on Roman gravestones.

[d] See p. 448, n. *a*; Norden, 78.

ENNIUS

28

Varro, *L.L.*, VII, 33 : Ennius scribit . . . una—

Ennius (Med., 246-7).

trabes remis rostrata per altum.

29

Varro, *L.L.*, VII, 23 :—

Ferme aderant ratibus repentibus aequore in alto.

Aequor mare appellatum. . . .

30

Varro, *L.L.*, VII, 46 : Apud Ennium . . . cata acuta . . . —

Tunc coepit memorare simul cata dicta

accipienda acuta dicta.

31

Barth, *Advers.*, XXVIII, 15 (' *ex m. s. optimo* ') : Bonus et
liberalis eo diversi sunt quod bonus est qui per naturam suam
non nocet; liberalis qui libenter prodest. . . . Ennius in
† eo †—

quod bonus et liber populus

32

Barth, *Advers.*, XXIII, 13 (*ex m. s. gloss. Vergil. ad Aen.*
XII, 19): ' O praestans animi iuvenis ' . . . est vero ex
† seno † Enni translatum.

---

^a Varro's words suggest that he takes his illustrations of
una trabes from different sources, as he does just before in
the case of *una canes*.

VARIA

28

Varro: Ennius writes . . . ('canes' *fem. sing.*; *see pp.* 432–3) 'trabes' feminine—

with oars through the deep a beaked bark [a] . . .

Then follows Ennius, Med., 246–7.

29

Varro :—

They were well-nigh at hand in their ships that came creeping over the level deep.[b]

'Aequor' is a term used of the sea . . .

30

Varro: In a passage of Ennius . . . 'cata' means sharp. . . . In the line [c] which runs—

Then at the same time he began to speak pointed words

by 'cata dicta' we are to understand 'acuta dicta.'

31

Barth claimed to have found a fr. of Ennius in a 'very good MS.': A 'good' and a 'free' man differ in that a good man is one who through his very nature does no harm, and a 'free' man is one who gives benefits in a 'free' way. . . . Ennius— [d]

which a people good and free

32

Barth claimed to have had access to a MS. note on Virgil's 'O youth of foremost valour': . . . 'it is further taken from Ennius'— [e]

---

[b] Or, 'high seas.' This fr. sounds like Ennius.

[c] Probably from Ennius, since it comes between two frs. of his *Annals*.

[d] See p. 448, n. *a*.

[e] *Ibid.*

ENNIUS

33-6

Ausonius, *Technopaegn.*, XIV, 3-4 :

Ennius ut memorat replet te—

laetificum gau,

livida meus hominum concretum felle coquat pus.

Ausonius, *Technopaegn.*, XIV, 17-19 :

Unde Rudinus ait—

divum domus altisonum cael

et cuius de more quod adstruit—

endo suam do

et de fronde loquens cur dicit—

populea frus

Cp. Charis., ap. *G.L.*, I, 278, 24 K : Diomed., ap. I, 441, 34 K : etc.

37

Commentator Cruquii, ad Hor., *Ep.*, I, 13, 10 : ' Lamas ' lacunas maiores continentes . . . pluviam . . . Ennius—

Silvarum saltus latebras lamasque lutosas

38

Festus, 468, 29 : ' Sagaces ' appellantur multi ac sollertis acuminis. . . . Lucretius lib. II (840) : Nec minus haec animum cognoscere * * * * etiam canem * * * —

Invictus can⟨is nare sagax et vi⟩ribus fretus

[33-6] Cp. Homer., *Il.*, I, 533 : εἰς ἅλα ἆλτο βαθεῖαν ἀπ' αἰγλήεντος Ὀλύμπου, Ζεὺς δὲ ἑὸν πρὸς δῶμα. *Il.*, I, 426 : Διὸς ποτὶ χαλκοβατὲς δῶ *al.* Cp. *Il.* VIII, 564, *al.* : κρῖ λευκόν. Vergil., *Aen.*, X, 101 : deum domus. Varro., *R.R.*, III, 17, 10 : ille endo suam domum. Cp. Vergil., *Aen.*, V, 134 : populea velatur fronde. *Aen.*, X, 190.

---

[a] Some do not believe that Ennius wrote these phrases, and Ausonius alone attributes them to him. They may have

VARIA

33–6

Ausonius : As Ennius [a] says—

happy-making joll

fills you; let the jaundiced minds of men distil gall-clotted
pus. *And again* : How is it that the man of Rudiae says—

home of the gods, high-sounding heav,

and after whose manner is the phrase which he adds—

into his dom

or again, in speaking of a leaf, why does he say—

poplar-fol

37

From a scholiast referred to by Cruquius : ' Lamas,' pools
of the bigger sort containing . . . rain-water. . . . Ennius—

Glades and lurking-holes and muddy pools in the
forests

38

Festus : ' Sagax ' is a term applied to persons who possess
plenty of sharp cunning . . . even a hound . . . —

a matchless hound, cunning of nostril, trusting
too in his strength [b]

come in the *Satires,* in which case we might translate ' merry-
making gladder,' ' high-sounding hevver,' ' into his digs '
or the like. But ' endo suam do ' looks like a borrowing
from Homer where words like this occur (see opposite).
In No. 36 *frus* is *fruns* (Oscan—cf. fr. 241) and is probably
genuine, though some read *fros.* Any attempt at translating
these frs. makes one inclined to associate them with the
Satires and not with *Annals.*

[b] This fragment has long been attributed to Ennius, but
his name does not appear in Festus' defective text.

ENNIUS

39

Censorinus, ap. *G.L.*, VI, 615, 18 K : Duodecasyllabŏs spondiazon—

Olli crateris ex auratis hauserunt.

40

Diomedes, ap. *G.L.*, I, 447, 16 K : Homoeoptoton fit cum oratio excurrit in eosdem casus et similes fines, ut Ennius—

maerentes flentes lacrumantes commiserantes

Cp. Charis. ap. *G.L.*, I, 282, 13 K, etc.

41

Auctor, ad Herenn., IV, 13, 18 : Compositio . . . conservabitur . . . si non utemur continenter similiter cadentibus verbis hoc modo—

flentes plorantes lacrumantes obtestantes

42

Columna, 498 : *ex antiq. gloss. affert tanquam Enniana*—

regredi gressum

43

Varro, *L.L.*, VII, 25 : Cornua a curvore dicta, quod pleraque curva—

Musas quas memorant nosces nos esse ⟨Camenas⟩.

Camenarum priscum vocabulum ita natum ac scriptum est alibi. Carmenae ab eadem origine sunt declinatae.

---

[43] Musas S   ac quas *Varr.*   nosce *Varr.*   nosces nos esse ⟨Camenas⟩ Jordan   *supplend. potius* Casmenas *vel* Carmenas   Musas quas memorant nos noscimus Casmenas *coni.* St.   *trib. Enn.* S, *Naev.* Mr.

VARIA

39

Censorinus: A spondaic hexameter [a] of twelve syllables—

Deep they drank their draughts from gold-encrusted wine-bowls.

40

Diomedes: 'Homoeoptoton' comes about when the words all finish in the same case and have a like ending; for example, Ennius— [b]

mourning, sobbing, weeping, pitying

41

The author of *To Herennius*: 'Good composition' . . . will be preserved . . . if we do not use a continuous series of words which end in a like sound, in this way—

sobbing, imploring, weeping, protesting

42

Colonna professes to quote a fragment of Ennius from an ancient commentator:—

To restep one's step

43

Varro: 'Cornua' is a term derived from crookedness, because most 'cornua' are crooked—

You shall know that we whom men call the Muses are Camenae. [c]

This is the origin of the archaic word Camenae, and we find it spelt elsewhere by writers. The form Carmenae is derived from the same original.

---

[a] Invented by Censorinus?

[b] This fr. is probably an invention. Cf. V., p. 103.

[c] This has been taken as the second line of the *Annals* (V., p. 1 and CXLVI–CXLVII), and as the second line of Naevius' *Bellum Punicum*. It is clear from Varro that we must supply *Casmenas* or *Carmenas* and take the words as prose (?) of unknown authorship. St., p. 234.

ENNIUS

44

Donatus, ap. *G.L.*, IV, 401, 14 : ' Tmesis ' unius conpositi aut simplicis verbi sectio, una dictione vel pluribus interiectis, ut . . .—

Massili portabant iuvenes ad litora tanas

hoc est . . . ' Massilitanas.'

Cp. Pompei., ap. *G.L.*, V, 310, 3 K.

---

[a] Probably an invention. It follows ' *cere comminuit brum* ' of Ennius (see p. 451). I remember that when I was still a schoolboy I said to myself—I would have written ' Portabant

VARIA

44

Donatus : ' Tmesis ' is the splitting up of one simple or composite word by thrusting in one or more utterances; for example . . . —

> Massili- by young men were transported to the beach -tans [a]

that is, ' Massilitans.'

---

iuvenes ad litora Massilitanas.' So would Ennius the man unless he did it in a Satire. Pompeius says that by Massilitanae, ' lagonae' (bottles) are meant. Perhaps the bottles were empty and broken.

CAECILIUS STATIUS

CAECILIUS STATIUS

AETHRIO

1

Festus, 202, 18 : ' Orae ' extremae partes terrarum. . . —
Caecilius in Aethrione usus est pro initio rei cum ait—

Oram reperire nullam qua expediar queo.

2

Nonius, 536, 8 : ' Prosumia,' navigii genus. Caecilius. . . .
Aethrione—

De nocte ad portum sum provectus prosumia.

3

Festus, 502, 8 : ' Sentinare,' sat agere, dictum a sentina,
quam multae aquae navis cum recipit periclitatur . . . —

Cum Mercurio capit consilium postquam sentinat
satis.

Cp. Paul., ex F., 503, 3.

---

[1] qua Spengel   qua me Carrio   quam cd.   expediar W
expediam cd.
[2] a portu Quich.   profectus Lu. al.   provectus rell.

CAECILIUS STATIUS

THE ETHEREAL [a]

1

Festus : ' Orae ' is a term applied to the outermost parts of lands. . . . Caecilius in *The Ethereal* used the term ' ora ' for the outset of a thing when he wrote—

I can't find a shore to start from.

2

Nonius : ' Prosumia,' a kind of ship. Caecilius . . . in *The Ethereal*—

By night I was carried on my spy-boat into port.

3

Festus : ' Sentinare,' to have one's hands full. It is a term derived from ' sentina ' (bilge-water); when a ship that gathers [b] much water takes in bilge, it is in danger . . . —

After he was sick of trying ' all hands to the pump ' [c] he took advice with Mercury.

[a] Possibly a play in which Jupiter and other gods (Mercury ? fr. 3) were introduced as characters. Cf. Plautus' *Amphitruo*.
[b] *multae aquae* may mean ' of large tonnage,' ' low in the water.'
[c] Paulus explains *sentinare* as ' *sat agere*, derived from a ship's bilge which one strives to empty out to ease the ship of water.'

CAECILIUS

4

Diomedes, ap. *G.L.*, I, 386, 17 K : Apud veteres reperimus
† id quod nolumus, non vultis † ut est in Aethrione apud
Caecilium—

– actutum, voltis, empta est; noltis, non empta est.

5

Festus, 178, 5 : Panurgus Antonius haec ait : 'Numero'
nimium cito, celeriter nimium. . . . —

(A) Ei perii!   (B) Quid ita?   (A) Numero venit.
(B) Fuge domum!

ANDRIA

6

Nonius, 152, 18 : ' Putidum,' putre. . . . . Caecilius Andria—
Conducit navem putidam.

ANDROGYNOS

7

Festus, 548, 19 : 'Taenias' Graecam vocem sic interpretatur
Verrius ut dicat ornamentum esse laneum capitis honorati,
ut sit apud Caecilium in Androgyno—

sepulchrum plenum taeniarum ita ut solet.

Diomed. 386   id quod non vultis noltis *edd. v!t.*   Caecilium Statium *coni.* Becker   Lucilium activum *cdd.*   (actutum *Monac. m.* 2)   *seclud.* activum *edd.*
   5 perii *vulg.*   peri *cd.*   domum *cd.*   modo *coni.*
Kiessling
   Non. 152 Andreia Dziatsko   andrea *cdd. fortasse recte*
   6 putidam *Flor.* 2 (3 ?), *edd.*   putridam *cdd.*

470

PLAYS

4

Diomedes: In the works of old writers we find 'noltis'; for example, the passage in *The Ethereal* of the works of Caecilius—

Quick, gentlemen! Will ye?—Done! She's bought. Nill ye? She's not.

5

Festus: Panurgus Antonius writes as follows: 'Numero,' very quickly, very swiftly . . . —

(A) Hey! I'm done for! (B) Why so? (A) He has come so very quickly.[a] (B) Run away home!

THE ANDRIAN [b] WOMAN

6

Nonius: 'Putidum,' the same as 'putre.' . . . Caecilius in *The Andrian Woman*—

He hires a rotten ship.

THE MAN-WOMAN [c]

7

Festus: 'Taeniae,' a Greek word, is explained by Verrius to mean a woollen adornment of an honoured head, as is the case in a passage of Caecilius in *The Man-Woman*—

a tomb covered with headbands, as is the custom.

---

[a] 'Numero' here may have its other meaning of 'at this very moment,' 'just now.'
[b] Probably from Menander's play Ἀνδρία, but it is not certain whether the title is *Andria* or *Andreia* ('Bravery').
[c] From Menander's Ἀνδρόγυνος?

471

CAECILIUS

8

Festus, 460, 12 : 'Stolidus,' stultus. . . . Caecilius . . . in Androgyno—

Sed ego stolidus; gratulatum med oportebat prius.

ASOTUS

9

Nonius, 517, 10 : ' Desubito.' . . . Caecilius Asoto—

Nam ego duabus vigiliis transactis duco desubito domum

10

Nonius, 258, 11 : ' Callet ' etiam dictum a callositate. . . . —

Tu iam callebis, ille festus desidet.

11

Nonius, 471, 11 : ' Populat.'   Est et passivum populatur. . . . —

iamdudum depopulat macellum

12–13

Nonius, 474, 2 : ' Mutuet,' mutuum sumat. . . . —

(A) Ad amicos curret mutuatum. (B) Mutuet mea causa.

Fest. 460 Androgyno Augustin.   Andronico *cd.*
[8] med oportebat Bothe   tibi me oportebat Umpfenbach (oportebat Augustin.)   me * * * oporteat *cd.*
[9] nam *cdd.*   eam S   duco *cdd.*   ducor *quid. ap. ed. Bas.*
[10] tu *ed. princ.*   tun Ribb.   tum *cdd.*   festum Palmer. (*Spic.*)   fessus Bothe

472

8

Festus: 'Stolidus,' silly. . . . Caecilius . . . in *The Man-Woman*—

But I'm a blockhead! I ought to have wished you joy before now.

THE DEBAUCHEE [a]

9

Nonius: 'Desubito.' . . . Caecilius in *The Debauchee*—

For I took her home on a sudden when the second watch was done

10

Nonius: 'Callet.' This word also has a meaning derived from callosity . . . —

You will now become a hardened sinner and he will sink low [b] by his merry-making.

11

Nonius: 'Populat.' There is also a deponent form 'populatur.' . . . —

He has long been pillaging the butchers' shops.

12–13

Nonius: 'Mutuet,' let him take as a 'mutuum,' or loan. . . —

(A) He'll run to friends to get a money-loan. (B) Let him get a loan for me.

[a] Cp. Ἄσωτος of Timostratus and Ἄσωτοι of Antiphanes and of Eutyches.
[b] *sc.* in morals. Cp. *desidentes mores*, Livy, praef., 9.

[12-13] mutuet causa mea Quich.

CAECILIUS

14

Nonius, 507, 5 : ' Edim ' pro edam. . . . —

Parasitus

Nihilne nihil tibi esse quod edim?

15

Nonius, 474, 35 : ' Opino ' pro opinor . . . (475, 6) . . . —

Nil fore opino inter me atque illum.

16

Nonius, 139, 18 : ' Meritissimo.' . . . —

Meritissimo hic me eiecit ex hae decuria!

CHALCIA

17

Nonius, 464, 21 : ' Parere ' etiam viros dici posse Caecilius auctor est Chalciis—

Ait hic vicinus se eas peperisse et vobis datum.

Id prudenter mutuatum ab Homero : αὐτὰρ Γλαῦκος ἔτικτεν ἀμύμονα Βελλεροφόντην (*Il.*, VI, 155).

18

Nonius, 491, 23 : ' Soniti' et ' sonu ' pro sonitus et sono. . . . Caecilius Chalciis—

Num quidnam fores fecere soniti?

Non. 464 Chalciis Spengel   Calchis *cdd.*
[17] ait Grauert   sat *cdd.*   at Spengel   at ait Mr. scit Havet   se eas peperisse Iun.   se has Buecheler asses *olim* Ribb.   peperisset Ribb.   se asperisse *cdd.* (asperasse *Par.* 7666, *Lugd.*, *Bamb.*)   et *cdd.*   id Mr.   it coni. Linds.   *alii alia : cf. Ribb., Com. Fr.,* 38-9

PLAYS

14

Nonius: ' Edim ' for ' edam.' . . . —

Sponger

What, you've got nothing, nothing for me to eat?

15

Nonius: ' Opino ' for ' opinor.' . . . —

There'll be nothing doing, I think, between him and me.

16

Nonius: ' Meritissimo.' . . . —

He's chucked me out of that tithing and it serves me jolly well right!

THE COPPERSMITHS' HOLIDAY [a]

17

Nonius: ' Parere.' That this verb can be used of a man we have the authority of Caecilius in *The Coppersmiths' Holiday*—

This neighbour of yours says he gave birth to them, and the gift has been made to you.[b]

This usage is skilfully borrowed from Homer: ' But Glaucus gave birth to blameless Bellerophon.'

18

Nonius: ' Soniti,' genitive, for ' sonitus ' and ' sonu ' for ' sono.' . . . Caecilius in *The Coppersmiths' Holiday*—

Has there been any knocking at the doors?

[a] Cf. Menander's Χαλκεῖα. The scene would be Athens.
[b] An obscure fragment; the readings are uncertain.

---

[18] num Grauert   nam *cdd.*   nam quid Bothe   nam quid iam *vel* n. q. nunc Spengel

CAECILIUS

CHRYSION

19–21

Gellius, VI, 17, 3 *s.* : Quis adeo tam linguae Latinae ignarus est quin sciat eum dici 'obnoxium' cui quid ab eo cui esse obnoxius dicitur incommodari et noceri possit. . . (13) Caecilius . . . in Chrysio . . . —

[*Coquus*]

. . . quamquam ego mercede huc conductus tua advenio, ne tibi me esse ob eam rem obnoxium reare ; audibis male si male dicis mihi.

DARDANUS

22

Nonius, 392, 15 : 'Spissum' significat tardum. . . . Caecilius Dardano—

Nihil Spei credo : omnis res spissas facit.

DAVOS

23

Festus, 284, 24 : 'Probrum,' stuprum, flagitium. . . . Caecilius in Davo—

Ea tum compressa parit huic puerum, sibi probrum.

[21] dixis *ed. Gronov.* (*recte ?*)
[22] nihil ego spei credo *LuG. Harl.* 2 *al.*   nihil rei e. c. *Gen. Bern.* 83 *al.*   nil re ego spe credo Mr.   nihil spei ego credo Linds.

PLAYS

CHRYSION [a]

19-21

Gellius: Who is so very ignorant of the Latin language that he does not know that 'obnoxius' is a term applied to a man to whom some disadvantage or hurt can be caused by the man to whom he is said to be 'obnoxius.' . . . Caecilius in *Chrysion* . . . —

[*Cook*]

Although your wages hired me to come here,
Do not suppose that puts me at your mercy.
Call me bad names—you'll hear bad names from
  me.[b]

DARDANUS [c]

22

Nonius: 'Spissum' means slow. . . . Caecilius in *Dardanus*—

I've no belief in Hope; she befogs everything.

DAVUS [d]

23

Festus: 'Probrum,' disgrace, shame. . . . Caecilius in *Davus*—

She then was forced and bore, to him a son, to herself disgrace.

---

[a] A woman's name. There is no corresponding Greek title, but cp. Χρυσίς of Antiphanes.
[b] Or, ' if you give me a bad character, you'll get one too.'
[c] From Menander's Δάρδανος.
[d] *Davo* may be a corruption of *Dardano*.

CAECILIUS

DEMANDATI

24

Nonius, 123, 33 : ' Icit ' significat percutit, ab ictu. . . .
(124, 7) Caecilius Demandatis—

Si umquam quisquam vidit quem catapulta aut
 balista iecrit,

EPHESIO

25-6

Nonius, 1, 2 : ' Senium ' est taedium et odium. . . .
Caecilius in Ephesione—

Tum in senectute hoc deputo miserrimum,
sentire ea aetate cumpse esse odiosum alteri.

Cp. Cic., *de Senect.*, 8, 25.

EPICLEROS

27-8

Priscianus, ap. *G.L.*, II, 354, 7 K : Apud antiquos hic et
haec memoris it hoc memore proferebatur, in quo testis est
Caper antiquitatis doctissimus inquisitor. Ostendit enim
Caecilium in Epiclero sic protulisse—

Itane Antipho est inventus profluvia fide ?
Itanest inmemoris, itanest madida memoria ?

Cp. Prisc., ap. 235, 13 K.

Non. 1 Ephesione tum *cdd.*   Ephesio nae tum Spengel
Hephaestione Iun.
   [25] tum <equidem> in s. Ribb.   senecta *Cic.*
   [26] cumpse esse o. Fleckeisen   ipsum esse odiosum Bothe
eumpsum *coni.* Linds.   eum ipsum esse o. *Non.*   esse
odiosum se *vel sim. cdd. Cic.*

PLAYS

THE WARDS

24

Nonius : ' Icit ' means ' strikes,' derived from ' ictus.' . .
Caecilius in *The Wards*—

If anyone has ever seen a man
Struck by a balister or catapult,

EPHESIO [a]

25-6

Nonius : ' Senium ' means loathing and dislike. . . .
Caecilius in *Ephesio*—

And then this is what I think is the wretchedest
thing in old age—when a man feels that at that time
of life he himself is an object of loathing to his
neighbour.

THE HEIRESS [b]

27-8

Priscianus : In the works of archaic writers we find ' memor '
used in the form ' memoris,' masculine and feminine singular,
and ' memore ' neuter. In this we have a witness in Caper,
a most learned researcher into archaic lore; for he shows that
Caecilius used this form in *The Heiress*—

Is this true? Is Antipho found to be a slippery
customer? Is he really so unremembering? Is his
memory so sodden?

[a] From Menander's 'Εφέσιος ? But the nominative Ephesio
suggests another play.
[b] Several Greek writers wrote a play having this title.

---

[27] est inventus Bothe   inventus *cdd.* 354, 235   invenitur Spengel *ex cdd. duobus* 354

CAECILIUS

29

Priscianus, ap. *G.L.*, II, 514, 15 K : Invenitur tamen etiam claudeo. . . . Caecilius in Epiclero—

An ubi vos sitis, ibi consilium claudeat?

Cp. *Thes. nov. Lat.* ap. Mai, *Class. Auct.* VIII, 107, 142.

EPISTATHMOS

30

Priscianus, ap. *G.L.*, II, 334 : ' Hic ' et ' haec celer ' vel celeris ' et ' hoc celere.' . . . Caecilius in Epistathmo—

Si properas, escende huc meam navem; ita celeris est.

EPISTULA

31-2

Festus, 100, 3 : ' Mantare ' saepe manere. Caecilius in Epistola—

(A)

Iamne adeo? Manta!

(B)

Iam hoc vide; caecus animum . . .

. . . adventus angit.

33

Priscianus, ap. *G.L.*, II, 229, 10 K : ' Iovis ' nominativo quoque casu invenitur. Caecilius in Epistula—

nam novus quidem iam deus repertus est Iovis

---

[29] an u. v. s. i. *Prisc.*   an ut sciatis ubi *Thes.* 107   vos nescitis ubi *Thes.* 142

Prisc. 334 Epistathmo Spengel   episathomo *vel sim. cdd.*
[30] escende *vel* exscende Gulielmus   extende *cdd.*
[31] iamne *cd.*   iamque Boshe   iam me *Ald.*   caecu's *coni.* Ribb.
[31-2] *lacun. viginti fere litt. suppl.* Leo : incertat metus ten patris   *fortasse* i. a. m. i. h. v. | c. a. a. a.

PLAYS

29

Priscianus : The form ' claudeo ' is found. . . . Caecilius
in *The Heiress*—

Is it really true that wherever you happen to be,
there falters all wise counsel?

THE QUARTERMASTER [a]

30

Priscianus : ' Celer ' or ' celeris ' masculine and feminine,
celere ' neuter. . . . Caecilius in *The Quartermaster*—

If you are in a hurry, climb up here on board my
ship, she is so fast.

THE LETTER [b]

31–2

Festus : ' Mantare ' often means ' manere.' Caecilius in
The Letter—

(A)

What, so soon? Wait! Wait!

(B)

Look at that now! Blind in his wits. . . . His
approach chokes him.

33

Priscianus : ' Iovis ' is also found as a nominative case.
Caecilius in *The Letter*—

for there was found then a new god Jove [c]

---

[a] Or, ' *The Lodger.*' Cp. Ἐπίσταθμος of Poseidippus.
[b] Cp. Alexis' Ἐπιστολή.
[c] Or, ' Jove was then indeed found to be a new god.'

---

[33] novus quidem *edd.*   iam *add.* Brugmann   nobis
equidem Ribb. (equidem Osann)   nobis quidem novos re-
pertu's Iovis deus *olim* Ribb.

CAECILIUS

EXHAUTUHESTOS

34-5

Donatus, ad Ter., *Adelph.*, IV, 5, 34 : ' Praesens praesenti
eripi.' Adiuvant significationem haec ex abundanti addita
. . . sic Caecilius in Exhautuhestoti—

. . . haec caterva plane gladiatoria
cum suum sibi alius socius socium sauciat.

EXUL

36

Nonius, 75, 21 : ' Abscondit ' pro abscondidit. Caecilius
Exule—

nam hic in tenebris intus sese abscondit.

37

Nonius, 369, 29 : ' Putare,' animo disputare. . . . Caecilius
Exule—

– non haec putas, non haec in corde versantur tibi ?

FALLACIA

38-9

Nonius, 511, 27 : ' Aliquantisper.' . . . Caecilius in Fallacia—

Nam si illi, postquam rem paternam amiserant,
egestate aliquantisper iactati forent,

Ex HAUTU ESTOS, *i.e.* Ἐξ αὐτοῦ ἑστώς (*non* Ἐκτὸς αὐ. ἑ.)
Spengel   *Donat.*: Caelius vel Celius *cdd.*   Exhautuhestoti
Spengel   Eratosthene *vulg.*   in exatostoti *Gand.*
mexato scoti *Dr.*   in hesatoshetim *Lugd.*
[34] plane Lindenbrog   plena *cdd.*
Non. 75 abscondidit p. abscondit *Flor.* 1

PLAYS

WISE IN HIS OWN CONCEIT [a]

34–5

Donatus, on ' In person snatched from him in person ' in
Terence : These words, added redundantly, reinforce the
meaning . . . so Caecilius in *Wise in his own Conceit*—

This is plainly a crowd of gladiators, where each
ally wounds his own ally.

THE EXILE [b]

36

Nonius : ' Abscondit ' for ' abscondidit.' Caecilius in
The Exile—

for this fellow hid himself away inside, in the
darkness.

37

Nonius : ' Putare,' to dispute in the mind . . . Caecilius in
The Exile—

Haven't you a thought for all this ? Don't you
turn it over and over in your heart ?

THE FRAUD [c]

38–9

Nonius : ' Aliquantisper.' . . . Caecilius in *The Fraud*—

For if they were to be flung about for a while by
Want after they had sqaundered their heritage,

---

[a] This title is uncertain; but I adopt Spengel's reading.
Ἐξ αὑτοῦ ἑστώς. This might mean *The Self-made Man*.
[b] Cp. Alexis' Φυγάς and Philemon's Ἄπολις.
[c] Several Greek writers composed a Καταψευδόμενος.

---

[36] abscondidit *Lu.*   [38] amisĕrunt *coni.* Ribb.

CAECILIUS

40-1

Nonius, 512, 1 : ' Duriter ' pro dure. . . . —

                          (A) Nam quam duriter
vos educavit atque asperiter!
                    (B) Non negat.

42

Nonius, 127, 22 : ' Incursim ' pro celeriter. . . . —

Nullus sum nisi meam rem iam omnem propero
    incursim perdere.

43-4

Nonius, 430, 10 : ' Iniuria ' a contumelia hoc distat; iniuria
enim levior res est . . . —

Facile aerumnam ferre possunt si inde abest inuria;
etiam iniuriam, nisi contra constant contumeliam.

45-6

Nonius, 511, 27 : Aliquantisper. . . . —

                    (A) Velim paulisper te opperiri.
(B) Quantisper?
        (A) Non plus triduum.

47

Nonius, 147, 24 : ' Ossiculatim,' ut si minutatim. . . . —

Ossiculatim Parmenonem de via liceat legant.

[40-1] nam. q. d. v. e. *cdd.*   atque asperiter Bothe
aspereque S   atque aspere *cdd.*   atque aspere vos
educarit Grauert   nam quin d. v. educarit Bothe
[43] possunt *cdd.*   possum Mr.

PLAYS

40-1

Nonius: ' Duriter ' for ' dure.' . . . —

(A) But how sternly and harshly he brought you up!

(B) He doesn't deny it.

42

Nonius: ' Incursim ' for quickly . . . —

It's all up with me, unless I make haste and squander all my wealth now by leaps and bounds.

43-4

Nonius: ' Iniuria ' differs from ' contumelia ' in this— injury is the slighter hurt . . . —

Men can easily bear hardship if there is no injury with it; and they can bear even an injury, unless they have to face insults also.

45-6

Nonius: ' Aliquantisper.' . . . —

(A) I should like you to wait a while.
(B) How long a while?
(A) Not more than three days.

47

Nonius: ' Ossiculatim,' as it were ' minutatim.' . . . —

Give them a chance to pick up Parmeno
Bonemeal out of the road.

---

⁴⁴ constant *LuG* 2 *al. Harl.* 3   constat *rell.*   contumeliam *edd.*   contumeliā Bothe   si citra constat
contumeliam C. Fr. Hermann

CAECILIUS

48

Nonius, 514, 7 : ' Pugnitus ' pro pugnis. . . . —

nisi quidem qui sese malit pugnitus pessum dari.

GAMOS

49

Festus, 536, 18 : ' Toxicum ' dicitur cervari<um venenum, quo> quidam perungere sagitta <s soliti sunt>.   Caecilius Gamo—

ut hom⟨inem . . .⟩ toxico transegerit.

HARPAZOMENE

50

Nonius, 155, 18 : ' Pulchritas ' pro pulchritudo.   Caecilius Harpazomene—

Di boni !   Quid illud est pulchritatis !

51

Nonius, 200, 16 : ' Collus ' masculino . . . —

hunc collum Ludo praecidi iube !

---

⁴⁸ sese Guietus, Bothe   se cdd.   nisi quis est qui sese
Madvig
⁴⁹ hominem miserum S   h. amoris Spengel

PLAYS

48

Nonius: ' Pugnitus ' for ' pugnis,' with fists . . . —

unless one who prefers a knock-out to perdition.

THE MARRIAGE [a]

49

Festus: ' Toxicum ' is a term applied to a poison obtained from the deer-wort; with it some tribes have long been accustomed to smear their arrows. Caecilius in *The Marriage*—

so that he shot the fellow through with arrow-poison.

THE ABDUCTED MAIDEN [b]

50

Nonius: ' Pulchritas ' for ' pulchritudo.' Caecilius in *The Abducted Maiden*—

Good heavens! What beauteousness is that!

51

Nonius: ' Collus ' in the masculine . . . —

Order a cutlet of that neck to be carved for Sport!

---

[a] Γάμος was the title of plays written by Antiphanes, Diphilus, and Philemon.
[b] From Philemon's Ἁρπαζομένη (-όμενος).

CAECILIUS

52-3

Charisius, ap. *G.L.*, I, 144, 19 K : ' Schema ' quasi mono-ptoton sit, proinde declinasse Caecilium in Ἁρπαζομένῃ denotatur—

Utinam † tescioli † te schema sine cruribus
videam. . . .

pro schemate.

54-5

Nonius, 10, 10 : ' Inlex ' et ' exlex ' qui sine lege vivat . . . —

Quid narras barbare cum indomitis moribus,
inlitterate inlex ?

56

Nonius, 128, 12 : ' Ineptitudo ' pro ineptia . . . —

Qui, homo ineptitudinis cumulatus, cultum oblitus es ?

57-8

Donatus, ad Ter., *Eun.*, IV, 4, 4 : ' Quid vestis mutatio.' . . . Caecilius 'Ἁρπαζομένῃ—

Quid tibi aucupatiost
argumentum aut de meo amore verbificatiost patri ?

Charis. 144 Ἁρπαζομένῳ *cd.*
[52] piscicuii Ribb. bestiolae Machly to schema Ribb. te sine schema *ed. pr.* te servoli schema Buecheler utinam inquit tescioli schematä sine *cd.* te sciole istac schema *olim* Ribb.
[54] cum indomitis *cdd.* indomitis cum Ribb.
[55] inlex hist (hi sunt) *Par.* 7666 *Lugd. Bamb. Tur.* inlex hes *Lu.* 1 inlex Sisenna Hist. Mr. *sequitur* Sisenna lib. IV illex es Spengel
[56] qui *cdd.* quid Mercier equi (ecqui) Ribb. qui tu Mr. cultum *cdd.* cultrum Bothe

PLAYS

52–3

Charisius: 'Schema.' Caecilius in *The Abducted Maiden* is observed to have inflected this word as though it were an indeclinable noun. He says—

I wish I could see you without legs, in the shape of a little . . .

where [a] 'schema' stands for 'schemate.'

54–5

Nonius: 'Inlex' and 'exlex' are terms applied to a man who lives without the law . . . —

What's that you make such a savage tale of, you fellow of untamed manners, unlettered and un-lawed?

56

Nonius: 'Ineptitudo' for 'ineptia.' . . . —

You mound of ineptitude, how came you to forget good manners?

57–8

Donatus, on 'What's the meaning of this change of dress' in Terence: . . . Caecilius in *The Abducted Maiden*—

Why should you be hawking after a proof? Why this wordification from your father about my love-affair?

---

[a] *schema* in the quotation is really ablative feminine singular.

Donat. Celius *cdd.*
[58] argumenti *Par. Lugd.*   argumentum *rell.*   de meo amore *cdd.* (*om.* meo *Gand.*)

489

CAECILIUS

HYMNIS

59–60

Diomedes, ap. *G.L.*, I, 383, 10 K : Quod vulgo ' obsepio '
dicimus veteres obsipio dixerunt. Caecilius in Hymnide—

Habes

Miletida ; ego illam huic despondebo et gnato saltum
obsipiam.

61

Nonius, 135, 2 : ' Luculentitatem ' a luculento. Caecilius
Hymnide—

. . . Vide luculentitatem eius et magnificentiam!

62–3

Nonius, 78, 30 : Blaterare. . . . Blandities . . . —

sine blanditie nihil agit
in amore inermus.

64

Cicero, *de Fin.*, II, 7, 11 : Reperiemus asotos . . . ita
mortem non timentes ut illud in ore habeant ex Hymnide—

Mihi sex menses satis sunt vitae ; septimum Orco
spondeo.

⁶⁰ Miletida Bothe   mulierculam *edd. vett.*   miletidam
cdd.   et gnato (nato *vulg.*) Spengel   et ex nato *vel* tanto
cdd.
   Non. 78 Blaterare. . . . <Blandities> *nov. lemm.* Onions
non. prob. Linds.   imnide sine *Lu.* 1 *Flor.* 2 *Harl.* 1   imnis
desine *GH2L3*   Hymnide Bentin.   blanditie *Harl.*
blanditiae *rell.*   sine blaterare Victor   sine blandirier
Stowasser   desine blanditias blaterare Osann

PLAYS

HYMNIS [a]

59-60

Diomedes : ' Obsepio,' commonly used by us, was ' obsipio ' in the speech of antiquity. Caecilius in *Hymnis*—

You've got a Milesian girl. I am going to betroth her to this fellow and hedge my son in—he shan't be out of the wood.[b]

61

Nonius : ' Luculentitas ' from ' luculentus.' Caecilius in *Hymnis*—

Look at her gorgeosity, her magnificence !

62-3

Nonius : ' Blaterare '(to blather) . . . ' Blandities ' . . . —

A man in love, when he is all unarmed,
Gets nothing done without some blandishment.

64

Cicero : We shall find that debauchees . . . are so unafraid of death that they always have on the tip of their tongues that phrase from *Hymnis*—

For me six months of life are enough ; the seventh I pledge to Death.[c]

[a] From Menander's Ῡμνις. For Lucilius on this play see Bergk. *Phil.*, XIV, 390. Hymnis is a woman's name. Lines 62-3 were probably spoken by a bawd ; 59-60, 67-9 by a father ; and 64-6, (69)-70 by his son.
[b] This is our saying. For the Latin, cf. Plaut., *Cas.*, V, 2, 43 (922), *ubi illum saltum video obsaeptum.* *Men.*, V, 6, 25 *ex hoc saltu . . . ut educam.*
[c] Lucilius has a reminiscence of this line. See *Remains, etc.*, Vol. III.

CAECILIUS

65

Festus, 188, 7: 'Nictare' et oculorum et aliorum mem-
brorum nisu saepe aliquid conari dictum est ab antiquis . . . —

Garruli sine dentes iactent, sine nictentur perticis.

66

Festus, 502, 30: 'Senium,' a senili acerbitate et vitiis
dictum, posuit Caecilius in Hymnide—

Sine suam senectutem ducat usque ad senium sorbilo.

67

Festus, 284, 19: 'Prodegeris,' consumpseris, perdi-
deris . . . —

Prodigere est cum nihil habeas te inriderier.

68-70

Nonius, 134, 11: 'Licitari,' congredi, pugnare . . . —

[*Pater*] Quae
narrare inepti est ad scutras ferventis.

[*Filius*] Quin machaera
licitari adversum ahenum coepisti sciens.

---

⁶⁵ garruli sine dentes S   garrulis medentes *cd.*
⁶⁶ usque Bentley   utique *cd.*   sorbilo Bentley   sor-
bito Spengel   sonticum Grauert   sorbitio *cd.*
⁶⁷ et Ribb.   est *cdd.*   te inriderier Dacier   ted i.
Nevius   te inridier *cd.*
⁶⁹ ad *suppl.* Ribb. (est ferventi scutra *olim*)   *alii alia*
cf. Ribb., Com. Fr. 46

PLAYS

65

Festus : ' Nictare ' (to blink) by a twitch of the eyes or some other part of the body, is a term often used by old writers for ' to try to do ' something. . . . —

Let the babblers ply their jaws, let them jerk along with their sticks.

66

Festus : ' Senium,' a term derived from the sourness and faults of old age, is used by Caecilius in *Hymnis*—

Let him draw out his old age to dotage drop by drop.

67

Festus : ' Prodegeris,' you have wasted, squandered . . . —

To be a spendthrift is to be laughed at
When you have nothing left.

68–70

Nonius : ' Licitari,' to come to blows, to fight . . . —

[*Father*] It's a clumsy clown's game, telling all this to boiling dishes. [*Son*] Rather have you begun to make a bid against bronze with a sword— and you know it.[a]

[a] Presumably the father complains that it is useless to argue with his son, who replies that they are quarrelling on equal terms. Cp. our ' pot calling kettle black.'

CAECILIUS

HYPOBOLIMAEUS (SUBDITIVOS) vel HYPOBOLIMAEUS CHAERESTRATUS vel HYPOBOLIMAEUS RASTRARIA

Varro, *R.R.*, II, 11, 11 : Neque non quaedam nationes harum (*sc.* caprarum) pellibus sunt vestitae . . . cuius usum apud antiquos quoque Graecos fuisse oportet, quod in tragoediis senes ab hac pelle vocantur διφθερίαι, et in comoediis qui in rustico opere morantur, ut apud Caecilium in Hypobolimaeo habet adulescens, apud Terentium in Hautontimorumeno senex.

Cicero, *pro Rosc. Amer.*, 16, 46 : Ecquid tandem tibi videtur, ut ad fabulas veniamus, senex ille Caecilianus minoris facere Eutychum filium rusticum, quam illum alterum Chaerestratum ? Nam ut opinor hoc nomine est. Alterum in urbe secum honoris causa habere, alterum rus supplicii causa relegasse ?

71

Schol. Gronov., *ad loc.* : Apud Caecilium comoediographum inducitur pater quidam qui habebat duos filios, et illum, quem odio habebat, secum habebat, quem amabat, ruri dedit.

Festus, 536, 4 : <Tugu>ria a tecto.   Caecilius in Hypobolimaeo—

Habita⟨bat * * * * tugurio pau⟩ perculo   ᵃ

⁷¹ habitabat in tuguriolo pauperculo Ribb.   tugurio sine operculo Ursinus t. nullo o. O. Mr.

ᵃ It will be seen from the following quotations that all these titles probably belong to one play adapted from Menander's Ὑποβολιμαῖος ἢ Ἄγροικος, whereas *The Changeling* *Aeschinus* (see 503) was another play altogether.

ᵇ *sc.* a play about country-life.

ᶜ See note *e*.

ᵈ nom. sing. διφθερίας

494

PLAYS

THE CHANGELING [a] OR
THE CHANGELING CHAERESTRATUS OR
THE CHANGELING, A PLAY OF THE HOE [b]

Chaerestratus [c] country-bred :

Varro: There are too some nations who clothed themselves in the skins of goats . . . and this custom must have existed among the ancient Greeks also, because in tragedies old men, and in comedies men who pass their time in rustic tasks, are called ' leather-coated ' [d] from the use of this kind of skin. In scenes of Caecilius' *Changeling*, for example, a young man wears one, and in scenes of Terence's *Self-punisher*, an old man.

The father of Chaerestratus and Eutychus :

Cicero: Well now, to take an example from plays, do you really think that your old man in Caecilius thinks less highly of Eutychus his countrified son than his other son Chaerestratus? That is his name, I believe.[e] Do you think he kept one of them at home with him in town as a token of favour and packed the other one off to the country to punish him ?

71

Gronovius' Scholiast on the preceding : In a play of the comedy-writer Caecilius there is brought on the stage a certain father who had two sons, and the one, whom he disliked, he kept at home with him and the one whom he loved he consigned to the country.[f]

From the prologue ?

Festus : ' Tuguria,' from ' tectum.' . . . Caecilius in *The Changeling*—

He was dwelling in a poor little hut

[e] I conclude from Festus, 186, 1 ff. and also from Quintil., I, 10, 18 that Cicero has interchanged the names, and that the country-reared son was Chaerestratus, and the town-reared son Eutychus. See pp. 496, 500.

The scholiast in all probability does no more than conclude this from Cicero's words. Yet the scholiast's words *odio habebat* and the rest sound rather like a septenarius.

495

CAECILIUS

72

Nonius, 147, 6 : 'Obsorduit,' obsolevit. Caecilius Hypobolimaeo Rastraria—

Obsorduit iam haec in me aerumna miseria.

73–4

Priscianus, ap. *G.L.*, II, 190, 17 K : 'Schema' pro 'schemate.' . . . Caecilius in Hypobolimaeo—

. . . filius . . . in me incedit satis
hilara schema.

75

Festus, 460, 12 : 'Stolidus,' stultus. . . . Caecilius in Hypobolimaeo—

Abi hinc tu, stolide ; vis ille ut tibi sit pater.

76

Nonius, 178, 14 : 'Tetulit,' tulit. . . . Caecilius Hypobolimaeo—

. . . aerumnam pariter tetulisti meam.

Quintilianus, I, 10, 18 : Apud Menandrum in Hypobolimaeo senex reposcenti filium patri velut rationem impendiorum quae in educationem contulerat opponens psaltris se et geometris multa dicit dedisse.

---

[72] obsorduit *cdd.*   obsurduit (*in lemm. quoque*) Ribb.
me *cdd.*   mea Fleckeisen, *recte* ?   iuvene Bothe
  Prisc., 199 Hypobolimaeo Stephanus   hippo *vel sim. cdd.*
[73–4] Filius meus eccum incedit in me sat *vel* f. m. in me incedit eccum s. Ribb.   filius in med incedit Bothe   hilari *Bamb. Amien.*   hilaria *Par.* 7496   schema *Par.* 7496 scema *rell. recte* ?
[75] vis *vel* visne *suppl.* Ribb.   dic Buecheler   ille Bothe illic Augustin. illi *cd.*

496

PLAYS

72

Chaerestratus wants to return to his real father ? :

Nonius: 'Obsorduit,' has worn out. Caecilius in *The Changeling, A Play of The Hoe*—

By now within me has this hardship mouldered
Through very misery.

73-4

Aged peasant, guardian of the changeling Chaerestratus :

Priscianus: 'Schema' for 'schemate.' . . . Caecilius in *The Changeling*—

Here comes my son towards me in merry shape.

75

He is angry at Chaerestratus' desire to leave him ? :

Festus: 'Stolidus,' silly. . . . Caecilius in *The Changeling*—

You get away from here, blockhead. It's *he* you
want to be your father.

76

Chaerestratus is not ungrateful ? :

Nonius: 'Tetulit,' the same as 'tulit.' . . . Caecilius in
The Changeling—

You have borne my hardships equally with me.

Settlement between the peasant and the real father :

Quintilian: In a scene in Menander's *Changeling* an old
man [a] puts before a father, when he asks to have his son back,
a kind of account of the expenses which he had incurred
towards the boy's education, and says he has given many a
fee to musicians and geometricians.

---

[a] *sc.* not the son's father (*senex ille Caecilianus* in Cic. p. 494),
but the peasant who was responsible for the upbringing of
Chaerestratus.

CAECILIUS

77

Nonius, 40, 1 : ' Rabere ' dictum est a rabie. . . . Caecilius Hypobolimaeo Rastraria—

Rabere se ait.

78

Nonius, 514, 31 : ' Iracunditer.' Caecilius Subditivo—

Quaeso ne temere hanc rem agas ne iracunditer.

79

Nonius, 89, 14 : ' Coepere,' incipere. Caecilius Hypobolimaeo Rastraria—

Ere, obsecro, hercle, desine, mane ; cocpiam.

80

Nonius, 16, 14 : ' Lactare ' est inducere vel mulgere, vellere, decipere. . . . Caecilius Hypobolimaeo Rastraria—

Quod prolubium, quae voluptas, quae te lactat largitas ?

Cp. Ter., Adelph., V, 9, 28.

81–2

Gellius, XV, 9, 1 : Vere ac diserte Caecilius hoc in Subditivo scripsit—

Nam hi sunt inimici pessumi fronte hilaro corde tristi

quos neque ut adprendas neque uti dimittas scias.

Cp. Non., 205, 1–2.

---

[78] et ne *cdd.*   et *seclud. ed. princ.*
[79] obsecro Spengel   obscuro *cdd.*
[82] adprendas *Non.*   adprehendas *Gell.*   uti dimittas Spengel   ut mittas *Gell.* (dimittas *Mon.*)   ut vitare *Flor.*
3 *Non.*   vitare *rell. Non.*

PLAYS

77

Nonius : ' Rabere ' is a term derived from ' rabies.' . . .
Caecilius in *The Changeling*, *A Play of the Hoe*—

He says he's raving.

78

Nonius : ' Iracunditer.' Caecilius in *The Changeling*—

Please don't dispatch this business heedlessly, no,
nor angrily.

79

A slave is forced to speak out :
Nonius : ' Coepere,' to begin. Caecilius in *The Changeling*,
A Play of the Hoe—

Oh, sir! Oh my! Please, stop it! Wait [a]—I'll
begin.

80

Nonius : ' Lactare ' means to lead on or coax, fleece, cheat.
. . . Caecilius in *The Changeling*, *A Play of the Hoe*—

What whim, what pleasure, what openhandedness
is it that's diddling you?

81–2

Gellius : Correct and elegant is the passage of Caecilius in
The Changeling—

For the worst of foes are those that have bright
faces, gloomy hearts,
You don't know how to hold 'em and you cannot
let 'em go.[b]

[a] Possibly the master's reply—' Stay there! I'm only
just going to begin ! '
[b] Gellius proceeds to comment on *frons* used in the masculine gender.

499

CAECILIUS

83

Nonius, 176, 6 : ' Singulatim ' et ' singillatim ' a singulis. Caecilius Hypobolimaeo Rastraria—

Hos singulatim sapere, nos minus arbitror.

84

Nonius, 505, 29 : ' Mantat ' pro manet. Caecilius Hypobolimaeo Rastraria—

In voltu eodem, in eadem mantat malitia.

85

Charisius, ap. *G.L.*, I, 132, 4 K : ' Hebem.' Caecilius in 'Υποβολιμαίῳ—

      subito res reddent hebem.

86

Festus, 376, 29 : ' Ravim ' . . . < . . . Caeciliu>s in Hypobolimaeo—

prius ⟨quam * * ad ravim * *⟩ . . . citam feceris.

87

Festus, 186, 1 : ' Noxa ' peccatum aut pro peccato poena. . . . Caecilius in Hypobolimaeo Chaerestrato—

Nam ista quidem noxa muliebre est magis quam viri.

[83] nos s. s. non Bothe
[85] reste reddent *ed. princ.* res te Bothe
[87] istaec Grauert muliebre est Bothe muliebris est Ursinus muliebrist O. Mr. mulierist Grauert muliebrem et *cd.* mulieris magis quam viri est Meineke

PLAYS

83

Nonius: 'Singulatim' and 'singillatim,' from 'singuli.'
Caecilius in *The Changeling, A Play of the Hoe*—

Taken one by one [a] they are all wise, I think, but
we are not.

84

Nonius: 'Mantat' for 'manet.' Caecilius in *The Changeling,
A Play of the Hoe*—

In the same look he keeps, in the same malice.

85

Charisius: 'Hebem.' Caecilius in *The Changeling*—

The facts will promptly blunt his ardour.

86

Festus: 'Ravim.' . . . Caecilius in *The Changeling*—

before you cause . . . to hoarseness.

87

Festus: 'Noxa,' a sin or a penalty for sin. . . . Caecilius
in *The Changeling Chaerestratus*—

For that sort of harm is a thing more natural in a
woman than in a man.[b]

---

[a] Or, possibly 'they are singularly wise, we are not.'
[b] Cp. Menand., *Hyp.*, frs. 8 and 9.

CAECILIUS

AESCHINUS

SIVE

HYPOBOLIMAEUS AESCHINUS

88

Gellius, XV, 14, 5 : Sese pecunias inquit (*sc.* Q. Metellus Numidicus) maximas exactos esse. . . . Caeciliusque eadem figura Hypobolimaeo Aeschino usus videtur—

Ego illud minus nihilo exigor portorium.

Id est : nihilo minus exigitur de me portorium.

Cp. Non., 106, 22.

IMBRII

89

Nonius, 159, 5 : ' Pecua ' et ' pecuda ' ita ut pecora veteres dixerunt . . . (19) Caecilius Imbriis—

et homini et pecubus omnibus

90

Festus, 220, 25 : ' Obstipum,' obliquum . . . —

Resupina obstipo capitulo sibi ventum facere tunicula.

91-2

Nonius, 188, 11 : ' Uter ' pro uterus . . . —

nunc uter

crescit, non potest celari.

---

[89] pecubus *vel* pecudis Spengel   pecudibus *cdd.*   et
et hominibus et pecudis Grauert
[90] tunicula Ursinus   cunicula *cdd.*

PLAYS

AESCHINUS

OR

THE CHANGELING AESCHINUS [a]

88

Gellius: Quintus Metellus Numidicus says that they had been exacted very large sums of money. . . . Caecilius seems to have used the same idiom in *The Changeling Aeschinus*—

I none the less am exacted that customs-due.

That is, 'none the less the customs-due is exacted from me.' [b]

THE IMBRIANS [c]

89

Nonius: 'Pecua' and 'pecuda' are terms used by old writers in the same ways as 'pecora.' . . . Caecilius in *The Imbrians*—

To man and all cattle

90

Festus: 'Obstipum,' slanting. . . . —

Lying on her back, her little head aslant, she fans herself with her little tunic.

91–2

Nonius: 'Uter' for 'uterus.' . . . —

Now her womb swells. It can't be hidden.

[a] Clearly not the same play as the preceding. It is natural to suppose that if Caecilius wrote several plays on the subject of changeling children, he distinguished them in their titles.
[b] Compare our 'He was given a book by me' for 'a book was given him by me.'
[c] Cp. Menander's Ἴμβριοι, which was a play about two poor men of Imbros who married twin sisters (*Oxyr. Pap.*, 1235).

CAECILIUS

93

Priscianus, ap. *G.L.*, II, 231, 13 K : ' Hic puerus ' . . . —

Age age i puere, duc me ad patrios fines decoratum
opipare !

Cp. *Thes. Nov. Lat.* ap. Mai, *Cl. Auct.*, VIII, 390, 407.

94–6

Priscianus, ap. *G.L.*, II, 512, 24 K : ' Expergiscor ' exper-
rectum facit . . . —

Surdo mihi
suadet ut eam quisquam dormitum ? Et si ego
obdormivero,
tute idem ubi eris experrectus ?

97

Nonius, 194, 7 : ' Balneae ' generis feminini. . . . Caecilius
in Imbris—

Quid ? Mihi non sunt balneae ?

98

Nonius, 524, 18 : ' Turbam ' et ' turbas.' . . . Nos . . .
invenimus . . . indiscrete positum et pro turbis turbam. . . .
(525, 3) Caecilius in Imbriis—

Mirum adeo nisi frater domi ebriatus turbam aliquam
dedit.

[93] age age i puere *Carolir., Lugd. Bat. Grut., Sang., Vind.
Prisc. om.* i *rell. Thes.* 390, 407   age age puer *Thes.* 390
puere puere 407   duc Spengel *ex uno cd.*   duce *rell.
Prisc.*   deduc *Thes.* 390, 407
[94-5] surdo mihi Fleckeisen   mihi surdo *vel* dum sorbilo *coni.*
Ribb.   sobrio Buecheler   sordi *vel* sordo *cdd. pler.*
sordido *ed. Ven.* 1 sordida *Lips.* 1   dormitum suadet ut
eam quisquam et si ego obdormivero *vel sim. cdd.*   dormitum
ut e. q. suadet Ribb.

PLAYS

93

Priscianus : ' Puerus,' nominative masculine . . . —

Come come, boy, get along ! Escort me, smartened up.[a] gorgeously, to the bounds of my father's estate !

94–6

Priscianus : ' Expergiscor ' . . . makes its perfect ' experrectus ' . . . —

Is anyone coaxing me (I turn a deaf ear) to retire to sleep? And in case I do fall asleep, when will *you* wake up, you ?

97

Nonius : ' Balneae,' of the feminine-gender. . . . Caecilius in *The Imbrians*— [b]

What's that? Haven't I got baths?

98

Nonius : ' Turba ' and ' turbae ' . . . We have found . . . the terms used without distinction and ' turba ' put for ' turbae.' . . . Caecilius in *The Imbrians*—

It will be just wonderful if my brother in a drunken frolic has not raised a riot at home.

[a] Or, ' so that I can smarten up ' . . .
[b] Or possibly we should accept the correction in the Florentine MS. which attributes the fr. to *Synephebi* (p. 537).

Non. 194 infoebis (= Synephebis) *Flor.* 3 *Harl.* 1   inimbris *rell.*
[93] ebriatus Buecheler   ebrius *cdd.*   *alii alia*

CAECILIUS

99

Nonius, 465, 1 : ' Grundire ' . . . etiam hominum esse grunditum Caecilius Imbriis designavit—

    cruento ita ore grundibat miser.

Cp. Diomed., ap. *G.L.*, I, 387, 22 K.

KARINE

100-1

Festus, 388, 28 : ' Reluere,' resolvere, repignerare. Caecilius in Carine—

. . . ut aurum et vestem, quod matris fuit,
reluat, quod viva ipsi opposivit pignori.

102-3

Festus, 460, 8 : ' Stalagmium ' genus inaurium videtur significare Caecilius in Karine cum ait—

    tum ex aure eius stalagmium
domi habeo.

Cp. Paul., ex F., 461, 2.

KRATINUS?

104-5

Priscianus, ap. *G.L.*, II, 282, 11 K : ' Concors, concordis.' Antiquissimi tamen solebant genetivo similem proferre nominativum. Caecilius in Cratino—

Modo fit obsequens hilarus comis
communis concordis, dum id quod petit potitur.

[101] ipsa Augustin.   opposivit S   opposuit *cd.*
Prisc. 282 Carine Meineke   Carino Bothe   crastino *Amien.*, *Sang.*   cratino *rell.*

PLAYS

99

Nonius: 'Grundire.'. . . . Caecilius in *The Imbrians* has indicated that grunting can be used even of men—

so loudly was the poor wretch grunting with his mouth all bloody.

THE KEENER [a]

100–1

Festus: 'Reluere,' to release, to redeem from pledge. Caecilius in *The Keener*—

that he may redeem the gold and clothing which belonged to her mother and which, before she died, she deposited with me, no other, as a pledge.

102–3

Festus: 'Stalagmium.' By this word Caecilius in *The Keener* seems to mean a kind of ear-rings when he writes—

and again I have at home an ear-drop from her ear.

CRATINUS?

104–5

Priscianus: 'Concors,' gen. 'concordis.' But the most archaic writers, in such compounds as these, used to employ the same form for the nominative as for the genitive. Caecilius in *Cratinus* [b]—

Sometimes, when he is getting what he wants,
He's cheery, kind, compliant, sociable,
Agreeable.

[a] 'The Carian Woman.' From Menander's or from Antiphanes' Καρίνη. The name was used particularly of a woman hired to sing funeral songs called Καρικὰ μέλη.
[b] Meinecke reads Carine, and this may be right.

CAECILIUS

MERETRIX

106

Nonius, 536, 68 : 'Prosumia,' navigii genus. Caecilius Meretrice—

Cypro gubernator propere vertit prosumiam.

107

Nonius, 202, 12 : 'Candelabrum' . . . masculini . . . —

. . . memini ibi candelabrum ligneum ardentem.

NAUCLERUS

108

Nonius, 505, 35 : 'Audibo' pro audiam. . . . Caecilius Nauclero—

Nunc abeo; audibis praeterea si dicis 'filia redeat.'

109

Nonius, 126, 27 : 'Infelicent' . . . —

Ut te di omnes infelicent cum male monita memoria!

110

Nonius, 12, 21 : 'Suppilare' est involare vel rapere, a pilorum raptu, unde et furtum passi conpilati dicuntur. . . . —

. . . subpilat vestem atque ornamenta omnia.

[106] Cupro Buecheler   cum ultro Ribb.   cui pro *cdd.* (*om.* pro *Par.* 7665, *Montepess., Ox.*)
[107] ibi <fuisse> Ribb. (*vel.* <videre>)   illic Grauert
[108] ab eo Buecheler   dicis *cdd.*   ditis Ribb.   dices Buecheler   si eius redeat filia *olim* Ribb.   sed vin redeat filia ? Grauert
Non. 126 infelicent Guietus infelicitent *cdd.*   molita *Par.* 7665–6, *Montepess., Ox., Lugd., Turic., Bamb.*   monita *rell.*   infelicent male moenita Spengel

508

PLAYS

THE HARLOT

106

Nonius: 'Prosumia,' a kind of ship. Caecilius in *The Harlot*—

The helmsman hurriedly put about the spy-boat from Cyprus.

107

Nonius: 'Candelabrum' . . . of the masculine gender . . . —

I remember a wooden chandelier burning there.

THE SHIPMASTER [a]

108

Nonius: 'Audibo' for 'audiam.' . . . Caecilius in *The Shipmaster*—

Now I'm going. You'll hear later on if you say 'let the daughter come back.' [b]

109

Nonius: 'Infelicent' . . . —

Well, may all the gods unbless you, ill-informed memory and all!

110

Nonius: 'Suppīlare' means to make seizure of or snatch; derived from the idea of pulling out 'pīli' (hairs). Whence to those who have suffered a theft the term 'conpilati' (plucked, fleeced) is applied . . . —

The clothes and all the ornaments he plucks away.

[a] From Menander's Ναύκληρος?
[b] The metre is anapaestic, apparently; but the words *si dicis* are doubtful.

---

[110] subpilat vestem *vel* s. v. aurum Onions   suppilatum est aurum *coni.* Bothe   suppilatum est aurum argentum atque Maehly (vestis atque *coni.* Ribb.)   subpilatum est eum atque *cdd.*

CAECILIUS

NOTHUS NICASIO

111

Nonius, 97, 25 : ' Decollare,' ex collo deponere. Caecilius Notho Nicasione—

Habes, vide ; tibi tradidi ; in tuo collo est. Decolles cave.

112

Nonius, 324, 34 : ' Ilico,' significat statim, mox . . . —

Ilico ante ostium hic erimus.

113

Nonius, 325, 6 : ' Ilico,' in eo loco . . . —

manete ilico !

OBOLOSTATES vel
FAENERATOR

114

Nonius, 508, 7 : ' Reperibitur ' pro reperietur. . . . Caecilius Obolostate—

Nunc enimvero est cum meae morti remedium reperibit nemo.

115–16

Nonius, 279, 24 : ' Deponere ' est desperare . . . —

depositus modo sum anima, vita sepultus sum.

---

111 vide vel viden *coni.* Ribb.   habes quidem Mr. *Non.* 508 Obolostate Mercier   obolo *cdd.*
116 animo *coni* Ribb.   vita *cdd.*   vivos Mr.   sum *seclud.* Ribb.   *alii alia*

510

PLAYS

THE BASTARD NICASIO [a]

111

Nonius : ' Decollare,' to put down from the neck or
' collum.' Caecilius in *The Bastard Nicasio*—

It's yours, look! I've given it up to you; it's
on your neck. Mind you don't unneck it.

112

Nonius : ' Ilico ' means at once, soon . . . —

Straightway we'll be in front of the door, here.

113

Nonius : ' Ilico,' the same as ' in eo loco.' . . . —

Stay all of you on that very spot!

THE MONEY-LENDER [b]

114

Nonius : ' Reperibitur ' for ' reperietur.' . . . Caecilius in
The Money-Lender—

Now is the time indeed when none shall find
A remedy against my death.

115–16

Nonius : ' Deponere ' means to despair of . . . —

Lately, though breathing, I have been laid out,[c]
Though living, have been buried.

[a] Possibly from Philemon's Νόθος. The title suggests that
Caecilius wrote another play entitled simply ' *The Bastard*.'
[b] The two frs. assigned to *The Hunter ?* (pp. 544–7) ought
perhaps to be included in this play.
[c] *sc.* for burial. This is what Caecilius means, in spite of
Nonius' interpretation.

CAECILIUS

117–18

Nonius, 149, 27 : ' Peniculamentum ' a veteribus pars
vestis dicitur. . . . Caecilius Feneratore—

Volat exsanguis, simul anhelat
peniculamentum ex pallio datur.

119

Nonius, 543, 20 : ' Pelvis,' sinus aquarius in quo varia
pelluuntur . . . —

Pelvim sibi poposcit.

120

Festus, 416, 18 : <' Silicernium ' dicitur cena fu>nebris,
quam <Graeci . . . περίδειπνον vo>cant. . . . <Caecilius
Ob>olostate—

Credidi silicernium eius me esse esurum

Cp. Paul., ex F., 417, 6.

121–3

Nonius, 277, 28 : ' Delica ' est aperi et explana. . . .
Caecilius Obolostate—

?

Si linguas decem
habeam, vix habeam satis te qui laudem, Lache.

Laches

Immo vero haec ante solitus sum.

?

Res delicat.

Cp. Non., 98, 7.

---

[117] exsanguis Bothe   sanguis *cdd.*
[118] ex Linds.   e Buecheler   et pallio datur *cdd.*   et
palliolatur Iun.   tenet | palliolatim Ribb. *cf. Com. Fr.,*
corollar. XXIV–XXV
Fest., 416 *suppl. ex Paul.*
[121] decem Bentin.   dete *cdd.*

512

PLAYS

117–18

Nonius: 'Peniculamentum' is a term used by old writers for part of a garment. . . . Caecilius in *The Money-Lender*—

Pale as a corpse he flies and puffing too;
A cloth trails out behind his cloak.

119

Nonius: 'Pelvis,' a water-bowl in which various things are washed, or 'pelluuntur,'[a] hence its name . . . —

She demands a wash-basin for her use.

120

Festus: 'Silicernium' is a term used of a funeral supper, which the Greeks . . . call περίδειπνον . . . . Caecilius in *The Money-Lender*—

I was sure I was going to eat his funeral-feast

121–3

Nonius: 'Delica' means make clear and explain. . . . Caecilius in *The Money-Lender*—

?

Even if I had ten tongues, I would hardly have enough to praise you with, Laches.

Laches

Not at all, surely. I've often done the same before.

?

That's clear from the facts.

[a] Of course this derivation is wrong.

---

[122] Lache Mercier   ache *edd.*   [123] res *add. ex* 98

CAECILIUS

124–5

Nonius, 154, 10 : ' Populatim.' Caecilius Obolostate—
Ego perdidi te, qui omnes perdo servolos
populatim. Quaeso, ne ad malum hoc addas malum.

PAUSIMACHUS

126

Nonius, 515, 24 : ' Rarenter.' Caecilius Pausimacho—
Edepol voluntas homini rarenter venit.

127

Nonius, 548, 16 : ' Molochinum,' a Graeco, color flori similis
malvae . . . —

carbasina molochina ampelina

128–9

Nonius, 127, 13 : ' Iamdiu ' pro olim . . . —

[*Meretrix*]
        libera essem iam diu
si istoc habuissem ingenio amatores mihi.

130–1

Nonius, 334, 2 : ' Limare ' etiam dicitur coniungere . . . —

[*Pater*]
        Hoc a te postulo,
ne cum meo gnato posthac limassis caput.

[124] perduo Bothe   perdito *coni.* Ribb.   perdo servolos Mr.
[126] voluptas Palmer. (*Spic.*)   [128] libera Iun.   liber *cdd.*
[129] s. i. h. i. Onions (si isto Mercier)   si ston habuissem ingenio *Flor.* 3   *om.* h. i. *Lu.*   h. i. siston *G.Harl.* 2 *Lu.* 3   h. i. si sto L   si stoc Roth   si isto Mercier

PLAYS

124–5

Nonius: 'Populatim.' Caecilius in *The Money-Lender*—

I've ruined you, as I ruin all my little slaves in tribes. Please don't add this trouble also to my troubles.

MAKEPEACE [a]

126

From the prologue ? :

Nonius: 'Rarenter.' Caecilius in *Makepeace*—

By heaven it is rarely that willingness comes to a man.

127

Dress of a courtesan :

Nonius: 'Molochinum,' from a Greek word; a colour like the mallow-flower. . . . —

dresses of flax, mauve and vine-hued

128–9

She speaks to a father about his son :

Nonius: 'Iamdiu' for once upon a time . . . —

[*Courtezan*]

Free woman would I long ago have been
If such had been the nature of my lovers.

130–1

The father addresses her :

Nonius: 'Limare' is also used for to join . . . —

[*Father*]

This I demand of you—do not from now on rub heads with my son.

[a] Probably a proper name ('Stop-the-fight'), but possibly an epithet.

CAECILIUS

PHILUMENA

132

Nonius, 197, 24 : ' Corbes.' ' Corbulas' Varro de Re
Rustica lib. I . . . Caecilius Philumena—

qui panis solidi corbulam

133

Nonius, 304, 24 : ' Factio ' iterum significat opulentiam
abundantiam et nobilitatem. . . . Caecilius Philumena—

. . . ita eorum famam occultabat factio.

PLOCIUM

This play was based on Menander's Πλόκιον, *The Little
Necklace*, and appears to have had roughly the following plot :
The daughter of a poor peasant was outraged one night by a
kinsman; neither recognised the other, and the girl kept her
secret. The youth became betrothed to the girl whom he had
outraged. Near the beginning of the play the guilty youth's
father complains about Crobyle, his rich but ugly wife, to a
neighbour. By her orders he had been forced to sell a pretty
handmaiden whom his wife suspected of being his mistress.
Meanwhile the daughter, who was with child secretly, was
attacked by birth-pangs on the eve of her wedding with her
betrayer. Parmeno, a good slave of her father's, heard her
cries and wondered because it was now ten months since his
master had moved in from the country and it was thought she
had known no man since the move. He discussed the mystery
with a friend. Inevitably the secret was revealed (though the
author of the girl's shame remained unknown), and her
father took Parmeno into his confidence. The youth, not

---

[132] quid ? *coni.* Mr.   solidi Ribb.   soli *cdd.* (*recte ?*
gen.)

Non. 304 Philumena ita eorum Grauert   lata Iun.
altam Bothe   filium in alta eorum *cdd.* (filumina ita *Bern.*
83)   *fortasse* Caecilius Philumena * * * * idem Plocio

516

PLAYS

THE FIANCÉE

132

Nonius : ' Corbes.' Varro has ' corbulae ' in the first book *on Farming.* . . . Caecilius in *The Fiancée*—

who brought a little basket of hard bread

133

Nonius : ' Factio ' again means opulence, abundance and nobility. . . . Caecilius in *The Fiancée*—

so well did their set [a] hide their bad report.

THE LITTLE NECKLACE

knowing that his betrothed was the girl he had himself ruined and that the baby was his, decided to repudiate her, and the wedding was stopped, but the girl's father decided to bring the matter into court. Then came the dénouement—through a necklace the girl and the youth recognised each other as the parents of the baby; the betrothal was renewed, and Parmeno was made free.

In the fragments of Caecilius we can distinguish the following characters :

(A) the guilty youth's father, husband of Crobyle. (B) an elderly neighbour of (A). (C) a friend of the slave Parmeno ? (see below). (D) a poor peasant, father of the betrayed girl. Parmeno, slave of (D). Crobyle, wife of (A). (Cf. Allinson, *Menander*, p. 432, 407 K.)

---

[a] This quotation might be an inaccurate reproduction of a line from another play—*The Little Necklace* (see below). The quotation from *The Fiancée* illustrating a usage of *factio* may have' dropped out together with the title *The Little Necklace* presumably prefixed to the quotation given here in Nonius' text. It is possible, however, that *The Fiancée* is the same play as *The Little Necklace*, into which the first fr. of *The Fiancée* could fit.

CAECILIUS

134-5

Nonius, 468, 20 : ' Auspicavi ' pro auspicatus sum. . .
Caecilius Plocio—

Insanum auspicium!   Aliter histrionium est
atque ut magistratus publice cum auspicant.

Gellius, II, 23, 4 : Libitum et Menandri quoque Plocium
legere, a quo istam comoediam verterat.   Quantum stupere
atque frigere quantumque mutare a Menandro Caecilius visus
est ! . . . Accesserat dehinc lectio ad eum locum in quo
maritus senex super uxore divite atque deformi querebatur
quod ancillam suam, non inscito puellam ministerio et facie
haut inliberali, coactus erat venundare suspectam uxori quasi
paelicem. . . . Menander sic :

(A) ἐπ' ἀμφότερα νῦν ἡ 'πίκληρος ἡ καλὴ
μέλλει καθευδήσειν. κατείργασται μέγα
καὶ περιβόητον ἔργον· ἐκ τῆς οἰκίας
ἐξέβαλε τὴν λυποῦσαν ἣν ἐβούλετο,
ἵν' ἀποβλέπωσι πάντες εἰς τὸ Κρωβύλης
πρόσωπον ᾖ τ' εὔγνωστος οὖσ' ἐμὴ γυνὴ
δέσποινα· καὶ τὴν ὄψιν ἣν ἐκτήσατο
ὄνος ἐν πιθήκοις τοῦτο δὴ τὸ λεγόμενον
ἔστιν. σιωπᾶν βούλομαι τὴν νύκτα τὴν
πολλῶν κακῶν ἀρχηγόν. οἴμοι Κρωβύλην
λαβεῖν ἔμ' ἑκκαίδεκα τάλαντα προῖκα καὶ
τὴν ῥῖν' ἔχουσαν πηχέως. εἶτ' ἐστὶ τὸ
φρύαγμά πως ὑπόστατον; μὰ τὸν Δία
τὸν Ὀλύμπιον καὶ τὴν Ἀθηνᾶν, οὐδαμῶς.
παιδισκάριον θεραπευτικὸν δὲ δεῖ λόγου
τάχιον ἀπάγεσθαι † . . . (Allinson, Men., p. 428)

Caecilius autem sic—

---

¹³⁴ auspicium <num> aliter coni. Linds.   <haud>
aliter Spengel   histrionium Guietus   istrionum cdd.
¹³⁵ aeque Mr.   publice cum cdd.   p. quoque Spengel
quando Bothe   publicitus cum Maehly   publicae rei
cum Ribb.   auspicant cum publice Mr.

ᵃ So I take it.   Compare some of Plautus' and Terence's
prologues.

PLAYS

134-5

From the prologue ; Caecilius ° *to his audience ? :*

Nonius : ' Auspicavi ' for ' auspicatus sum.' . . . Caecilius in *The Little Necklace*—

It's an unhealthy augury; quite different is the actors' augury from that of a magistrate when he takes the auspices for the state.

The father of the guilty youth, after a soliloquy, converses with a neighbour about troublesome wives :

Gellius : We had a fancy to read also *The Little Necklace* of Menander, which Caecilius had adapted for *his* comedy. . . . How dull and stiff was Caecilius revealed right from the beginning! What great alterations he made in Menander's material! . . . Our reading in due course had reached the passage in which an old husband was making a great to-do about his wife, who was rich and ugly, complaining that he had been forced to put up for sale a handmaid who rendered skilled service and was very good-looking; his wife suspected her of being his mistress. . . . Menander writes thus :

(A) So now my lovely heiress *ᵇ* can go to sleep on both cheeks. She has done a doughty deed which will make a big noise everywhere; she has cast out of the house the girl who wanted to, one who provoked her, so that the whole neighbourhood may gaze on the face of, why—Crobyle, and that she, my illustrious wife, may be a tyrant over me. As for the looks which she got herself, well, she's an ass amongst apes, as the saying is. I'd rather say nothing about the night which was the prime cause of many troubles. Oh! Damn it! That I should have chosen to marry Crobyle with a dowry of sixteen talents and a nose a yard long! And besides, is her snortiness by any means to be put up with? No! By Zeus in heaven and by Athena, not at all! And the little serving girl must be led away before you can say a word.

But Caecilius writes thus *ᶜ*—

ᵇ sc. his rich wife Crobyle.

ᶜ The following verses have been variously arranged. The first four are anapaestic. Cf. Ribbeck, *Com. Fr.*, 58–62, and corollar., XXV–XXIX.

CAECILIUS

136–50

(A)

Is demum miser est qui aerumnam suam nesciat
    occultare
foris; ita me uxor forma et factis facit, si taceam,
    tamen indicium,
quae nisi dotem omnia quae nolis habet. Qui sapiet
    de me discet,
qui quasi † ad hostis † captus liber servio salva urbe
    atque arce.
Quae mihi quidquid placet eo privatum it me ser-
    vatam velim ?   140
Dum ego eius mortem inhio, egomet inter vivos
    vivo mortuus.
Ea me clam se cum mea ancilla ait consuetum; id
    me arguit,
ita plorando orando instando atque obiurgando me
    optudit
eam uti venderem. Nunc credo inter suas
aequalis cognatas sermonem serit :   145
    ‘ Quis vostrarum fuit integra aetatula
        quae hoc idem a viro
    impetrarit suo, quod ego anus modo
effeci, paelice ut meum privarem virum ? ’
Haec erunt concilia hocedie; differar sermone
    misere.   150

Cp. Non., 502, 12 (147).

126–150 cf. *Ribb. Com. Fr.* 58 *s. corollar., XXV s.*
136 nesciat Ribb.   non potis Fleckeisen   nescit Thysius
nesquit *Burn.*   nequit *rell.*
137 foris Ribb.   efferre Spengel   fere *edd.*   ferre *cdd.*
140–1 *transpos.* Ribb.

PLAYS

136–150

(A)

A poor wretch is he surely who doesn't know how he can hide his troubles out of doors. You see, my wife, even if I say nothing, gives the show away by her looks and by her acts—she who has every thing you wouldn't want her to have except a dowry. He who'll be a wise man will learn a lesson from me —I'm free but still a slave to the will of enemies, though yet my town and stronghold are safe. What, am I to wish long life to the woman who is always going to rob me of whatever gives me joy? While I gape for her death, I am a living corpse among the living. She says that unknown to her there is intimacy between me and my handmaid. That's what she accuses me of; and so by moaning and groaning and bothering and pothering she thumped me into selling her. And now I believe she's sowing this sort of gossip among her cronies and kinsfolk: ' Of all you women who is there, who, in the tender flower of her age, got out of her husband what I, an old woman, have lately accomplished—robbed my husband of his wench? ' That's the sort of mothers' meetings there'll be these days. I shall be damnably torn to pieces by gossip.

---

140 quae *cdd.*   quaen Ribb.   privatum it me servatam Ribb. (p. i. m. servatum Thysius)   *alii alia*   privatu vim me servatum *vel* privatum in me servat *vel sim. cdd.*

141 d. e. e. Non. *om. ego cdd. Gell.*   inibo *cdd. Non.* inter vivos vivo mortuus Ribb.   vivo m. i. vivos *cdd.*

145 aequalis atque *vel* et *cdd.*   aequalis cognatas Ribb.

146 nostrarum *cdd. nonnulli*

150 convitia Maehly   hocedie Bergk   hodie *cdd.* differar Ribb.   differor *cdd.*   misere Ribb.   miser *cdd.* *alii alia*

CAECILIUS

151-5

Gellius, II! 23, 11 : Praeter venustatem autem rerum atque verborum in duobus libris nequaquam parem in hoc equidem soleo animum attendere, quod quae Menander praeclare et apposite et facete scripsit, ea Caecilius ne qua potuit quidem conatus est enarrare, sed quasi minime probanda praetermisit et alia nescio quae mimica inculcavit et illud Menandri de vita hominum media sumptum simplex et verum et delectabile nescio quo pacto omisit. Idem enim ille maritus senex cum altero sene vicino colloquens et uxoris locupletis superbiam deprecans haec ait :

(A)   Ἔχω δ' ἀπίκληρον Λάμιαν· οὐκ εἴρηκά σοι
τοῦτ', εἶτ' ἄρ' οὐχί; κυρίαν τῆς οἰκίας
καὶ τῶν ἀγρῶν καὶ τῶν ἀπάντων ἄντικρυς
ἔχομεν, Ἄπολλον, ὡς χαλεπῶν χελεπώτατον,
ἅπασι δ' ἀργαλέα 'στίν οὐκ ἐμοὶ μόνῳ,
υἱῷ, πολὺ μᾶλλον θυγατρί.

(B)   πρᾶγμ' ἄμαχον λέγεις.
(A) εὖ οἶδα. (Allinson, *Men.*, pp. 428, 430.)

Caecilius vero hoc in loco ridiculus magis quam personae isti quam tractabat aptus atque conveniens videri maluit. Sic enim haec corrupit—

(B) Sed tua morosane uxor quaeso est? (A) Va! Rogas?
(B) Qui tandem? (A) Taedet mentionis quae mihi ubi domum adveni, adsedi, extemplo savium dat ieiuna anima. (B) Nil peccat de savio; ut devomas vult quod foris potaveris.

Cp. Non., 233, 12 (152-4).

151 Va! Rogas? Ribb. (*coni.* quam, rogas?) q[an] *Rott.* quam erogas *Reg.*   q. errogas *Vat.*   quam erogas *coni.* Spengel
152 qui Ribb.   qui quia *Reg.*   quas qui *Rott.*

---

[a] So I take it. (A) uses the phrase in the sense of 'breath that makes you want to vomit,' 'nauseous breath,' and means

PLAYS

151-5

Gellius goes on : Quite apart from charm of ideas and diction, which is by no means the same in the two works, I am generally impressed by the fact that where Menander wrote brilliantly and wittily and to the point, Caecilius has not tried to reproduce even where he might have, but has passed them over as not in the least worthy of approbation, and has crammed in some farcical tricks, and in some way or other has altogether missed that simple and delightful effect of Menander's, which is so true to nature and is taken from the very heart of human life. For that same old husband, in conversation with a second person, another old man, calls down curses on the haughtiness of his wealthy wife in these words :

(A) I've got an heiress-witch. Haven't I told you this? Haven't I really then ? Well, as the mistress of the house and fields and absolutely everything, we have, by Apollo, a thing most tiresome of the tiresome. She's a nuisance to everyone, not only to me, but her son too and much more to her daughter.
(B) There's no fighting with that kind of thing.
(A) Don't I know it well !

But Caecilius in this passage preferred to act the buffoon rather than fit and accommodate himself to the character he was dealing with. For this is the way in which he has spoiled all that passage—

(B) But tell me, please, is your wife moody? (A) Wow! What a question!
(B) Well, how about it? (A) I don't like to talk about it. Whenever I have come home and sat down beside her, first thing she gives me a kiss with fasting breath.[a] (B) She makes no mistake about that kiss; she wants you to belch up what you have been drinking out of doors.

his wife's. But (B) thinks of the phrase in the meaning of ' with a starved soul.' The wife wants to smell (A's) breath. Nonius gives most of this passage to illustrate *anima* in the sense of *alitus oris et odor.*

CAECILIUS

156

Nonius, 314, 21 : Et graviter multum intellegitur. . . . —

(B)

Placere occepit graviter, postquam emortuast.

Gellius, II, 23, 14 : Quid de illo quoque loco in utraque comoedia posito existimari debeat manifestum est, cuius loci haec ferme sententia. Filia hominis pauperis in pervigilio vitiata est. Ea res clam patrem fuit. Et habebatur pro virgine. Ex eo vitio gravida mensibus exactis parturit. Servus bonae frugi, cum pro foribus domus staret et propinquare partum erili filiae atque omnino vitium esse oblatum ignoraret, gemitum et ploratum audit puellae in puerperio enitentis; timet irascitur suspicatur miseretur dolet. Hi omnes motus eius affectionesque animi in Graeca quidem comoedia mirabiliter acres et illustres, apud Caecilium autem pigra istaec omnia et a rerum dignitate atque gratia vacua sunt.

157-8

Gellius, III, 16, 3 : Hoc idem tradit etiam Menander poeta vetustior, humanarum opinionum vel peritissimus. Versus eius super ea re de fabula Plocio posui :
γυνὴ κυεῖ δέκα μῆνας * * * * Sed noster Caecilius cum faceret eodem nomine et eiusdem argumenti comoediam ac pleraque a Menandro sumeret, in mensibus tamen genitalibus nominandis non praetermisit octavum, quem praeterierat Menander. Caecilii versus hice sunt—

Parmeno

Soletne mulier decimo mense parere?

156 emortuast Ribb.   emortuas *Lu.* 1, *Gen., Bern.* 83 emortua *Harl.* 1   est mortua *rell.*   157 *vide* p. 526

---

^a The rest of Menander's lines have dropped out.

PLAYS

156

The neighbour on his wife :

Nonius : By ' graviter ' also is understood ' much ' . . . —

(B)

She began to please me mightily after she was dead and gone.

Parmeno is puzzled at the girl's childbirth :

Gellius : It is quite clear what opinion we ought to hold on that scene also—it occurs in both comedies—of which the following is more or less the purport. The daughter of a poor man was outraged during a sacred vigil. The occurrence was kept secret from her father, and she was still taken for a virgin. Made big with child by that outrage she gave birth when the sum of months was past. A slave of good character, while he was standing before the doors of the house, not knowing that his master's daughter was approaching delivery, and being quite unaware that she had suffered outrage, heard the cries and entreaties of the girl in the throes of childbirth. He is frightened, angry, suspicious, full of pity, and sad. All these emotions and feelings of his mind are, at any rate in the Greek comedy, wonderfully vivid and clear. But in Caecilius' play all this is dull and void of all the dignity and grace of expression which the occasion demands.

157–8

Gellius again : The same thing is recorded by the older poet Menander, a man very well informed about the general opinion. I have added here some lines on that subject from the play *The Little Necklace.* ' A woman is with child for ten months.' . . .[a] But our poet Caecilius, though he wrote a comedy having the same title and the same plot and took most of his material from Menander, did not, in stating the months of pregnancy, leave out the eighth, which Menander had passed over. Caecilius' lines are as follows—

Parmeno

Does a woman usually give birth in the tenth month?

CAECILIUS

(C)?
Pol nono quoque
etiam septimo atque octavo.

159–60
Nonius, 209, 13 : ' Insomnium . . . feminini. . . . —

(D) Consequitur comes insomnia ;
ea porro insaniam affert.

161
Nonius, 153, 12 : ' Properatim,' id est properanter.
Caecilius—

(A) Properatim in tenebris istuc confectum est opus.

Cp. Non., 155, 4 (. . . Caecilius Plocio).

162
Nonius, 84, 3 : ' Commemoramentum ' . . . —

Parmeno
Pudebat credo commemoramentum strupri.

163–6
Gellius, II, 23, 20 : Post ubi idem servus percontando quod
acciderat repperit, has apud Menandrum voces facit :

ΠΑΡΜ. ὦ τρὶς κακοδαίμων ὅστις ὢν πένης γαμεῖ
καὶ παιδοποιεῖ. ὡς ἀλόγιστός ἐστ᾿ ἀνήρ,
ὃς μήτε φυλακὴν τῶν ἀναγκαίων ἔχει,
μήτ᾿ ἂν ἀτυχήσας εἰς τὰ κοινὰ τοῦ βίου
ἐπαμφιέσαι δύναιτο τοῦτο χρήμασιν,
ἀλλ᾿ ἐν ἀκαλύπτῳ καὶ ταλαιπώρῳ βίῳ
χειμαζόμενος ζῇ, τῶν μὲν ἀνιαρῶν ἔχων
τὸ μέρος ἁπάντων, τῶν δ᾿ ἀγαθῶν οὐδὲν μέρος·
ὑπὲρ γὰρ ἑνὸς ἀλγῶν ἅπαντας νουθετῶ.

(Allinson, *Men.*, p. 430.)

---

[157] soletne olim Hertz   insuetne Bothe   insoletne *cdd.*

PLAYS

(C)?

'Gad, yes; or the ninth or even the seventh or eighth.

159–60

The girl has confessed to her father, who takes Parmeno into his confidence ; the half-drunken youth :

Nonius : ' Insomnium ' . . . of the feminine gender . . . —

(D) There followed a companion to it [a]—sleeplessness ; and this further brought on madness.

161

How he outraged the girl :

Nonius : ' Properatim,' that is, the same as ' properanter.' Caecilius—

(A) Hastily, in the dark—that's how yonder business was done.

162

The girl's secrecy :

Nonius : ' Commemoramentum ' . . . —

Parmeno

I expect she was ashamed to make any mentioning of her disgrace.

163–6

Parmeno's comments :

Gellius : Afterwards when the same slave by inquiring had found out what had happened, in Menander he makes the following speech :

PARMENO. Oh! Thrice unhappy is he who though poor yet marries and gets children. How improvident is the man who keeps no watch over his necessities, and, when he has been unlucky in the common run of life, could not wrap it up in a cloak of money, but lives a storm-tossed, unprotected and unhappy life, and gets a share of all the grievous misfortunes, but no share of the blessings. Of course, when I grieve like this for one, I'm warning all men.

---

[a] *sc.* too much drinking.

CAECILIUS

Ad horum sinceritatem viritatemque verborum an aspiraverit Caecilius consideremus. Versus sunt hi Caecili trunca quaedam ex Menandro dicentis et consarcinantis verba tragici tumoris—

Parmeno

Is demum infortunatust homo
pauper qui educit in egestatem liberos,
cui fortuna et res nuda est continuo patet;
nam opulento famam facile occultat factio.

Cp. Non., 304, 36 ?

167–9

Cicero, *de Senect.*, 8, 25 : Melius Caecilius de sene alteri saeculo prospiciente quam illud idem—

(D)

Edepol, senectus, si nihil quicquam aliud viti
adportes tecum, cum advenis, unum id sat est
quod diu vivendo multa quae non volt videt.

Cp. Non., 247, 4 (Caecilius Plocio).

170

Nonius, 97, 13 : ' Danunt,' dant . . . —

Patiere quod dant, quando optata non danunt.

171

Donatus, ad Ter., *Andr.*, IV, 5, 10 : ' Quando ut volumus non licet ' . . . —

Vivas ut possis quando nec quis ut velis.

---

[163] infortunatust Spengel   infortunatus est *edd. vett.* e. i. *cdd.*
[165] nuda (ut ut *olim*) Ribb.   ut *cdd.*   res est ut Spengel
[167] si *Cic.*   ut si *Non.*   etsi Bothe   ut Onions
[169] quod diu *cdd.*   diu quis Manutius
[170] potire *olim* Ribb.   potiere Bothe (*vel* patere quod di dant)

PLAYS

Now let us consider whether Caecilius had enough inspiration to attain the sincerity and truth of these words. Here are Caecilius' lines; he reproduces some tatters from Menander and patches them up with words swelling with tragic bombast—

Parmeno

He's surely an unlucky fellow who is poor yet brings up children to neediness. When a man's fortune and estate are bare, he is exposed at once; but with a wealthy man his set keeps hid his bad report with ease.

167-9

Comments of the father ? :

Cicero : A better effect is produced by Caecilius when he speaks about the old man whose mind is looking forward to another age (*see line* 200) than he does with the following—

(D)

Ah! By heaven, Old Age, if there's no other mischief which you bring with you when you come— well—this one's quite enough—that a man by living long sees many things he doesn't want.

170

Parmeno to the father ? :

Nonius : ' Danunt,' the same as ' dant.' . . . —

You will put up with what the gods grant, since they do not grant all you long for.

171

Donatus on 'since we can't as we'd like' in Terence : . . . —

Live as you may, since you can't as you'd like.

---

171 ne quis Ribb.   non quis Fabric.   nequit *ed. Med.*
nequitur Spengel   nequis *cdd.*

CAECILIUS

172

Nonius, 297, 35 : ' Extollere,' differre . . . —

(D)

Abi intro atque istaec aufer; tamen hodie extollat
nuptias.

173

Nonius, 484, 24 : ' Sumpti ' pro sumptus . . . —

Quid hoc futurum obsonio est ubi tantum sumpti
factum ?

174

Nonius, 164, 21 : ' Rarenter ' pro rare . . . —

Crobyla ?

Tu nurum non vis odiosam tibi esse quam rarenter
videas ?

Cp. Men. (Allinson, p. 430 (929 K)): Κρωβύλη τῇ μητρὶ
πείθου καὶ γάμει τὴν συγγενῆ.

175

Nonius, 513, 1 : ' Publicitus ' pro publice . . . —

(D)

Ibo domum; ad plebem pergitur; publicitus defen-
dendum est.

---

[172] aufer *vulgo*   aufert *cdd.*   auferto Bothe (*recte ?*)
aufer si Ribb.   adfer tamen ut hodie Mr.   extollet *coni.*
Ribb.
[173] est Bothe   et *cdd.*
[175] ibo domum *cdd.*   domum ibo Grauert   ibi demum
Bothe   pergitur *cdd.*   peragetur *coni.* Ribb.   peragitur
vel peragitor Mr.   pergitor Spengel

PLAYS

172

The wedding will not take place :

Nonius : ' Extollere,' to postpone . . . —

(D)

Away with you inside and clear off those dishes;
let him put off the wedding to-day in spite of all.

173

The wedding fare :

Nonius : ' Sumpti ' for ' sumptus.' . . . —

What's to be done with this meat after all that
expense on it ?

174

Effort to persuade the youth to relent :

Nonius : ' Rarenter ' for ' rare.' . . . —

Crobyle ? [a]

Surely you don't want the young lady, whom
you see so rarely, to become a thing of hate to you ?

175

The girl's father decides to go to law about his jilted daughter :

Nonius : ' Publicitus ' for ' publice.' . . . —

(D)

I'll go home; the case will go before the commoners; it must be defended publicly.

[a] Probably. Or the words may be spoken to Crobyle, not
by her. Cf. the fr. of Menander quoted opposite.

CAECILIUS

176

Nonius, 220, 4 : ' Paupertas ' . . . neutri . . . —

(D)

Ibo ad forum et pauperii tutelam geram.

177–8

Nonius, 146, 11 : ' Opulentitas ' pro opulentia . . . —

Crobyla ?

opulentitate nostra sibi iniuriam
factam.

179

Nonius, 124, 24 : ' Inibi ' pro sic et mox . . . —

(C)

Liberne es ?

Parmeno
Non sum liber, verum inibi est quasi.

POLUMENI

180

Nonius, 114, 15 : ' Floces,' faex vini. Caecilius—

At pol ego neque florem neque floces volo mihi;
vinum volo.

Cp. Gell. XI, 67, 6 (floces . . . aput Caecilium in Polumenis).

---

[176] pauperii Ribb.   pauperio Spengel   pauperie Bothe
pauperi *cdd*.
[177-8] sibi <esse> i. Ribb.   s. <eam> i. Mr.   *alii*
alia   factam Mercier   faciam *cdd*.

532

PLAYS

176

Nonius : ' Paupertas ' . . . of the neuter [a] gender . . . —

(D)

I'll go to court and champion my cause—it's
Poverty's brief.

177–8

The whole truth has come to light :

Nonius : ' Opulentitas ' for ' opulentia ' . . . —

Crobyle ?

that it was through our wealthiness that the outrage was committed against her.

179

Parmeno is freed from slavery :

Nonius : ' Inibi ' for ' thus ' and ' soon.' . . . —

(C)

Are you a free man?

Parmeno

No, I'm not free, but I'm there or thereabouts, as
you might say.

MEN FOR SALE [a]

180

Nonius : ' Floces,' lees of wine. Caecilius—

But by god I want neither leaves nor lees, please ;
what I want is wine.

---

[a] *pauperii* is really old genitive of *pauperies*.
[b] Cp. Menander's Πωλούμενοι.

---

[179] liber *Flor.* 3 *om. cdd.*   quasi *Flor.* 3 *om. cdd.*

CAECILIUS

PORTITOR

181

Nonius, 118, 23 : ' Gcrrae,' nugae, ineptiae. . . . Caecilius
Portitore—

Cur depopulator ?   Gerrae !

PROGAMOS

182

Nonius, 346, 13 : ' Moliri,' retinere, morari ac repigrare.
Caecilius Progamo—

Ita quod laetitia me mobilitat, maeror molitur metu.

PUGIL

183–4

Festus, 188, 7 : Quidam ' nictationem,' quidam ' nictum,'
ut Caecilius in Pugile—

Tum inter laudandum hunc timidum tremulis
    palpebris
percutere nictu ; hic gaudere et mirarier.

SYMBOLUM

185

Nonius, 279, 43 : ' Destitui ' rursum statui. . . . Caecilius
in Symbolo—

Destituit omnes servos ad mensam ante se.

[181] fur d. — gerrae ! Kiessling   f. d. gerro Rost
[182] laetitia Palmer (*Spic.*)   letale Grauert   letiale *cdd.*
[183] luctandum Ribb.   ludendum Fruter.   laudandum *cd.*
Non. 279 Symbolo Mercier   sembono *vel* embono *cdd.*

PLAYS

THE CARRIER

181

Nonius: 'Gerrae,' nonsense, ineptitudes. . . . Caecilius in *The Carrier*—

Why a pillager? Bosh!

WEDDING-PRELIMINARIES [a]

182

Nonius: 'Moliri,' to keep back, delay and slacken. Caecilius in *Wedding-Preliminaries*—

Yes, because gladness sets me all agog, and sorrow sets me all aclogged with dread.

THE BOXER [b]

183–4

Festus: Some write 'nictatio,' some 'nictus,' for example Caecilius in *The Boxer*—

Then in the midst of his complimenting, while that fellow's eye-lids quiver in mortal funk, he knocks him out with a wink. He's pleased and surprised.

THE TOKEN

185

Nonius: 'Destitui' means also the same as 'statui.' . . . Caecilius in *The Token*—

He set down all the slaves in front of him at table.

---

[a] Probably from Menander's Πρόγαμοι or Προγάμια, a sacrifice before a wedding.
[b] Cp. Πύκτης by Timotheus and another by Timocles.

CAECILIUS

186

Nonius, 246, 9 : ' Auscultare ' est obsequi. . . . —

Audire ignoti quom imperant soleo non auscultare.

SYNARISTOSAE

187-8

Gellius, XV, 15 : Veteres dixerunt ' expassum,' non
' expansum.' Caecilius in Synaristosis—

heri vero prospexisse eum se ex tegulis,
haec nuntiasse et flammeum expassum domi.

Cp. Non., 370, 17.

SYNEPHEBI

189-99

Cicero, *de Nat. Deor.*, III, 29, 72 : Ille vero in Synephebis
Academicorum more contra communem opinionem non
dubitat pugnare ratione, qui—

In amore suave est summo summaque inopia
parentem habere avarum inlepidum, in liberos
difficilem, qui te nec amet nec studeat tui.

Atque huic incredibili sententiae ratiunculas suggerit—

Aut tu illum fructu fallas aut per litteras
advertas aliquod nomen aut per servolum

[186] quom Ribb.   quae Bothe   quod *cdd.*
[188] haec nuntiasset *cdd.*   h. nuntiasse *vulg.*   ecnunti-
asse et Hertz   et nuntiasse Bergk
[189] i. a. s. e. s. s. i. | p. Bothe   in amore summo sum-
maque inopia suave esse dicit parentem *Cic.*
[192] fructu *cdd.*   furto Buecheler

PLAYS

186

Nonius: ' Auscultare ' means to comply with . . . —

When persons I don't know give commands, I am accustomed to hear, not to heed.

LADIES AT LUNCH[a]

187-8

Gellius: The old writers used the form ' expassum,' not ' expansum.' Caecilius in *Ladies at Lunch*—

but that yesterday he looked in at him from the roof-tiles; he brought news of this and then the bridal veil was spread out at home.

COMRADES IN YOUTH[b]

189-99

Cicero : But the well-known character in *Comrades in Youth*, after the manner of the Academics, does not hesitate to fight against the general opinion with the weapon of reason. He says—

When one is deep in love and deep in poverty, it is a nice thing to have a father who is stingy and disagreeable and troublesome towards his children, who neither loves you nor takes interest in you.

And he brings a poor sort of reasons to support this incredible opinion—

You must either diddle him out of some profit or misappropriate some item of debt by a forged document or by[c] help of a slave-boy strike terror into

---

[b] From Menander's Συνέφηβοι? We ought perhaps to add to this play fr. 97 of *The Imbrians* (pp. 504-5).

[c] He means by sending him a slave with bad news.

537

CAECILIUS

percutias pavidum ; postremo a parco patre
quod sumas quanto dissipes libentius !   195

Idemque facilem et liberalem patrem incommodum esse
amanti filio disputat—

Quem neque quo pacto fallam nec quid inde auferam
nec quem dolum ad eum aut machinam commoliar
scio quicquam ; ita omnes meos dolos fallacias
praestrigias praestrinxit commoditas patris.

200

Cicero, *de Senect*, 7, 24 : Nemo est tam senex qui se annum
non putet posse vivere; sed idem in eis elaborant, quae
sciunt nihil omnino ad se pertinere—

Serit arbores quae saeclo prosint alteri,

ut ait Statius noster in Synephebis. Nec vero dubitat agri-
cola, quamvis sit senex, quaerenti cui serat respondere. . . .

Cf. Cic., *Tusc Disp.*, I, 14, 31.

201–4

Cicero, *de Nat. Deor.*, I, 6, 13 : Convocandi omnes videntur
qui quae sit earum (*sc.* sententiarum) vera indicent. . . .
Itaque mihi libet exclamare, ut est in Synephebis—

Pro deum popularium omnium omnium adulescentium
clamo postulo obsecro oro ploro atque inploro fidem ;

[196] nec quid inde Schoemann   neque qui inde Heindorf
neque quid Bothe   nequid inde *vel* neque ut inde *vel sim.*
(neque aliquid *Glog.*) *cdd.*
[199] praestrigias Buecheler   praestigias (*infra quoque*
praestigiae *praet. Vindob.*) *cdd.* (*recte ?*)
[200] saeclo prosint alteri Spengel   serit | a. q. a. saeculo
prosient Hermann (prosint Bergk)   a. saeculo prosint *cdd.*

538

him. My last word is—how much more fun it is to squander what you have screwed out of a stingy father!

And that same person argues that an easy-going and generous father is a disadvantage to a son in love—

. . . A man whom I know not in the least in what way I can cheat or rob; nor do I know any artful dodge or contrivance which I can bring to bear upon him. So utterly has the generosity of my father trumped [a] all my tricks and dodges and juggleries.

200

Cicero : No one is so old that he does not believe he can live for a year. But these same men spend all their labour on things which they know have no application to them—

He sows the seed of trees that they may be a profit to another age,

as our Statius says in *Comrades in Youth*. Nor too does the husbandman, even though he be an old man, hesitate to answer the person who inquires for whose sake he is sowing. . . .

201–4

Cicero : It seems to me that I must invite all mankind to judge which of these opinions is the true one . . . and so I should like to exclaim, as we read in *Comrades in Youth*—

Oh! I shout, wail and bewail, I beg, treat and entreat for the help of the gods and all my countrymen, all our youths;

[a] ' taken the edge off.'

---

[201] omnium omnium Manutius   omnium *cdd. pler.*

CAECILIUS

non levissima de re, ut queritur ille—

  . . . in civitate fiunt facinora capitalia,
nam ab amico amante argentum accipere meretrix
  noenu volt.

205

Nonius, 200, 16 : ' Collus ' masculino. . . . Caecilius. . . .
Synephebis—

(A) Ad restim res redit. (B) Immo collus, non
  res, nam ille argentum habet.

SYRACUSII

206

Nonius, 176, 29 : ' Similitas,' similitudo. Caecilius
Syracusiis—

Vide Demea, hominis quid fert morum similitas ?

207

Nonius, 96, 27 : ' Dulcitas,' ' dulcitudo ' pro dulcedo. . . . —

tanta hinc invasit in cor Davi dulcitas.

208

Nonius, 391, 28 : ' Stare ' iterum horrere significat. . . . —

Hic amet, familiae fame pereant, ager autem stet
  sentibus.

[203] fieri *Cic.*   fieri in civitate Orelli
[204] nam *suppl.* Ribb.   noenu volt Bergk (nunc nevolt
olim, nevolt Wolf)   non vult *cdd.* (ñuult *Leid.* 63)   abs
amico amante meretrix accipere argentum nevolt *coni. olim*
Mayor
[206] fert *edd.*   feret *cdd.*
[207] tanta *Flor.* 3 *Harl.* 1   tantam *rell.*   tantan Mercier
hinc Victor   huic *cdd.*   in cor Davi Mercier   i. c.

PLAYS

on a matter of very weighty import, according to his complaint—

Capital crimes are being committed in this State; for there's a whore who doesn't want to take money from a love-sick sweetheart.

205

Nonius: 'Collus' in the masculine. . . . Caecilius . . . in *Comrades in Youth*—

(A) This business comes to the gallows. (B) A neck rather, not the business. For he has got the money.

THE SYRACUSANS [a]

206

Nonius: 'Similitas,' the same as similitude. Caecilius in *The Syracusans*—

Look, Demea, what's the import of the similarity in this fellow's conduct?

207

Nonius: 'Dulcitas' and 'dulcitudo' for 'dulcedo.' . . . —

So much sweetness has entered Davus' heart because of this.

208

Nonius: 'Stare' again means to bristle . . . —

Let him love, let his households perish with hunger and his fields stand thick with thornbushes.

[a] Alexis wrote a play called Συρακόσιος.

---

dandi Buecheler   in corollam Ribb.   in corda in *cdd.*
fortasse tanta invasit huic in corda indulcitas   in cor
damni dulcitas Bothe
[208] fame familiae Mr.   *alii alia*

CAECILIUS

TITTHE

209–10

Nonius, 258, 37 : 'Contendere' significat conparare. . . .
Caecilius Titthe—

Egon vitam meam
Atticam contendam cum istac rusticana Syra ?

211

Nonius, 196, 5 : 'Compita' . . . masculino . . . —

adiacentem compitum

212–13

Nonius, 183, 23 : 'Utrasque' pro utrimque vel utrobique. . . . —

. . . atque hercle utrasque te cum ad nos venis
subfarcinatam vidi.

214–15

Nonius, 118, 9 : 'Gravidavit,' implevit . . . —

Per mysteria
hic inhoneste . . . gravidavit probro.

216

Nonius, 483, 1 : 'Lacte' nominativo casu . . . —

Praesertim quae non peperit lacte non habet.

[210] atticam *cdd.*   asticam Bergk   rusticana tua Syra
Bergk, Quich.   rustica dura (*vel* vana) Spengel   rustica
Syra C. F. W. Mr.
  [211] ubi adicientem *cdd.*   *seclud.* ubi Ribb. (*natum ex
initio praeced. ex Varr. citationis videtur*)   adiacentem *quid.
ap. Steph.*   ubi adi ad adiacentem Spengel
  [212-13] te Mercier   et *cdd.*   subfarcinatam Mercier
subfraginatam *cdd.*

PLAYS

THE WET-NURSE [a]

209–10

Nonius: 'Contendere' means to compare. . . . Caecilius in *The Wet-Nurse*—

What, am I to compare my Attic [b] life with that countrified Syrian life of yours?

211

Nonius: 'Compita' . . . in the masculine . . . —

The roadsmeet that lay near.

212–13

Nonius: 'Utrasque' for 'utrimque' or 'utrobique' . . . —

and by God when you came to our house I could see you were stuffed out both times.

214–15

Nonius: 'Gravidavit,' has filled . . . —

During the Mysteries this man dishonourably got her heavy by lewdness.

216

Nonius: 'Lacte,' a form in the nominative case . . . —

She especially who has not given birth does not have milk.

[a] Several Greek writers wrote a play on this theme.
[b] Perhaps, however, we should read *asticam* and take Syra as the name of a slave, in the vocative case.

---

215 inhoneste <inceste> Mr.   inhoneste <honestam> Bothe

CAECILIUS

217

Nonius, 270, 5 : 'Concedere,' recedere vel cedere. . . .
Caecilius Titthe—

. . . Hic dum abit, huc concessero.

TRIUMPHUS

218

Gellius, VI, 7, 9 : ' Adprobus ' tamen, quod significat valde
probus non infitias eo quin prima syllaba acui debeat. Caecilius in comoedia quae inscribitur Triumphus vocabulo isto
utitur—

Hierocles hospes est mi adulescens adprobus.

219-20

Festus, 442, 25 : ' Succenturiare ' est explendae centuriae
gratia supplere, subiecre. . . . Caecilius in Triumpho—

Nunc meae militiae Astutia
opus est. Subcenturia!

Cp. Paul, ex. F., 443, 8.

VENATOR?

221-2

Nonius, 483, 18 : ' Quaesti' vel 'quaestuis' dictum pro
quaestus. . . . Caecilius Venatore—

(A) Satine huic ordini
etsi nihil ego egi, quaesti? (B) Quaesti? (A) Quia
sunt aemuli.

[219-20] malitiae *Paul.*   militiae *Fest.*   astutiam O. Mr.
astutiae Kiessling   subcenturia *Fest.*   succenturia
Paul.   subcenturiare O. Mr.   subcenturiari Bergk
subcenturiata Buecheler   est succenturiata opus Bothe
Non. 483, 18 Venatore *cdd.*   Feneratore Spengel
[221] huic Bothe   huc *cdd.*
[222] ego egi Ribb. (egisti *olim*)   egi *cdd.* (ego *Escorial.*
1, *Par.* 7667)   quaesti quaesti *Par.* 7666 *Lugd. Bamb.*
quaesti *rell.*   sunt aemulae *Ald.*   sunemuli *cdd.*

PLAYS

217

Nonius : ' Concedere,' the same as ' recedere ' or ' cedere.'
. . . Caecilius in *The Wet Nurse*—

While he withdraws, I'll step aside just here.

THE TRIUMPH

218

Gellius : In the word ' adprobus,' however, which means very ' probus,' I do not deny that it ought to be accented on the first syllable. Caecilius uses this word in the comedy which is called *The Triumph*—

My guest Hierocles is a most honourable young man.

219–20

Festus : ' Succenturiare ' means to supply or submit for the purpose of filling up a ' century.' . . . Caecilius in *The Triumph*—

Now my warfare has need of Dame Cunning. Enlist her ! [a]

THE HUNTER [b] ?

221–2

Nonius : ' Quaesti ' or ' quaestuis,' genitive; used for ' quaestus.' . . . Caecilius in *The Hunter*—

(A) Although I have done nothing, has this society made enough profit ? (B) Profit ? (A) The fact is, they're niggards.

[a] I retain the readings of the MS. of Festus, but possibly *malitia* of the MSS. of Paulus should be accepted.
[b] The MSS. of Nonius point definitely to a play called *Venator*, but it is usual to correct them to *Faeneratore* (see pp. 510–5). The first fragment given here supports such a correction.

CAECILIUS

223

Nonius, 42, 19 : ' Verniliter ' pro adulatorie, a vernis quibus haec vivendi ars est. Caecilius Venatore—

Credo, nimis tandem hoc fit verniliter.

EX INCERTIS FABULIS

224–35

Cicero, *pro Caelio*, 16, 37 : Redeo nunc ad te, Caeli, vicissim, ac mihi auctoritatem patriam severitatemque suscipio. Sed dubito quem patrem potissimum sumam. Caeciliumne aliquem vehementem atque durum ?—

Nunc enim demum mi animus ardet, nunc meum cor
  cumulatur ira ;

aut illum—

O infelix, o sceleste !

Ferrei sunt isti patres !—

Egone quid dicam ? Egon quid velim ? Quae tu omnia
tuis foedis factis facis ut nequiquam velim.

Vix ferenda diceret talis pater !—

Cur in vicinitatem istam meretriciam
te contulisti ? Cur illecebris cognitis
non effugisti ? . . .   230
. . . cur alienam ullam mulierem
nosti . . . . . .   dide ac disiice
per me licebit . . .

Non. 42 Venatore (-i) *cdd.*   Feneratore Spengel
[223] hoc <hercle> Ribb.   hocce *vel* tamen istuc fit Bothe
tandem hoc fiet (*vel* fuit) Spengel   tamen hoce *olim* Ribb.
[226] egone quid velim *cdd.*   om. quid velim *Brux.*   *seclud.*
egone Spengel   quae *cdd.*   qui Spengel   *fortasse* nae

546

PLAYS

223

Nonius: 'Verniliter' for flatteringly; derived from 'vernae' to whom flattery is a trick of their trade. Caecilius in *The Hunter*—

My belief is there's too much slavishness about this business by now.

FRAGMENTS NOT ASSIGNED TO ANY PLAY

224-35

Cicero: I come back to you, Caelius; now it is your turn. And I take upon myself a father's authority and severity. I am in doubt, however, as to what kind of father I ought to choose as the best example. Shall it be some father [a] in Caecilius, hot-tempered and stern?—

For now at length my soul burns and my heart is a mountain of anger;

or this famous example—

You unhappy boy! You rascal!
Made of iron, those fathers!—

What *am* I to say, you ask? What are my wishes? Why, things which you, by your dirty doings, make me wish for in vain now.

Such a father as this would say things hardly to be borne—

Why did you betake yourself to that whorish neighbourhood? Why didn't you run right away when you learnt of the allurements there? . . . Why did you get to know any strange woman? . . . Scatter and squander your money for all I

[a] Cp. Quintil., XI, 1, 39.

228-9 c. i. v. i. m. | t. c. Spengel   cur t. in i. v. m. con-ulisti *cdd.* (civitatem *Brux.*)   istam i. v. t. m. cur c. Ribb.
230 effugisti Spengel   refugisti *cdd.*
232 cognosti Spengel

CAECILIUS

. . . si egebis, tibi dolebit, mihi sat est
qui aetatis quod reliquom est oblectem meae.   235

Cp. Cic., *de Fin.*, II, 4, 14.   *

236-7

Cicero, *de Amicit.*, 26, 99 : Quid turpius quam inludi?
Quod ut ne accidat magis cavendum est—

Ut me hodie ante omnes comicos stultos senes
versaris atque inluseris lautissime.

Cp. Cic., *de Senect.*, 12, 36 (quos ait Caecilius comicos stultos
senes. . . .).

238-42

Cicero, *Tusc. Disp.*, IV, 32, 68 : Totus . . . iste qui volgo
appellatur amor . . . tantae levitatis est ut nihil videam
quod putem conferendum.   Quem Caecilius—

deum qui non summum putet
aut stultum aut rerum esse inperitum existumem.
Cui in manu sit, quem esse dementem velit,
quem sapere, quem insanire, quem in morbum inici
. . . . .
quem contra amari, quem expeti, quem arcessier.

Cp. Eur., *Auge*, 269 N.

243-4

Isidorus, *Orig.*, XIX, 4, 5 : ' Scaphon ' funis in prora
positus; de quo Caecilius—

Venerio cursu veni, prolato pede
usque ad scaphonem.

²³⁴ si egebes *seclud.* Spengel
²³⁵ quod mi est reliquom *coni.* Ribb.
²³⁶ ut *cdd.*   tu Halm
²³⁷ illuseris Augustin.   elusseris Halm   ut lusseri‹
Buecheler   emunxeris Bentley   iusseris *vel* ut iusseri‹
cdd. (lusseris *P*   unxeris *Pal.* 1)
²³⁸ <ego vero Amorem> deum *coni.* Bentley

care! . . . If you fall into want, it's *your* funeral;
I've got enough to keep me content for the rest of
my life.

236-7

Cicero : What is more humiliating than to be made sport
of? We must be all the more careful to see that this does
not happen—

So that to-day you have most gorgeously muddled
me and poked fun at me more than all the stupid
old fools to be found in comedies.

238-42

Cicero : All of him who is commonly called love . . . is
of such paltriness that I see nothing which could, in my belief,
be compared with him. Caecilius speaks of him thus—

The man who does not believe that Love is the
greatest of gods, I should think he's either a fool
or else untried in worldly affairs. It is in his power
to make mad whom he will, to make him wise or
crazed, or cast him straight into disease . . . and
on the other hand to make him, whom he will, loved,
sought out and in demand.

243-4

Isidorus : 'Scaphon,' a rope fixed on a ship's prow. Caecilius on this writes—

I came running on Love's course, with my sail-
sheet hauled right to the forestay.

---

²³⁹ rerum *cdd.*   venerum *coni.* Meineke   existumet
Gud. Pith. Reg.   existumem *rell.*   existumo Bentley
existimat *vulg.*
²⁴⁰ cui *cdd.*   cuii Ribb.   cuius Ernesti
²⁴¹ insanire *cdd.* (sanari *cdd. Ox.* ? *an recte* ?)   sanire
Usener   *post* 241 *lac. un. vers. stat.* Bentley
²⁴² arcessier *Bern.*   arcessiri *rell.* (accersiri *aut* accessiri
Pith.)   ²⁴³ *fortasse* cursu Venerio

CAECILIUS

245

Charisius, ap. *G.L.*, I, 122, 11 : ' Amantum ' Caecilius . . .
. . . —

quantum amantum in Attica est.

246

Nonius, 101, 23 : ' Deintegrare,' deminuere. . . . Caecilius —
nomen virginis, nisi mirum est, deintegravit.

247

Nonius, 197, 28 : ' Quis ' et generi feminino attribui posse
veterum auctoritas voluit. . . . Caecilius—

Quaeso igitur, quisquis es mea mulier . . .

248

Nonius, 119, 14 : ' Gramiae,' pituitae oculorum. Caecilius—

grammonsis oculis ipsa atratis dentibus.

249

Paulus, ex F., 559, 13 (21) : Truo avis onocrotalus. Caecilius irridens magnitudinem nasi—

Pro di inmortales ! Unde prorepsit truo ?

250

Gellius, V, 6, 12 : ' Civica corona ' . . . fuit ex illice, . . .
sicut scriptum est in quadam comoedia Caecilii—

Advehitur cum iligna corona et chlamyde. Di
vostram fidem !

245 Attica Ribb.   natica *cd.*   riatica *ed. princ.*
Non. 119 gramae Buecheler
248 gramiosis Mercier   graminosis Spengel   dentibus
Flor. 1   gentibus *cdd.*
250 advehitur Bothe   advehuntur *vel*   adeuntur *cdd.*
advehunt | eum C. F. W. Mr.   iligna Fleckeisen   ilignea
cdd.

PLAYS

245

Charisius: 'Amantum,' genitive plural, is the form used by Caecilius . . . —

As many lovers as there are in Attica.

246

Nonius: 'Deintegrare,' to diminish. . . . Caecilius—

I should not wonder if he has impaired the girl's fair name.

247

Nonius: 'Quis.' The authority of the old writers sanctions the attribution of this form to the feminine gender as well as to the masculine. . . . Caecilius—

I pray you then, whoever you are, my dear woman . . .

248

Nonius: 'Gramiae,' phlegm in the eyes. Caecilius [a] has 'grammonsus'—

herself has phlegmy eyes and blackened teeth.

249

Paulus: 'Truo,' a bird—the ὀνοκρόταλος. Caecilius,[b] making fun of a big nose—

By the gods in heaven, from where has the pelican crept upon us?

250

Gellius: The civic crown . . . was at one time made of the leaves of the holm, . . . as we find in a certain comedy [c] of Caecilius—

He is driving up all decked with crown of holm and cloak of state. Heaven help us!

[a] Possibly in The Little Necklace (pp. 516 ff.); the old man describing his wife Crobyle.
[b] Cf. preceding note and Menander quoted on pp. 518-9.
[c] The Triumph ? (pp. 544-7).

551

CAECILIUS

251–3

Cicero, *de Orat.*, II, 64, 257 : Saepe etiam versus facete interponitur vel ut est vel paululum mutatus, aut aliqua pars versus, ut Statii a Scauro stomachante—

St! Tacete! Quid hoc clamoris? Quibus nec
    mater nec pater
tanta confidentia estis? Istam enim superbiam
auferte!

254

Cicero, *ad Fam.*, II, 9 : Repente . . . —

Incessi omnibus laetitiis laetus.

Cp. Cic., de *Fin.*, II, 4, 13 (. . . ille Caecilianus . . .).

255

Cicero, *Tusc. Disp.*, III, 23, 56 : Hic Socrates commemoratur, hic Diogenes, hic Caecilianum illud—

Saepe est etiam sub palliolo sordido sapientia.

Apuleius, *Apolog.*, 5 : Statium Caecilium in suis poematibus scripsisse dicunt innocentiam eloquentiam esse.

256

Isidorus, *Orig.*, X, 40 : 'Confidens,' quod sit in cunctis fiducia plenus; unde et Caecilius—

Si confidentiam adhibes, confide omnia.

257

Symmachus, *Epist.*, IX, 114 : Recte Caecilius comicus—

Homo homini deus est si suum officium sciat.

[251] sed *vel* si *cdd.*   mater nec pater *vel* p. n. m. *cdd.*
n. p. n. m. est Leo
[252] estis *cdd.*   *seclud.* Schütz   istam e. s. | a. W
a. i. e. s. *vel sim. cdd.*   estis? aufertin superbiam? Leo
auferte nunc i. s. *ed. Rom.*

PLAYS

251-3

Cicero : Often too a line is wittily inserted, either as it stands or slightly altered : or else some part of a line like the example from Statius quoted by Scaurus in a rage . . .—

Sh! Quiet, all! What's all this shouting? Are you so bumptious—you that can't boast of mother or father? Why, away with such haughtiness!

254

Cicero : Suddenly—

I came strutting along as merry as merry could be.[a]

255

Cicero : Now Socrates is quoted, now Diogenes, now that famous saying of Caecilius—

There's often wisdom even underneath
A shabby little cloak.

Apuleius : They say Statius Caecilius wrote in his poems that innocence and outspokenness are the same.

256

Isidorus : 'Confidens.' When a man is so called it is on the ground that he is full of ' fiducia ' in everything. Whence, for example, Caecilius—

If you bring Confidence with you, confide everything to her.

257

Symmachus : Rightly does Caecilius, a writer of comedies, say—

Man to man is a god if he knows his job.

[a] I take it that Cicero quotes Caecilius' own words.

---

[254] o. l. l. incedo Ribb.
[257] homo inquit *Symm.*

CAECILIUS

258

Iulius Rufinianus, ap. *G.L.*, 19, 43 : 'Αποφώνημα, sententia responsiva, ut apud Caecilium—

Fac velis : perficies.

259

Varro, *L.L.*, VII, 103 : Multa ab animalium vocibus tralata in homines. . . . Caecilius—

tantam rem dibalare ut pro nilo habuerit.

260

Festus, 340, 12 : ' Quisquiliae ' dici putantur quidquid ex arboribus minutis surculorum foliorumque cadit velut ' quidquidcadiae.' Caecilius—

(A) Quisquilias volantis venti spolia memorant.

(B) I modo !

261

Cicero, *ad Att.*, VII, 3, 10 : Venio ad Piraeea. . . . Nostrum si est peccatum, in eo est quod non ut de oppido locutus sum sed ut de loco, secutusque sum non dico Caecilium—

Mane ut ex portu in Piraeum . . .

—malus enim auctor Latinitatis est—sed Terentium.

262-4

Charisius, ap. *G.L.*, I, 201, 10 : ' In mundo ' pro palam et in expedito, ac cito. Plautus . . . Caecilius quoque, ut Annaeus Cornutus . . . —

profertoque nobis in mundo futurum
lectum.

item idem—

namque malum in mundost, ere.

---

[259] tantam S   tantum *cdd.*   [260] memoras S
[262] profertoque Ribb.   profecto qui *cd.*
[264] namque *cd.*   namque <mihi> Ribb.   nam cui *coni.* Buecheler   num qui Lindemann   nam quia *coni.* Keil in mundost ere Buecheler   in mundo is ire *cd.*   i. m. esse sciret *coni.* Keil

PLAYS

258

Julius Rufinianus: ʼΑποφώνημα, an aphorism that contains a reply; for example, in a play of Caecilius—

Make yourself want to : you'll make good.[a]

259

Varro: There are many sounds proper to animals which have been used figuratively of men. . . . Caecilius—

to bleat abroad so great a secret, that he surely held it as nothing.

260

Festus: ‘Quisquiliae’ is believed to be a term [b] applied to any little twigs and leaves which fall from very small trees, ‘quidquidcadiae,’ ‘whateverfalls,’ as it were. Caecilius—

(A) Floating what-d'ye-call 'ems, mere spoils of the wind—that's what all their talk means. (B) Get along now!

261

Cicero: I come ‘ad Piraeea.’ . . . If I am at fault, it lies in the fact that I spoke of Piraeus as though I were speaking not of a town but of a region, and I followed good authority, I do not say Caecilius—

in the morning as from the port into Piraeus . . .

—for he is a bad authority on Latinity—but Terence.

262-4

Charisius: ‘In mundo’ for openly and without hindrance; also quickly. Plautus . . . Caecilius also, according to Annaeus Cornutus . . . —

and bring you out a bed that is to be in readiness for us.

The same writer likewise—

for there's hell all ready, master.

[a] Cp. our ‘Where there's a will, there's a way.’
[b] The word is probably derived from *quisque*.

CAECILIUS

265

Diomedes, ap. *G.L.*, I, 345, 4 : ' Hiare ' et ' hietare ' veteres dixerunt. . . . Caecilius—

(A) Sequere me. (B) Perii hercle ! (A) Tu quid mi oscitans hietansque restas ?

266

Servius auctus, ad Verg., *Georg.*, I, 74: 'Quassante,' quae sonet cum quassatur. Caecilius—

si quassante capite tristes incedunt.

267

Paulus, ex F., 25, 5 : ' Bardus,' stultus, a tarditate ingenii appellatur. Caecilius—

. . . nimis audacem nimisque bardum barbarum

Comment. Cruqui ad Horat. *Art. Poet.*, 236–239 : Pythias persona comica in comoedia Caecilii quae inducitur per astutias accipere argentum a Simone domino suo in dotem filiae.

Cp. Pseudoacro *ad loc.*

268

Rufinus, ap. *C.G.L.*, VI., 556, 7 K : Non nunquam ab his initium fit ut apud Caecilium—

Di boni ! Quid hoc ?

269

Fronto, *Epist.*, I, p. 142, Haines : Igitur paene me opicum animantem ad Graecam scripturam perpulerunt homines, ut Caecilius ait—

incolumi inscientia

[265] praei hercle Putschius   periercle *Par.* 7494   pehercle *Par.* 7498   quid Ribb.   qui *cdd.*   mi Spengel   enim (*vel* nam) Ribb.   mihi *cdd.*
[266] sic *coni.* Ribb.
Comment. *Cruq.* : Caecilii Orelli   Lucilii *comment.*

PLAYS

265

Diomedes : ' Hiare ' and ' hietare.'   Both forms were used
by old writers. . . . Caecilius—

(A) Follow me.   (B) O Lord, I'm done for !
(A) Here you!   Bless me, why stand still and keep
yawning and gaping?

266

Servius (supplemented) on ' quassante ' in Virgil : ' Quassante,' which makes a noise when ' quassatur.'   Caecilius—

if they mournfully march on with wobbling heads.

267

Paulus : ' Bardus,' applied to a man who is silly, is derived
from the slowness ($\beta\rho\alpha\delta\upsilon\tau\acute{\eta}s$) of his wits.   Caecilius—

a very bold and block-headed barbarian

A commentator on a passage in Horace : Pythias is a comic
character in a comedy of Caecilius; she is brought on to the
stage as a person who gets, by a crafty trick, some money [a]
from her master Simo for her daughter's dowry.

268

Rufinus : Sometimes it is a beginning that is made with
' clausulae '; for example, in a play of Caecilius—

Good heavens!   What's this?

269

Marcus Aurelius to Fronto : And so I (who am, as one
might almost say, a living barbarian) have been forced to
write in Greek by men—

of unimpaired ignorance

as Caecilius has it.

---

[a] A talent, says Pseudo-Acro on this same passage; he
adds that she was a whore.

CAECILIUS

Macrobius, *S.*, III, 15, 9 : Sed quis neget indomitam apud illos et, ut ait Caecilius, vallatam gulam fuisse ?

270

Cicero, *de Orat.*, II, 10, 40 : Hesterno sermone, ut ait Caecilius—

operis unius cuiusdam remigem aliquem aut baiulum, nobis oratorem descripseras, inopem quendam humanitatis atque inurbanum.

271

Donatus, in Ter., *Eun.*, IV, 7, 45 : ' Domi ' et ' foci ' genetivi sunt. Caecilius—

Decora domi

272

Nonius, 229, 5 : ' Tapete ' generis neutri. . . . Caecilius—

glabrum tapete

273

Diomedes, ap. *G.L.*, I, 385, 22 : Caecilius praeterea—

si non sarciri quitur

274

Festus, 286, 25 : ' Profesti dies.' . . . Caecilius in †—

. . . ⟨dies profe⟩sti tantundem

SPURIA ?

275

Festus, 584, 19 : ' Taenias ' Graecam vocem sic interpretatur Verrius ut dicat ornamentum esse laneum capitis honorati, ut sit apud Caecilium in Androgyno . . . et alias—

dum taeniam qui volnus vinciret petit.

[270] operis unius cuiusdam *coniicio*   u. c. o. ut ait C. r. a. a. b. *Cic.*
Non. 229 Turpilius et Caecilius *Non.*   *seclud.* et Caecilius Mr.
[273] sarcire *edd. vett.*

PLAYS

Macrobius : But who would deny that among those men gluttony was unconquerable, and, as Caecilius writes, ' intrenched ' ?

270

Cicero : In the way you talked yesterday you had described to us an orator who was in the words of Caecilius—

some galley-slave or porter doing one mechanical task,

someone who was unendowed with human kindness and unmannerly.

271

Donatus : ' Domi ' and ' foci ' are genitives. Caecilius—

fineries of the house

272

Nonius : ' Tapete,' of the neuter gender. . . . Caecilius—

a smooth carpet

273

Diomedes : Caecilius further writes ' quitur '—

if it cannot be patched

274

Festus : ' Profesti dies.' . . . Caecilius—

non-festive days just as much

SPURIOUS FRAGMENTS ?

275

Festus : ' Taeniae,' a Greek word, is explained by Verrius to mean a woollen adornment of the head of a person of rank, as is the case in a passage of Caecilius in *The Man-Woman* . . . and in another passage— [a]

while he begged for a headband to tie up the wound.

[a] This might imply ' in another author,' and the quotation suggests a tragedy; it might, however, come from a comedy such as Naevius' *Acontizomenos*.

CAECILIUS

276

Seneca, *Epist.*, CXIII, 26 : Haec disputamus adtractis superciliis, fronte rugosa? Non possum hoc loco dicere illud Caecilianum—

o tristes ineptias!

Ridiculae sunt.

277–8

Nonius, 80, 32 : ' Bellosum,' bellicosum. Caecilius—

Tantum bellum suscitare conari adversarios
contra bellosum genus!

279

Servius, ad *Aen.*, II, 777 : ' Sine numine divum,' sine fati necessitate. Ut enim Statius dicit—

Fata sunt quae divi fantur.

vel quae indubitanter eveniunt.

280

Gloss. Terent. ap. Barth. Advers., 38, 14 : Aliquid monstri plus est quam aliquid monstrum . . . ut Caecilius—

Quid hominis uxorem habes?

Seneca, Ep. CXIII cicilianum *vel* celanum *vel* caeciliani *vel* celiani *edd.* (caelianum *Bamb. ?*)
Non. 80 cecilius *G. Harl.* 2 *Lugd.* 3   caelius *rell.*   *trib.*
Cael. Antipat. edd.
   [279] divi Bothe
   [280] uxoremne Ribb.

PLAYS

276

Seneca : Is this the sort of things we discuss with knitted brows and wrinkled forehead ?   I cannot at this point bring myself to quote that famous passage in Caecilius [a]—

Oh ! what dismal fooleries !

Ridiculous—that's what they are.

277–8

Nonius : ' Bellosum,' bellicose. Caecilius [b]—

The idea that they should try to stir up so big a war, as foes against a breed so warrish !

279

Servius, on ' without the will of the gods ' in Virgil : Without the necessity caused by fate. As Statius [c] says—

Dooms are what the gods doom.

or they are events which infallibly come to pass.

280

A gloss quoted by Barth [d] : ' Aliquid monstri ' is something more than ' aliquid monstrum ' . . . as Caecilius has—

What sort of a human being have ÿou for a wife ?

[a] Probably.   But the MSS. do not make it certain.
[b] Here again the MSS. leave us in doubt, and the quotation, in spite of its septenarian metre, suggests the prose of Caelius Antipater the annalist.
[c] Possibly Papinius Statius or some other grammarian.
[d] who is not to be trusted.

WORDS FROM ENNIUS AND CAECILIUS
NOT INCLUDED IN THE TEXT OR
THE NOTES OF THIS VOLUME

ENNIUS

Annals, Book XVI : 'hebes,' acc. 'hebem' instead of 'hebetem' (blunt). Charisius, *G. L.*, I, 132, 6.

Annals, Incerta : 'Anio,' acc. 'Anionem' instead of 'Anienem' (River Anio). Serv., ad *Aen.*, VII, 683.

'haec abnueram' (?) (I had refused this.) Schol. Veron., ad *Aen.*, X, 8.

Tragedies, '*Telamon*' : 'abnuebunt' (they will deny). Diomedes, *G. L.*, I, 382, 11.

Holy History : 'gluma' (husk). Varro, *R. R.*, I, 48, 1.

Not assigned to any work

'consiluere' (they fell silent). Paul., ex F., 41, 5.

'Cretenses', for 'Cretes' (Cretans). Charis., *G. L.*, I, 124, 12.

'ambactus' (vassal; a Celtic word). Fest., 4, 2 ; *Gloss. Lat. Graec.*, *C. G. L.*, II, 16, 3.

'⟨philo⟩logam' (learned). Fest., 310, 27.

'sancti' (hallowed) applied to poets. Cic., *pro Arch.*, 8, 18.

'longi,' epithet of epic verses. Cic., *de Leg.*, II, 27, 68.

'daedala' (skilful), epithet of Minerva. Paul., ex F., 48, 7. 'domina, hera' (Lady, mistress), applied to Minerva. Achilles Tat., ad Cat., I, 9.

562

'Vesper' (evening star). Censorinus, *de die nat.*, 24, 4.

'sospes' in the sense of saviour. Fest., 430, 15; Paul., 431, 3.

'crebrisuro' (stockade). Paul., ex F., 41, 23 ('a rampart fortified by " crebri suri," crowded stocks ').

'aplustre' (stern-streamer of a ship). *Gloss. Lat. Graec.*, *C. G. L.*, II, 48, 33.

'corpulentus' (corpulent). Paul., ex F., 44, 2.

'bona' (goodly) for magna. Porphyrio, ad Hor., *S.*, I, 1, 61.

'repostos' (stored—Virg., *Aen.*, VI, 655) and 'porgite' (hold ye out—*Aen.*, VIII, 274), examples of syncope. Serv., *ad Aen.*, I, 26.

'vidĕn' (do you see ?). Serv., ad *Aen.*, VI, 779 (780).

'solui' instead of 'solitus sum' (I was wont). Varro, *L. L.*, IX, 107.

'insexit' (from 'inseco,' go on to tell) for 'dixerit.' Paul., ex F., 79, 29.

'remorbescat' (should relapse into sickness). Fest., 382, 22; Paul., 383, 9.

'redinunt' (they return). Fest., 400, 12; Paul., 401, 1.

'inter ponendum' (in the midst of placing). Serv. auct., ad Verg., *Ecl.* IX, 23.

'insomnia' (sleeplessness). Serv., ad *Aen.*, IV, 9.

'torrus' (firebrand). Serv., ad *Aen.*, XII, 298.

'festra' (small window in a shrine). Macrob., *S.*, III, 12, 8.

'tapetae' (nom. pl. masc.; carpets). Fest., 528, 5.

'cicur' (mild, tame), used of men. Hieronym., *Apol. adv. Rufin.*, II, 11.

'locum' (nom. sing. neuter; place). Fr. Bob., *G. L.*, VII, 542, 9.

WORDS NOT INCLUDED IN THE TEXT

' vita vitalis ' (life worth living). Cic., *de Amic.*, 6, 22.

' bombus pedum ' (rumble of feet). Augustin., *de Dialect.*, 9.

' pede (?) ruit ' (rushes on foot). Fest., 312, 11.

' fidus ' for ' foedus ' (treaty). Varro, *L. L.*, V, 86 (from Ennius the grammarian, not the poet ?).

' acanthus ' (thorn-tree). *Schol. Bern.*, ad Verg., *G.*, II, 119, on the authority of M. Antonius Gnipho in a commentary on ' the tenth book of the *Annals*.'

' erumna ' (for ' aerumna '; hardship). Charis., *G. L.*, I, 98, 12.

Annals? Servius, on *Aen.*, XI, 608 ff. says that this passage is based on Ennius.

CAECILIUS

' *Hymnis* ' : ' nudius tertius ' (three days ago). Charis., *G. L.*, I, 207, 20.

' *Pausimachus* ' : ' velitatio ' (petty quarrelling). Nonius, 3, 3.

' *Plocium* ' : ' catellae ' (small chains). Nonius, 199, 7.

' *Progamos* ' : ' audibo ' for ' audiam.' Nonius, 505, 35.

Incerta : ' facilioreis ' and ' sanctioreis ' for facilioris, sanctioris. Charis., *G. L.*, I, 130, 4.

' gnoscit ' for ' noscit ' (come to know). Diomedes, *G. L.*, 383, 18.

' Leontium ' as a woman's name. Charis., *G. L.*, I, 104, 2.

CONCORDANCES

I GIVE here two concordances of Ennius and two of
Caecilius. In the case of both authors, Concordance
I is designed to help those who, using a copy of a
standard Latin text, wish to find information about
any fragment in this volume : while Concordance II
is designed to help those who, using this volume,
wish to refer to a standard Latin text about any fragment. In these concordances, V³ indicates the
numeration of lines in Vahlen's third edition of
Ennius; Ribb.²⁻³ the second and third editions of
Ribbeck's *Comicorum Romanorum Fragmenta* (Caecilius
Statius) ; W the numeration in this volume ; *n.* means
that the fragment is, in this volume, only referred to
in a note ; and *catal.* means that the fragment will
be found in the catalogue or list of single words which
precedes these concordances.

ENNIUS

Concordance I

V³	W	V³	W
Annales	*Annals*	9	*Ex inc. scr.* 6
1	1	10–12	*Ann.* 7–10
2	*Spur. ?* 43	13–14	11–12
3–4	*Ann.* 2–3	15	13
5	4	16	14
6	5	17	15
7	*vide* p. 430	18–19	18–19
8	*Ann.* 6	20	22–23

565

V³	W	V³	W
21	20	107–108	112–113
22	21	109	108
23	24	110–114	117–121
24	25	115–116	114–115
25	26	117	116
26–27	27–28	118	catal.
28	29	119	Ann. 124
29	59	120–121	125–126
30–31	16–17	122–124	127–129
32	78	125	130
33	31	126	139
34	30	127	525
35–51	32–48	128	122
52–53	49–50	129	132
54	51	130	137
55	52	131	136
56–57	53–54	132	131
58	56	133	133
59	55	134	134
60	57	135	138
61	58	136	135
62–63	60–61	137	140
64	62	138–139	141–142
65–66	63–64	140	143
67	67–69	141	144
68	71	142	145
69	65	143	149
70–72	72–74	144–145	146–147
73–74	75–76	146	150
75	77	147–148	151–152
76	104	149	154
77–96	88–100	150	155
97	101	151	156
98	105	152	159
99–100	102–103	153–154	160–161
101	107	155	157
102	79	156	158
103	Spur. ? 40	157	123
104	Ann. 111	158	163
105	109	159	162
106	110	160	475

CONCORDANCE I

V³	W	V³	W
161	164	232–233	256–257
162	165	234–251	210–227
163	166	252	247
164–165	251–252	253	250
166	167	254–255	242–243
167	170	256	244
168	506	257	254
169	*Spur. ?* 2	258	253
170	*Ann.* 474	259	228
171	169	260	255
172	168	261	241
173	171	262–263	239–240
174	173	264	70
175–176	207–208	265	316
177	178	266–267	258–259
178	172	268–273	262–268
179–181	174–176	274–275	272–273
182	179	276	*Spur. ?* 5
183–185	526–528	277	*Ann.* 283
186	180	278	274
187–191	181–185	279	275
192–193	*Spur. ?* 21–22	280–281	276–277
194–201	*Ann.* 186–193	282	279
202–203	194–195	283	278
204	196	284	281
205–206	198–199	285	280
207	197	286	282
208–210	200–202	287–289	284–286
211	205	290	269
212	206	291	293
213–217	231–235	292–293	294
218–219	229–230	294	295
220	236	295	287
221	237	296	289
222	271	297	288
223	238	298	290
224	204	299	291
225	248	300	307
226	177	301	296
227–229	297–299	302	546
230–231	245–246	303–308	300–305

V³	W	V³	W
309	540	367–369	363–365
310	306	370–372	360–362
311	*Spur. ?* 4	373	209
312–313	*Ann.* 313–314	374–375	388–389
314	315	376	*vide* p. 434
315	308	377	*Ex inc. scr.* 10
316	312	378	*Ann.* 369
317–318	320–321	379	551
319–320	318–319	380	370
321–322	310–311	381–383	366–368
323	317	384–385	372–373
324	309	386	374
325	270	387–388	375–376
326–327	322–323	389	377
328	324	390	*n.* p. 141
329	325	391–392	*Ann.* 378–379
330	*catal.*	393	380
331	*Ann.* 326	394–395	381–382
332–333	337–338	396	383
334	331	397	384
335–337	327–329	398–399	385–386
338	330	400	491
339	332	401–408	409–416
340–342	339–341	409	387
343–345	333–335	410	390
346–347	336	411–412	393–394
348	345	413	392
349–350	343–344	414	423
351	342	415	417
352	352	416–417	425–426
353	*Spur. ?* 23	418	424
354	*n.* p. 7	419	371
355	*Ann.* 346	420	398
356–357	347–348	421	397
358–359	349–350	422	422
360–361	354–355	423	396
362	353	424	395
363	356	425	391
364	357	426	*catal.*
365	351	427	*Ann.* 405
366	359	428	408

CONCORDANCE I

V³	W	V³	W
429	407	486	445
430	406	487	531
431	399	488	542
432	418	489	564
433	400	490	565
434-435	401-402	491	292
436-437	403-404	492	533
438	203	493	485
439	429	494	486
440	427	495	524
441	428	496	543
442	433	497-498	534-535
443-445	430-432	499	539
446-447	434-435	500	467
448-449	514-515	501-502	468-469
450-452	436-438	503	358
453	439	504	249
454	440	505	490
455	555	506	492
456	Spur. ? 8	507	493
457-458	Ann. 450-451	508	483
459	487	509	Ex inc. scr. 22
460	455	510	Ann. 498
461-462	419-420	511	552
463	462	512	460
464	463	513	550
465-466	471-472	514-518	517-521
467-468	458-459	519-520	499-500
469	480	521-522	260-261
470-471	Ex inc. scr. 3-4	523	—
472-473	Ann. 501-502	524	544
474	513	525	484
475-476	catal.	526	Plays 395-396
477	Ann. 148	527	Ann. 454
478	442	528	Ex inc. scr. 7
479	447	529	Spur. ? 30
480	441	530	Ann. 488
481	446	531	421
482	537	532	479
483	538	533	Spur. ? 38
484-485	443-444	534	Ann. 530

V³	W	V³	W
535	554	587	509
536	553	588	*Ex inc. scr.* 19
537	529	589	*Ann.* 497
538–539	481–482	590	*catal.*
540	457	591–592	*Ann.* 522
541	*Spur. ?* 11	593	556
542–543	*Ann.* 452–453	594	561
544	494	595	562
545	557	596	536
546	470	597	523
547–548	*Ex inc. scr.* 8–9	598	*Ex inc. scr.* 26
549	*Ann.* 478	599	*Ann.* 473
550	489	600	560
551–552	504–505	601	496
553	516	602	*catal.*
554	510	603	*catal.*
555	456	604	*catal.*
556	563	605	*catal.*
557	559	606	*vide* pp. 442–3
558	558	607	*Ann.* 512
559	476	608	503
560	549	609	*Spur. ?* 13
561–562	547–548	610	*Spur. ?* 44
563–564	*Ex inc. scr.* 12–13	611–612	*Ex inc. scr.* 20
		613	*Ann.* 153
565	*Ann.* 477	614–615	——
566	532	616	*Spur. ?* 28
567	545	617	*Spur. ?* 25
568	*Spur. ?* 37	618	*Spur. ?* 19
569	*Ann.* 541	619	*Spur. ?* 18
570	495	620	*Spur. ?* 12
571	511	621	*Spur. ?* 24
572	507–508	622	——
573	*Spur. ?* 27	623	*Spur. ?* 3
574–577	*Spur. ?* 33–36	624	*Spur. ?* 39
578	*Ann.* 461	625	*Spur. ?* 26
579	*Ex inc. scr.* 21	626	*Spur. ?* 31
580	*Ann.* 449	627	——
581	448	628	*Ex inc. scr.* 15
582–583	*Ex inc. scr.* 18		
584–586	*Ann.* 464–466		

CONCORDANCE I

V³	W	V³	W
Scenica	*Plays*	105	109
1–3	1–3	106	112
4	4–5	107–110	113–116
5	13	111	111
6	6	112–113	117–118
7–9	10–12	114	121
10–11	16–17	115	120
12	7–9	116	122
13–14	14–15	117	119
15	18	118–119	123–124
16	19	120	126
17	20	121	127
18	22	122	125
19	21	123–127	128–132
20	23	128	133
21	24	129	136
22–26	25–29	130	139
27–33	30–36	131–132	134–135
34	37	133	137
35–46	38–49	134	138
47–48	50–51	135–136	140–141
49	53	137–138	142–143
50	52	139	144
51	54	140	145–146
52	55	141–144	150–153
53	56	145–146	147–148
54–68	57–72	147	149
69–71	73–75	148	154
72–75	76–79	149	155
76–77	80–81	150	156
78	82	151–155	157–161
79	85	156	162
80–81	83–84	157	163
82	93	158–159	164–165
83–84	88–89	160	166
85–91	94–100	161–172	169–181
92–99	101–108	173	167
100–101	91–92	174	168
102	90	175	182
103	110	176	183
104	86–87	177	187–188

ENNIUS

V³	W	V³	W
178	192	257–258	264–265
179	191	259–261	266–268
180	193	262–263	269–270
181	196	264–265	272–273
182–183	194–195	266–272	274–280
184	189	273	271
185	197	274–275	282–283
186	198	276–277	284–285
187	199	278	286
188–189	200–201	279	281
190–192	184–186	280	287
193	190	281	288
194	(ante 202)	282–283	289–290
195	202	284–286	291–293
196	203	287–288	294–295
197–198	204–205	289–290	296–297
199–201	206–208	291	298
202	209	292	301
203–204	210–211	293	303
205	212	294	302
206	213	295	299–300
207	214	296	304
208	215	297	305
209	219	298	306
210	216	299	307
211–212	217–218	300–303	308–311
213–214	220–221	304–305	312–313
215–218	222–225	306	316
219–221	226–228	307	315
222–223	229–230	308	314
224	231	309	317
225–227	232–234	310	318
228–229	235–236	311	323
230–231	237–238	312–314	319–322
232	239	315	324
233	240	316–317	328–329
234–241	241–248	318	330
242–244	249–251	319–323	332–336
245	252	324	327
246–254	253–261	325–326	325–326
255–256	262–263	327	337

CONCORDANCE I

V³	W	V³	W
328	338	382	398
329	catal.	383	397
330	339	384–385	423
331	340	386–387	418
332	343	388–389	424–425
333	342	390–391	392–393
334–335	347–348	392–393	408–409
336	344	394	331
337–338	345–346	395	407
339	341	396	394
340	349	397	415
341	354	398–400	412–414
342–343	371–372	401	388
344	373	402	410
345	351	403	389
346–347	350	404–405	402–403
348	355	406	390–391
349–351	358–360	407	411
352	361	408	417
353	362	409	416
354–356	363–365	410	419
357–358	356–357	411	421
359	vide p. 352	412–413	405–406
360	Plays 352	414	385
361	353	415	426
362–365	366–370	416	420
366	376	417–418	399
367	374	419	431
368	377–378	420	433
369	375	421	429
370–371	379–380	422	432
372	381	423	428
373	382	424	430
374	383	425	434
375	384	426	436
376	400	427	435
377	(post 400)	428	437
378	404	429	427
379	401	430	422
380	386		
381	387		

V³	W	V³	W
Saturae	*Satires*	*Varia,*	
1	1	*Protrepticus*	*Exhortation*
2	2	30	*n.* p. 406
3–4	3–4	31–33	1–3
5	5	*Varia,*	
6–7	6–7	*Hedyphagetica*	*Delikatessen*
8–9	8–9	34–44	1–11
10–11	10–11	*Varia,*	
12–13	12–13	*Epicharmus*	*Epicharmus*
14–19	14–19	45	1
20	*post* 31	46	2
21–58	*vide* pp. 388–9	47	3
59–62	*Sat.* 28–31	48–50	4–6
63	22	· 51	7
64	21	52–53	8–9
65	20	54–58	10–14
66	24	59	*n.* p. 415
67–68	25–26	*Varia,*	
69	23	*Euhemerus*	*Euhemerus*
70	27	60–61	1–4
Varia, Scipio	*Scipio*	62–63	5–7
1–2	10–11	64–82	8–38
3	7	83–86	39–45
4–5	8–9	87–97	46–63
6–8	12–14	98	64–65
9–12	1–4	99–106	66–77
13	5	107–108	78–80
14	6	109–112	81–87
Varia, Epi-		113–115	88–92
grammata	*Epigrams*	116–131	93–118
15–16	7–8	132–141	119–133
17–18	9–10	142–145	134–138
19–20	5–6	146	*catal.*
21–22	1–2	*Incerta*	
23–24	3–4	1	*Ex inc. scr.* 1
Varia, Sota	*Sotas*	2	*catal.*
25	2	3	*Ex inc. scr.* 2
26	1	4	*Ex inc. scr.* 33
27	3	5	*Ex inc. scr.* 5
28	4	6	*Ex inc. scr.* 23
29	5	7	*Ex inc. scr.* 14

ENNIUS

V³	W	V³	W
8	*Ex inc. scr.* 31	33	*n. p.* 331
9	*Ex inc. scr.* 16	34	*catal.*
10	*Ex inc. scr.* 17	35	*catal.*
11	*Ex inc. scr.* 25	36	*catal.*
12	*Ex inc. scr.* 28	37	*catal.*
13	*Ex inc. scr.* 29	38	*catal.*
14	*Ex inc. scr.* 36	39	*Ex inc. scr.* 35
15	*Ex inc. scr.* 27	40	*Ex inc. scr.* 30
16	*Ex inc. scr.* 24	41	*catal.*
17	*catal.*	42	*catal.*
18	*Ex inc. scr.* 32	43	post *ex inc. scr.* 32
19	*catal.*		
20	*catal.*	44	post *ex inc. scr.* 11
21	*Ex inc. scr.* 34		
22	*catal.*	45	—
23	*catal.*	46	*catal.*
24	*vide p.* 434	47	*Spur. ?* 32
25	*catal.*	48	*catal.*
26	*catal.*	49	*catal.*
27	*catal.*	50	*catal.*
28	*catal.*	51	*catal.*
29	*catal.*	52	*Spur. ?* 42
30	—	53	*Ex inc. scr.* 11
31	*catal.*		
32	post *ex inc. scr.* 17		

ENNIUS

Concordance II

W	V³	W	V³
Annals	*Annales*	11–12	13–14
1	1	13	15
2–3	3–4	14	16
4	5	15	17
5	6	16–17	30–31
6	8	18–19	18–19
7–10	10–12	20	21

ENNIUS

W	V³	W	V³
21	22	110	106
22–23	20	111	104
24	23	112–113	107–108
25	24	114–115	115–116
26	25	116	117
27–28	26–27	117–121	110–114
29	28	122	128
30	34	123	157
31	33	124	119
32–48	35–51	125–126	120–121
49–50	52–53	127–129	122–124
51	54	130	125
52	55	131	132
53–54	56–57	132	129
55	59	133	133
56	58	134	134
57	60	135	136
58	61	136	131
59	29	137	130
60–61	62–63	138	135
62	64	139	126
63–64	65–66	140	137
65	69	141–142	138–139
66–67	[ad 67]	143	140
67–69	67	144	141
70	264	145	142
71	68	146–147	144–145
72–74	70–72	148	477
75–76	73–74	149	143
77	75	150	146
78	32	151–152	147–148
79	102	153	613
88–100	77–96	154	149
101	97	155	150
102–103	99–100	156	151
104	76	157	155
105	98	158	156
106	vide V., p. 16	159	152
107	Ann. 101	160–161	153–154
108	109	162	159
109	105	163	158

CONCORDANCE II

W	V³	W	V³
164	161	248	225
165	162	249	504
166	163	250	253
167	166	251–252	164–165
168	172	253	258
169	171	254	257
170	167	255	260
171	173	256–257	232–233
172	178	258–259	266–267
173	174	260–261	521–522
174–176	179–181	262–268	268–273
177	226	269	290
178	177	270	325
179	182	271	222
180	186	272–273	274–275
181–185	187–191	274	278
186–193	194–201	275	279
194–195	202–203	276–277	280–281
196	204	278	283
197	207	279	282
198–199	205–206	280	285
200–202	208–210	281	284
203	438	282	286
204	224	283	277
205	211	284–286	287–289
206	·212	287	295
207–208	175–176	288	297
209	373	289	296
210–227	234–251	290	298
228	259	291	299
229–230	218–219	292	491
231–235	213–217	293	291
236	220	294	292
237	221	295	294
238	223	296	301
239–240	262–263	297–299	227–229
241	261	300–305	303–308
242–243	254–255	306	310
244	256	307	300
245–246	230–231	308	315
247	252	309	324

577

W	V³	W	V³
310–311	321–322	375–376	387–388
312	316	377	389
313–314	312–313	378–379	391–392
315	314	380	393
316	265	381–382	394–395
317	323	383	396
318–319	319–320	384	397
320–321	317–318	385–386	398–399
322–323	326–327	387	409
324	328	388–389	374–375
325	329	390	410
326	331	391	425
327–329	335–337	392	413
330–331	338, 334	393–394	411–412
332	339	395	424
333–335	343–345	396	423
336	346–347	397	421
337–338	332–333	398	420
339–341	340–342	399	431
342	351	400	433
343–344	349–350	401–402	434–435
345	348	403–404	436–437
346	355	405	427
347–348	356–357	406	430
349–350	358–359	407	429
351	365	408	428
352	352	409–416	401–408
353	362	417	415
354–355	360–361	418	432
356	363	419–420	461–462
357	364	421	531
358	503	422	422
359	366	423	414
360–362	370–372	424	418
363–365	367–369	425–426	416–417
366–368	381–383	427	440
369	378	428	441
370	380	429	439
371	419	430–432	443–445
372–373	384–385	433	442
374	386	434–435	446–447

CONCORDANCE II

W	V³	W	V³
436–438	450–452	488	530
439	453	489	550
440	454	490	505
441	480	491	490
442	478	492	506
443–444	484–485	493	507
445	486	494	544
446	481	495	570
447	479	496	601
448	581	497	589
449	580	498	510
450–451	457–458	499–500	519–520
452–453	542–543	501–502	472–473
454	527	503	608
455	460	504–505	551–552
456	555	506	168
457	540	507–508	572
458–459	467–468	509	587
460	512	510	554
461	578	511	571
462	463	512	607
463	464	513	474
464–466	584–586	514–515	448–449
467	500	516	553
468–469	501–502	517–521	514–518
470	546	522	591–592
471–472	465–466	523	597
473	599	524	495
474	170	525	127
475	160	526–528	183–185
476	559	529	537
477	565	530	534
478	549	531	487
479	532	532	566
480	469	533	492
481–482	538–539	534–535	497–498
483	508	536	596
484	525	537	482
485	493	538	483
486	494	539	499
487	459	540	309

ENNIUS

W	V³	W	V³
541	569	20	17
542	488	21	19
543	496	22	18
544	524	23	20
545	567	24	21
546	302	25–29	22–26
547–548	561–562	30–36	27–33
549	560	37	34
550	513	38–49	35–46
551	379	50–51	47–48
552	511	52	50
553	536	53	49
554	535	54	51
555	455	55	52
556	593	56	53
557	545	57–72	54–68
558	558	73–75	69–71
559	557	76–79	72–75
560	600	80–81	76–77
561	594	82	78
562	595	83–84	80–81
563	556	85	79
564	489	86–87	104
565	490	88–89	83–84
		90	102
		91–92	100–101
		93	82
		94–100	85–91
		101–108	92–99
		109	105
Plays	*Scenica*	110	103
1–3	1–3	111	111
4–5	4	112	106
6	6	113–116	107–110
7–9	12	117–118	112–113
10–12	7–9	119	117
13	5	120	115
14–15	13–14	121	114
16–17	10–11	122	116
18	15	123–124	118–119
19	16	125	122

CONCORDANCE II

W	V³	W	V³
126	120	200–201	188–189
127	121	202	195
128–132	123–127	203	196
133	128	204–205	197–198
134–135	131–132	206–208	199–201
136	129	209	202
137	133	210–211	203–204
138	134	212	205
139	130	213	206
140–141	135–136	214	207
142–143	137–138	215	208
144	139	216	210
145–146	140	217–218	211–212
147–148	145–146	219	209
149	147	220–221	213–214
150–153	141–144	222–225	215–218
154	148	226–228	219–221
155	149	229–230	222–223
156	150	231	224
157–161	151–155	232–234	225–227
162	156	235–236	228–229
163	157	237–238	230–231
164–165	158–159	239	232
166	160	240	233
167	173	241–248	234–241
168	174	249–251	242–244
169–181	161–172	252	245
182	175	253–261	246–254
183	176	262–263	255–256
184–186	190–192	264–265	257–258
187–188	177	266–268	259–261
189	184	269–270	262–263
190	193	271	273
191	179	272–273	264–265
192	178	274–280	266–272
193	180	281	279
194–195	182–183	282–283	274–275
196	181	284–285	276–277
197	185	286	278
198	186	287	280
199	187	288	281

W	V³	W	V³
289–290	282–283	351	345
291–293	284–286	352	360
294–295	287–288	353	361
296–297	289–290	354	341
298	291	355	348
299–300	295	356–360	357–358,
301	292		349–351
302	294	361	352
303	293	362	353
304	296	363–365	354–356
305	297	366–370	362–365
306	298	371–372	342–343
307	299	373	344
308–311	300–303	374	367
312–313	304–305	375	369
314	308	376	366
315	307	377–378	368
316	306	379–380	370–371
317	309	381	372
318	310	382	373
319–322	312–314	383	374
323	311	384	375
324	315	385	414
325–326	325–326	386	380
327	324	387	381
328–329	316–317	388	401
330	318	389	403
331	394	390–391	406
332–336	319–323	392–393	390–391
337	327	394	396
338	328	395–396	*Ann.*, 526
339	330	397	*Scen.*, 383
340	331	398	382
341	339	399	417–418
342	333	400	376
343	332	401	379
344	336	402–403	404–405
345–346	337–338	404	378
347–348	334–335	405–406	412–413
349	340	407	395
350	346–347	408–409	392–393

CONCORDANCE II

W	V³	W	V³
410	402	20	65
411	407	21	64
412–414	398–400	22	63
415	397	23	69
416	409	24	66
417	408	25–26	67–68
418	386–387	27	70
419	410	28–31	59–62
420	416	*Scipio*	*Varia ; Scipio*
421	411	1–4	9–12
422	430	5	13
423	384–385	6	14
424–425	388–389	7	3
426	415	8–9	4–5
427	429	10–11	1–2
428	423	12–14	6–8
429	421	*Epigrams*	*Varia ;*
430	424		*Epigrammata*
431	419	1–2	21–22
432	422	3–4	23–24
433	420	5–6	19–20
434	425	7–10	15–18
435	427	*Sotas*	*Varia ; Sota*
436	426	1	26
437	428	2	25
		3	27
		4	28
		5	29
		Exhortation	*Varia ;*
			Protrepticus
		1–3	31–33
Satires	*Saturae*	*Delikatessen*	*Varia ;*
1	1		*Hedyphagetica*
2	2	1–11	34–44
3–4	3–4	*Epicharmus*	*Varia ;*
5	5		*Epicharmus*
6–7	6–7	1	45
8–9	8–9	2	46
10–11	10–11	3	47
12–13	12–13	4–6	48–50
14–19	14–19	7	51

W	V³	W	V³
8–9	52–53	26	Ann., 598
10–14	54–58	27	*Incerta.* 15
Euhemerus	Varia ;	28	12
	Euhemerus	29	13
1–4	60–61	30	40
5–7	62–63	31	8
8–38	64–82	32	18
39–45	83–86	33	4
46–63	87–97	34	21
64–65	98	35	39
66–77	99–106	36	14
78–80	107–108	Spur. ?	
81–87	109–112	1	—
88–92	113–115	2	Ann. 169
93–118	116–131	3	Ann., 623
119–133	132–141	4	Ann., 311
134–138	142–145	5	Ann., 276
Ex incertis		6–7	
scriptis		8	Ann., 456
1	Incerta, 1	9–10	—
2	Incerta, 3	11	Ann., 541
3–4	Ann., 470–471	12	Ann., 620
5	Incerta, 5	13	Ann., 609
6	Ann., 9	14	—
7	Ann., 528	15	
8–9	Ann., 547–548	16–17	—
10	Ann., 377	18	Ann., 619
11	Incerta, 53	19	Ann., 618
12–13	Ann., 563–564	20	vide V., p. 33
14	Incerta, 7	21–22	Ann., 192–193
15	Ann., 628	23	Ann., 353
16	Incerta, 9	24	Ann., 621
17	Incerta, 10	25	Ann., 617
18	Ann., 582–583	26	Ann., 625
19	Ann., 588	27	Ann., 573
20	Ann., 611–612	28	Ann., 616
21	Ann., 579	29	—
22	Ann., 509	30	Ann., 529
23	Incerta, 6	31	Ann., 626
24	Incerta, 16	32	Incerta, 47
25	Incerta, 11	33–36	Ann., 574–577

CONCORDANCE II

W	V³	W	V³
37	*Ann.*, 568	41	*vide V.*, p. 16
38	*Ann.*, 533	42	*Incerta*, 52
39	*Ann.*, 624	43	*Ann.*, 2
40	*Ann.*, 103	44	*Ann.*, 610

CAECILIUS

Concordance I

RIBB. 2-3	W	RIBB. 2-3	W
1	2	41	37
2	5	42–43	40–41
3	1	44–45	38–39
4	3	46	42
5	4	47–48	43–44
6	6	49	48
7	7	50	47
8	8	51–52	45–46
9–10	9	53	49
11–12	12–13	54–55	50
13	11	56	51
14	10	57–58	52–53
15	16	59–60	54–55
16	14	61	56
17	15	62–63 (64)	57–58
18–19	17	(64)–65	59–60
20–21	18	66–67	62–63
22–24	19–21	68–69	68–70
25	22	70	64
26	23	71	61
27	24	72	65
28–29	25–26	73	66
30–31	27–28	74	67
32	29	75	76
33	30	76	73–74
34–35	31–32	77	75
36	33	78	78
37–38 (39)	34–35	79–80	81–82
40	36	81	85

CAECILIUS

Ribb. 2-3	W	Ribb. 2-3	W
82	71	139–140	130–131
83(–84)	86	141	132
85	87	141 [1]	133
86	72	142–157	136–150
87	84	158–162	151–155
88	83	163	156
89	77	164–165	157–158
90	79	166	162
91	80	167	161
92	88	168	159–160
93	89	169–172	163–166
94–95	91–92	173–175	167–169
96(95)–97	94–96	176	170
98	97	177	171
99	90	178–179	172
100	93	180	173
101–102	98	181–182	134–135
103	99	183	174
104–105	100–101	184	176
106–107	102–103	185	175
108–109	104–105	186–187	177–178
110	106	188	179
111–112	107	189	*catal.*
113	108	190	180
114	109	191	181
115	110	192	182
116	111	193–194	183–184
117	112	195	185
118	113	196	186
119–120	114	197–198	187–188
121	115–116	199–209	189–199
122–123	120	210	200
124–125	124–125	211–214	201–204
126–128	121–123	215	205
129–130	221–222	216	206
131	223	217	207
132–133	117–118	218–219	208
134	119	220	216
135	126	221–222	209–210
136–137	128–129	223	214–215
138	127	224–225	212–213

CONCORDANCE I

Ribb. [2-3]	W	Ribb. [2-3]	W
226	211	268	248
227	217	269	250
228	218	270	249
229	219–220	271–272	266
230–242	224–235	273–274	265
243–244	236–237	274[1]	270
245–246	251–253	275	275
247	256	276–278	262–264
248	*post* 255	279	273
249	259	280	268
250	267	281	276
251	260	282	269
252	254	283	*post* 269
253	245	284	271
254–255	246	285	272
256–257	243–244	286	*catal.*
258	261	287	*catal.*
259–263	238–242	288	*catal.*
264	257	289 ed.[2]	280
265 ed.[2]	279	290–291	258
266	255	291 [1]	274
267	247	292–293 ed.[3]	277–278

CAECILIUS

Concordance II

W	Ribb. [2-3]	W	Ribb. [2-3]
1	3	12–13	11–12
2	1	14	16
3	4	15	17
4	5	16	15
5	2	17	18–19
6	6	18	20–21
7	7	19–21	22–24
8	8	22	25
9	9–10	23	26
10	14	24	27
11	13	25–26	28–29

CAECILIUS

W	RIBB. 2-3	W	RIBB. 2-3
27–28	30–31	84	87
29	32	85	81
30	33	86	83–84
31–32	34–35	87	85
33	36	88	92
34–35	37–38 (39)	89	93
36	40	90	99
37	41	91–92	94–95
38–39	44–45	93	100
40–41	42–43	94–96	96(95)–97
42	46	97	98 ·
43–44	47–48	98	101–102
45–46	51–52	99	103
47	50	100–101	104–105
48	49	102–103	106–107
49	53	104–105	108–109
50	54–55	106	110
51	56	107	111–112
52–53	57–58	108	113
54–55	59–60	109	114
56	61	110	115
57–58	62–63 (64)	111	116
59–60	(64)–65	112	117
61	71	113	118
62–63	66–67	114	119–120
64	70	115–116	121
65	72	117–118	132–133
66	73	119	134
67	74	120	122–123
68–70	68–69	121–123	126–128
71	82	124–125	124–125
72	86	126	135
73–74	76	127	138
75	77	128–129	136–137
76	75	130–131	139–140
77	89	132	141
78	78	133	141[1]
79	90	134–135	181–182
80	91	136–150	142–157
81–82	79–80	151–155	158–162
83	88	156	163

CONCORDANCE II

W	RIBB. 2-3	W	RIBB. 2-3
157–158	164–165	221–222	129–130
159–160	168	223	131
161	167	224–235	230–242
162	166	236–237	243–244
163–166	169–172	238–242	259–263
167–169	173–175	243–244	256–257
170	176	245	253
171	177	246	254–255
172	178–179	247	267
173	180	248	268
174	183	249	270
175	185	250	269
176	184	251–253	245–246
177–178	186–187	254	252
179	188	255	266
180	190	256	247
181	191	257	264
182	192	258	290–291
183–184	193–194	259	249
185	195	260	251
186	196	261	258
187–188	197–198	262–264	276–278
189–199	199–209	265	273–274
200	210	266	271–272
201–204	211–214	267	250
205	215	268	280
206	216	269	282
207	217	270	274 [1]
208	218–219	271	284
209–210	221–222	272	285
211	226	273	279
212–213	224–225	274	291 [1]
214–215	223	275	275
216	220	276	281
217	227	277–278	292–293 ed. [3]
218	228	279	265 ed. [2]
219–220	229	280	289 ed. [2]

INDEX

(The numbers refer to pages)

A

abnneo 102, 562
abscondit 482
Abydus 408–9
acanthus 564
acarnae 408
Achaeans 227, 249
Acherusia, Acheron 254–5, 310–1
Achilles 218 ff., 253, 272–7, 283–7,
    290–1, 307, 309, 341–2
Achivi 226, 282–3, 292–3
acris (nom. masc.) 132
adgretus 440
aditavere 380
Adrastus 228–9, 328
Adriatic 359
Aeacus 67, 101, 338–9
Aegeus 323
Aegisthus 357
Aelius (C.) Teucrus 144, 146–7, 153–7
Aelius (Sextus) Paetus 120–1
Aelius (T.) Paetus 147
Aemilius (L.) Barbula 69
Aemilius (L.) Paullus 95, 101 ff.
Aemilius Lepidus 149
Aemilius Regillus 139
Aeneas, 8 ff., 28, 287, 428–9
Aenus 408–9
Aeolus 326–9
Aesculapius 278–9
Aesopus 280–1
Aetolia(ns) xx, 143, 358–9
Africa 114–5, 386–7, 394–5, 409
Agamemno(n) 218, 221, 274–5, 284–5,
    298 ff., 300 ff., 344–5, 347, 437
agea 200–1
Aias see Ajax
Ajax 221, 223, 226 ff., 276–7, 287,
    337 ff.
Alba, Albani 9, 28, 45, 50–1, 446–7;
    Albai Longai 31

Alcmeo. Alcmaeon 228 ff.
Alexander (Paris) 234 ff., 279
aliquantisper 482
Alphesiboea 232
altivolantum 30
amantum 550
ambactus 562
Ambivius Turpio xxvii–viii
Ambracia xx, 143–4, 358–9, 408–9
Ambracia (poem), xx, xxv, 358–61
Amphiaraus 228–9
Amulius 19, 33
Amyntor 330 ff.
Anchises 8–11 (Anchisen 8)
Ancus Marcius 50–1, 54–5
Andromacha, Andromache 244 ff., 291
Andromeda 254 ff
anguivillosi (?) 376
Anienem 562
Annals xxv, 2 ff., 430 ff.
ansatae 58, 62
Antilochus 284–5
Antiochus III 127, 134–7, 209
anuis 292
Anxur 61
aplustre 563
Apollo 23, 67, 229, 232–5, 240–1,
    269–71, 342–3, 350–1
Appius see Claudius
aprienium 408
araneae 442
Arcadia 229, 231
arcessier 548
Archestratus 406–7
Areopagitae 272; Areopagus 272
Ares 272
Argeos 42
Argives, Argivi 275, 281, 312–3, 334–5
Argo 312–3
Argos 259, 307, 343
argutarier 332
Arimaspi 393

INDEX

Aristarchus 218–9
armentas 442
Arsinoe 232–3
Asia 137, 139, 193
Assaracus 8, 9
Astyanax 247–9
Athamas 260–1
Athena 226–7, 268 ; *see* Minerva
Athens 204–5, 311, 323–5
Atlas 21
Atlas, Mt. 444–5
Atreus 346 ff.
Attic, Attica 542–3, 550
aucupant 322
audibis 362 ; audibo 564
augificat 252
auguro 326
Aulacia 418–9
Aurelius Cotta 120–1
Ausculum 75, 77
auspicant 518
Automedon 283
Aventine xviii–ix, 29–31
axim 118
Azov 401

B

Bacchus 260–1, 377
balneae 504
bardum 556
bellicrepa 34
bellipotentes 66
bellosum 560
Beneventum 77, 94
bipatentibus 20
blanditie 490
bombus 564
bovantes 174
brabium (?) 348–9
Brachyllas 129
bradys 148
Bromius 260
Bruges 282
Brugio, Brugian 276–7, 283
Brundisium xviii, xxiii, 202, 408–9
Bruttace 202
Bruttian 203
Burrus 64, 100–1, 454–5 ; *see* Pyrrhus
buxum 86
buxus 442

C

Caecilius Statius, *life* xxiii, xxvii ff.;
    works 467 ff.

Caecilius (*or* Caelius) Teucrus *see* Aelius
    Teucrus
cael (*for* caelum) 460–1
Caelus 12, 418–9, 422–4
caementae 368
Calchas 309, 339
Callinicus 159, 161
calvaria 408
Camenas 462
Camillus 177
Campani, 446–7
Campi Magni 398–9
canes (*fem. sing.*) 432
Cannae 78, 100–5
Canusium 105
capessere 16
Capua 107, 109
Capys 8, 9
carinantes, carinantibus 436–7
Carthage 65, 78 ff., 159 ; New C. 164
casci 12
Cassandra 234–5, 240 ff.
Cassiepeia, Cassiope 254
cassita 388
cata 182, 458
Cato *see* Porcius
Caupuncula 360–1
celere (*adv.*) 384; cele is (*nom. sing.
    fem.*) 480
celerissimus 170, 194
Cepheus 254
Cerberus 377
cere comminuit brum 450–1
Ceres 324–5, 412–3, 418–9
cette 322
Charopus 121–3
Cineas 73, 75
Cisseis 290–1
Cisseus 234–5, 291
claudeat 480
Claudius (Appius) Caecus 72–3, 75;
    Caudex 86–7
Claudius (C.) Pulcher 157
Claudius Marcellus 95
Claudius Nero 111
cluebat 358; cluebunt 2; cluo 454
Clupea 408–9
Clytaemnestra 301, 306–7, 347
Cnossus 429
coclites 392
coepiam 498
cohus, cohum 210
Colchis 312–3, 320–1
collus 486
comedies 360–3, 378 ff., 468 ff.

INDEX

commemoramentum 526
commiserescite 288
compitum 542
concordis (*nom. sing.*) 506
conque fricati (?) 34
consipta 330; consiptum 331
contrā 172-3, 436-7
convestirier 272
convivat 182
Corcyra 408-9
Corinth 311, 314-5
Cornelius (M.) Cethegus 112-3; *see also* Scipio
corporaret 256
corpulentus 563
Corsica 65, 87
Cotta 120-1
Cotys 161
cracentes 182
crebrisuro 563
Creon 316-7, 319
Cresphontes 262 ff., 356
Cretans, Cretensium, Crete 422-3, 428-9
criminat 386
Cumae 408-9
cunctato 360
cunctent 284
cupienter 330
Curetes 428-9
Curiatii, Curii 44 ff., 197
Curius, M'. 78-9
Cyclops 114-5
Cynoscephalae 123-5
Cyprus 402-3, 430-1, 508-9

D

Danai 288
danunt 528
Dardaniis 128
Dardanus 129
debil 114
Decius Mus 75
decolles 510
degrumari 162 (163)
deintegravit 550
Deiphobus 238-9
delicat 512
Delphi 351
de me hortatur 136
Demetrius of Pharos 95; D. son of Philip 127

depopulat 472
deque totondit 196
derepente 286
destituit 534
dia 10, 18; die 40
dibalare 554
Dido 98
Diomedes 221
do (*for* domum) 460-1
duellis 178
dulcitas 540
duriter 334, 484

E

edim 474
edolavi 307, 436-7
Egeria 43; Egeriai 42
eliminas 312
elopem 408
Empedocles 97, 348-9, 433
endo 400, 460-1; *see* indu
Ennius, *life* xvii ff.; *works* 1 ff.
Ennius (*grammarian*) xxvi
enodari, 346
Ephesus 134
Epicharmus 410-1
Epicharmus (*poem*) xxi, 6-7, 410 ff.
epigrams 398-403
Epirus, 351
Epulo 148, 157
eques 94-5, 160
equitatus 194
Erechtheus 264-7
Eriboea 337
Eriphyle 228-9
erumna 564
Ethiopia 252
Etruria, Etruscans 56-8
euax 188
Euhemerus 414
Euhemerus (*poem*) xxi, 13, 414 ff.
eumpse 478
Europa, Europe 204-5
Eurypylus 278-81
evenat 294
evitari 252
exanclando 268; exanclavi 243
exerugit 208
expassum 536
expectorat 230
expedibo 270
explebant 202
extetulisses 320

593

INDEX

F

Fabius Maximus Cunctator 95, 100–1, 106–7, 132–3, 149
Fabius Maximus Rullianus 95
Fabricius 71
face (*from* facio) 10
facessite 270; facessunt 18
facilioreis 564
falarica 184
famul 116
faxim 334; faxit 402
festra 563
Festus xi; *passim*
fici 26
ficus Ruminalis 26–7
fidus (*for* foedus) 564
fiere 6–7
filiis (*for* filiabus) 258
flamines 44–5
Flaminia, via 93
Flamininus *see* Quinctius
Flaminius 93
floces 532
fortunatim 38
Fregellae 63
frundes 86; frus 460–1
frux 116, 150
fuat 282
Fulvius, Cnaeus 89
Fulvius (M.) Nobilior xx, xxi, xxv, 95, 143, 149, 358–9, 435
Fulvius (Q.) Nobilior xx–xxi, 435
Furies 229, 243
futtile 334

G

Gallia 120; *see* Gaul
gau (*for* gaudium) 460–1
Gaul(s) xxvii, 63, 66, 90, 92–3, 111, 121, 177
gerrae 534
Gibraltar 205
Glabrio 137
Glauca 420–1
glaucum 408
gluma 562
gnoscit 564
Gnossus 428
Gracchus, Tiberius 158
gracilentum 90
Graecia 120, 336; *see* Greece
Graecus 128, 276, 414–5

Graium 54; Graius 68, 128
grammonsis 550
gravidavit 542
Greece 121 ff., 158, 193, 337
Greeks 126, 128, 247, 277, 415 *etc.*
guttatim 296

H

halitantes 284
Hamilcar Rhodanus 100
Hannibal xxv, 66, 85, 90, 95 ff., 134–7, 145, 209, 396–7
Hasdrubal 105
hebem 500, 562
Hector 244–5, 248–9, 250–1, 253, 272 ff., 276, 280–1, 283–7
Hecuba 234–7, 242–3, 247, 290 ff.
Hedyphagetica 406–11
hehae 368
heia 196
Helen 304–5
Helenus 221
Helicon 3, 7
Hellen 327
Hellespont 136–7, 141
Heraclea 71
Herem, Here 36–7
Hersilia 37, 39
Hesione 337
Hesperia 12
hietans 556
Hippodamea 352–3
Histrians 144–5, 154–5; *see* Istrian War
Homer 2 ff.
homonem 50
Hora 38–9
Horatii, Horatius 44 ff., 197
Horatius Cocles 18
horitatur 122
horitur 156
hortatur (de me h.) 136
hostibitis 286–7
Hostilius, Tullus 45–6, 49, 51
hostimentum 264
Hyginus xiv–xv
Hyperion 210–1

I

iactarier 248
ignotus 260–1
Ilia 14 ff.
Illyrians 91, 111

INDEX

immemoris (*nom. sing.*) 478
incursim 484
indalbabat 76–7
indotuetur 26
indu 80, 160
induperantum 152
induperator 30, 118, 122, 178
induvolans 158
ineptitudo 488
infertis 388
inibi 532
inlex 488
inriderier 492
insece, inseque 118; insexit 563
Insubrian xxvii
Interamna Lirenas 65
Iovis (*nom.*) 480
Iphigenia 298–9, 305, 310–1
ipsei 284
iracunditer 498
Istrian War 144–59
Itali, Italy 2, 13, 69, 119, 422–3, 449
itiner 346
Iup(p)iter *see* Jupiter

J

Jason 311, 313, 321–3
Juno 22–3, 109, 420–1
Jupiter, Iup(p)iter 20–5, 35, 77, 92, 168, 288–9, 298–9, 324–5, 338–9, 348–9, 352–3, 408–9, 414 ff., 448–9, 450–1, 454–5, 469, 480–1

K

Karthaginiensibus 86; *see* Carthage
Κύμη 408–9

L

labat 368
Lacedaemon(ia) 242–3
lactat 498
lacte (*nom.*) 128, (*acc.*) 542
lamas 460–1; lamis 442
lapi 142
Lares 450
Latini, Latins 12 ff., 57, 188–9
Latium 176
laudarier 206
Laurentis, Laurentum 14, 15
laverent 248
Leucatan, Leucate 118–9

Liber 376–7
Libya 204–5
Licinius (P.) Crassus 159, 161
licitantur 26; licitari 492
Liguria 144
limassis 514
Liris 65
Livius Andronicus xviii, xxii, 108–9
Livius Salinator 110–1
locum (*nom. sing.*) 563
longiscere, longiscunt 162
Luceres 38
Lucilius 36, 96–7
Lucretia 59
luculentitatem 490
Luna 8–9; Lunai 8
Lyaeus 260

M

Macedon, Macedonian Wars 119 ff., 159, 197
mactassint 344
mactatus 110
Maeotis 400–1
Magnesia 134, 139, 141
Manlius (Titus) Torquatus 63; *his son* 62; Cn. Manlius Vulso 144
manta 480; mantat 500
Marcellus 457
Maro 376–7
Mars 17, 20–3, 36–7
Marsa, Marsian 448–9
Massili-... -tanas 464–5
Massinissa 158–9
Mavortis 36
med 242, 410, 472
Medea 310 ff.; Mede 320; Medeai 314
Mediolanum xxvii
Melanippe 326 ff.
melanurum 408
Melo 444–5
memorderit 390
Menelaus 277, 302–5, 311
mentis (*nom. sing.*) 412–3
Mercurius, Mercury 468–9
Merope 262–3, 265
Messapus xvii, 434–5
Messenia 262–3
Metaurus 111
Mettoeoque Fufetioeo (?) 48–9
Mettus (Mettius) Fufet(t)ius 46, 48–9
Minerva 270–3
Minturnae, Minturnenses 446–7

INDEX

mirarier 534
mis 44–5
miserete 292
Mitylene 408–9
moene 438
moenimenta 398
moero 248; moeros 136
momen 212
moraret 378
morimur 140
mu 438; μῦ 438
muriculi 408
Musa, Musae, Muses 2–3, 82–3, 108, 118, 462
mussabant 68; mussare 162, 253; mussaret 122; musset 378
muttire 344
Mycenae 347, 356
Myonnesus 139
Myrmidones 288–9

N

Naevius xviii, xxii, 16, 64, 82–3
Nar 92–3
navus 68
Nemea 328–31
neminis 266
Neoptolemus 368–9
Neptune 246–7, 255, 394–5, 420–1, 424–5
Nereus 255, 258–9
Nerienem, Nerio 36–7
Nesactium 157
Nestor 221, 408–9
nictentur 492
Nile 444–5
ningulus 48
nitidant 264
noctu (abl.) 56, 92
noenu 162, 540; noenum (?) 132
noltis 470
nōmus 276
Nonius ix–xi; passim
nox (adv.) 150
Numa Pompilius 43–5
Numidae, Numidians 76, 105, 110
Numitor 29

O

obatus (? for orbatus) 204–5
obnoxiosae 332–3

obnoxium 476
obsidionem 280, 338
obsipiam 490
obsorduit 496
obstipis 150; obstipo 102; obstipum 27, 502
obstringillant 384
obvarant 220
occasus 46, 62, 110
Oceania 418–9
Oenomaus 352–3
olli 42, 170, 462
Olympia, Olympic Games 144–5
Olympus 2, 3, 424–5, 454–5
opino 474
opis 400; Ops 418–21, 424–7
Opscus 106
opulentitate 532
Orcus 254–5, 490
Orestes 268–71
Ossa 161
ossiculatim 484
Ostia 53

P

Pacuvius xxiii
Paeligna, Paelignian 448–9
palm (for palmis) 296–7
paluda 96
Pan 422–3
Panchaea 423
Pancratiastes 362
pannibus 406
parire 6
Paris see Alexander and 234 ff.
partivit 342
partum (for partium) 210
Parum, Paros 204–5
parumper 16–17, 26, 190, 208
Patroclus 221, 273, 278–87
Patricoles 278; see Patroclus
pauperies 294; pauperii 532
pavum 6
peniculamentum 130, 512
Pelias 312–3, 320–1
Pelio, Pelion 312–3
Pelopia 356–7
Pelops 352–3, 356–7
perbiteret 298
perduellibus 366
Pergamum, Pergama 135, 137, 234–5, 244–5
permarceret 198–9
perpetuassit 118

596

INDEX

Perseus 257 ff.
Perseus (of Macedon) 94, 159, 161
Phalanna 165
Phegeus 229, 231, 233
Phemonoe 454–5
Philip V of Macedon 118–9, 125, 127
philologam 562
Phoenicians 85, 99, 449; *see* Poeni
Phoenix 221–3, 330 ff.
pilatas 384
pinsibant 376; pinsunt 124
Piraeum, Piraeus 554–5
Plautus xxii
Pluto 420–1
Poeni 84, 98, 104–5, 116–7, 448; *see* Phoenicians
poetor 390
Polydamas 275
Polydorus 290–1
Polymestor 291, 299
Polyphontes 262–3, 265
polypus 408
Polyxena 253, 255, 291, 295
Polyxenidas 139
Pompilius, Numa 43–5
populatim 514
porcet 342
Porcius Cato xviii, xxi, 95, 127, 129, 131, 145
porgite 563
portisculus 110
Poseidon 326; *see* Neptune
Postumius, (A.) Albinus xxii
Postumius, Lucius 89
pote 154; potis 376; potis est 278, 372; potis sunt 152
potestur 440
Praecepta 406–7
praecox 100–1
praepete 202–3
praeterpropter 308
praestrigias praestrinxit 538
Praxithea 265–7
Priam 8, 9, 234–7, 239 ff., 250–1, 272–3, 288–91
Proculus 39
prodinunt 56
proeliant 222
prognariter 74
prohibessis 324
proletarius 196–7
propagmen 178
properatim 526
propinas 386
propitiabilis 360

propritim 30
proterviter 362
Protrepticum (?) 406–7
Proserpina 415
prosumia 468, 508
Psophis 229, 231
publicitus 196, 530
puelli 84
puere 504
pugnitus 486
pulchritas 486
Punic Wars 64 ff., 78 ff., 193, 394 ff.
putas 244
Pyrrhus 65 ff., 101, 129, 193, 454

Q

quaesendum 258, 262
quaesti (*gen. sing.*) 541
quamde 32, 46
quianam 80, 196
Quinctius (T.) Flamininus 120–5, 127, 129
quippe 126, 146
Quirinus 38
quisquilias 554–5
quitur 558
quoi 80

R

rabere 498
Ramnenses 38
raptarier 248
rarenter 246, 514, 530
ratus 28
ravim 500
reciprocat 258
redinunt 563
remorbescat 563
Remuria 29
Remus 17, 27–33, 457
reperibit 510
repostos 563
restat 166–7
restitat 304
Rhaeti 448–9
Rhea 424–5
Rhodians 139
rimantur (?) 132
Ripaean 392–3
Rome, Romans xviii ff., 31, 42, 60, 66 ff. *etc.*, 172, 176–7, 180, 182, 198, 202, 398–9, 434, 416–9

INDEX

Romulus 15–7, 27–43, 157
Rudiae, Rudini, Rudian xvii–xviii
rumpiae 141
runata 186–7

S

Sabinae (poem) 360–1
Sabini, Sabines 34 ff., 361
saeviter 286
sagus 180, 440
Salamis 337
sale (nom.) 138–9
Salmacis 226–7
salum (acc.) 290–1
sam 82
Samnites 63
sanctioreis 564
sanguen 40, 294
sapientipotentes 66
sapsa 152
Sardinia xviii, 65, 87–9, 158
Sarra 84
sas 34
Satires, Saturae xxv, 8, 382 ff., 436 ff.
Saturn(us) 12, 23, 418 ff., 448–9
scabrent 256
Scamander 288–9
scamna 30
scaphonem 548
schema 488–9, 496
sciciderit 328
Scipio Africanus xx, xxiv–v, 95, 110–7, 139, 141, 145, 164–5, 387, 394 ff.
Scipio Nasica xix
Scipio (poem) xx, xxv, 394–9
Scythia 393
sēd (for sinc) 80
Seleucus IV 135, 137
Sempronius, (P.) Tuditanus 105, 113
sentinat 468–9
Seppius Loesius 109
Servilius Geminus 78–81
Servius Galba xxii, 410–1
Servius Honoratus xi–xii
Servius Tullius 43, 57, 59
sibynis 90
Sicilia, Sicily 81, 87, 428–9
sicilibus 184
silicernium 512
silvai frondosai 70
similitas 540
singulatim 500

sis 54
Sky 419, 423, 425
solui 563
sonit 288; sonunt 140, 254
soniti (gen. sing.) 474
sortiunt 262
sos 10, 56, 88, 128
sospes 563; sospitem 366
sospitent 326
Sota, Sotas (poem) 402–5
Sotades 403
Spain, Spanish 131, 144
speres (plur. of spes) 40, 152
spiras 186
spoliantur 452
Statius see Caecilius
stlataria 68
stola 342, 344, 374
strepiti 274
suai 122
subcenturia (?) 544
subices 224
sublimat 322
subulo 388
Sulpicius (P.) Galba 120; Servius Galba xxii, 410–1
sum 32, 46, 432
summussi 252–3
sumpti (for sumptus) 530
superescit 182
Surrentum 408–9
Syracuse 165, 410–1, 457

T

Talthybius 294–5
Tanaquil 55, 57
Tantalus 352–3
tapete 558; tapetae 563
taratantara 143
Tarentum xviii, 69, 408–9
Tarquinius Priscus 55–7, 431
Tarquinius Superbus 59
Tarracina 61
ted 282
telamo 444–5
Telamo(n) 93, 336 ff.
Telephus 342–7
Tempe 159
Terentius Varro 101
tergus 180
termo 164–6
terrai frugiferai 212

INDEX

tesca 376
tetulisti 18, 496
Teucer 228–9, 337 ff.
Thebes 229
Thelis 306–7
Thermopylae 135, 137
Thersites 219
Thesprotus 346, 351, 356–7
theta 456–7
Thetis 284–5, 287, 306–7
Thrace 144, 377; Thracians 141, 161
Thraeca 376
Thyestes 346 ff.
Tiber 18–21, 24–5, 52–3
Tiberinus 18
Ticinus 102, 186
Timavus 149, 151
Titan(us) 12–3, 261, 418–21
Titanis 260
Titienses 38
Titus Tatius 36–39
toleraret 46
tongent 404
tonsam 110, 404; tonsas, tonsis 88
topper 382–3
torrus 563
torviter 32
totondit (deque t.) 196
trabali 186
tractatus 48
tragedies xxv–vi, 218 ff., 362 ff.
trifaci 198
Trivia 260–1
Troia 234, 244, 336, 347, 432
Troy, Trojans 129, 181, 221, 235, 241, 244, 247, 282–3, 286, 287, 337, 433
truo 550
tuditantes 48
tullii 228
Tullius, Servius 43, 57, 59
Tullus Hostilius 45–6, 49, 51
tumulti 274
tute 36
tutulatos 42
Tyre 85

U

ulciscerem 268
Ulixes 276, 292; *see* Ulysses
Ulysses 221–3, 227, 253, 255, 277, 292–3, 311
urvat 256
uter (*for* uterus) 502
utrasque 542

V

vacant (?) 288
vagit 156
vagore 158
Valerius Laevinus 119
vallatam 558
vastae 306
veges 358
vei 274
velitatio 564
Venus 10, 16–9, 430–1
verant 136
verniliter 546
Vesper 563
Vesta 418–21
Vestina, Vestinian 448–9
viai 72
vias (*for* viae, *gen.*) 160
vidén 563
viere 404
Villius (P.) 134
visceratim 258
vitulans 238–9
Volscians 61
Vulcanus 284–5
Vulsculus 60
vulta 174
vulturus 50

X

Xerxes 135, 137

Z

Zama xxv, 115–7, 395–7

PRINTED IN GREAT BRITAIN BY
RICHARD CLAY & SONS, LIMITED,
BUNGAY, SUFFOLK.

THE LOEB CLASSICAL LIBRARY

VOLUMES ALREADY PUBLISHED

Latin Authors

APULEIUS: THE GOLDEN ASS (METAMORPHOSES).
W. Adlington (1566). Revised by S. Gaselee. (*6th Imp.*)
AULUS GELLIUS. J. C. Rolfe. 3 Vols.
AUSONIUS. H. G. Evelyn White. 2 Vols.
BEDE. J. E. King. 2 Vols.
BOETHIUS: TRACTS AND DE CONSOLATIONE
PHILOSOPHIAE. Rev. H. F. Stewart and E. K. Rand.
(*2nd Imp.*)
CAESAR: CIVIL WARS. A. G. PESKETT. (*3rd Imp.*)
CAESAR: GALLIC WAR. H. J. Edwards. (*6th Imp.*)
CATO AND VARRO: DE RE RÚSTICA. H. B. Ash and
W. D. Hooper. (*2nd Imp.*)
CATULLUS. F. W. Cornish; TIBULLUS. J. B. Post-
gate; AND PERVIGILIUM VENERIS. J. W. Mackail.
(*10th Imp.*)
CELSUS: DE MEDICINA. W. G. Spencer. 2 Vols.
Vol. I.
CICERO: DE FINIBUS. H. Rackham. (*3rd Imp. re-
vised.*)
CICERO: DE NATURA DEORUM AND ACADEMICA.
H. Rackham.
CICERO: DE OFFICIIS. Walter Miller. (*3rd Imp.*)
CICERO: DE SENECTUTE, DE AMICITIA, DE
DIVINATIONE. W. A. Falconer. (*3rd Imp.*)
CICERO: DE REPUBLICA AND DE LEGIBUS. Clinton
W. Keyes.
CICERO: LETTERS TO ATTICUS. E. O. Winstedt.
3 Vols. (Vol. I. *4th Imp.*, II. *3rd Imp.* and III. *2nd Imp.*
CICERO: LETTERS TO HIS FRIENDS. W. Glynn
Williams. 3 Vols.

1

CICERO: PHILIPPICS. W. C. A. Ker.
CICERO: PRO ARCHIA, POST REDITUM, DE DOMO, DE HARUSPICUM RESPONSIS, PRO PLANCIO. N. H. Watts. (2nd Imp.)
CICERO: PRO QUINCTIO, PRO ROSCIO AMERINO, PRO ROSCIO COMOEDO, CONTRA RULLUM. J. H. Freese.
CICERO: TUSCULAN DISPUTATIONS. J. E. King.
CICERO: PRO CAECINA, PRO LEGE MANILIA, PRO CLUENTIO, PRO RABIRIO. H. Grose Hodge.
CICERO: PRO MILONE, IN PISONEM, PRO SCAURO, PRO FONTEIO, PRO RABIRIO POSTUMO, PRO MARCELLO, PRO LIGARIO, PRO REGE DEIO-TARO. N. H. Watts.
CICERO: VERRINE ORATIONS. L. H. G. Greenwood. 2 Vols.
CLAUDIAN. M. Platnauer. 2 Vols.
FLORUS. E. S. Forster, and CORNELIUS NEPOS: J. C. Rolfe.
FRONTINUS: STRATAGEMS AND AQUEDUCTS. C. E. Bennett and M. B. McElwain.
FRONTO: CORRESPONDENCE. C. R. Haines. 2 Vols.
HORACE: ODES AND EPODES. C. E. Bennett. (10th Imp. revised.)
HORACE: SATIRES, EPISTLES, ARS POETICA. H. R. Fairclough. (3rd Imp. revised.)
JEROME: SELECTED LETTERS. F. A. Wright.
JUVENAL AND PERSIUS. G. G. Ramsay. (5th Imp.)
LIVY. B. O. Foster and E. Sage. 13 Vols. Vols. I.-V. and IX. (Vol. I. 2nd Imp. revised.)
LUCAN. J. D. Duff.
LUCRETIUS. W. H. D. Rouse. (3rd Imp. revised.)
MARTIAL. W. C. A. Ker. 2 Vols. (3rd Imp. revised.)
MINOR LATIN POETS: from PUBLILIUS SYRUS to RUTILIUS NAMATIANUS, including GRATTIUS, CAL-PURNIUS SICULUS, NEMESIANUS, AVIANUS, and others with "Aetna" and the "Phoenix." J. Wight Duff and Arnold M. Duff. (2nd Imp.)
OVID: THE ART OF LOVE AND OTHER POEMS. J. H. Mozley.
OVID: FASTI. Sir James G. Frazer.
OVID: HEROIDES AND AMORES. Grant Showerman. (3rd Imp.)
OVID: METAMORPHOSES. F. J. Miller. 2 Vols. (5th Imp.)
OVID: TRISTIA AND EX PONTO. A. L. Wheeler.

2

PETRONIUS. M. Heseltine; SENECA: APOCOLO-
CYNTOSIS. W. H. D. Rouse. (5th Imp. revised.)
PLAUTUS. Paul Nixon. 5 Vols. Vols. I.–IV. (Vol. I.
4th Imp., Vols. II. and III. 3rd Imp.)
PLINY: LETTERS. Melmoth's Translation revised by
W. M. L. Hutchinson. 2 Vols. (4th Imp.)
PROPERTIUS. H. E. Butler. (4th Imp.)
QUINTILIAN. H. E. Butler. 4 Vols. (Vol. I. 2nd Imp.)
REMAINS OF OLD LATIN. E. H. Warmington. 3 Vols.
Vol. I. (ENNIUS AND CAECILIUS.)
ST. AUGUSTINE, CONFESSIONS OF. W. Watts
(1631). 2 Vols. (Vol. I. 4th Imp., Vol. II. 3rd Imp.)
ST. AUGUSTINE, SELECT LETTERS. J. H. Baxter.
SALLUST. J. Rolfe. (2nd Imp. revised.)
SCRIPTORES HISTORIAE AUGUSTAE. D. Magie.
3 Vols. (Vol. I. 2nd Imp. revised.)
SENECA: APOCOLOCYNTOSIS. Cf. PETRONIUS.
SENECA: EPISTULAE MORALES. R. M. Gummere.
3 Vols. (Vol. I. 3rd Imp., Vol. II. 2nd Imp. revised.)
SENECA: MORAL ESSAYS. J. W. Basore. 3 Vols.
Vols. I. and II. (Vol. II. 2nd Imp. revised.)
SENECA: TRAGEDIES. F. J. Miller. 2 Vols. (2nd
Imp. revised.)
SILIUS ITALICUS. J. D. Duff. 2 Vols.
STATIUS. J. H. Mozley. 2 Vols.
SUETONIUS. J. C. Rolfe. 2 Vols. (4th Imp. revised.)
TACITUS: DIALOGUS. Sir Wm. Peterson and AGRI-
COLA AND GERMANIA. Maurice Hutton. (4th Imp.)
TACITUS: HISTORIES AND ANNALS. C. H. Moore
and J. Jackson. 3 Vols. Vols. I. and II. (Histories
and Annals I–III.)
TERENCE. John Sargeaunt. 2 Vols. (5th Imp.)
TERTULLIAN: APOLOGIA AND DE SPECTACULIS.
T. R. Glover. MINUCIUS FELIX. G. H. Rendall.
VALERIUS FLACCUS. J. H. Mozley.
VELLEIUS PATERCULUS AND RES GESTAE DIVI
AUGUSTI. F. W. Shipley.
VIRGIL. H. R. Fairclough. 2 Vols. (Vol. I. 11th Imp.,
Vol. II. 9th Imp. revised.)
VITRUVIUS: DE ARCHITECTURA. F. Granger.
2 Vols.

3

Greek Authors

ACHILLES TATIUS. S. Gaselee.

AENEAS TACTICUS: ASCLEPIODOTUS AND ONA-
SANDER. The Illinois Greek Club.

AESCHINES. C. D. Adams.

AESCHYLUS. H. Weir Smyth. 2 Vols. (Vol. I. 3rd *Imp.*,
Vol. II. 2nd *Imp.*)

APOLLODORUS. Sir James G. Frazer. 2 Vols.

APOLLONIUS RHODIUS. R. C. Seaton. (4th *Imp.*)

THE APOSTOLIC FATHERS. Kirsopp Lake. 2 Vols.
(Vol. I. 5th *Imp.*, Vol. II. 4th *Imp.*)

APPIAN'S ROMAN HISTORY. Horace White. 4 Vols.
(Vol. I. 3rd *Imp.*, Vols. II., III. and IV. 2nd *Imp.*)

ARATUS. Cf. CALLIMACHUS.

ARISTOPHANES. Benjamin Bickley Rogers. 3 Vols.
(3rd *Imp.*) Verse trans.

ARISTOTLE: "ART" OF RHETORIC. J. H. Freese.

ARISTOTLE: ATHENIAN CONSTITUTION, EUDE-
MIAN ETHICS, VICES AND VIRTUES. H. Rackham.

ARISTOTLE: METAPHYSICS. H. Tredennick. 2 Vols.

ARISTOTLE: NICOMACHEAN ETHICS. H. Rackham.
(2nd *Imp.* revised.)

ARISTOTLE: OECONOMICA AND MAGNA MORALIA.
G. C. Armstrong; (with Metaphysics, Vol. II.)

ARISTOTLE: ON THE SOUL, PARVA NATURALIA,
ON BREATH. W. S. Hett.

ARISTOTLE: PHYSICS. Rev. P. Wicksteed and F. M.
Cornford. 2 Vols. (Vol. II. 2nd *Imp.*)

ARISTOTLE: POETICS AND LONGINUS. W. Hamil-
ton Fyfe; DEMETRIUS ON STYLE. W. Rhys
Roberts. (2nd *Imp.* revised.)

ARISTOTLE: POLITICS. H. Rackham.

ARRIAN: HISTORY OF ALEXANDER AND INDICA.
Rev. E. Iliffe Robson. 2 Vols.

ATHENAEUS: DEIPNOSOPHISTAE. C. B. Gulick.
7 Vols. Vols. I–V.

CALLIMACHUS AND LYCOPHRON. A. W. Mair;
ARATUS. G. R. Mair.

CLEMENT OF ALEXANDRIA. Rev. G. W. Butter-
worth.

COLLUTHUS. Cf. OPPIAN.

DAPHNIS AND CHLOE. Thornley's Translation revised
by J. M. Edmonds; AND PARTHENIUS. S. Gaselee.
(3rd *Imp.*)

DEMOSTHENES: DE CORONA AND DE FALSA
LEGATIONE. C. A. Vince and J. H. Vince.

DEMOSTHENES : OLYNTHIACS, PHILIPPICS AND
MINOR ORATIONS : I–XVII AND XX. J. H. Vince.
DIO CASSIUS : ROMAN HISTORY. E. Cary. 9 Vols.
(Vol. II. 2nd Imp.)
DIO CHRYSOSTOM. J. W. Cohoon. 4 Vols. Vol. I.
DIODORUS SICULUS. C. H. Oldfather. In 10 Volumes.
Vol. I.
DIOGENES LAERTIUS. R. D. Hicks. 2 Vols. (Vol. I.
2nd Imp.)
EPICTETUS. W. A. Oldfather. 2 Vols.
EURIPIDES. A. S. Way. 4 Vols. (Vol. I., II., IV.
5th Imp., Vol. III. 3rd Imp.) Verse trans.
EUSEBIUS : ECCLESIASTICAL HISTORY. Kirsopp
Lake and J. E. L. Oulton. 2 Vols.
GALEN : ON THE NATURAL FACULTIES. A. J.
Brock. (2nd Imp.)
THE GREEK ANTHOLOGY. W. R. Paton. 5 Vols.
(Vol. I. 3rd Imp., Vols. II. and III. 2nd Imp.)
GREEK ELEGY AND IAMBUS WITH THE ANACRE-
ONTEA. J. M. Edmonds. 2 Vols.
THE GREEK BUCOLIC POETS (THEOCRITUS,
BION, MOSCHUS). J. M. Edmonds. (5th Imp. revised.)
HERODES. Cf. THEOPHRASTUS : CHARACTERS.
HERODOTUS. A. D. Godley. 4 Vols. (Vol. I. 3rd Imp.,
Vols. II.–IV. 2nd Imp.)
HESIOD AND THE HOMERIC HYMNS. H. G. Evelyn
White. (5th Imp. revised and enlarged.)
HIPPOCRATES AND THE FRAGMENTS OF HERA-
CLEITUS. W. H. S. Jones and E. T. Withington. 4 Vols.
HOMER : ILIAD. A. T. Murray. 2 Vols. 3rd Imp.
HOMER : ODYSSEY. A. T. Murray. 2 Vols. (4th Imp.)
ISAEUS. E. W. Forster.
ISOCRATES. George Norlin. 3 Vols. Vols. I. and II.
JOSEPHUS. H. St. J. Thackeray and Ralph Marcus.
8 Vols. Vols. I.–V. (Vol. V. 2nd Imp.)
JULIAN. Wilmer Cave Wright. 3 Vols. (Vol. I. 2nd
Imp.)
LUCIAN. A. M. Harmon. 8 Vols. Vols. I.–IV. (Vols.
I. and II. 3rd Imp.)
LYCOPHRON. Cf. CALLIMACHUS.
LYRA GRAECA. J. M. Edmonds. 3 Vols. (Vol. I.
3rd Imp., Vol. II. 2nd Ed. revised and enlarged.)
LYSIAS. W. R. M. Lamb.
MARCUS AURELIUS. C. R. Haines. (3rd Imp. revised.)
MENANDER. F. G. Allinson. (2nd Imp. revised.)
OPPIAN, COLLUTHUS, TRYPHIODORUS. A. W.
Mair.

5

PAPYRI (SELECTIONS). A. S. Hunt and C. C. Edgar. 4 Vols. Vols. I. and II.
PARTHENIUS. Cf. DAPHNIS AND CHLOE.
PAUSANIAS : DESCRIPTION OF GREECE. W. H. S. Jones. 5 Vols. and Companion Vol. (Vol. I. 2nd Imp.)
PHILO. F. H. Colson and Rev. G. H. Whitaker. 9 Vols. Vols. I.–VI.
PHILOSTRATUS : THE LIFE OF APOLLONIUS OF TYANA. F. C. Conybeare. 2 Vols. (Vol. I. 3rd Imp., Vol. II. 2nd Imp.)
PHILOSTRATUS : IMAGINES; CALLISTRATUS : DESCRIPTIONS. A. Fairbanks.
PHILOSTRATUS AND EUNAPIUS : LIVES OF THE SOPHISTS. Wilmer Cave Wright.
PINDAR. Sir J. E. Sandys. (5th Imp. revised.)
PLATO : CHARMIDES, ALCIBIADES, HIPPARCHUS, THE LOVERS, THEAGES, MINOS AND EPINOMIS. W. R. M. Lamb.
PLATO : CRATYLUS, PARMENIDES, GREATER HIPPIAS, LESSER HIPPIAS. H. N. Fowler.
PLATO : EUTHYPHRO, APOLOGY, CRITO, PHAEDO, PHAEDRUS. H. N. Fowler. (7th Imp.)
PLATO : LACHES, PROTAGORAS, MENO, EUTHYDEMUS. W. R. M. Lamb.
PLATO : LAWS. Rev. R. G. Bury. 2 Vols.
PLATO : LYSIS, SYMPOSIUM, GORGIAS. W. R. M. Lamb. (2nd Imp. revised.)
PLATO : REPUBLIC. Paul Shorey. 2 Vols.
PLATO : STATESMAN, PHILEBUS. H. N. Fowler; ION. W. R. M. Lamb.
PLATO : THEAETETUS AND SOPHIST. H. N. Fowler. (2nd Imp.)
PLATO : TIMAEUS, CRITIAS, CLITOPHO, MENEXENUS, EPISTULAE. Rev. R. G. Bury.
PLUTARCH : MORALIA. F. C. Babbitt. 14 Vols. Vols. I.–III.
PLUTARCH : THE PARALLEL LIVES. B. Perrin. 11 Vols. (Vols. I., II., III. and VII. 2nd Imp.)
POLYBIUS. W. R. Paton. 6 Vols.
PROCOPIUS : HISTORY OF THE WARS. H. B. Dewing. 7 Vols. Vols. I.–VI. (Vol. I. 2nd Imp.)
QUINTUS SMYRNAEUS. A. S. Way. Verse trans.
ST. BASIL : LETTERS. R. J. Deferrari. 4 Vols.
ST. JOHN DAMASCENE : BARLAAM AND IOASAPH. Rev. G. R. Woodward and Harold Mattingly.
SEXTUS EMPIRICUS. Rev. R. G. Bury. In 3 Vols. Vols. I. and II.

SOPHOCLES. F. Storr. 2 Vols. (Vol. I. 6th Imp., Vol. II. 4th Imp.) Verse trans.
STRABO: GEOGRAPHY. Horace L. Jones. 8 Vols. (Vols. I and VIII. 2nd Imp.)
THEOPHRASTUS: CHARACTERS. J. M. Edmonds; HERODES, etc. A. D. Knox.
THEOPHRASTUS: ENQUIRY INTO PLANTS. Sir Arthur Hort, Bart. 2 Vols.
THUCYDIDES. C. F. Smith. 4 Vols. (Vol. I. 3rd Imp., Vols. II., III. and IV. 2nd Imp. revised.)
TRYPHIODORUS. Cf. OPPIAN.
XENOPHON: CYROPAEDIA. Walter Miller. 2 Vols. (2nd Imp.)
XENOPHON: HELLENICA, ANABASIS, APOLOGY, AND SYMPOSIUM. C. L. Brownson and O. J. Todd. 3 Vols. (2nd Imp.)
XENOPHON: MEMORABILIA AND OECONOMICUS. E. C. Marchant.
XENOPHON: SCRIPTA MINORA. E. C. Marchant.

IN PREPARATION

Greek Authors

ARISTOTLE: DE CAELO, etc. W. C. K. Guthrie.
ARISTOTLE: ON HISTORY, MOTION AND PRO-GRESSION OF ANIMALS. E. S. Forster and A. Peck.
ARISTOTLE: ORGANON. H. P. Cooke and H. Treden-nick.
ARISTOTLE: RHETORICA AD ALEXANDRUM. H. Rackham.
DEMOSTHENES: MEIDIAS, ANDROTION, ARISTO-CRATES, TIMOCRATES. J. H. Vince.
DEMOSTHENES: PRIVATE ORATIONS. A. T. Mur-ray.
DIONYSIUS OF HALICARNASSUS: ROMAN ANTI-QUITIES. Spelman's translation revised by E. Cary.
GREEK MATHEMATICAL WORKS. J. Thomas.
MINOR ATTIC ORATORS (ANTIPHON, ANDOCIDES DEMADES, DINARCHUS, HYPEREIDES). K. Maidment.
NONNUS. W. H. D. Rouse.

7

Latin Authors

AMMIANUS MARCELLINUS. J. C. Rolfe.

S. AUGUSTINE : CITY OF GOD. J. H. Baxter.

CICERO : AD HERENNIUM. H. Caplan.

CICERO : IN CATILINAM, PRO FLACCO, PRO MURENA, PRO SULLA. Louis E. Lord.

CICERO : DE ORATORE. Charles Stuttaford and W. E. Sutton.

CICERO : ORATOR, BRUTUS. H. M. Hubbell.

CICERO : PRO SESTIO, IN VATINIUM, PRO CAELIO, DE PROVINCIIS CONSULARIBUS, PRO BALBO. J. H. Freese.

COLUMELLA : DE RE RUSTICA. H. B. Ash.

PLINY : NATURAL HISTORY. W. H. S. Jones.

PRUDENTIUS. J. H. Baxter and C. J. Fordyce.

SIDONIUS : LETTERS & POEMS. E. V. Arnold and W. B. Anderson.

VARRO : DE LINGUA LATINA. R. G. Kent.

DESCRIPTIVE PROSPECTUS ON APPLICATION

London   -   -   -   -   **WILLIAM HEINEMANN LTD**
Cambridge, Mass. -   -   - **HARVARD UNIVERSITY PRESS**

1983 4